PATTERNS IN WESTERN CIVILIZATION

Third Edition

Managing Editor: Sarah Trulove
Senior Editor: James Woelfel

Editors for Volume II

Section III Editor: Peter Casagrande
Section IV Editor: Thomas Heilke

Contributors:

Robert Anderson
Stephen Auerbach
S. Daniel Breslauer
Katherine P. Clark
Richard De George
Joanathan Earle
Diane R. Fourny
Thomas Heilke
James Leiker
Rex Martin
Lewis McKinney
Norman Saul
Emily Wicktor

PEARSON
Custom Publishing

Cover Photo: *Excavations*, by Brian Stevens.

Maps Drafted by George Nichols

Printed in the United States of America

10 9 8 7 6 5 4 3 2 1

Please visit our web site at www.pearsoncustom.com

ISBN 0–536–67962–2

BA 996579

PEARSON CUSTOM PUBLISHING
75 Arlington Street, Suite 300, Boston, MA 02116
A Pearson Education Company

CONTENTS

MAPS

INTRODUCTION TO THE THIRD EDITION

For the past eleven years *Patterns in Western Civilization* has served as the textbook for the Western Civilization courses at the University of Kansas and at some other institutions. It was designed to serve as background for a course that makes significant use of primary sources of the Western tradition. Students are required to read both the textbook and the primary sources texts. The list of primary texts is reviewed every three to five years and some changes are made, which requires alterations in the background textbook.

In 2000 the Curriculum Committee of the Humanities and Western Civilization Program spent a semester reviewing the primary texts and the textbook, *Patterns*. After selecting the texts, they turned their attention to *Patterns* and decided that a revised textbook should be more reading specific. It was also decided that the shorter primary source readings published as *Collected Readings* become a part of the text. Much of the material from the previous editions of *Patterns* has been reworked but there is also new material. The chapters are shorter and generally follow a similar format. Maps have been added and the existing ones improved. There are also some new illustrations. The formerly one-volume *Patterns* is now in two volumes, divided into WC I and II.

This new edition is the work of many people. Trulove and Woelfel have been joined by four section editors. Chapters follow a general set of guidelines. We have also tried to make sure that the authors write for the introductory-level student—defining terms, clearly identifying and explaining things, and not assuming more knowledge than the student is likely to have.

Studying Western civilization at KU means focusing on some of the main patterns—of ideas, values, and institutions—that make up the complex and varied fabric of Western cultures and institutions, rather than broadly surveying Western history. We pay special attention to main currents in Western thought.

In planning the 3rd edition of *Patterns in Western Civilization*, the editors have sought to produce a textbook that would provide students with both historical background and some guidance for their reading of the primary sources. Our purpose was to create an approach to the study of Western civilization that would be of interest and value to faculty and students involved in Western Civilization programs that emphasize intellectual history and use a range of primary sources.

We also give serious attention to three important challenges confronting the modern West: the historic subordination and neglected contributions of women, the emergence of modern racism and its close links with European and American imperialism, and the Jewish heritage and anti-Semitism. What we have accomplished in this regard does not attain to the editors' ideal, but we believe we have moved a good distance in the right direction.

Patterns in Western Civilization is divided into two volumes each containing two parts: Volume One consists of: I. The Ancient World: Greece & Rome (Homer, Plato, Sophocles, Aristotle, Cicero and Seneca), and the Beginnings of Judaism and early Christianity (Hebrew and Christian Scriptures). II. The Middle Ages (Augustine, Aquinas, Chaucer), Islam (Qu'ran), the Reformation (Martin Luther), the Renaissance (Machiavelli), and the Scientific Revolution (Galileo).

Volume Two includes: III. John Locke and the origins of modern political thought, Voltaire and the Enlightenment, the American experiment, John Stuart Mill and individual liberty, Mary Shelley and Romanticism, and Darwinism. IV. Marxism, W. E. B. Du Bois and modern racism, Dostoevsky and Russia's relationship to the West, Frederick Nietzsche, precursor to existentialism, Sigmund Freud and psychoanalysis, Virginia Woolf and feminism, and Gerda Weissmann Klein and the Holocaust.

Introducing each of the chapters is a survey of the people, movements, events, and ideas to be covered, building on what has gone before and showing the connections among the chapters. Each chapter contains questions for study and discussion and a bibliography for further reading. We have also selected a variety of illustrations related to what is talked about in the text, along with timelines and maps to help students orient themselves to the times and places about which they are reading. An Index provides ready reference to many of the main terms, names, and topics.

Throughout the textbook we have tried to standardize the use of gender-inclusive language. We have also adopted the abbreviations "B.C.E." (Before the Common Era) and "C.E." (Common Era) rather than the more familiar "B.C." (Before Christ) and "A.D." (*Anno Domini*, Latin for "in the year of our Lord"). Jewish scholars and writers have long used B.C.E. and C.E., and a growing number of Christian and other scholars now use them. The reason is that B.C. and A.D. are specifically Christian inventions, with explicit references to Jesus understood as the Christ or Messiah. The designations B.C.E. and C.E. also divide history with the birth of Jesus. But in this era of greater dialogue and ecumenical spirit among world religions, and the special importance of greater understanding between Christians and Jews, the terms "before the common era" and "common era" point in a slightly less particularist way to what unites rather than divides two of the main living religious traditions of the Western world.

THE STUDY OF WESTERN CIVILIZATION

What is Western civilization, and why study it? "Western civilization" is a very broad term intended to designate some of the common features of the human cultures that have dominated Europe and been transplanted to the Americas and other parts of the world. Those common features have their roots in ancient Mesopotamia and Egypt, Israel, Greece, and Rome—all very diverse cultures whose heritages came to be woven together and transmitted by the Christian European civilization of the Middle Ages. That original diversity, enriched by the diversity contributed by native European populations such as the Franks, Goths, Saxons, Lombards, and Celts, and later by races and peoples from other parts of the world, should caution us against thinking of Western civilization as a monolith even as we seek to understand its common ideas and values. Western civilization is itself a richly diverse mix of cultures and peoples.

Furthermore, from their origins to the present day the cultures that have contributed to the shaping of Western civilization, like almost all human cultures, have not existed in isolation but in interaction with other cultures. This pattern of mutual influence and conflict has been continuous. The ancient Israelites were influenced by and struggled with surrounding Middle Eastern and North African cultures such as Mesopotamia (Iraq), Syria, Persia (Iran), Egypt, and Ethiopia, and for a long time the Jews were subject to the Romans. In the fourth century B.C.E. Alexander the Great conquered and brought Greek culture to lands as far away as India, and today one can see ancient Indian statues of the Buddha showing Greek influence. The Roman Empire included an enormous variety of peoples, religions, and cultural traditions stretching from Spain and Britain in the west to Syria in the east. Throughout the Middle Ages Christian Europe and the empire of Islam engaged in centuries of struggle with each other for control over parts of Europe and the Middle East, a contact which at the same time opened up trade for Europe and bequeathed to Europe the ideas of Muslim philosophers, theologians, and scientists and the works of Aristotle they had preserved. Intercultural conflict and exchange have continued to the present day, on the one hand through the global dominance of Western imperialism, colonialism, capitalism, warfare, science, technology, and communications; and on the other hand by immigration to Western countries and the reaffirmation by other cultures of their distinctive heritage and contributions.

The culturally diverse richness of Western civilization, and its ongoing interaction with other cultures, are facts the student of Western Civilization needs always to keep in mind. A number of our authors provide reminders of these facts within the context of a focus on the distinctive development and character of that heritage we call Western. At the same time, in a course emphasizing Western thought, we are centrally concerned with those distinctive ideas, values, and institutions that have become the common property of the Western world. That common property is itself a plurality of different and often conflicting responses to the perennial human questions. Every human civilization asks these questions and comes up with answers that show great variety and also overlap and similarity. In Western Civilization courses we learn about and critically examine the answers that have taken shape over millennia in one complex world civilization, while recognizing that these Western answers take their place within a larger human conversation on the great questions and have their counterparts and alternatives in other civilizations.

But it has also become essential to recognize that the characteristically Western responses to the great human questions are even more richly pluralistic than we used to think. Through a wealth of research in areas such as African and African-American and other ethnic and world area studies, Judaic studies, and women's studies over the past thirty years, we are now acutely aware of voices in the Western conversation that have not been heard, because historically they have been marginalized and suppressed. We have tried to incorporate some of that research into this textbook, offering glimpses, explanations, and sometimes sustained treatments of the historic situation and the achievements of women in various Western societies, the modern phenomenon of Western racism and the response to it of Africans and African-Americans, and the story of the Jewish people and of anti-Semitism in the Western world.

We now realize, for example, that because of their historic subordination—which has often meant exclusion from educational opportunity and public life and legal discrimination—women's experience and outlooks have been seriously underrepresented in the influential writings of the Western world. Those women who have managed to contribute publicly, as political and religious leaders, writers, artists, scientists, and philosophers, have often had their contributions neglected, denigrated, and denied—not because of the quality of their work but because of their gender. This recognition makes the study of the influential writings of Western civilization more complex and also more stimulating and rewarding.

People used to read the "great books of the Western world"—written almost entirely by caucasian European men—as definitive statements on various aspects of the human condition. Now we recognize the need to balance a continuing recognition of their greatness and enduring insights with what some scholars call a "hermeneutics of suspicion." What this means, first, is that we must examine closely their assumptions about the roles of women and men and about sexuality generally. Secondly, we must consider their assumptions about human groups other than their own—other social classes, races and cultures. Thirdly, we must ask how these assumptions affect their ideas about humans and the world and their claims to universality. At the same time, we must become aware of how women and other marginalized and oppressed groups in Western civilization have based their struggles for dignity and equality precisely on ideas and values that are enshrined in the "great works" of Western religion, philosophy, and art, seeing in those ideas and values universal implications that even their authors often did not see. In addition, we have the task, in today's Western Civilization courses, of including some of these hitherto suppressed voices in the Western heritage alongside the "classic texts," to enrich and make more fully "whole" the Western world's discussion of the great human issues.

And what are those great human issues? There are various ways we might formulate the basic questions that all human cultures ask, but they include the following: What can we know about the world and ourselves, and what is true and false? What is the meaning of our brief existence in the world, and is it to be found in nature and ourselves or in higher, even transcendent powers? What is the good life for the individual, and what are our responsibilities toward one another? Do humans choose freely, or are we determined by fate, divine will, or heredity and environment? What is the good society, and how is justice to be defined? What is the meaning of being male and female and in other ways diverse as humans? What are the roles of love and work in our lives? What is beauty, and why do we enjoy it and create what is beautiful? Is the realm of human events a history with a meaning and a goal, or a mere unfolding of events, or repeating cycles? Why do we suffer and inflict suffering? What is the significance of death for human life? Is there a destiny beyond death, and if so what is it? At the bottom of all these questions is the most fundamental question of all: What are we human beings, these strange creatures who ask so many questions of life?

Now of course cultures and individuals have asked and answered these questions implicitly and explicitly, inchoately and articulately, simply and sophisticatedly. They have also typically asked and answered them quite concretely and not in the general way indicated above. Humans have lived in families and tribes, democracies and monarchies; they have worshipped gods and goddesses; they have created songs and pictures and stories; they have toiled in fields and towns; they have struggled to get along with one another; they have observed the movement of the planets and stars. That is to say that humans raise the great issues of human life and grapple with them largely through the practical realities of human community, religious faith and tradition, politics and law, artistic expression, intellectual curiosity, the customs and mores of society, work and family.

Out of this concrete matrix emerge some individuals who quite consciously and single-mindedly ponder the foundational questions and try to give expression to the best answers they can. Among these men and women are prophets and mystics, poets and artists, philosophers and theologians, scientists and historians. They are the main sources of the oral traditions, writings, and works of art that have shaped and interpreted the common ideas and ideals, principles and aspirations of civilizations. In this book and in a course on the civilization of the West our interest is in those who have played such a role in the Western world, looking at them and their achievements against the background of the social, economic, political, religious, and cultural life of their time and place.

But *why* study Western civilization, and particularly its ideas, values, and institutions? The most obvious answer is that most of us who learn and teach in colleges and universities in the United States are children of and participants in that civilization, and one of the marks of a well-educated human being is to have knowledge of the roots and development of her or his own cultural heritage. Those students who also claim another cultural legacy, such as Native Americans and Asian-Americans, have been profoundly shaped by Western civilization even as it has often tried to reject or suppress their other cultural traditions and as these traditions have, in turn, criticized the West. Similarly, in a world that has come to be heavily influenced by so many things European and American, it is important for students from non-Western nations and cultures to learn of the history, ideas, and values of this civilization that has had such an influence—in both positive and negative ways—on their own lives and the lives of their people.

But the study of Western civilization alone is not nearly enough. It is equally important for American and European students to learn of civilizations other than their own. Indeed, in our ever-shrinking "global village" knowledge of other human cultures has become imperative for informed persons, and in international relations we continue to make serious mistakes even at the highest levels of diplomacy out of ignorance of other countries and peoples. Courses in the language, geography, politics, history, religion, philosophy, and arts of other civilizations should be an integral part of one's education together with courses in Western civilization.

To be human is to have a personal story and to be part of a larger story, and the past—history—is everything about me and the larger world in which I live up to the moment I am telling the story. When I "open up" to another person about who I am, I inevitably begin to tell a story—to be a historian in miniature. I talk about the place or places I came from, where I went to school, something about my parents and siblings. If I really ponder in depth who I am, I realize that my story includes not only my immediate family but also a wider family (aunts, uncles, and cousins) and earlier generations of family (grandparents and great-grandparents). I become aware that I am a link in a chain of human generations stretching back through time and forward through the children and grandchildren I may have.

Probing still further, I come to recognize that my personal identity is inseparable from the fact that I am, say, black rather than white, female rather than male, middle-class rather than working-class, and what it means to be one or the other in the society in which I grew up. Then I come to all the things that I simply take for granted in my self-definition because they are part of the very fabric of my society: democratic ideas and institutions, religious freedom together with the dominance of Christianity, characteristically American customs and prejudices, capitalism and consumerism, science and advanced technology, colleges and universities, certain traditions and tastes in music and literature. I begin to grasp that the story of who I am is part of a much larger story going back generations without number and encompassing a whole civilization. I may begin to wonder how all these things that I have always taken for granted started, how they came to be in the form in which I know them, and how they compare to other alternatives. That kind of curiosity is what the study of Western civilization tries to help stimulate and satisfy.

A Western Civilization program is a vitally important part of a liberal education. This is so because a basic assumption of liberal education is that people can be liberated from the tyranny of attitudes controlled entirely by custom and convention and can make informed and independent choices concerning those questions of fundamental human concern about which we spoke earlier. The root of the word "liberal" is the Latin word meaning "free," and we may think of a liberal education as one designed to enlarge human freedom. Free choices can only be informed choices, made in the context of the knowledge of alternative possible answers to the questions and in view of a careful study of the arguments and evidence that are relevant to evaluating the worth of those answers.

The role of a Western Civilization program within a liberal education is to acquaint us with the history, variety, and content of the responses that some of the influential and representative authors of the Western world have given to those perennial human questions. We in the present enter thereby into a dialogue with them in a great conversation through the ages—learning from them, questioning them, weighing the strengths and weaknesses of the alternatives they present, discovering their impact on issues of our day and how we think about those issues. The perspectives we develop personally from our dialogue with the past may be other than those which the ancient, medieval, and modern shapers of Western civilization have forged. But in the process of our study, we discover that we cannot develop our own views in an informed manner without their aid. We find that our views—whether unconscious, half-formed, or carefully thought out—are inescapably indebted to traditions of thought those men and women have created, carried forward, built on, revised, and criticized.

The ancient Greek philosopher Socrates is famous for his exhortation, "Know yourself." For the liberally educated person, an important part of acquiring self-knowledge is learning the sources and history of the ideas and institutions that have molded the modern Western world and all who grow up in it or are affected by it.

INTRODUCING VOLUME TWO

In Volume One of *Patterns in Western Civilization*, we followed the story of the ideas and ideals of the Western world from their beginnings in the ancient world down to the Scientific Revolution of the sixteenth and seventeenth centuries. In Volume Two, we will follow the continuation and seeming fragmentation of that story. As the story presented in Volume One already revealed, Western civilization has never been monotonal nor monolithic, proceeding in a straight line. Rather, its story, since at least the time of Socrates in Athens and the Hebrew prophets in Israel and Judah, has always been a story of opposing tendencies: simultaneously status quo and critique, idea and counter-idea, establishment and disruption, affirmation and rejection. For instance, Socrates was ostracized by the ruling elite of Athens and eventually put to death. Several Hebrew prophets and many later thinkers and writers whom we now consider to be among the leading lights in the story of Western civilization shared a similar fate.

In Volume Two, we see not only the ongoing back-and-forth struggle in Western civilization between what is and what could be or should be, we also see that the modern project of Western civilization contains admirable and sinister qualities alike. Both are revealed in the thought of the philosopher and intellectual figure with whom we begin—René Descartes.

In Part One of Volume Two, the "light" or optimistic side of modern Western Civilization is more prominent. In the closing chapter of the *Discourse on the Method for Rightly Conducting One's Reason and for Seeking Truth in the Sciences* (1637), René Descartes describes a particular kind of knowledge that he seeks and the value of this kind of knowledge. Divided between knowledge that will serve posterity in some as yet unknown way, and knowledge that will serve immediate social and human needs, Descartes invokes what he calls "the law that obliges us to procure as best we can the common good of all men." His studies have taught him, he says, that it is "possible to arrive at knowledge that is very useful in life and that [replaces] . . . the speculative knowledge taught in the Schools." The "Schools" are for Descartes and for many who follow after him the representatives of traditional religious and philosophical teachings, which Descartes (and many who follow after him) want to reject. His chief example of "very useful" knowledge is neither philosophy nor theology, but medicine. Why medicine? Because, he writes, "the maintenance of health . . . is the first good and the foundation of all other goods in this life."[1]

It is always somewhat surprising (and pleasing) to discover that the philosopher who is famous for the egoistic basis of his thought (*Cogito, ergo sum* ["I think, therefore I am"]) has at the same time such an other-regarding purpose, closing the *Discourse* by declaring an unwavering commitment to what we might now call medical research.[2] Why should Descartes favor applied knowledge? Because "each man is obliged to see as best he can to the good of others," because "being useful to no one . . . is actually to be worthless."[3]

Descartes' concern for "the good of others," or "the common good of all men," over against the easy life of a privileged few anticipates certain defining conflicts in Western thought—political, social, and mythopoetic—over the next 250 years. In the writings of Locke and Voltaire, in *The Federalist Papers*, in the several declarations of human rights created between 1775 and 1848, in John Stuart Mill's passionate cry for personal liberty, in Mary Shelley's depiction of a research scientist's frightening failure to create a "fully human" human being, in Charles Darwin's patient attempts to delimit the natural origin of human life itself, and in Thomas Huxley's similar and related attempts to discover the ethical end of human life, a new, revolutionary idea of human nature emerges. One traditional idea sees that nature as limited and flawed. The new, emerging view is that human persons, however imperfect, possess intrinsic value, regardless of race, gender, class, wealth, or religion. To borrow some words from Jonathan Swift, author of *Gulliver's Travels* (1726), human beings, although they are "odious little vermin . . . smitten with pride" are also, if not reasonable creatures, certainly creatures "capable of reason," and therefore capable of improving an imperfect order of things. They are capable, Descartes might say, of seeing as best they can to the good of others, to the common good of all, and of doing so by the light of their own reasoning faculties alone, without the aid of religious or philosophical tradition.

This claim is, of course, overstated. Descartes probably did not have *all* men in mind (and he says nothing about women); what's more, many who believed in what Thomas Paine in *Common Sense* (1776) would later call "the rights of man" were unable or unwilling to put such beliefs into practice. Thomas Jefferson, as an owner of slaves, is only one example. No matter that "the common good of all men" was at first said with a limited understanding—the idea nevertheless pointed the thinkers that followed in a new direction.

A human revolution—or better, a Humanitarian Revolution—encompasses, informs, and in certain ways *drives* the massive socio-political upheavals in the seventeenth-, eighteenth-, and nineteenth-century Europe that produced modernity. One sign of this link is that the word "humanitarian" was coined during this period.[4] Behind the American and French Revolutions, within the Industrial Revolution, informing both the Enlightenment and the Romantic Movements, and behind the women's movement, the labor movement, and the movement to abolish slavery, a growing, new understanding of what a person is simmers near boiling. He (and increasingly "she") is now a citizen rather than a subject, an agent rather than an instrument, an infinity rather than an earthen clod. Most remarkably, an increasing number of both secular and religious thinkers found that they could agree about this rising egalitarian idea. This ethic of compassion—this humanitarian humanism—also met and continues to meet with fierce resistance: the desire *to* empower struggles against the desire *for* power. In the language of myth, this is an epic struggle, a struggle between the "Promethean" and "Faustian" impulses that coexist in Western culture from its earliest beginnings, and that may well identify what we mean by the West. According to ancient Greek mythology, Prometheus was a god who stole fire from the gods to benefit humanity; in some versions of the story he also gave humans arts and crafts. The medieval European legend of Faust or Dr. Faustus is the story of a scholar who sold his soul to Satan in return for unlimited knowledge and power.

In Part Two of this volume, we see more prominently the dark, "Faustian" impulse that lurks in Descartes' original project. The other-regarding intent and the quest for individual autonomy at the core of the modern project of Western civilization that Descartes first proclaimed was followed, amended, and amplified in numerous ways by thinkers and writers who came after Descartes. Many of the figures considered in Part One expressed this intent and this quest in one way or another in their work. At the same time, however, Descartes also revealed a dark side to that same modern project. In the same paragraph of *Discourse on Method* that articulates his "humanitarian" purposes and his desire for a science that will provide for the "maintenance of health," Descartes says this: " . . . just as we understand the various skills of our craftsmen, we could, in the same way, use these objects for all the purposes for which they are appropriate, and thus make ourselves, as it were, masters and possessors of nature."[5] This intent may sound praiseworthy to our modern ears. The mastery of nature, however, can include the mastery of human nature. The desire for mastery of both the natural and human worlds—the Faustian impulse—may, for any number of reasons, ignore the possibility that there are limits to human knowing and human action. It may also ignore the possibility that attempting to master nature can have unforeseen and unwanted consequences. According to such Greek, Roman, and Christian thinkers as Plato, Aristotle, Sophocles, Seneca, Augustine, and Aquinas, among others, both human beings and the natural world have ultimate, divinely appointed purposes that limit what we may do with, to, and in them. The thought of these and other writers continued to comprise part of the woof and warp of Western civilization, even after Descartes' rejection of "the Schools." In Descartes' conception, however, it is not clear that the purposes and limits of human nature and the natural world that these thinkers had discovered are actually real.

Let us suppose that we have torn ourselves loose, as Descartes explicitly and purposefully does, from the moorings of a human and natural world that has boundaries that are revealed, for example, by natural reason, natural law, or divinely revealed truth. Are there now any inherent limits to human freedom and to the human mastery of nature, including human nature (and, by extension, of other humans)? One could understand the readings of Part Two in this volume as a chronicle of the development of human freedom and human possibilities in Western civilization. As human beings explore the nature of the universe and their own nature more and more closely in a quest for both freedom and mastery, these same readings may also be read as roadmarkers on the way to a disaster. The death camps of the National Socialists, the labor camps of the Soviet Communists and Maoists, the killing fields of Cambodia, the genocides of Kosovo and Rwanda, and the monstrously oppressive tactics of numerous right- and left-wing social, political, and economic movements (all based on ideas derived from the tradition of Western civilization) are but a few examples of such a disaster. The thinning and coarsening of political and public life in capitalist democratic societies that are increasingly ruled by technological and commercial imperatives, about which many social critics complain, is another, perhaps less physically deadly, but nevertheless spiritually oppressive example.

Another way of expressing the general problem posed by the modern quest for human freedom and for mastery of everything, whether scientific, philosophical, social, economic, or political, is found in Friedrich Nietzsche's now-famous parable of a madman who runs into the marketplace with a lantern, looking for God:

> The madman jumped into their midst and pierced them with his eyes. "Whither is God?" he cried: "I will tell you. *We have killed him*—you and I. All of us are his murderes. But how did we do this? How could we drink up the sea? Who gave us the sponge to wipe away the entire horizon? What were we doing when we unchained the earth from its sun? Whither is it moving now? Whither are we moving? Away from all suns? Are we not plunging continually? Backward, sideward, forward, in all directions? Is there still any up or down? Are we not straying as through an infinite nothing? Do we not feel the breath of any empty space? Has it not become colder? Is not night continually closing in on us? Do we not need to light lanterns in the morning? Do we hear nothing as yet of the noise of the gravediggers who are burying God? Do we smell nothing as yet of the divine decomposition? Gods, too, decompose. God is dead. God remains dead. And we have killed him.[6]

All that Nietzsche may have meant with this blasphemous description is open to interpretation. We can say with some assurance, however, that the ideological and genocidal warfare of the twentieth century, which, it seems at times, can only be expressed in terms of body-counts, would be one example of the gravediggers burying God. The religious fundamentalist movements of this and the past century, with their quest for a certainty that attempts to imitate the knowledge of Enlightenment science and that most Christian, Jewish, and Islamic religious leaders and thinkers of the pre-modern period would have considered highly questionable, might be another example. The current increasing reduction of all political and social questions into economic ones might be a third. To add to the images, Nietzsche's "divine decomposition" arguably symbolizes the disintegration of a Western civilization that, until the time of the Protestant Reformation and, in most ways, up until two hundred years ago, was generally based on a commonly shared set of premises concerning the proper nature of relationships among human beings and their relationship to the divine and to their surrounding world. Nearly all such common premises have now been deeply questioned and, in many quarters, rejected. As you will see in your reading, Nietzsche is himself one of the most severe interrogators of this Western tradition and of the "idea" of a Western civilization at all, including the various twentieth- and twenty-first century Enlightenment and Romantic versions of that idea.

At the same time, you will encounter thinkers like W.E.B. Du Bois, who criticize the injustices embedded in Western civilization, but who also extol its virtues and advantages, which they wish only to extend to everyone.

Another way to describe the ambiguous achievement of the modern project in Western civilization is to consider three of the "blows" to the human sense of self that result from the various intellectual developments of that civilization. In the first blow, Nicholas Copernicus developed a mathematical model of the cosmos that removed the earth from the center of that cosmos. Along with casting doubt on the perfect nature of the heavenly bodies, Galileo's empirical observations helped to consolidate that removal. The earth, which human beings called home, was no longer at the center of a perfectly arranged heavenly array of perfect, orbiting bodies, each divinely placed in its respective sphere in a carefully arranged cosmos. Rather, the earth, now itself a planet, gradually came to be seen as a fortuitous arrangement of solids, liquids, and gases in an impersonal universe of vast, empty spaces. It turned out that the inhabitants of that planet—human beings—had not been placed by God at the center of an orderly cosmos. They were now lost in the seemingly infinite reaches of the universe. In a second blow, Charles Darwin seemed to destroy the idea that there was a natural hierarchy among living things, with human beings at its pinnacle. Put another way, Darwin seemed to remove once and for all any notions of an ultimate purpose from our image of both human and non-human nature. He did so by putting in doubt the idea of any kind of fixed human nature that had a knowable purpose and meaning within the wider context of a fixed order of living things. In Darwin's conception, all living things are in constant flux and they are the product of immutable, material, impersonal forces. Third, the psychological speculations and explorations of Sigmund Freud put into question whether human beings are ultimately motivated and guided by a faculty of reason or understanding that is unique to our species, or by instincts and impulses that we share in common with other forms of life. All three of these "blows" were prepared by previous philosophical and scientific work, expanded or objected to by later work, and all three led to further widespread scientific, philosophical, social, and political consequences. You will encounter some of these preparations, consequences, and objections in the readings that follow.

If Western civilization is a coherent set of ideas, then one may argue that the history of the modern period is a history of its disintegration. At the same time, it is also the case that self-reflection, self-critique, and change have nearly always been among the hallmarks of that civilization. Coupled with a well-developed idea of the individual, these were precisely among the characteristics that many of the Greeks, one of the two most important tributaries of Western Civilization, believed set them apart from their surrounding civilizations, especially the Persian and the Egyptian. We might therefore suggest that even in the face of the disasters of the twentieth century, Western civilization continues both as a coherent set of ideas and as an attempt to realize those ideas in concrete social and political forms. Neither the Holocaust, nor nihilism, nor a technological society in which the human spirit is overwhelmed by the *danse macabre* of technocratic managers and aesthetes are, as yet, the last, dying gasps of that civilization. Whether we renew emphasis on the optimistic side of Descartes' original project and its modern inheritors and critics, or reach back to other spiritual and intellectual resources in the Western tradition that are much older than Descartes, the story of Western civilization is still being written.

---

[1] Descartes René. *Discourse on Method*. Donald A. Cress, trans. Indianapolis, IN: Hackett Publishing Co., 1980, 33.

[2] Ibid., " . . I have resolved to spend my remaining lifetime only in trying to acquire a knowledge of nature which is such that one could deduce from it rules for medicine that are more certain than those in use at present. . . .," 41.

[3] Ibid., 35.

[4] Coined in the late eighteenth century, the word "humanitarian" was first used to describe a person who affirmed the humanity of Christ and denied Christ's divinity. From roughly 1830 to 1890, a humanitarian professed "the Religion of Humanity" (e.g. French philosopher and mathematician Auguste Comte [1798-1857]). Comte and his followers believed that it was their duty to advance the well-being of the human race, and that humanity was worthy of worship and the highest reverence. Contemporary with the Comtean definition was its complete opposite: "humanitarian" was also a slanderous term, interchangeable with "sentimentalist" and "abolitionist"; all three terms described extremism on behalf of humanity. From about 1900 onward, the word gradually lost both its Comtean and

its slanderous uses, and came to mean broadly philanthropic, i.e., concerned with the needs of men and women and the alleviation of their suffering. The American humorist Ambrose Bierce defined a philanthropist as "a rich (and usually bald) old gentleman who has trained himself to grin while his conscience is picking his pocket."

[5] *Discourse*, 33.

[6] Nietzsche, Freidrich. *The Gay Science*, aph. 125.

BIOGRAPHIES

Managing Editor

Sarah Chappell Trulove co-authored an NEH grant that brought about sweeping changes in the then-Western Civilization Program at the University of Kansas, and since 1997 has been a Lecturer in the Humanities and Western Civilization Program. She helped develop the program's Semester Abroad in Florence and Paris in 1995 and co-directed the program in 2001.

Senior Editor

James Woelfel is Professor of Philosophy and Professor and Director of the Humanities and Western Civilization Program at the University of Kansas. He has done extensive teaching and research in modern European philosophical and religious thought.

SECTION EDITORS:

Peter Casagrande is Professor of English and Humanities and Western Civilization and a former associate dean of the College of Liberal Arts and Sciences. He is a specialist in the writings of Thomas Hardy and in the study of literary creativity.

Thomas Heilke is Associate Professor of Political Science and former Distinguished Lecturer in Humanities and Western Civilization. He is a Nietzsche scholar and specializes in the study of politics and religion.

CONTRIBUTORS:

Robert Anderson
Stephen Auerbach
S. Daniel Breslauer
Karlyn Kohrs Campbell
Peter Casagrande
Katherine Clark
Richard De George
Jonathan Earle
Diane Fourny
Thomas Heilke
James Leiker
Rex Martin
H. Lewis McKinney
Norman Saul
Benjamin Sax
Sarah Trulove
Emily Wicktor
James Woelfel

SECTION THREE

LIFE OF RENÉ DESCARTES

1596
  Born in La Haye in Touraine

1614
  Completes early eduction at College Henri IV
    in La Flèche (Jesuit)

1616
  Studies canon law at Poitiers

1618
  Joins army of Prince Maurice of Nassau as a
    "gentleman soldier"

1619
  Experience in stove-heated room

1620s
  Pursuit of "good life"

1628
  Turns to more sober pursuits and moves to
    Holland

1635
  Birth of daughter, Francine (dies 5 years later)

1637
  Discourse on Method

1640–41
  Meditations on First Philosophy

1644
  Principles of Philosophy

1649
  The Passions of the Soul
  Moves to Sweden to become tutor to Queen
    Christiana

1650
  Dies of pneumonia in Sweden

CHAPTER ONE

RENÉ DESCARTES AND SEVENTEENTH-CENTURY EUROPE

INTRODUCTION

Born in a French province not far from Paris, fighting as a "gentleman officer" in Germany, living most of his adult life in the Netherlands (Holland)—René Descartes' world was the center of European politics, trade, and society. The seventeenth century ushered in the era of **royal absolutism** and strong, centralized nation-states, such as England, France, the Dutch provinces, and later Prussia. This was accompanied by the slow undoing of the Holy Roman Empire. Throughout the seventeenth and eighteenth centuries, the old imperial territory and power would split and grow wider between the Austrian-Hungarian kingdom to the east, under the Hapsburg dynasty, and the Brandenburg-Prussian states to the west, ruled by the Hohenzollern dynasty (Frederick William to Frederick the Great). With the defeat of the Spanish Armada by the British navy in 1588, the all-powerful Spanish and Portuguese overseas empires would give way to English, Dutch, and French claims in the Americas, Africa, and the South Pacific. Economic might and political right were shifting northward, leaving the Mediterranean basin—the traditional sphere of a Europe conceived as one large Catholic Christian empire, with Rome as its capital—to settle instead in the Protestant countries that looked more to the Atlantic Ocean. If France alone remained the powerful Catholic state, its clergy enjoyed a large degree of autonomy from Rome, pledging loyalty instead to the French crown.

Western Europe gave way to these strong national monarchies and scattering of republics, due in large part to the development of centralized administrations able to collect and manage taxes more effi-ciently, standing armies, and effective means of fostering and maintaining commercial, banking, and trade interests. Central and Eastern Europe for the most part remained frozen in its feudal identity and manners. However, all across Europe the threat of an expanding Ottoman Turkish Empire to the east (which had made important incursions into the Balkans, even threatening to reach Vienna in the eighteenth century), fueled real fear among Europeans and their governments of future Muslim incursions. Relations among the various European states remained contentious and generalized warfare was the norm, with the protracted Thirty Years War, 1618-1648, definitively ending Catholic supremacy in Europe. However, underlying causes of foreign wars shifted from primarily religious ones to disputes over territory, trade interests, and rights of succession. England and France became the two superpowers, with overseas empires, large standing armies, and royal courts and urban social life (in London and Paris/Versailles) the envy of every weaker principality or kingdom. The newcomer among powerful states would be Russia, as it expanded its territories westward into the Ukraine and Poland and began to restructure its society and institutions, under bold rulers like Peter the Great and later Catherine the Great, and to emulate the Western monarchies.

René Descartes' life (1596–1650) was framed by two important events that provide us with some historical insight into the philosopher's lifelong concern with rational inquiry and world systems. The 1598 **Edict of Nantes**, granting France's Protestants (the **Huguenots**) limited rights in a predominantly Catholic country, should have marked the end of a

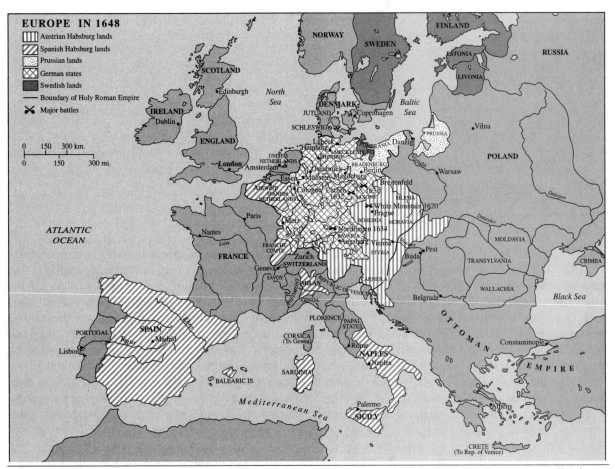

Europe in 1648. Redrawn from *A History of World Societies*, Fifth Edition, by John P. McKay, Bennett D. Hill, John Buckler, and Patricia Buckley Ebrey, (2000), Houghton Mifflin Co.

bloody thirty-six-year civil war of religion that witnessed murderous conspiracies and regicide and pitted Catholicism against reformed religion and monarchy against nobility. But though tempered, the politics of religion would continue to plague France, as well as the rest of Europe, well into the seventeenth century, with Louis XIV revoking the Edict of Nantes in 1685. Much of the century's success in resolving the problems of religious division through the consolidation of nation-states under a strong, centralized authority came at the price of royal absolutism and state religion. Especially in Catholic states, "free thinkers" were regarded with suspicion and their works often censured. An exception to the model of absolutism, where intellectuals and professionals enjoyed much greater freedom, remained the

Netherlands, a union of rich and powerful commercial provinces that had won independence from Spain by 1581. Descartes would spend most of his adult life in the Netherlands, where universities were open to greater intellectual exchange, especially in mathematics and natural philosophy. The seventeenth century was also plagued by frequent poor harvests and food shortages due to colder climatic conditions, fueling frequent waves of famine, disease, and thus peasant revolts.

The second event, the **1648 Treaty of Westphalia** ended the **Thirty Years War (1618–1648)** that had involved most European states and left much of the continent, especially the German states, devastated. (Descartes briefly participated in this war as an officer in the army of

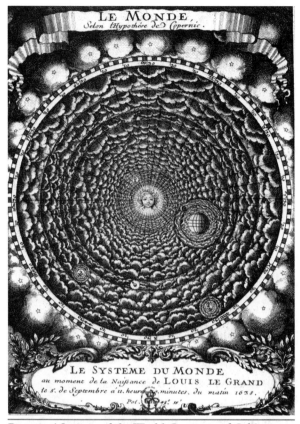

LE MONDE,
Selon l'Hypothèse de Copernic.

LE SYSTÊME DU MONDE
au moment de la Naissance de LOUIS LE GRAND
le 5. de Septembre à 11. heures 45. minutes. du matin 1638.
Pol. 48° 51'

Decartes' *System of the World*. Courtesy of Cabinet des Estampes, Bibliotheque National, Paris

Maximilian, Duke of Bavaria in 1619). Descartes' work, which reflected a search for order, solid foundations, and rules, was embedded in a social and political context fraught by turbulence and uncertainty.

Despite this bleak picture of the times, real gains had been achieved in the intellectual and economic sectors. Given the growth of overseas trade and colonization, and national monarchies and states shifting priorities from religious disputes and wars to economic activities, the emerging middling classes of professionals and bureaucrats, together with enlightened members of the clergy and aristocracy, gave new impetus and resources to the **Scientific Revolution**.

While Descartes' France still suffered from terrible religious struggles between Catholics and Protestants, it also saw a flourishing of artistic and intellectual production, fueled in large measure by the politics of the Reformation and Counter-Reformation of the previous century. With greater emphasis placed on individual desire, initiative, and

reflection on the one hand and on the other, the struggle by the temporal powers of Church and State to maintain their hold on the spiritual, intellectual, and political spheres of society, seventeenth-century Europe's elites profited from several things: a proliferation of privately constituted societies of learning, the expansion of universities and royal academies accommodating the new sciences, and institutional and national support of the arts. At the same time, the general population, especially the rural masses, remained fixed in their crude manners, ignorance, superstitions, and precarious living conditions (famine, epidemics, devastation from war).

While developed by the ancient Greeks, **skepticism** (especially in areas of religious certainty), which had been widely used in the writings of the Humanists of the Renaissance, also fed the rise of science and a renewed interest in the ethical dimension of human society. From the Dutch philosopher Desiderus Erasmus (d.1566) to the French essayist Michel de Montaigne (d. 1592), the new turn toward critical assessment of received ideas, use of **subjective experience**, and confidence in individual motivation and enterprise remained permanent influences in seventeenth-century thought and writing. It comes as no surprise, then, that the manner in which Descartes chose to share his theory of scientific method in his famous *Discourse on Method* was that of a quasi-autobiographical tale of a subject in search of its own grounding in truth and experience. Later in the century, the English political philosopher John Locke would also be universalizing his theories of human understanding and political authority to address human beings as equal, free, and unique individuals, unfettered in areas of ethics, political rights, or psychology by caste, tradition or other preconceived notions.

Unfortunately, this was not the general case among the largely illiterate populations of Europe whose beliefs and activities remained tied to traditional social hierarchies, superstition, and prejudice. Belief in and fear of **witchcraft** not only remained prevalent across Europe but grew in intensity in the seventeenth century. Witchcraft persecutions were carried on by both Catholics and Protestants and were directed overwhelmingly against women. Feminist historians have called the persecutions the "holocaust of women" and "the most hideous example of misogyny in European history." Estimates of

IMPORTANT EVENTS OF THE SCIENTIFIC REVOLUTION

1543: Nicolas Copernicus asserts heliocentrism.

1572: Tycho Brahe establishes accurate data on planetary/lunar orbits and first modern star catalog.

1596: birth of René Descartes.

1600: Wm. Gilbert on magnetic properties of bodies (earth).

1609: Johannes Kepler and laws of planetary motion.

1610: Galileo Galilei and first telescopic observations of celestial phenomena, supports Copernican theory.

1628: William Harvey demonstrates circulation of blood.

1632: Galileo's trial and recantation before Roman Inquisition.

1637: Descartes publishes Discourse on Method and mathematical treatise setting forth analytic geometry.

1642: Blaise Pascal constructs first adding machine.

1644: Descartes publishes Principia philosophiae giving mechanistic explanations for matter and motion for physical, chemical, and biological phenomena.

1650: death of Descartes.

1654: Pascal and Pierre de Fermat begin probability theory.

1657: foundation of first organized scientific center for new experimental science based on work by Galileo, the Accademia del Cimento (Florence).

1660: Robt. Boyle's work on pressure/volume and pneumatic pump.

1662: founding of the Royal Society of London.

1664: posthumous publication of Descartes' L'Homme (Man) expounding a mechanistic interpretation of the animal body.

1665: first scientific journal in the English-speaking world, Philosophical Transactions (Royal Society of London).

1666: Louis XIV establishes the Académie Royale des Sciences and its journal (Journal des Savants).

1669: Isaac Newton develops calculus and reflecting telescope (1672).

1684: Gottfried Wilhelm Leibniz publishes work on differential calculus.

1687: Newton's law of motion and principle of universal gravitation.

1688: Francesco Redi challenges ancient belief in spontaneous generation, beginning a two-century debate on the subject.

the total number who were tortured and killed vary widely because of the difficulty of compiling enough evidence from that period. Anywhere from 100,000 to a million individuals were persecuted and killed, about 80% of whom were women.

The backdrop to the witchcraft persecutions is the uncertainty, conflict, and confusion created by the religious, social, and political turmoil of the sixteenth and early seventeenth centuries. In the mid-dle of the sixteenth century there was a sudden, dramatic increase in arrests and trials for witchcraft, which just as suddenly and dramatically decreased in the middle of the seventeenth century. All over Europe, pre-Christian religious and folklore traditions had continued throughout the Middle Ages and would continue until the twentieth century. These traditions centered on figures whom people called the "cunning folk": usually wisewomen and

Bernini, Apollo and Daphne. Courtesy of Art Resource.

they copulated with Satan. Many ingenious forms of torture and "Catch-22" tests of guilt and innocence were used in trying, convicting, and executing them. By the early seventeenth century witch-hunting was completely out of control, and church and civil authorities attempted to restrain the persecutors. It continued here and there until the eighteenth century. The famous Salem witch trials occurred in the American colonies in the late seventeenth century. After the witchcraft furor died down, many country people returned to their old ways. They saw no problem in being a Catholic or a Protestant and at the same time consulting the cunning folk and practicing the old pre-Christian magic.

Racism was also introduced in European colonies in the Americas, fueled by the alarming growth of indentured and slave labor exploited as commercial and agricultural investments in the new colonies. Time-worn racial stereotypes gleaned from Christian and Muslim theological speculation and the copious collections of three centuries of travel literature, later to be finessed by questionable political and scientific theories of Enlightenment philosophers, often portrayed "peoples of color" (black Africans, Amerindians) as amoral heathens, cannibals, barbarians, and sexually lubricious individuals, good for doing the work of animals, "owing to their low degree of humanity and their proximity to the animal stage." Estimates of the number of black Africans sold into slavery are difficult to confirm; however, historians roughly estimate a minimum of twelve million slaves being sent to the Americas over four centuries (mid-fifteenth to mid-nineteenth). The use and abuse of slaves was so prolific and horrifying in the French colonies of the seventeenth century that Louis XIV's administration finally passed into law the infamous **Black Code** (1685) which legislated the "rights of slaves" to be uniformly (and forcibly) converted to the true faith (Catholicism) and uniformly treated (disciplined) in the area of punishable crimes. Owners could not arbitrarily whip, maim, torture or kill slaves. Every offense would carry a specific penalty, perhaps "softening" the inhumane treatment of slaves to a small degree, yet legalizing their status as human chattel to be corporally punished and stripped of any political rights.

The Arts: The early part of the seventeenth century ushered in the **Baroque esthetic** style in painting, music, theatre, and literature. From the fantasy

midwives who with their magic, spells, and cures were perceived as seers and healers. "Witch" was not originally a negative term; it is from "wicca," which means simply a wizard or wise person. The cunning folk practiced mostly "white magic" (good), but their power was believed to be capable of "black magic" (evil) as well. Women who practiced these arts usually lived alone and were single, which made them suspect in an age when marriage or the convent were the only conventionally acceptable roles for women. A standard charge against women accused of witchcraft was that their lust was insatiable and visions of Christian or atheist utopias such as Campanella's *City of the Sun* (1601), Francis Bacon's *New Atlantis* (1614-26), or Cyrano de Bergerac's *Voyage to the Moon* (1657), to Johann Sebastian Bach's (1685-1750) massive output of cantatas, fugues, choral masses, and concertos, to Bernini's baldacchino (1624-33) over the high altar in Saint Peter's in Rome or his sculpture of an enraptured Saint Teresa (1645-52), the Baroque esthetic reveled in expression of movement, the freedom of form and ornamentation, excess, and metamorphosis, especially in its adornment of palaces and gardens and in Church architecture and music. Shakespeare's notion that "all the world is a stage" or Pierre Corneille's dramatic use of the "play within a play" (*The Comic Illusion*) underscored the Baroque's fascination with such contradictory themes as reality and illusion, genius and folly, and struggles between the dying feudal society of chivalric valor and the new world order of *raison d'Etat* (reasons of state). Such plays as Shakespeare's *A Midsummer's Night Dream* and *Hamlet*, and Corneille's *The Cid* are fitting examples of the precarious nature of a society in a constant state of flux. Finally, no other artistic medium could more fully illustrate the confusion of orders in everyday life wrought by religious, social, and political conflict than the world of **opera**—a play to be sung, a choral piece to be acted—a hybrid spectacle inaugurated by the Italian composer Monteverdi's *Orfeo* in 1607.

Yet the ever-widening consolidation of political authority by powerful princes would mean a substantial increase in royal patronage of the arts, and with it, the birth of a new esthetic, **Classicism**, that triumphed over Baroque sensibilities. Heavily dependent upon new readings of Greek and Roman literature, Classicism infused "national" art with grandeur, rule, and harmony appropriate to royal absolutism. For example, dramatists returned to Aristotle's *Poetics* with its definitions of time, place, and action according to classical Greek tragedy and comedy. The playwright desiring success at court also had to create a plot and characters that conformed to the rules of verisimilitude and good taste. Greek, Roman, and historical plots were resuscitated; declamatory verse of an elevated style encouraged; and overly emotional or violent action was forbidden on stage. In architecture, the geometric gardens of Versailles, the classical regu-

larity of the palace's façades, and the cult of Louis XIV as reincarnation of the Sun King as portrayed in the enormous fountain sculpture of Apollo in Versailles' gardens, all answered to the spirit of the new Classical esthetic.

An increasingly prosperous and educated bourgeoisie had acquired the means to engage in leisured activities similar to those of the aristocracy. Nobles across Europe were being pushed to the margins of political power by strong monarchical rulers (Great Britain perhaps being the exception). For example, dueling among the French nobility was outlawed in 1613, and by 1661, Louis XIV had imposed regular attendance and a strict code of etiquette upon an emasculated nobility at his court in Versailles, effectively impoverishing nobles who were pressured to emulate the king's expensive, princely existence. More enlightened nobles (or those having fallen from favor) found common cause and outlets with the wealthy merchant and administrative classes, preferring together to develop their talents and tastes through cultural and intellectual exchanges. The formation of private scientific **academies** and **salons**, the latter run by wealthy and influential women, fostered an ongoing desire for widening the scientific community and opening the culturally well-bred and urban elite to new ideas (see part 6 of the *Discourse on Method*). In the eighteenth century, especially with the advent of the café, more open discussion of political issues would be added to the mix.

Upper-class women become increasingly influential in shaping taste and ideas, fostering the early development of feminist circles of thinkers and writers intent on crediting women for their part in having "civilized" the modern nation-state in areas of manners, language, style, and domestic life. The well-known playwright Molière satirized both the vulgar manners of the aspiring merchant class and the exaggerated gentility of these women, known as précieuses, in such comedies as *The Bourgeois Gentleman* and *The Learned Ladies*.

Women of the Scientific Revolution: The excitement generated by the new scientific methods and discoveries in the seventeenth and eighteenth centuries stimulated numbers of upper- and middle-class European men and women to take up the study of science. The fact that the women were women, and often wives or sisters of male scientific investigators, caused them to be stereotyped as "scientific ladies": strictly amateurs, useful assistants to men, who could fill their time satisfyingly in such pursuits but lacked both the education and the intellectual capacity to do creative theoretical science. But behind the stereotype was the reality that a number of women in the upper strata of society became scientifically knowledgeable and some made noteworthy contributions to the new science.

The Scientific Revolution produced a large number of women astronomers. The contribution of most was in the realm of observation and calculation rather than of new discovery, but by no means entirely. To mention a few: Sofie Brahe (c. 1556–1643), the sister of the influential Danish astronomer Tycho Brahe (1546–1601), was a self-taught astronomer and alchemist who worked with her brother at his observatory and helped him in making the observations that led to Kepler's determination of the elliptical orbits of the planets. Maria Winckelmann Kirch (1670–1720), a German astronomer, discovered the comet of 1702 but did not receive recognition as its discoverer. She also made observations on the aurora borealis in 1707 and wrote on the conjunction of the sun with Saturn and Venus in 1709.

The one woman astronomer who achieved wide fame and respect—and during her lifetime—was Caroline Herschel (1750–1848), a German who for fifty years lived and did scientific study in England. In 1782, Herschel began her career as an independent observer and became an expert on comets. In 1786 she became the first woman to be recognized for discovering a comet; she discovered seven in all. By the end of the eighteenth century Caroline Herschel was known and respected as an astronomer throughout Europe.

In the seventeenth and eighteenth centuries women likewise played a role in furthering the mechanistic model in science and popularizing the work of scientific pioneers such as Newton. In England Margaret Cavendish (1623–1673), Duchess of Newcastle, numbered among her associates René Descartes, Thomas Hobbes, and Robert Boyle. While her own scientific speculations, expressed in several books, can only be described as fancifully original, she was an aggressive exponent of mechanism, materialism, and atomism.

One of the most notable European women of the eighteenth century was Gabrielle-Emilie Le Tonnelier de Breteuil, the Marquise du Châtelet-

Lomont (1706–1749). Highly regarded among the scientists and mathematicians of her day, it may have been Emilie du Châtelet who more than anyone else brought about the end of the dominance of French science by Descartes and replaced it with Newtonian science. She is also a classic example of the denigration and even theft of women's achievements. History remembers her best as the lover of the famous French Enlightenment writer and thinker Voltaire (1694–1778), and an associate named Samuel Koenig falsely claimed that he had dictated to her her book *Institutions de physique*, which she first published anonymously in 1740. When she and Voltaire remodeled a family estate at Cirey, they installed one of the finest collections of books in France and a large laboratory where the marquise carried out experiments in Newtonian optics. They collaborated in writing the book that played an important role in introducing Newtonian science to the French, stimulating debate on it among intellectuals, and displacing the influence of Descartes. *Eléments de la philosophie de Newton*, first published in 1738, appeared under Voltaire's name and has always been officially attributed to him, despite his repeatedly stating that "Lady Newton," as he called her, knew more about Newtonian science and his clearly implying in the Dedication that hers was the larger contribution to the book. We know for a fact that the chapters on Newton's optics were largely her work. Emilie du Châtelet's last influential project was her two-volume translation of Newton's *Principia*, including her mathematical commentaries on it together with a greatly improved revision of the *Eléments*. With its posthumous publication in 1759, Newtonian science became firmly established as the approach to knowledge that would dominate the French Enlightenment, and it remains the only French translation of Newton's great work.

"Scientific ladies" were also active in other branches of the new methods of scientific investigation, such as chemistry, medicine, and biological classification. A very few examples: Throughout their marriage the Frenchwoman Marie Lavoisier (1758–1836) collaborated closely with her husband Antoine (1743–1794), the founder of modern chemistry, such that her contributions became inseparable from his. Lady Mary Wortley Montagu (1689–1762), a scientific researcher and outspoken early feminist, introduced smallpox vaccination to Britain and Western Europe, despite strong opposition from the medical profession and the church, after carefully studying its successful practice in Turkey. Her work on variation (inoculation with a small amount of smallpox virus) was an early contribution to the eventual development of the germ theory of disease. Maria Sybille Merian (1647–1717), of Dutch-Swiss parentage, was a pioneering entomologist and botanist and an excellent scientific artist who, assisted by her daughter Dorothea, illustrated her books with her own engravings. She wrote a three-volume work on insects of Europe and a book on insects of Surinam (Dutch Guiana, in South America), where she and her daughter studied insects and plants for two years (1698–1700). Merian's books on insects became standard works in entomology.

What feminist historians of science have uncovered in recent years is the considerable role that patriarchal or sexist bias has played in scientific investigation—predominantly, and for obvious reasons, in the fields of biology, human anatomy and physiology, psychology, and medicine—and the negative impact this has had on women. This has been true in terms both of perpetuating ancient prejudices in new forms, with their restriction of women's rights and opportunities, and of directly affecting women's physical and mental health and reproductive life. One out of many examples is the widely held medical opinion, which appeared in standard medical textbooks until the early years of the twentieth century, that too much education was harmful to women because it drained away vital energy needed for their reproductive role. Because most of us think of the methods and conclusions of the natural sciences as objective, neutral, impersonal, and unbiased, it is important to be reminded that science too is a human activity that grows out of and is shaped and sometimes distorted by the values and limitations that always characterize human cultures. The considerable value of science as a reliable way of gaining knowledge of the world is not only that its methods have proven enormously fruitful in terms of their explanatory and predictive power, but also that it is an essentially self-correcting enterprise—testing, improving, and discarding its hypotheses in the light of new data or better interpretations of existing data. This self-critical atti-

Descartes as Faust. Courtesy of Oxford University Press

tude that is so vital to scientists in their inquiries must and at its best does include the disclosure of bias in their previous investigations.

At the most fundamental level, the Scientific Revolution brought about a fateful change in Western humanity's attitude toward nature that affects our lives very directly as contemporary human beings. For thousands of years most cultures imagined and thought of nature as an *organism*, a nurturing "mother." Humans were creatures among creatures, and their role was to adapt to and live in harmony with nature. This attitude toward nature, expressed in a variety of ways in systems of knowledge and ethics and in religious myths, continued to be influential in the Western world long after the advent of Greek philosophy and Christianity. The Scientific Revolution brought about a "paradigm shift" in Western attitudes toward nature. Nature came to be imagined and thought about as a vastly complex *machine*.

Through the power of the rational mind humans were set apart from and over nature, and the human role became the dominating one of wresting its secrets from it, conquering and exploiting it for human benefit. In his *Novum Organum* Francis Bacon influentially expounded this new view of nature and the human relationship to it. The advantages of the new attitude were obvious in terms of the widespread human benefits of the rapid expansion of scientific knowledge and the dramatic technological revolution that began in the eighteenth century and is still going on. The liabilities we have only recently begun to acknowledge and deal with: the serious depletion of earth's resources; the human encroachment on more and more of the natural environment; the destruction of thousands of animal species; global air and water pollution including well-known phenomena such as acid rain, the greenhouse effect, and ozone depletion; the dangers of nuclear weapons, nuclear accident, and nuclear waste; overpopulation.

OUR AUTHOR: René Descartes was born on March 31, 1596 in the small French town of La Haye, France, situated in the rich province of Touraine, widely visited today for its magnificent châteaux and gardens. As an adolescent, he spent several years studying at the best Jesuit institution, the Royal College in La Flèche. Descartes writes about the education he received there in part one of the *Discourse on Method.* By 1616, Descartes was enrolled at the University of Poitiers where he received his law degree two years later. In 1618, he embarked on a two-year career as a "gentleman soldier" that eventually took him north to Holland and then to Germany. The opening pages of part two of the *Discourse* recount Descartes's thoughts while staying in his military camp in Ulm, Germany during the month of November, 1619. Descartes's first trip to Holland marked a turning point in his intellectual life since it was there that he met the mathematician and logician, Isaac Beeckman, whose work was to stimulate and redirect Descartes's interests toward mathematics and the new science. After dropping his short military career, Descartes returned to France, spending most of his time in Paris with intermittent trips to other regions (Brittany) and to Italy and again Holland. The environment in Holland was much more intellectually tolerant than in France, and Descartes moved there permanently in 1629.

Although Descartes never married, he conceived a child with a serving maid who bore a daughter, Francine, born in 1635. He seems to have provided support for mother and daughter, though his having fathered a child was never made public. Very little else is known about Descartes' relationship with them; however, he expressed feelings of apparent distress in a letter to a friend upon the death of his daughter at the age of five, saying that it had left him "with the greatest sorrow that he had ever experienced in his life." Other than this one affair, Descartes was never known to have maintained any other intimate relationships with women. By contrast, Descartes' intellectual relations with fellow thinkers across Europe were numerous and sometimes contentious. He remained very much a solitary individual, preferring written exchanges to face-to-face conversation. He guarded his ideas jealously and was known to accuse others of frequently misunderstanding and sometimes plagiarizing his theories. Despite the very cold, impersonal, and exacting style of most of his writing, Descartes revealed himself a man of strong emotions and convictions as his times dictated. Later in life, starting in 1643, Descartes kept up an active correspondence with a royal princess, Elizabeth of Bohemia, who herself was a gifted and well-read 25-year-old woman with a keen interest in mathematics, physics, theology, and philosophy. Their letters reveal a mutually felt, deep friendship, if not altogether a platonic love for each other. While Descartes apparently went to great pains to avoid meeting with Elizabeth in person (for fear of exacerbating his affections for a woman well above his own station?), he dedicated his last work to her, *The Passions of the Soul* (published 1650), a treatise on the general relation between the mind and the body from moral and psychological as well as physiological perspectives. Having gained an international reputation for his work in mathematics and philosophy, in 1649 Descartes was invited by Queen Christina of Sweden to join her at court in Stockholm. He had been in Sweden less than a year when he succumbed to the harsh winters of Scandinavia and fell ill with pneumonia, dying in 1650 at the age of 54.

GUIDE TO THE READING: *DISCOURSE ON METHOD*

Descartes was deeply and creatively involved in the Scientific Revolution. The inventor of analytic geometry, he was also an experimental scientist who studied physiology (see the *Discourse*, Part 5) and wrote scientific treatises on meteorology and a theory of vision. As he promises in the title, *Discourse on the Method for Rightly Conducting One's Reason and for Seeking Truth in the Sciences*, in Parts 5 and 6 Descartes describes and illustrates his understanding of scientific method. In the *Discourse* Descartes sounds like Francis Bacon in his enthusiasm for science as giving humans the power to be "masters and possessors of nature."

The Scientific Revolution raised **three philosophical issues in new ways. The first** was the problem of appearance and reality. The new science challenged the common-sense realism of Aristotle and demonstrated—as in the case of Copernican astronomy—that we cannot rely uncritically on the evidence of our senses. This contributed to the centrality of skepticism in modern philosophy: How do we know when we have accurate knowledge of the world? How do we bridge the gap between the knowing mind (subject) and the external world (object)? **The second** issue was the status of the human soul (self, mind) and free will. The new science explained all natural phenomena in terms of causal laws and physical activity. Could not the mind and human choice also be explained as properties of matter? Another hallmark of modern philosophy has been this preoccupation with the nature of the human self. **A third** problem was the relationship between reason and revelation. The success of the new science seemed to show that reason was capable of understanding everything. The bitter conflict within Christianity and a general decline of its influence, along with the new science, raised questions about the authority of the Bible and the Church. Critical questioning of claims to revelation became central to eighteenth-century Enlightenment thought and has continued as an important theme of modern thought generally.

Discourse on Method, which Descartes published in 1637, was—together with his other philosophical writings—an attempt to find solutions to these problems. (We call Descartes' ideas, and ideas based on them, *"Cartesian."* Thus people speak, for example, of the Cartesian theory of the relation between mind and body.) Descartes cast this writing in the form of an intellectual autobiography, describing how philosophical problems arose for him and how he tried to solve them. He also wrote the *Discourse* in French, to reach a wider audience (including women) than professional scholars.

Descartes' project involved rethinking the foundations of human knowledge. In Part One of the *Discourse* Descartes describes his education and the doubts he had about what he had learned. He believes that most people are roughly equal in their capacity to reason, and his approach is to rely on ordinary reason and direct experience. The belief that every normal person has the ability and the obligation to think for him- or herself became a central theme of Enlightenment thought.

In Part 2 Descartes describes his day in the "stove-heated room" in 1619, during the Thirty Years War. Here, as a young man, he formulated his project for rethinking the foundations of knowledge. Although he does not indicate it in this account, this was a visionary experience in which the ideas came to him with the force of revelation. The following night he had dreams that seemed to convey the divine seal of approval to his project. Note Descartes' statement of the fourfold method he would use to guide his thinking, and see how he carries it out in succeeding chapters.

In Part 3 Descartes describes how he formulated a "provisional moral code" to guide his practical life while he was working on his project. Look carefully at the four principles or maxims in the moral code. Notice in the first maxim that Descartes does not intend to apply his method of radical doubt to the government and religion of his country. Later thinkers such as Voltaire and Montesquieu, influenced by Descartes' method, did not stop, as he did, with questioning theoretical knowledge, but also questioned the politics and religion of their day. Despite being accused of atheism for his philosophical writings, Descartes always considered himself a faithful Catholic, doing for the faith in the seventeenth century what Thomas Aquinas had done in the thirteenth. Descartes was also a man of circumspection and caution, as can be seen in his decision not to publish a book defending Copernican astronomy when he heard of the trial of Galileo. In examining the four maxims we can see the influence of Aristotle and of Stoicism.

Part 4 is the pivotal chapter of the *Discourse*. With his new method Descartes questioned whether there is anything that cannot possibly be doubted, anything that is not merely possible or probable but certain. He uses the method of *formal or methodological doubt*: using radical skepticism in order to overcome skepticism and attain certainty. (Using a skeptical method and arriving at skeptical conclusions are not the same thing. Descartes uses a skeptical method but comes to certain conclusions. By contrast, Hume uses a skeptical method and also comes to skeptical conclusions. Hence we consider him a skeptic.) Descartes provides a much more detailed account of his reasonings in his book *Meditations on First Philosophy*, which he published in 1641.

Having doubted everything he can conceivably doubt—even the truths of mathematics—Descartes hits bedrock: The one thing he cannot doubt is that he is doubting, which is a form of thinking. The proposition "I think, therefore I am" is his foundational truth, the certainty from which he will proceed to build up the edifice of knowledge. This is one of the most famous statements in philosophy, and it is called the *Cogito* after its Latin formulation: *Cogito ergo sum* (in the original French, *Je pense, donc je suis*). What is the "I" whose existence Descartes cannot doubt—the mind or the whole person? It is important that you understand that before you proceed. When Descartes thinks about his basic proposition, he derives from it two criteria for determining whether something is true. What are they?

From his own existence Descartes then proceeds to demonstrate the existence of God—twice. Carefully review the two arguments for God's existence. Remember that at this point the objective reality of the external world is still a matter of doubt. How does Descartes proceed from the reality of God to the reality of the external world and the trustworthiness of our knowledge?

In Parts 5 and 6 Descartes applies his method to gaining knowledge in the sciences. Examine carefully how he understands scientific knowledge. His understanding of how science works is *deductive*, and his model is mathematics. The deduction process involves deriving from general premises specific conclusions that are contained in the premises. From the nature of God and general natural laws we can deduce the nature of the universe, according to Descartes, but we need observation and experiment to determine the actual effects among the possible effects of various causes. Descartes illustrates his understanding of scientific method from the anatomy and physiology of the heart. This concept of scientific reasoning was challenged by Newton's *inductive* understanding of science as beginning with observation of or experiment on particular things and inferring generalized conclusions on that basis.

How are Descartes' methods and conclusions a response to the three issues posed by the Scientific Revolution? (1) Regarding the problem of appearance and reality, Descartes uses skepticism to overcome skepticism by uncovering "clear and distinct ideas" (his own existence as a thinking being and the existence of God) which he believes cannot be doubted and are therefore the foundations of all thought. (2) Descartes's answer to the problem of the human soul or self is what is called *Cartesian dualism*. Two absolutely different substances make up the universe: *res cogitans* or "thinking things"—minds—which are non-material, independent, free, and immortal; and *res extensa* or "extended things," physical objects (including the human body) which are material, composite, changing, perishable, and causally determined. Descartes uses the model of the machine to characterize the physical universe, a model that was to dominate all thinking about nature in the Enlightenment. Descartes speculated that the point at which mind and body interacted—where the physical and non-physical universes were synchronized—was the pineal gland (a cone-shaped structure in the brain whose precise function is still unknown). (3) Regarding the relation between revelation and reason, Descartes confidently believed that he had only confirmed and strengthened Catholic doctrine by his independent demonstrations of the independence, freedom, and immortality of the soul and of the existence of a supremely perfect Being.

Descartes became the source of what is called *Continental Rationalism*. Its exponents were all from the Continent of Europe: Descartes from France, Baruch Spinoza from Portugal and Holland, and Gottfried Leibniz from Germany. Central to Rationalism was Descartes's belief that the human mind contains *innate ideas* or "certain seeds of truth that are in our souls." All clear and distinct ideas are innate: the *Cogito*, God, the laws of thought such as the principle of identity ("A thing is what it is and not something else"), the idea of causality, mathematical and geometrical principles such as "the whole is equal to the sum of its parts," and the universal laws of nature. Our sense experience provides the occasions for the mind to call on its innate ideas to organize and understand experience. The theory of innate ideas has its ancient roots in Plato's theory that learning is recollection, but the Continental Rationalists reformulated it. They argued that the human mind or reason (hence "rationalism") is richly "furnished" and powerful in its ability to know itself, God, and nature. This means that for the Rationalist the ideal of knowledge is certainty.

Responding critically to the Continental Rationalists were the *British Empiricists*—John Locke in the seventeenth century and Bishop George Berkeley and David Hume in the eighteenth. (Newton was also an empiricist in his scientific writings.) They argued that there are no innate ideas. All knowledge is derived from experience ("empiricism" is from the Greek word meaning "experience"): from sense impressions, mental intuitions, and feeling states. The human mind is limited in the scope of its knowledge, and the ideal of knowledge is probability and not certainty.

QUESTIONS FOR STUDY AND DISCUSSION

1. What was Descartes' project, and what method did he adopt in pursuing it? Be specific about the stages and progression of the method. What was the connection between his project and the Scientific Revolution? Why is Descartes called the founder of modern philosophy?
2. Compare and contrast Descartes' philosophical method and conclusions with those of Plato and Aristotle. With which of the two ancient philosophers does Descartes seem to have the closer affinities, and why? Do you see any relationship between the answer to this question and Descartes' involvement in the Scientific Revolution?
3. Descartes "set the agenda" for subsequent philosophers, even those who disagreed with him. Describe the differences between *rationalism* and *empiricism* as the two dominant philosophical approaches Descartes influenced. Which approach did Descartes initiate, and which did Locke initiate? Which one came to prevail among French Enlightenment thinkers?
4. How did transformations of the political landscape of seventeenth-century Europe encourage new ways of thinking? In what ways did the Scientific Revolution not contribute to the social and political progress of the age?
5. In what ways were women involved in the Scientific Revolution?

SUGGESTIONS FOR FURTHER READING

Alic, Margaret. *Hypatia's Heritage: A History of Women in Science from Antiquity through the Nineteenth Century*. Boston: Beacon Press, 1986.

Briggs, Robin. *The Scientific Revolution of the Seventeenth Century*. New York: Harper and Row, 1969.

Cohn, I. Bernard. *Revolution in Science*. Cambridge, MA and London, England: the Belknap Press of Harvard University, 1985.

Dekosky, Robert K. *Knowledge and Cosmos: Development and Decline of the Medieval Perspective*. Washington, D.C.: University Press of America, 1979.

Gaukroger, Stephen. Descartes: *An Intellectual Biography*. Oxford: Clarendon Press, 1995.

Hall, A.R. *The Scientific Revolution 1500–1800. The Formation of the Modern Scientific Attitude*. Boston: Beacon Press, 1956.

Kearney, Hugh. *Science and Change, 1500–1700*. New York: McGraw-Hill, 1971.

Merchant, Carolyn. *The Death of Nature: Women, Ecology, and the Scientific Revolution*. San Francisco: Harper & Row, 1980.

Rossi, Paolo. *Philosophy, Technology, and the Arts in the Early Modern Era*. Translated by Salvator Attanasio. New York: Harper and Row, 1970.

Spencer, Samia, ed. *French Women and the Age of Enlightenment*. Bloomington: Indiana University Press, 1985.

Westfall, Richard. *The Construction of Modern Science: Mechanisms and Mechanics*. New York: John Wiley & Sons, Inc., 1971.

Wightman, W. P. D. *Science and the Renaissance*. 2 vols. New York: Hafner, 1962.

LIFE OF JOHN LOCKE

1632
John Locke born at Wrington, Somerset

1642–49
English Civil War

1647-1665
Education of John Locke first at Westminster School, London, then Christ Church College Oxford

1649–1660
Commonwealth under Oliver Cromwell

1660
Restoration of monarchy under Charles II

1666
Locke begins a long association with the First Earl of Shaftesbury

1668
Elected a Fellow of the Royal Society

1675–78
Travels and studies in France

1682
Shaftesbury flees to Holland, dies 1683

1683–1689
Locke takes refuge in Holland

1685–1688
James II succeeds his brother as king

1688–89
Glorious Revolution, monarchy of William and Mary

1689
Letter on Toleration and *Two Treatise of Government*

1690
An Essay Concerning Human Understanding and *A Second Letter Concerning Toleration*

1693
Some Thoughts Concerning Education

1695
The Reasonableness of Christianity

1696–1700
Serves as commissioner of Board of Trade

1700–1704
Lives in retirement at the country estate of Sir Francis and Lady Damaris Masham.

1704
Dies

CHAPTER TWO

JOHN LOCKE AND MODERN POLITICAL THOUGHT

INTRODUCTION

Seventeenth-century ideas of natural rights and of government by consent are often held to have fueled the two great revolutionary movements of the eighteenth century, the American and the French Revolutions, which inaugurated the modern era in political and social thought and institutions. The belief that individual civil rights and representative, multi-branched government, can form part of a program for re-creating political authority were undoubtedly part of the background to what happened in Philadelphia in 1787-1791, when the framers of the U. S. Constitution embodied in that document the separation of powers, the federal system, and the Bill of Rights. These ideas flowed into the language of other documents following the establishment of the Constitution and are alive and active in the twenty-first century. The expression "human rights," however, has largely replaced "natural rights." A few examples of many in the past hundred and fifty years are the *Declaration of Rights and Sentiments* of the first women's rights convention in 1848, the United Nations' *Universal Declaration of Human Rights* of 1948, and the many appeals to the language of human rights in the Eastern European revolutions of 1989. It matters greatly, therefore, exactly what the origins of these modern ideas are and that we can trace them back to their seventeenth-century roots. Seen historically, we can often appreciate the meanings of writers of the past as twofold: the meanings of what they wrote at the time, and the meanings that later ages read into them.

We begin this enquiry, therefore, with the historic meaning of the ideas of John Locke (1632-1704). These addressed the situation in England during his lifetime, but after his death his seventeenth–century English ideas were used as if he had spoken to and for people at all times and everywhere.

THE LONG SHADOW OF
THE REFORMATION AND THE RISE OF
ABSOLUTISM

The reforming movements of Martin Luther (1483-1546) and John Calvin (1509-64) brought about devastating religious conflicts throughout Europe. These included the so-called Peasants' Revolt in Germany (1524-6), the French wars of religion (1562-98), the revolt of the Netherlands against Spanish rule (c. 1572-9), and the Thirty Years' War in central Europe (1618-48). This menace of instability coincided across Europe with the steady strengthening of the state and especially of the institution of monarchy. In France, the key figure in the development of royal power was Louis XIII (1601-43), although the most resplendent of the monarchs was Louis XIV (1638-1715). Faced with the threat of civil war and the ruin of their fragile economies, many European political thinkers, notably the Frenchman Jean Bodin (1530-96), elaborated theories of strong, centralized monarchy as the only safeguard. Strengthening monarchies went with the recovery of European Roman Catholicism now known as the Counter Reformation, especially following the Council of Trent (*Trentino*) in Italy (sat 1545-63), where Roman Catholic doctrine was redefined. Protestants almost everywhere were driven back by resurgent Catholicism, backed by the military power first of Spain, then of France: this produced heightened fears, perhaps justified, of the extinction of "reformed religion" and the triumph of autocratic Catholic monarchy.

In England and Scotland, the key figures of a resurgent monarchy were James I (1566-1625) and Charles I (1600-1649). The British Isles experienced their own version of the horrors of civil war and religious conflict, beginning in 1642. They ended with the restoration of the monarchy in 1660; but no one knew if revolution would break out again. This was an age of lasting and profound insecurity. England too had its theorists advocating a strong state, notably Sir Robert Filmer (d. 1653) and Thomas Hobbes (1588-1679), author of a classic work, *Leviathan*, published in the middle of England's troubles in 1651.

Many modern constitutional historians have interpreted seventeenth-century English political history in terms of a stark contrast between monarchical absolutism and constitutionalism: that is, between the idea that the king was arbitrary and could do whatever he chose, and the idea that the king could only rule in conformity with fundamental law. More recent scholars have shown that this is a false antithesis. Most people at the time wanted a strong monarchy and a strong parliament together (they saw kings as absolute in their jurisdiction but not thereby arbitrary in their power), and England's "ancient constitution" had for centuries included both a monarchy and a parliament.

From the 1640s, however, some extremists did indeed side with one or the other alternative. Extreme royalists like Filmer argued that kings were both absolute and arbitrary, and that this was good. Extreme parliamentarians agreed that "absolute" and "arbitrary" were the same, but repudiated monarchy in an attempt to establish a republic. Most people in the middle, who held that kings were absolute but not arbitrary, thought that monarchs were obliged to rule in accord with natural, that is, divine, law.

The English monarchy, as restored in 1660, healed this rift: it abandoned its earlier attempts to raise certain taxes without parliamentary approval. Another major source of conflict now arose, however: the question of religious toleration. Few people in the first century after the Reformation thought religious toleration was a virtue: most claimed to have the correct answers in matters of religion, and thought they had a right and even a duty to impose those right answers on others. After his restoration to the throne in 1660, Charles II displayed a novel and worrying tendency: he preferred to settle the religious disputes of the age by the concession—as an act of royal prerogative—of religious toleration—even toleration of the feared Roman Catholics. The most virulent political slogan of the age was now to be "Popery and arbitrary power." Some people feared, or said they feared, that Charles II (reigned 1660-85) and James II (reigned 1685-88) intended not toleration but an attempt to institute arbitrary rule through an alliance with international Roman Catholicism.

THE INTELLECTUAL RESPONSE

How did seventeenth English thinkers respond to what was increasingly spoken of as "absolutism"? They reacted in very different ways. Thomas Hobbes came to support absolutism on essentially secular and pragmatic grounds. He posited as the starting point of his analysis the "state of nature," existing before government, in order to deduce conclusions from what he claimed were the essential attributes of human nature. Hobbes held that people were unchangingly egoistic, and ruthlessly sought their individual advantage; only a strong state could preserve civil peace among such individuals. Hobbes believed that his gloomy picture of human life without government was solidly based on what we can observe of human behavior generally, but he also had the England of his own day vividly in mind, wracked as it was by political and religious conflict and then torn apart by civil war.

We have witnessed civil wars in many places in the world in our own time—for example in former Yugoslavia, Rwanda and Burundi, and Afghanistan. In such situations people do things they would never normally do, even savage and violent things. If one were to imagine order gradually breaking down completely, so that eventually anarchy occurred, and there was no place to escape from it, then it is possible to see how Hobbes reached his very pessimistic conclusion that a state of nature (that is, life without government) is like a war, a "war of all against all." For Hobbes, civil society, even under conditions that would seem to us oppressive or restrictive, was infinitely preferable to life in the state of nature, and the preservation of human life and the securing of peace were the two highest values.

Other thinkers came to support the monarchy on religious grounds. The most authoritative political text in seventeenth-century England was the Bible,

Portrait of Thomas Hobbes. Courtesy of the Library of Congress.

and many argued that it showed that God had instituted monarchy rather than any other form of government. In 1680 one such book, Sir Robert Filmer's *Patriarcha*, was published posthumously. It was untypically extreme in one way: it argued that subjects must obey even the unjust commands of their monarch and did not have the right, as taught by the Church of England, of "passive obedience" (our term for this is "civil disobedience"). But Filmer was useful for royalists, most of whom were members of the Church of England ("Anglicans"), because he was a firm monarchist as well as an ardent anti-Catholic. His book was published during the "Exclusion Crisis," a parliamentary crisis of 1679–83 caused by the attempt of the opposition in Parliament to bar James, Duke of York, from the succession to the throne on the grounds of his open Catholicism. The opposition failed, and James succeeded his brother Charles II as James II in 1685. Locke, and his friends, were terrified.

John Locke, at least in his early writings around 1660, also supported a strong monarchy as the only antidote to chaos, but he moved to the opposite end of the spectrum by the 1670s. We now know that his book *Two Treatises of Government* (although not published until 1690) was drafted during the Exclusion Crisis. It therefore focused on dynastic questions and said little about many of the other political questions that generally concern people and would be raised in the Revolution of 1688. Locke's immediate aim was to find arguments to justify resistance to monarchs, and it has been suggested that he was involved in conspiracies to assassinate Charles and James (the failed "Rye House plot" of 1683). Although Charles survived assassination, and James survived two failed rebellions soon after his accession in 1685, his opponents were unremitting in their hostility. James swiftly alienated his natural supporters, the Anglican royalists, by favoring his co-religionists the Catholics, and when a son was born to the Queen in 1688, thereby possibly providing a Catholic succession and a permanent alliance with France, his enemies had to act. William of Orange, Stadtholder of the United Provinces and a sworn enemy of Louis XIV, transported an army to England. The English did little to support James, whose power therefore collapsed; he fled to France, and William and his wife became King and Queen. This coup of 1688–9 was soon known, by its admirers, as the "Glorious Revolution."

In the wake of the Revolution, the political landscape was transformed. Locke quickly adapted his *Two Treatises of Government* and published the book, with a Preface praising William III. Read in the light of the Glorious Revolution, it could be interpreted not as the call for armed resistance (and even radical revolution) that it had been in 1683 but as a rationale for the moderate, constitutional monarchy that William claimed to have safeguarded. Indeed, William III's supporters, called the Whigs, argued that England's ancient constitution of mixed and limited monarchy had been restored (a debatable claim) and that the Stuarts had all along stood for arbitrary government, Popery and tyranny (also debatable); but since the Whigs had won, so did their interpretation of events. Because Locke was now thought to be on the winning side, his book was interpreted in the light of the values that the new regime was claimed by its supporters to embody. Gradually, over decades, those values changed, and Locke was eventually held to be the champion or even the founding father of democracy, of mixed

Title page from Hobbes' Leviathan. Courtesy of Corbis Images.

government, of liberalism, and of capitalism. We need to examine his text carefully if we are to see just how his ideas fed into later ones, or how later ages misread him for their own purposes.

FROM SCHOLAR TO REVOLUTIONARY

John Locke (1632-1704) came from the west of England, born in Wrington, Somerset, the son of a minor landowner. Locke's family were Puritans rather than Royalists, and his father served as a captain in the Parliamentary army during the Civil War. After graduating from Oxford University Locke became a Student (i.e., a Fellow) of Christ Church, Oxford's largest college. There he taught Greek and moral philosophy, turned to the study of medicine in order to avoid taking Holy Orders, and was eventually licensed as a physician. He was early exposed to the philosophy of Descartes and influenced by the

new developments in science. Critical of Descartes' rationalism, in which the mind contains a number of "innate ideas" independently of experience, Locke developed what he considered to be a "common sense" empiricist approach in which all knowledge depends on sense experience. Thus he is often considered as the "father" of British empiricism, which in the seventeenth and eighteenth centuries was the main rival and alternative to the Continental rationalism associated with Descartes.

In 1665 Locke became physician and adviser to a member of the aristocracy, Lord Ashley, the first Earl of Shaftesbury. Shaftesbury was politically active as a prominent member of the Parliamentary opposition to the throne. In 1668 he became seriously ill from a liver ailment that had troubled him for twelve years. An excellent physician, Locke devised a silver and later a gold shunt to drain Shaftesbury's abscess. Shaftesbury's health completely recovered, and he wore the shunt the rest of his life. In 1672 Shaftesbury was appointed Lord Chancellor of England by Charles II, the highest office in the land under the king. From 1676-79 Locke was in France for reasons of health. He returned to the service of Lord Shaftesbury in 1679, and wrote his *Two Treatises on Government* during the period 1679-83. (While there is some scholarly disagreement about exactly when Locke wrote the two treatises, one widely accepted view is that he wrote the *Second Treatise* first, between 1679 and 1681, and the *First Treatise* in 1683. He did not publish them until 1690, after the Glorious Revolution.) Locke followed Shaftesbury into exile in Holland following an unsuccessful plot to keep James, Duke of York, from succeeding to the throne as James II. Shaftesbury died in Amsterdam early in 1683, and Locke arrived there later in the year.

It was during his six years in Holland, a republic with a tradition of religious toleration, that Locke wrote his most important philosophical work, which was not published until after his return to England: his *Essay Concerning Human Understanding*, the book that established him as the founder of the British empiricist tradition in philosophy. While in Holland he also wrote *A Letter Concerning Toleration* (published in 1689), a pioneering essay on behalf of religious toleration, and *Some Thoughts Concerning Education* (published 1695), which revealed Locke's ideas on childhood and education.

Locke returned to England in the wake of the Glorious Revolution, and after the accession of William and Mary he published, although anonymously, his *Two Treatises of Government* in 1690. Some have seen in this book a call, too late, for a more radical revolution; others have seen it as an endorsement of William's rule. After his return Locke served with distinction as a commissioner of trade until 1700, and continued to write and publish philosophical works, including *The Reasonableness of Christianity* (1695). Locke never married, although his writings on fatherly power and the education of children are sometimes today treated as practical rather than academic texts. Locke died one of the most honored philosophers in Europe; yet only at his death did he acknowledge authorship of what is now his most famous work, *Two Treatises of Government*. Scholarly opinion differs on the influence of Locke in the first two centuries after his death, but in the twentieth century he acquired the reputation of being a chief founder of our modern ideas of human rights and a philosopher who provided the foundations of political and economic liberalism.

KEY THEMES IN THE *TWO TREATISES OF GOVERNMENT*

Locke's *Two Treatises of Government* was his most important book on politics. Its immediate purpose was to destroy the late Stuart monarchy in England. However, while addressing the political situation in late seventeenth-century England, Locke subtitled the *Second Treatise* "an essay concerning the true original, extent, and end of civil government," and many have interpreted it as a general theory of government. That is the way many enduring ideas arise: although a response to a particular situation of the author's time and place, they transcend that situation and achieve universality (or are considered as doing so).

Locke wrote both treatises as a reply to Robert Filmer, whose posthumously-published book *Patriarcha* was an extreme and provocative defense of royal absolutism. The *First Treatise* is a detailed refutation of Filmer's arguments. Locke polemically misstated the essence of Filmer's views: "[Filmer's] system . . . is no more but this: *That all government is absolute monarchy*. And the ground he builds on is this: *That no man is born free.*" In the *Second Treatise*

Locke developed his own theory of government, arguing for just the opposite: that all humans are born equal in the state of nature, and that therefore all legitimate government is limited in power. The *First Treatise* is difficult and detailed, but the shorter and more generalized *Second Treatise* is often thought to lay the theoretical foundations of modern ideas of rights and representative democracy.

One basis of Locke's arguments in the *Second Treatise* is often taken to be his theory of human nature, which he set forth in his *Essay Concerning Human Understanding*. According to Locke, our behavior is propelled by our natural desires ("appetites") and aversions—generally speaking, by the desire for happiness and the avoidance of pain. Locke recognized the dominance of self-regarding or egoistic motives, which manifest themselves prominently in the desire for recognition, status, and possessions. But Locke also emphasized the inherent rationality of human beings: our natural ability to direct and control our behavior through knowledge and choice, and particularly to acknowledge and put into practice standards of morality. Others have argued that Locke's two books were inconsistent, for the *Essay Concerning Human Understanding* ignored the idea of natural law so important in the *Two Treatises*.

The state of nature. This famous phrase refers to *human existence without government*—that is, without any common political authority over people. This concept had roots in the late Middle Ages, but Locke developed the idea in what would become a powerfully influential way. He formulated a hypothesis about what human life would look like if stripped of all political institutions—what he called *civil society*—and imagined how people would behave and relate to one another without civil society, that is, in a *state of nature*. In this way, he believed, we can gain some understanding of the rationale for civil society, grounded as it is in human needs, relations, and reflections. While Locke often used the idea of the state of nature to help in understanding government in the abstract, he wrote in other passages as if there was originally a time when humans actually lived in that state. He also believed that there were isolated groups of people in his own time who lived in a state of nature (for example—and of course incorrectly—some Indian tribes in North America). In addition, he used the term to

Portrait of John Locke. Courtesy of the Library of Congress.

describe the relations that always exist between *different* civil societies, such as England and France, since different societies do not recognize any common political authority over them. Locke argued that in the state of nature humans are *free* (independent) and *equal*. What Locke meant by that is that in the state of nature there is no subordination or supremacy among individuals (equality), and no human authority over them (freedom). (In Locke's thinking all human beings, even those living in the state of nature, were under the authority of God, but here he was speaking only of *political* authority or government.) When Thomas Jefferson in the *Declaration of Independence* stated that "all men are created equal," he had in mind the Lockeian idea of equality in the state of nature.

The law of nature. According to Locke, the state of nature, even without society and government, is not the sheer anarchy it was for Hobbes. Whereas Hobbes characterized the state of nature *psychologically*, in terms of the individual's entirely egoistic powers and desires, Locke told his version of the "story" in terms of the inherently *moral* character of life in the state of nature. Even in this state,

wrote Locke, there was a moral law governing human conduct: the *law of nature*. Here Locke departed dramatically from Hobbes. When Hobbes wrote of the "law of nature," he meant a purely prudential or practical rule that individuals adopt: not to do anything that will harm their own self-preservation. By contrast, when Locke wrote of the "law of nature," he stood in the tradition of natural law developed by Christian thinkers such as Thomas Aquinas. Locke affirmed a universal moral law, with its source in God, of which all humans inherently have some knowledge as reasoning beings. In his interpretation of natural law Locke was influenced by the sixteenth-century Anglican theologian Richard Hooker, and Locke often quotes from Hooker in the *Second Treatise*. According to Locke, even in the state of nature individuals did not simply do anything they could to preserve their lives and possessions, as Hobbes would have it. Individuals are constrained in their behavior toward one another by natural moral principles. It is those principles—the law of nature—that in fact reveal what natural rights are.

Natural rights. Natural rights are *the rights that individual human beings would have in the state of nature*. These are rights a person has simply by being a member of the human race and therefore a rational and moral agent, *independently* of government. The idea of natural rights has an even older history than the idea of the state of nature. It grew out of the ancient theory of *natural law*, the view that there is a universal, objective moral law that all humans know through their natural capacity to reason. This idea was developed by the Stoic philosophers, incorporated by early Catholic Christianity, and through Thomas Aquinas in the Middle Ages became an influential way of thinking about ethics and politics down to our own day. The idea of natural law affirmed that all human beings, just by virtue of being rational animals, and quite apart from the particular laws, customs, and morals of the societies they happen to live in, know universal moral principles such as not harming or murdering others, and recognize (even if they often do not follow) their obligation to follow those principles.

But the idea of natural *rights* of individuals was only implicit in natural law theory until Locke made it the very center of his theory of government. In the medieval world, rights were typically seen as connected with the "estate" to which an individual belonged, whether clergy, aristocracy, or common-ers. Each estate had its own set of rights and its own set of obligations. But Locke, and later natural rights thinkers such as Jean-Jacques Rousseau, derived from their hypotheses of the state of nature ideas about what inherent or natural rights all individuals, equally and without exception, would have in the state of nature. The theory of natural rights, as famously expressed for example in the American *Declaration of Independence* in terms of "life, liber-ty, and the pursuit of happiness," is one of the most powerful political ideas of the modern world.

Having described the state of nature as regulat-ed by the law of nature, Locke then enumerated the main moral principles that comprise the law of nature: *not harming, robbing, subjecting, enslav-ing, or killing other human beings*. Such violations of others are, said Locke, violations of people's *nat-ural rights* of *life*, *liberty*, and *possessions*. It's impor-tant to note that in writing the *Declaration of Independence*, Jefferson saw his phrase "life, liberty, and *the pursuit of happiness*" as simply reiterating Locke's original triad of rights. Not only in Locke's writings and the eighteenth-century Enlightenment thought that influenced Jefferson, but also in the New England Puritan tradition that influenced many of those who signed the *Declaration*, "happiness" was equated with "property." That was because these traditions did not understand a person's labor and possessions in a purely economic way. The individ-ual's right to "pursue happiness" had as its essential core the right to his or her own labor and posses-sions, but Jefferson's usage embraced all the many and varied ways—not only economic but also social, aesthetic, intellectual, and spiritual—in which indi-viduals pursue happiness.

Locke regarded rights as *moral claims* each per-son has on other persons, which entail *moral oblig-ations* on the part of other persons. Locke's inter-pretation of rights as claims on others involving obligations on their part became one source of the dominant understanding of rights in modern politi-cal thought. As I naturally want to preserve my life, liberty, and possessions, so I recognize that I am obligated not to kill or harm you, enslave you to my will, or deprive you of your possessions. I know these things—which are the law of nature—because I have the capacity to reason, and in fact at one point Locke simply refers to the law of nature as "reason."

Locke understood the law of nature as both a rationally discoverable fact about human beings and the expression of the will of God. Throughout the *Second Treatise* he appealed to both reason and rev-elation. As a philosopher Locke believed that his arguments stood on their own on the basis of obser-vation and sound reasoning. As a reflective Christian, like Thomas Aquinas, he believed that the Bible con-tained divine confirmation of many things we know independently through reason.

The state of war. Locke's characterization of the state of war was directly related to his portrayal of the state of nature as governed by the law of nature. Hobbes defined war not only as actual con-flict but also as the predisposition to conflict. Given his picture of the state of nature as egoistic individ-uals aggressively doing whatever they can to pre-serve and enhance their lives, Hobbes simply identi-fied the state of nature with a state of war, the "war of all against all." By contrast, Locke defined war as actual "enmity and destruction," in which one person tries to rob another person of her liberty, to domi-nate and enslave her. Since the state of nature was characterized not simply by egoistic self-aggrandize-ment but by rational recognition of the law of nature, which morally constrained individuals to rec-ognize both rights and duties, it followed that the state of nature was not simply a state of war but also of peace and cooperation. The problem with the state of nature, said Locke, is that in cases of war—of aggression by one or more persons against others—every individual, whether aggressor or victim, was his own judge, jury, and punisher. Since humans were apt to be self-regarding, this meant that each person's natural rights were inadequately protected in the state of nature.

The meanings of property. "Property" is a key term in Locke's political philosophy. In reading Locke it is crucial to understand that he used the term in two senses, a broad and a narrow one, and the reader has to figure out which meaning from the context. The word "property" is from the Latin word *proprium*, which means "what is one's own." In the *broad* sense "property" includes anything that is one's own, including one's life and liberty, and Locke usually used the word that way. In this broad sense all natural rights—life, liberty, and possessions—are property rights. In the *Second Treatise* Locke argued that the preservation of property is the main reason humans leave the state of nature and form organized societies with governments. He explicitly stated that under "property" he includes people's "lives, liberties, and estates [possessions]."

In a long chapter of the *Second Treatise* entitled "Of Property," (V) however, Locke used the term "property" in the *narrow* sense in which we usually use it: to refer only to one of the natural rights, the right of "possessions" or "estates"—what we call "private property." Locke said that God originally gave the goods of the earth to humans in common; in other words, there were no private possessions. But in the state of nature individuals changed the original situation by appropriating land by their labor—by cultivating it and making it productive. Since it is essential to the preservation and maintenance of individuals' life and liberty, this appropriation of possessions through one's own work (e.g., farming a piece of land) was a natural right.

Initially the right to property in the narrow sense was strictly *limited*: the individual had a right only to what he or she could use before it spoiled, not to unlimited acquisition. Historically the introduction of *money* then changed everything. Money is a non-perishable medium of exchange that replaced direct bartering of goods and resolved the problem of spoilage. The introduction of money, Locke argued, meant that the right to private property through "mixing" one's own labor (or, he added, the labor of others one hires) with what occurs in nature now became an *unlimited* right of acquisition. This produced the great inequalities of wealth with which we are familiar. But because human ingenuity and labor have greatly improved human life for everyone from what it was originally in the state of nature, even the poor are better off than people generally were before the introduction of money, and those who acquire wealth through farming or manufacturing are society's benefactors.

The social compact and the nature of government. The idea that government is based on a social contract goes back to the argument of some medieval political thinkers that governments, including monarchies, ultimately rest upon the consent of the governed. Locke preferred the term "compact," which signified the creation of a legal trust, rather than "contract," which implied that both parties (and so perhaps a monarch) would receive benefits from it. Although Locke is today often seen as a "contract

theorist," his term "compact" did not imply short-term, easily revocable agreements; once civil society was formed, Locke's rationales for its social institutions were more often drawn from natural law than from the device of contract.

In the thought of Locke, the *social compact* is *an agreement by a group of people to leave the state of nature and live together in civil society for greater security and peace*. That compact is based upon the mutual *consent* of persons living independently in the state of nature to submit themselves to a common political authority. As we have seen, Locke argued that the main reason people leave the state of nature and create "civil society" is to preserve their property, that is, their life, liberty, and possessions. In the state of nature people were without established law and without judges to adjudicate disputes on the basis of law, and therefore lacked the power to enforce judicial decisions. That meant, given human tendencies to selfishness and injustice, that individuals' rights—their *proprium*—were never secure. The formation of civil society was designed to correct these deficiencies.

In the state of nature every individual had (1) the right to do whatever he or she thought was necessary for his or her own preservation and that of others, within the constraints of the law of nature; and (2) the right to punish crimes committed against the law of nature—that is, against one's own or other people's natural rights. In making a social compact a group of people agreed to transfer these powers from individuals to the community, thus creating *civil society*. But they relinquished the individual right to judge in their own cause precisely for the sake of preserving their natural rights: as Locke wrote, "for their comfortable, safe, and peaceable living amongst one another, in a *secure enjoyment of their properties*, and a greater security against any that are not of it." Or as Locke famously stated it, the "chief end" or purpose of government was the *preservation of property* in the broad sense, that is, the preservation of the natural rights to life, liberty, and estate of its citizens.

Each person must voluntarily consent to the compact, but Locke assumed that consent may be implicit as well as explicit. Sovereignty or authority ultimately lies with those consenting. (This is the idea, enshrined in the *Declaration of Independence*, that governments rest upon "the consent of the governed.") They agree to be governed and bound by the will of the majority, since for practical reasons unanimous agreement on all the decisions necessary to a civil society is impossible. The government created in this way, consisting of a *legislative* and an *executive* body, is the agent of the people's sovereignty, and looked to as the preserver of their rights.

Thus Locke argued that legitimate government is *limited in its powers* and *functions on behalf of* the members of the community. It may be that he defined things in this way in order to argue that absolute monarchy was not a legitimate form of government. Locke formally conceded that his analysis of political authority as ultimately lying with the people was compatible with any of the traditional three types of government—monarchy, oligarchy, or democracy. Yet he believed that absolute monarchy, in which all political power is placed in one person's hands, inevitably produced tyranny and argued instead for a constitution in which the "executive" was checked by the "legislative."

Locke considered the supreme power in the state to be the legislative power, since the making of laws directed to the public good was the fundamental task of government. The executive power carried out and enforced the laws, a role which included the prerogative of making decisions that mitigate or modify the application of the laws in specific circumstances. If either the legislative or the executive power violated the limited authority they possessed in trust to the people, it forfeited the people's obligations to be bound by his decisions and might be resisted and replaced. Yet Locke said little about when or how a *legitimate* government might forfeit that trust.

The right of resistance. The primary purpose of the *Second Treatise* was to define the "right of resistance," which Locke himself called the right of "rebellion." Jefferson and others who contributed to the *Declaration of Independence* appealed to this right (which they found not only in Locke but also in other sources) in presenting their reasons for breaking their allegiance to the British crown. Locke believed that the events of his own time had dramatically demonstrated that tyranny was the worst thing that could befall civil societies. When a monarch claimed absolute power, he violated everything a legitimate government exists to do: to exercise limited power on behalf of the people and in

preservation of their rights under natural law. Locke viewed absolute monarchy, as for example the rule of Louis XIV in France or Charles II in England, as an illegitimate form of government. Contrary to Hobbes, who argued that any state (even a tyranny) was legitimate and was preferable to the state of nature, and to Filmer, who argued that monarchy was the form of government preferred by God, Locke thought all absolute monarchies illegitimate. In a clear case of tyranny, the people have the right of rebellion.

Locke claimed that people generally would put up with a great deal before they resorted to revolt. For him, the fact of rebellion showed that the people had suffered the most extreme provocation. The people were the only judges of when resistance was justified. In writing of legitimate governments, he recognized that the executive power needed strong authority and must be allowed latitude in governing, and that the legislative body must be granted the right, after due discussion, to formulate laws in accordance with the majority of its members' perceptions of the public good. Only the most extreme circumstances, and the failure of all other means available within the social compact, justified rebellion. Yet this he envisaged in his writing, and may have tried himself to bring about in the reign of Charles II.

Grounds for rebellion, argued Locke, are constituted by any acts by which the monarch puts himself into a state of war against the people he is supposed to defend. He would thereby violate the trust reposed in him to preserve people's rights and to be limited by natural law. Rebellion would be justified when a monarch put his arbitrary will above the law or prevented the legislative body from performing its legitimate functions, as Charles II had done with Parliament. Other circumstances justifying rebellion included the monarch's allowing the people to be made subject to a foreign power, or neglecting or abandoning his responsibilities. All these generalized points were coded references to what Charles II, according to Locke's patron Shaftesbury, had actually done.

For Locke the right of rebellion was the canceling of all obligation on the part of the citizens. Locke placed the exercise of the right of rebellion in the hands of the people (though whether this meant individuals, a majority, or "the people" collectively is still debated). Since in rebellion the parties at odds are in a state of war with each other, the question arises as to who can adjudicate between them. Here Locke used the notion of an "appeal to Heaven." By this he meant that only God can ultimately judge between an aggrieved citizenry and a sovereign perceived as unjust: there is no higher earthly authority to which either side can appeal in pleading its cause. Living in an age of civil wars, he must have meant such an appeal to be decided by armed conflict, with God determining the victor.

When rebellion occurred, civil society was dissolved; though scholarly opinion differs on whether, in Locke's theory, people then returned to the state of nature or to some intermediate stage of community. In either case, when sovereignty reverted to the people, the people had the right to create new forms of government. Some commentators have seen in

Locke at this point a radical individualism that revealed anarchist elements in his thought; others have seen him as the architect of stable, limited government and the separation of powers.

According to some interpreters, from Locke and his contemporaries came three ideas that have had a major influence on modern political thought and action: the *state of nature*, the *natural rights* of individuals, and the *social contract*. These ideas are now familiar to us from political thought since Locke's day. We should consider them carefully, however. Are our terms identical with Locke's? How were they employed by Locke? Were there any inconsistencies between them? To what extent are they still really accepted in today's world?

QUESTIONS FOR STUDY AND DISCUSSION

1. Describe the difference between absolute and constitutional monarchy. What were the circumstances that led to the establishment of constitutional monarchy in England?
2. What is the idea of the state of nature, and how was it useful to Locke in analyzing the nature of government? Is the state-of-nature hypothesis useful today?
3. What, according to Locke, were natural rights? Cite some historic examples of the practical political implementation of the idea of natural rights, and suggest why it has been a powerful idea.
4. What were the broader and the narrower meanings of "property" in Locke's *Second Treatise*? How did he characterize the rise and development of property in the narrower sense?
5. How did Locke understand the nature and function of government, in the light of natural rights and the social compact?
6. What was the "right of resistance," and how did Locke explain and justify it? Do we enjoy such a right today?
7. The American *Declaration of Independence* of 1776 is often said to be a "Lockeian" document. How did the American colonists differ from Locke in their interpretation of the best kind of government?
8 What evidence would you use to argue that the U.S. Constitution, including the Bill of Rights, was inspired by Lockeian values?

SUGGESTIONS FOR FURTHER READING

Locke's key text is *Two Treatises of Government* (1690). The essential modern edition is edited by Peter Laslett (Cambridge University Press, 1960, 1988). It has a valuable introduction, and Laslett's editorial work is the starting point for modern Locke scholarship.

Important but advanced monographs on Locke include:

Ashcraft, Richard. *Revolutionary Politics and Locke's 'Two Treatises of Government.'* Princeton U. Press, 1986.

Dunn, John, *The Political Thought of John Locke*. Cambridge Press, 1969.

Marshall, John. Locke: *Resistance, Revolution and Responsibility* Cambridge Press, 1994.

Useful short summaries include:

Chappell, V. ed. *The Cambridge Companion to Locke*. Cambridge Press, 1994.

Dunn, John. *Locke*. Oxford Press, 1984.

Spellman, W. M. *John Locke*. London, 1997.

For background on seventeenth-century political thought, see:

Burgess, Glenn. *Absolute Monarchy and the Stuart Constitution.* Yale University Press, 1996.

Burns, J. H. ed. *The Cambridge History of Political Thought, 1450–1700.* Cambridge University Press, 1991.

Schochet, Gordon. *Patriarchalism in Political Thought.* Oxford Press, 1975.

For introductions to seventeenth-century England, see:

Coward, Barry. *The Stuart Age.* London, 1980.

Kenyon, J. P. *Stuart England.* Penguin, 1978.

Morrill, John, ed. *The Oxford Illustrated History of Tudor and Stuart Britain.* Oxford Press, 1996.

LIFE OF VOLTAIRE

1694 Born in Paris as François-Marie Arouet.

1704–11 Attends Jesuit college, Louis-le-Grand.

1715 Death of Louis XIV; France governed by a Regent, the duke of Orléans.

1716 Voltaire accused of a satire against the Regent and imprisoned in the Bastille (1717)

1718 Adopts the name "Voltaire." Stages his first play, *Oedipe.*

1721 Montesquieu publishes *La Ligue,* an epic poem about Henry IV, and is hailed as a great poet as well as a playwright.

1726 Voltaire quarrels with the Chevalier Rohan and is imprisoned in the Bastille, the exiled to England

1728 Returns to England

1734 Voltaire publishes *Lettres philosophiques;* the work is condemned by the Parlement of Paris. Voltaire flees to Cirey and begins living with Madame du Châtelet.

1736 Begins correspondence with Frederick of Prussia.

1745 Becomes historiographer to Louis XV at Versailles.

1746 Elected to the Académie Français

1747 Publishes *Zadig,* his first *conte* or short novel (the genre to which *Candide* belongs); loses favor at court.

1748 Montesquieu publishes *De L'Esprit des lois.*

1749 Death of Madame du Châtelet.

1750 Voltaire moves to Frederick the Great's court at Potsdam.

1751 First volume of the *Encyclopédie* appears in print.

1753 Voltaire leaves Frederick's court.

1755 Lisbon earthquake.

1756 Publishes a poem on the Lisbon earthquake.

1756–63 Seven Year's War.

1759 Publishes *Candide*; acquires château of Ferney near Geneva.

1762 Rousseau publishes *Du Contrat social* and the *Emile.*

1764 Voltaire publishes *Dictionnaire philosophique.*

1774 Death of Louis XV; succeeded by Louis XVI.

1778 Voltaire returns to Paris, dies May 30, buried secretly in Champagne.

1789 Beginning of the French Revolution.

1791 Voltaire's body transferred to the Panthéon in Paris.

CHAPTER THREE

VOLTAIRE AND THE ENLIGHTENMENT

"My trade," the eighteenth century's most famous intellectual is supposed to have said, "is to say what I think."[1] Voltaire was a *philosophe*, one of the intellectual leaders of the Enlightenment, the critical analysis of Western thought and society, also known as the European Age of Reason. While most scholars consider the eighteenth century representative of the European Enlightenment, some prefer a more nuanced periodization. Political historians often choose two dates, 1688 (England's Glorious Revolution) and 1789 (the beginning of the long French Revolution), to mark the opening and close of the Age of Reason. Still others extend it as far as 1815, the year Napoleon Bonaparte was finally defeated at Waterloo.[2] On the other hand, historians of science and philosophy often prefer to think of the Enlightenment as concomitant with the **Scientific Revolution** of the seventeenth century, equating enlightenment with the fervent activity of courts, society, and scholars who, since at least the late Renaissance, continued a cautious yet certain, humanistic and secular path toward a human-based knowledge of the world. Both long and short perspectives of the Enlightenment's timeline are accepted; however, the term "Enlightenment" is more commonly attached to those activities and theories which applied rational inquiry to issues of political and social reform rather than exclusively to scientific knowledge and technological innovation. Though most intense in France and Great Britain, the Enlightenment touched most parts of Europe and even extended to Russia and to North America.

RELIGION AND POLITICS—POLITICS AND RELIGION

The second half of the seventeenth century witnessed major political upheavals in England, almost all connected with religious problems. Oliver Cromwell rose to power, overthrew the king, and subsequently failed; the monarchy was restored in 1660; and, finally, the "Glorious Revolution" of 1688–90 brought with it a constitutional monarchy limiting considerably the powers of the king and queen. Though the English political system by century's end was still elitist and aristocratic, it differed enough from Louis XIV's absolute monarchy in France to make a number of liberal French thinkers envious and eager to see in their own country political changes patterned after those which had taken place in England. Their dreams were not to be realized, however, until much later, after the greater part of the following century had passed.

In matters of religion the English, however, were less admired by the French, who were puzzled by British tolerance, or at least passive acceptance, of almost any sort of Christianity *except* Catholicism. France had remained a predominantly Catholic country since the Reformation, and had welcomed the Catholic royalty of England who sought refuge from Anglican or Puritan persecution. The French were intrigued about a system that could tolerate the development of new religious systems in England, such as the Quakers.

Among the most influential religious doctrines to appear in England during the seventeenth century was **deism**, to a great extent another product of Rationalist philosophy. Deists accepted the existence of God either as innately known or known through reasoned arguments, but they rejected the tenets of any organized church. Christianity was viewed by deists as a politically powerful but theologically unnecessary complication of a simple *natural religion* accessible to all people everywhere through reason: worship of one God, living a moral

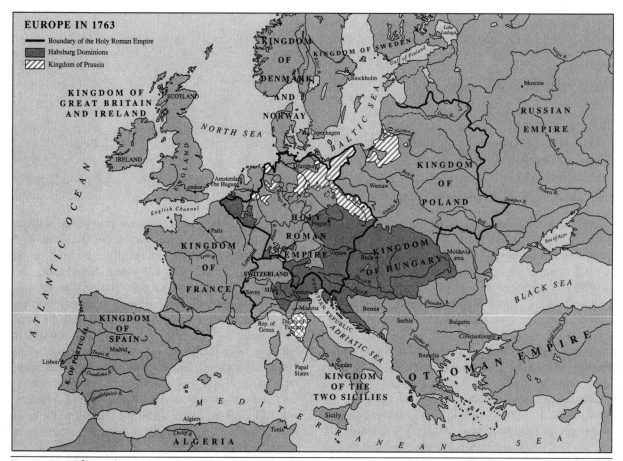

Europe in 1763. Redrawn from *Historical Atlas of the World,* Newly Revised Edition, (1997), Hammond Incorporated.

life, and life after death. In the late seventeenth and early eighteenth centuries, several important deistic works were published in England. The impact made itself felt not only at home but across the English Channel, winning over a number of supporters among the French and throughout the Continent.

In France, religious unrest had been part of politics and the average citizen's life since the Reformation, when Protestantism had won many supporters and incurred the wrath of the Catholic majority and the royalty. The Edict of Nantes, promulgated in 1598 by Henri IV, had ended the bloody wars of religion that had marred the second half of the sixteenth century, by granting religious freedom to Protestants. In 1685, however, Louis XIV, persuaded that religious uniformity was desirable, signed the revocation of this edict, ending religious tolerance.

After 1685, French Protestants could not live in France without concealing their true religious beliefs. The only legal marriage was a Catholic marriage; Protestant education was forbidden; persecution of known Protestants was rampant. French Protestants had a choice only between going underground and fleeing into exile. Large communities of Huguenots, as French Protestants were known, moved to Holland, England, and Prussia, maintaining their French identity and developing centers of French civilization outside of France. The role of these communities (in Amsterdam, London, and Berlin) proved to be crucial in the dissemination of new philosophical and scientific trends through the considerable correspondence among the communities themselves with family and friends who remained in France. The French community in Holland went so far as to establish a number of

French-language publishing houses whose books and pamphlets circulated throughout all of Europe.

Most influential of these French exiles was Pierre Bayle (1647–1706), whose *Dictionnaire historique et critique (Historical and Critical Dictionary)* appeared in 1697 and was regarded a milestone in progressive thought. Permeated with skepticism about revealed religion, Bayle's work was admired by some, attacked by others, but, most importantly, read and discussed by many.

NEW CURRENTS IN THE EIGHTEENTH CENTURY

During the first twenty years of the eighteenth century, both England and France were centers of intellectual and social ferment. Rationalist and Empiricist philosophies were compared and debated. Enthusiasm and optimism abounded about the role science might play in the betterment of human affairs, chiefly as a result of Sir Isaac Newton and his discoveries. Accounts of exploratory voyages to Turkey, India, and China became popular reading and kindled hopes of far-reaching and financially profitable trade circuits for European countries. Occurring as a by-product of broadened commercial horizons, a new relativism developed in the areas of moral and religious thought. Could it be possible that people who lived on this earth in total ignorance of Western philosophy and Christianity led moral, happy, productive lives?

Four North American Indian chiefs visited England in 1710 and were received in intellectual circles with great curiosity, furthering European interest in the concept of the "noble savage," that is, in a thinking, sensitive, and morally upright being who had become what he was without the benefits of "civilization." In France, the publication of travel diaries and a translation into French in 1704 of the Persian *Thousand and One Nights* focused attention on the Orient, its people, customs, religion, and political systems. An image of the "good sultan" emerged in both literature and philosophy, replacing that of the barbarous Muslim whom Europeans had fought so ferociously during the Crusades of the Middle Ages. National ethnocentrism and religious prejudice found themselves challenged as a result of this renewed interest in "foreign" countries and civilizations.

1713 saw France, England, Holland, and Spain all signing the Treaty of Utrecht, ending the War of Spanish Succession that had divided these important European powers for a number of years. Two years later came the death of Louis XIV of France, the king whose absolute political power, elegant court, and magnificent royal palace at Versailles, a city outside Paris, had become the envy of monarchs throughout Europe. Inside France itself, however, the last years of the old king's all-too-long reign (1643–1715) were marred by a conservatism that stifled intellectual and social activities. Following his death, a general sigh of relief rose among the French, and the period of the Regency (1715–1723), under Louis XIV's nephew Philippe d'Orleans, witnessed a return of the court from Versailles to Paris, and a loosening of political and religious constraints, engendering a new optimism—if not liberalism—toward recent developments in science, philosophy, and the arts. The rising upper middle class, or *haute bourgeoisie*, as prosperous and well-educated as most of the nobility, began to assert itself as an intellectual and political power whose concerns about the betterment of society could no longer be ignored. The stage was set, especially in Paris and London, for major social and political changes, to be made in the name of progress in human activity and the perfectibility of men and women as social beings.

Two influential intellectual institutions, products for the most part of the preceding century, began to assume pivotal roles in the development, discussion, and articulation of new ideas in politics, science, the theory of knowledge, and the righting of social wrongs. There were, in both France and England, the several academies of learned people formed by royal edict—the British Royal Society, The French Academy of Sciences and Academy of Inscriptions—and the *salon*, regular gatherings of intellectuals at the regal houses of socially prominent and influential women. The *salon* was a French phenomenon, while its British equivalent was the "club," groups of philosophers and writers meeting regularly to discuss modern trends in thought and literature.

In France during this period a number of women thoroughly committed to progress in literature, the arts, and politics, invited to their *salons* the most important and distinguished men of the age. Ironically, many of the women whose *salons* were so popular were as talented as or more talented than their male guests. The social milieu in which they lived, however, prevented them from becoming public rather than private citizens. Their influence on the philosophical, artistic, and literary works of the century was most assuredly impressive,[3] but cannot be documented because of the subservient position forced upon them by a male-dominated society.

NEW IDEAS IN THE ENLIGHTENMENT

The first published work to reflect the intellectual and philosophical ferment of the early eighteenth century appeared in 1721. *Les Lettres persanes* (*Persian Letters*), written by Charles Louis de Secondat, Baron de Montesquieu (1689-1755), best known for his much later book *L'Esprit des lois* (*The Spirit of the Laws*). In this work, published in 1748, Montesquieu advocated a government composed of different branches that would "check and balance" each other. This idea would significantly influence the framers of the United States Constitution.

Les Lettres persanes takes the form of a novel, an imaginary voyage made by two Persian noblemen into Western Europe for the purpose of acquiring knowledge about foreign political institutions, customs, and morals. As they travel, the Persians write letters to family and friends at home, expressing amazement at the "strange" people and customs they have encountered in Europe.

Montesquieu's purpose in *Les Lettres persanes* was to shake the French out of their provincialism and complacency, forcing them to confront simple, clear, and logical commentaries made by the Persians on the "bizarre" nature of French politics, religion, and social life, aspects of their existence which the French had always taken for granted as absolute models of civilization to be imitated, not questioned. The novel's philosophical bases are very clear: the desirability of a representative form of government and political liberty; examination and discussion of the emerging doctrine of materialism (a refinement of Descartes' *res extensa* theory: the whole universe, including the human soul, is composed exclusively of matter); and skepticism concerning revealed religion.

Tempering the shock of such direct criticism of "sacred" institutions is the literary device employed by Montesquieu in the work. He is a ventriloquist, speaking through the mouths of his admirably learned Persians, who quickly win the reader's sympathy. Such a device is transparent, of course, but quite useful in permitting expression of outspoken

sentiment. Humor, too, serves Montesquieu well as he seeks to convince his compatriots that France is perhaps not the center of the universe, absolute monarchy not the ideal form of government, and austere Catholicism not the only true religion. His Muslim travelers must return to Persia for fear of being "soiled" and perverted by contact with inhabitants of the Western World. The Italians and the French are as "barbaric" to the Persians in their politics, religion, and social customs as Orientals had seemed to the Westerners who had published accounts of their travels in the East. Usbek, the older of the two, declares at one point that he was so angry at his treatment by the French that he was on the verge of "swearing like a Christian," echoing in a delightful manner the French phrase of "swearing like an infidel."

Montesquieu's book met with immediate success and was translated, copied, and imitated throughout Europe. Though published anonymously by one of the French Huguenot communities in Holland, with Cologne (Germany) listed as place of printing on the title page, the identity of its author was widely known, and Montesquieu, in part because of his status as a noble, and also because of the liberal political climate of the period, never suffered politically or socially as a result of *Les Lettres persanes*.

In 1734, across the English Channel, another seminal philosophical work was published, this time from the pen of Alexander Pope (1688-1744), poet and member of the Scriblerus Club. Pope's purpose in his elegant verse essay, *Essay on Man*, was to proclaim that the universe, as it exists, follows the divine plan of an omniscient creator ("One truth is clear. WHATEVER IS, IS RIGHT," Epistle I, line 294) and that humankind's seeming dissatisfaction with the world stems from limited vision, an inability to see the whole of God's plan. The focus of human philosophical endeavors has been wrong, Pope contends: "Know then thyself, presume not God to scan; / The proper study of Mankind is Man." (Epistle II, lines 1-2). (The idea that "whatever is, is right" found expression also in the German philosopher Leibniz's argument that this is the "best of all possible worlds"—and argument mercilessly satirized by Voltaire in *Candide*.)

The *Essay on Man* is a humanistic work concerned principally with the human being's role as both individual and social being, and not so much with his or her relationship to a God and Creator whom he or she will never come to understand completely. It represents a deistic "distancing" of God from humanity, conflicting with contemporary Christian dogma, which stressed the immediate and continuous involvement of God in all earthly and human affairs. Pope's work quickly met with success in his native England, but it enjoyed even more fame in France, where it was translated into French six times and went through seventy separate editions before 1800.

The 1730s and 1740s also saw another major Enlightenment "wave" in the writing, copying, and clandestine circulation of a group of manuscripts, by authors named and unnamed, aimed at the dissemination of controversial ideas in philosophy. Because of the increasing government hostility to unorthodox or potentially inflammatory books, the liberal thinkers and writers of these decades resorted to the use of scribes and copyists for their works, convinced that this was less dangerous than having them printed. Permeating this body of clandestine manuscripts was the new critical spirit of the age—a reaffirmation of the potential of human reason. Influenced at first by Descartes' method, the authors' inspiration gradually changed to Locke and Newton, tending towards the idea that the experimental or empirical method alone was of value in philosophy. All ideas stem from the senses; revealed religion should be questioned; government must proceed from the principles of reason—these were the themes developed in these manuscripts.

The circulation of the clandestine manuscripts led to a unification, not just of the period's great thinkers, but of all readers who were sufficiently open-minded to realize that significant improvement of human life could be brought about through a change in philosophical, religious, and political outlook. An intellectual kinship arose from this commonality of purpose, as many people throughout France and the French-speaking Protestant settlements in Europe realized that they, too, could use their reason to better society, and not leave important decision-making up to established authority.

It is at this moment that the word *philosophe* (originally meaning "philosopher" in French) began to take on a new meaning for the French, and ultimately for most of Western Europe. To this generation of the 1730s, a *philosophe* was any intelligent person possessed of the courage to reject the influence of traditional philosophy and religion, accept the validity of inductive reasoning, and recognize his or her responsibilities as a social being. Voltaire, whose life and work we examine below, is often regarded as the epitome of the *philosophe*, his life spanning the major portion of the century, and given over to the service of humanity. No *philosophe* in the old sense, that is, creator of metaphysical systems or analytical methods, Voltaire combated with fervor, irony, and dedication the social ills of his age: religious intolerance and fanaticism, political inequalities and injustices, social prejudice, war, and every other social aberration resulting from misuse of human reason.

Beginning in the mid 1740s, the *philosophes* and their supporters took center stage in the dramatic confrontation between the new ideas and the old. Two figures, Denis Diderot and Jean-Jacques Rousseau, assumed the important roles they would play during the next thirty years in reshaping philosophy and society. Like Voltaire, with whom they alternately agreed and disagreed on specific points, they understood the dangers implicit in simply replacing one metaphysical system with another. In the years to follow, Diderot was to become France's principal champion of empirical philosophy, while Rousseau developed an increasing distaste for both Rationalism and Empiricism. Each was intent upon aiding humanity to better itself, but they differed radically in explaining how this could be done.

A third, the Edinburgh-born David Hume (1711–76), was at the same time dedicating himself to philosophy, politics, morals, and history. From 1734 to 1737 he lived in France, studying at La Flèche (where Descartes had studied), and shortly thereafter published his *Treatise of Human Nature* (1739–40), now considered the most significant representation of British Empiricist thought in the eighteenth century. This work, which went almost unnoticed after its initial publication, constituted both a refinement and a refutation of the conclusions concerning human reason reached previously by Locke. Hume argued that all knowledge is derived from perceptions, by which he meant "whatever can be present to the mind." There are two sorts of perceptions: impressions, which include sense data and feelings; and ideas, which are our reflections on objects or

French Enlightenment leaders: Descartes, Montesquieu, Diderot, Voltaire, and Rousseau. By Stephen Lahey.

feelings when they are not immediately present. Thus all ideas arise from impressions: "we can never think of any thing which we have not seen without us, or felt in our own minds." In his analysis of human knowledge, building on this basis, Hume showed that the scope of reason was very limited and that its most fundamental and universal assumptions could not be rationally justified. Our belief in cause and effect, for example, which is essential to all reasoning about the world, rests upon feeling and custom. At the same time, it is only by relying on these non-rational inclinations and assumptions that we avoid total skepticism and develop usable knowledge of the world and ourselves. (Hume greatly admired Newton's achievement in systematizing the study of nature and thought he was applying Newton's methods to the study of human nature.)

Born in 1713 into a fairly wealthy middle-class provincial family, Diderot received the classical Jesuit education in language, literature, and religion that was standard for a young man of his social standing.

Continuing his education on his own in Paris, he taught himself Latin and English, and concentrated on work in the natural sciences, which were to become of great importance as the foundation of his philosophical views. In Paris, Diderot supported himself by translating British works into French, frequented literary *salons*, and soon won the attention of prominent *philosophes*, including Voltaire.

Diderot's first "enlightened" work, *Pensées philosophiques* (*Philosophical Thoughts*), was published anonymously in 1746, and was quickly denounced by the French *Parlement* and condemned to be burned. A very short book expressing daring ideas of an anti-religious character, the *Philosophical Thoughts* reflected a deistic orientation more radical than that of the *Essay on Man*, distancing God from man to the point of questioning the philosophical necessity of God's existence. Three years later, Diderot published an even stronger attack on religion, the *Lettre sur les aveugles à l'usage de ceux qui voient* (*Letter Concerning the*

Blind, for the Use of Those Who See). This was a short study developing the Lockean theory that all ideas come to us through the senses, and stating that blind people, unable to see the wonders of nature, were unlikely to be convinced by religious theories that proved the existence of God through an examination of the natural perfection surrounding them. Attacked for the materialistic and atheistic implications of this work, Diderot was temporarily imprisoned in the Chateau de Vincennes, a political prison on the eastern edge of Paris.

While in prison Diderot received a visit from an acquaintance who, like himself, had made small waves among the intelligentsia of Parisian *salons*, Jean-Jacques Rousseau (1712–1778). Son of a Genevan watchmaker, Rousseau had made his way to Paris after a vagabond youth marked by little formal education, a lengthy love affair with an older woman, and, most importantly, an overwrought sensitivity which made it difficult for him to get along well with others, and equally difficult for him to accept wholeheartedly the Rationalist and Empiricist philosophies which had taken root in France.

Rousseau's visit to the imprisoned Diderot was a turning-point in his career. Reading a newspaper as he walked to Vincennes from Paris, he learned that the Academy of Dijon (an important intellectual group in Dijon, a city southeast of Paris) had announced an essay competition on the following subject: "Si le rétablissement des sciences et des arts a contribué à épurer les moeurs" ("If contemporary developments in the sciences and the arts have contributed to the betterment of morals"). Diderot is said to have advised Rousseau to attack the arts and sciences as morally corrupting forces, which Rousseau did, winning the competition. (His *Discourse on Science and the Arts*, 1750).

In this work, and in his *Discours sur l'origine et les fondements de l'inégalité parmi les hommes* (*Discourse on the Origin and Bases of Inequality among Men*, 1754), Rousseau laid out the tenets of his philosophy, the theory that humans were born free, naturally good, and happy, but have been enslaved, corrupted, and rendered unhappy through the process of civilization. Directly opposing the contemporary belief that humankind and society were perfectible through the proper use of reason, Rousseau proposes a "return to nature," a renuncia-

tion of the social, scientific, and artistic "progress" which has served only to distance humanity from its natural simplicity and goodness. Rousseau's theories, echoing the "noble savage" theme developed earlier in the century, did not constitute a naive demand for his fellow humans to repudiate their "civilization." Rather, they served to demonstrate that the key to human happiness lay not in social and technological advancement, but in the reconciliation of human beings with their own original nature, and with the natural world around them. Rousseau's writings emphasize the importance of the emotions in humanity's search for happiness, exhorting people to judge and to act according to their feelings, not cold reason, which he claimed led invariably to error. For Rousseau, Locke's "sensationalism" made human emotions all-important.

During the next eight years, Rousseau devoted himself to more elaborate articulation of his "natural," anti-Rationalist philosophy. By 1762, he had published what was to become the most popular novel of his century, *Julie, ou la nouvelle Hèloíse* (*Julie, or the New Eloise*); a controversial novel-philosophical tract, *Emile, ou de l'éducation* (*Emile, or On Education*); and a major work of political theory, *Du Contrat social* (*On the Social Contract*). The latter two of these works have proven, over time, to be remarkably "modern" in their orientation and subsequent influence.

In *Emile*, Rousseau totally rejects educational theory and practice since the Middle Ages. Recognizing that children are not simply adults in miniature, he constructs an educational program for his imaginary pupil, Emile, derived from study of the child's nature, his physical and emotional needs, and his capacity for learning at different stages of his childhood and adolescence. Emile's intellectual development (that is, his use of his rational faculties) is seen as only a part of his overall growth into a physically robust, economically productive, thinking and feeling citizen with an acute religious and political consciousness.

The first educational philosopher to explore at length the relationship between student and teacher, Rousseau emphasizes the necessity of a bond, or "contract," between the two, a mutual understanding and cooperation which will enable Emile to apply what he has learned to living his adult life. Such an approach to the teaching and learning processes contrasted dramatically with the training of young men at the time, a rigid and impractical holdover from the scholastic tradition.

Having created and educated his ideal citizen in Emile, Rousseau proceeded to study, in *Du Contrat social*, the nature of the political entity or state best suited for his pupil. Following Locke and other seventeenth- and eighteenth-century political theorists, Rousseau creates a fictional "state of nature" in order to study the origins of government. The ideal government for him stems from a social contract made willingly by all citizens of a society among themselves, that is, not forced upon them by a more powerful person or group. The people themselves are sovereign, and all law results from self-imposed limits freely agreed upon by this sovereign body. The form of government (whether democracy, monarchy, or oligarchy) is chosen and empowered by the people. Should this government at any time devolve into an entity no longer corresponding to the people's wishes, it may be modified or revoked.

Rousseau was also, at least for a time, a participant in the most ambitious intellectual project of the century, publication of *L'Encyclopédie, ou dictionnaire raisonné des sciences, des arts, et des métier* (*Encyclopedia, or "Reasoned" Dictionary of Sciences, Arts, and Crafts*). Begun by a group of Parisian printers as simply the translation of a popular British work (Ephraim Chambers' *Cyclopedia*, 2 volumes, 1728), *L'Encyclopédie* soon took on larger proportions, and Denis Diderot was hired as its editor-in-chief. Between 1751 and 1772, there appeared seventeen volumes of text and eleven volumes of engraved illustrations (all published with Diderot as editor), and these were followed by four supplementary volumes of text, a twelfth of illustrations, and two of index (1776-1780). In the hands of Diderot and his collaborators, the *Encyclopédie* became the first comprehensive "anatomy" of humankind and the world, a work based on Enlightenment faith in the powers of human reason, whose creators were determined to set down, in a clear and organized fashion, all the achievements of humanity, from the noblest—philosophy and religion—to the most mundane—crafts such as glassblowing and wine-making.

A complete list of contributors to the *Encyclopédie* will probably never be established, but it is clear that they numbered more than 200, including the great *philosophes* of the period—Montesquieu, Voltaire, Rousseau, and Diderot, himself author of many articles. Seeking the editorial collaboration of someone better known in philosophical and scientific circles than he himself was at the time, Diderot called upon the services of Jean le Rond D'Alembert (1717-1783), distinguished mathematician, member of the Academy of Sciences and author of the *Encyclopedie's Preliminary Discourse*, or introduction to the public, one of the great documents of the Enlightenment.

The boldest aspect of D'Alembert's *Preliminary Discourse* was its wholehearted endorsement of the Lockean doctrine that all human knowledge comes to us through the senses, asserting the supremacy of the Empiricists (Bacon, Newton, Locke) over the Rationalists (Descartes, Malebranche, Leibniz, Wolff). Such a philosophical position was generally regarded as indicative of the eighteenth century's "modernity" in the history of human thought, and the *Encyclopédie* was viewed as a concrete symbol of the age's dedication to progress in human affairs.

In reality, the *Encyclopédie* was all this and more, as became clear with publication of Volumes I (1751) and II (1752). Major articles dealing with philosophy and religion reflected a materialist—if not completely atheistic—orientation, while those treating politics were characterized by the libertarian and anti-monarchical trends of the century. This was accomplished not by direct statement of controversial ideas, but rather through inference, innuendo, and a creative use of the cross-reference system, encouraging readers of the more conservative articles to move on to others which applied methodological doubt to existing philosophical, religious, and political beliefs.

On February 7, 1752, King Louis XV issued a decree officially condemning the first two volumes of the *Encyclopédie* for containing "several maxims tending to destroy royal authority, establishing a spirit of independence and revolt, and, in obscure and equivocal terms, supporting the bases of error, the corruption of morals, anti-religious thought, and unbelief [in God]" (from the *Decree of the King's State Council*). Following censure of their work by public authority, the Encyclopedists went underground, and continued to maintain the support of many influential people, especially Guillaume Chrétien de Lamoignon de Malesherbes (1721-1794), royally-appointed director

The Palace of Versailles, a 17th century engraving. The Library of Congress.

of the printing trade and the official censorship of books. With Malesherbes' protection, five additional volumes appeared by 1757, despite the *Encyclopédie*'s condemnation.

In the same year, however, an attempt was made to assassinate Louis XV, and almost every political, religious, and philosophical faction was implicated, including the Encyclopedists. Louis XV retorted with an edict stating that the author of any subversive work would be put to death. To make matters even worse, the following year, 1758, saw the publication of *De L'Esprit* (*On The Mind*) by Claude-Adrien Helvétius (1715-1771), a wealthy *philosophe* who had only recently allied himself with the Encyclopedists. Thoroughly empirical in his methodology, Helvétius develops in this work the bases of *Utilitarian* philosophy that the Englishman Jeremy Bentham was to popularize a number of years later. Religion, absolute monarchy, the nobility of the human mind and reason—all were questioned by Helvétius in *De L'Esprit*, which was quickly condemned by the *Parlement*. This condemnation heav-

ily damaged the Encyclopedists' reputation, though they really had nothing to do with the publication of *De L'Esprit*.

In the realm of European politics matters had also taken a turn for the worse. The Seven Years War, a conflict involving five European powers (England and Prussia on one side and France, Russia and Austria on the other), devastated parts of Eastern Europe and resulted also in France's loss of its colonies of Canada and India to the British. With the principal powers of the Western world at war once again, it appeared that all the efforts of Enlightenment philosophers had come to naught. For a while, it seemed that the Enlightenment was over, and that retrograde, conservative forces had finally won.

Though none of the major *philosophes* lived to witness the French Revolution, it was clear that they had set the stage for the radical changes that would take place in 1789 and the decade which followed. Though strikingly different in their thought and methodology, men like Voltaire, Montesquieu, Diderot and Rousseau, convinced of the need to bring about change for the benefit of society and the individual, succeeded in modifying the European way of thinking.

PRE-REVOLUTIONARY FRANCE

To understand social and political life in France before the Revolution it is necessary to comprehend the *Ancien Régime* (the "Old Regime") to distinguish it from the new order that succeeded it. Its political form was "absolutism," a form of government in which the king and his agents ruled alone, without sharing power with various representative institutions of the realm. Under absolutism, politics was the private concern of the monarch and was regularly referred to as the "secret of the king." The *Ancien Régime* was a complex series of traditional laws, institutions, and social groupings that had grown up in France over the centuries. This pattern was further complicated by the fact that the French monarchy did not originally rule over all of the territory that it possessed in the eighteenth century. From the early Middle Ages it slowly incorporated more and more territories; and in the process it usually respected the local rights and privileges of these areas. For instance, the province of Brittany in northwestern France, which was fully integrated into the monarchy only in the sixteenth century, continued to be governed by its own set of privileges, that is, its own traditional laws, customs, and even political institutions. The kingdom of France as a whole was simply all those privileged groupings—of provinces, of social orders such as the nobility, as well as of corporations, including the incorporated towns—that owed allegiance to the king of France.

With the sole exception of the unity offered by the Catholic Church, which the king was required to protect, the crown offered the only practical and symbolic unity to France. This piecemeal formation of the French monarchy led to a great diversity of practices and institutions that limited all attempts at effective rule by the central authority of the king. The monarchy was charged with protecting all these local rights and privileges. The "state," then, was a passive rather than an active entity. The way in which it defined justice—the way, in other words, it exercised its legitimate power—was by preserving the traditional political, social, and religious order of things.

The rise of absolutism marked that stage of the monarchy in which it attempted to reduce the independence of these privileged groupings without, however, destroying the traditional fabric of society. For the purposes of strengthening France against its external enemies, the king and his ministers began in the seventeenth century to shift power away from these semi-autonomous bodies and toward the central government. As part of this process, they tried to suppress the political institutions of these privileged groups. By sending out into the provinces new royal agents, the *intendants*, who were directly responsible to the king, the monarchy created the first effective centralized bureaucracy in European history. In the late seventeenth century absolutism reached its highest stage of perfection in the France of Louis XIV (1638–1715; ruled 1643–1715). Louis's government became a model for other states in Europe that strove to be both efficient forces at home and effective powers abroad.

This new monarchical bureaucracy, however, began to break away from the passive and static definition of the monarchy and replace it with an active and evolving one. During the eighteenth century the balance between the traditional structure of society and the new role of the monarchy was beginning to break down. In part it was the result of the success of absolutism itself. Another way of looking at absolutism is to see it, with its centralization of power and establishment of the first efficient bureaucracy, as the creative harnessing of the economic, social, and political powers of the kingdom to meet the rapidly mounting costs of maintaining an effective military establishment. Although it created the conditions for the political and economic recovery of France, absolutism also sowed the seeds of its own destruction.

By the 1740s and 1750s a number of tensions were recognizable, the most significant of which was a breach between the conservative, particularistic forms of traditional society and the more active, regularizing and universalizing tendencies of the centralizing state. Specifically, the absolutist state of the eighteenth century increasingly had to infringe upon local privileges and curtail the operations of traditional bodies in the demand for greater uniformity.

The problem of taxation highlighted a number of the tensions inherent in this system. The root of these financial difficulties, however, lay in the very definition of the society itself. The great variety of divergent and overlapping segments that comprised the society of the *Ancien Régime* either paid or avoided paying certain taxes according to their particular relationship to the crown. This made the question of taxation and especially of changing the system of taxation overwhelmingly complex. To simplify this system would entail undermining the entire social structure as it then existed. Absolutism had already begun this process, in fact if not in theory, by subjecting the nobility to direct taxation and whittling away the privileges of the towns. These taxes were, nevertheless, neither heavy nor systematic enough to meet current needs. As a result monarchical absolutism was undermining the very social order upon which it was founded. In the second half of the eighteenth century, the French monarchy found itself caught between the older definition of its role as the fount of justice and its new function as an active political agent. In the last decades of the *Ancien Régime*, absolutism faced the need for further political and social reform, even if this meant even further undermining of the traditional order. It was precisely a severe financial crisis—in part caused by French financial support of the American Revolution—and the monarchy's inability to bring about the reforms necessary to deal with it, that led to the French Revolution.

Voltaire, an 18th century engraving by Benoit-Louis Henriquez.

VOLTAIRE

A writer of poetry, fiction, drama, history, popular science, political philosophy, and much, much more, Francois-Marie Arouet, known as Voltaire (1694–1778), was celebrated as much for his radical critique of the society of his time as for his literary brilliance. Of his many books, none is more widely known and imitated than *Candide* (1759), a picaresque, satirical novel about a naïve young man who manages to encounter hypocrisy, injustice, and folly in every country and every class of the eighteenth-century world.

Voltaire was born in Paris in 1694 to an upper-middle-class family: his father was a lawyer and his mother a member of the minor aristocracy. Educated in a prestigious Jesuit school from ages 10 to 17, Voltaire was a precocious student with a love of poetry and theater and a burning ambition. Rebelling against his father's desire that he become a lawyer, Voltaire became part of a pleasure-loving crowd, wrote poetry offensive to those in power, and was arrested and imprisoned in the Bastille for it in 1717. But in 1718 his first play, *Oedipe* (Oedipus), was produced and was a smash hit. He then tried to rival Virgil's *Aeneid* by writing France's first epic poem, the *Henriade* (1722), and would come to be regarded as the greatest French poet of the eighteenth century. By 1720, Voltaire's anti-establishment attitudes sent him to an eleven-month stay in the Bastille, the famous political prison that would be attacked in 1789 by an unruly mob in Paris, marking the beginning of the French Revolution. During his imprisonment he began a serious literary career that was to last through the greater part of the century. Known and admired for his wit and talent, he was soon reintegrated into the best of Parisian society, producing a number of poems and tragedies dealing with socio-political issues, which made him famous.

In 1726 an altercation with an aristocrat caused Voltaire to be beaten and expelled from France. He

Jean Huber (1711–1786), Le Lever de Voltaire a
Ferney. Courtesy of Art Resource.

spent the years 1726-29 in exile in England, where
he was "royally" welcomed and met all the leading
English writers and intellectuals. Voltaire admired
Britain's constitutional monarchy, individual liberty,
religious toleration, and comparative lack of strict
censorship of speech and published writings—all
things he desired for France. He came under the
influence of Locke's and Newton's ideas, and
became an important transmitter of their ideas to
France. He was drawn to the English Quakers for
their pacifism and simplicity of life. Voltaire learned
English well and wrote the first edition of his book
Letters Concerning the English Nation (published
in 1733 in London) in English. He later expanded it,
put it into French, and published it as his *Lettres
Philosophique* (Philosophical Letters). Voltaire, it
must be added, also made a lot of money in England
and became interested in accumulating wealth—
which he did for the rest of his life.

Returning to France in 1729, Voltaire was in trouble again within five years. He published his

Philosophical Letters in France in 1734, which of
course advocated such things as greater political freedom, religious toleration, and the ideas of Locke and
Newton. The book has the distinction of being the first
Enlightenment book to be banned! Copies were
seized and Voltaire was threatened with arrest. He fled
to the province of Lorraine and was not permitted to
return to Paris. By this point, and until 1748, Voltaire
had a refuge in Cirey, in a chateau owned by Madame
Emilie du Chatelet, one of the great women of the
Enlightenment. They were both lovers and intellectual
co-workers. She had a laboratory in the chateau where
they conducted scientific experiments, and they frequently discussed Newtonian physics. "Lady Newton,"
as Voltaire dubbed Madame du Chatelet, co-authored
Voltaire's *Elements of the Philosophy of Newton*
(1738), and her translation of Newton's *Principia
Mathematica* remained the standard in France until
the twentieth century. Madame du Chatelet died in
1749, by which time the two were no longer lovers
but still friends. It was through her influence that
Voltaire became more welcome at the royal court at
Versailles. During the Cirey years Voltaire also became
a friend and frequent correspondent of King Frederick
the Great of Prussia, perhaps the greatest of the eighteenth-century "enlightened despots" of Europe. For
three years Voltaire was Frederick's guest at the royal
palace of *Sans Souci* in Potsdam, but the friendship
soured and Voltaire left in anger. Despite being named
the official (royal) historiographer to the French king,
Louis XV in 1745, befriended by another monarch,
Frederick the Great of Prussia, and elected to the prestigious Académie Francaise for life in 1746, Voltaire
nevertheless remained extremely wary of kings and
clergy and of the arbitrary manner in which authority
chose to censure works and imprison authors.

Still forbidden to return to Paris, Voltaire lived in
Geneva, Switzerland, Rousseau's hometown, for
awhile, but he was too controversial for the
Genevans. By this time he was quite wealthy, and in
1753 he bought an estate at Ferney, where he lived
out his days as a "kingly patriarch" and the "Sage of
Ferney." Ferney was in France, but just over the border
from Switzerland so he could slip across the border if
the authorities were after him. The estate at Ferney
became an intellectual and cultural center, where
Voltaire housed many guests.

Voltaire was one of the famous contributors to
L'Encyclopédie, that great monument of the French

Enlightenment, and knew and frequently corresponded with other leading *philosophes* such as Diderot, D'Alembert, and Holbach. He also debated—with some exasperation—important issues with Rousseau, who (as we have seen) criticized the exaltation of reason by the *philosophes* and emphasized the importance of feelings. Voltaire continued to write a great deal—novels (such as *Candide*), short stories, and essays that called attention to and satirized social injustices. He also wrote histories, including *The Century of Louis XIV* (1751). Widely regarded as the greatest French playwright of the eighteenth century, his popularity as a dramatist was beginning to decline with the rise of popularity of Shakespeare's plays (which Voltaire had introduced to France). But he became known as the "conscience of Europe" because he put the full weight of his reputation and influence into the cause of social justice. He was actively involved throughout the rest of his life in fighting for justice for victims of persecution, and he was successful in rehabilitating many innocent people accused of crimes.

In his later years one of the most famous people in Europe, Voltaire triumphantly returned to Paris in 1778. This description by a historian, based on contemporary accounts, shows all too clearly the juxtaposition of acclaim and harassment that Voltaire had experienced throughout his life:

J.M. Moreau, Le Jeune, Candide s'enfuit au plus vite... .
Courtesy of Roger-Viollet

> At the age of 83 he returned to his native Paris for a triumph such as few authors have ever enjoyed. Delegations from the Académie Française and the Comédie Française, personages as diverse as Mme du Barry and Mme Necker [wife of Louis XVI's Minister of Finance], Diderot and [Benjamin] Franklin, Glück [the composer] and the English ambassador, came to pay him their respects. Crowds cheered him in the streets. At the sixth performance of his tragedy *Irene*, he in his box and later his bust on the stage were crowned with wreaths amid wild acclaim. Yet he had come to Paris with no clear authorization after 24 years of exile. When he died there ten weeks later (May 30, 1778) the religious authorities denied him burial, and his body was removed secretly at night to be interred in the abbey of Scellieres in Champagne.

Voltaire was greeted as a hero by this wildly enthusiastic public. He died in Paris that year at the age of 84. Several years later, during the tumultuous years of the French Revolution, his remains were transferred to the Panthéon, a national shrine in Paris that holds the remains of several great French intellectuals and statesmen.

GUIDE TO THE READINGS: VOLTAIRE, *CANDIDE*

Voltaire wrote the novel *Candide* at a particularly pessimistic time in his life. Emilie du Chatelet, his great love, had died in 1749. The terrible Lisbon earthquake, which plays a part in the story (chs. 5–6), had taken place in 1755. The *Encyclopedia* was suppressed by the French government in 1751 and again in 1757. France and Britain were engaged in the protracted Seven Years War (1756–63), a reference to the North American phase of which appears in chapter 23 of *Candide*.

Candide is a *satire*. A satire uses irony, derision, and caustic wit to expose human folly and stupidity. For example, in chapter 19 Candide defines "optimism" as "the madness that leads one to maintain that all is well when one's own life is dreadful." Satire is an entertaining and dramatic form of social criticism. As we have seen, the hallmark of Enlightenment thought, rooted in its commitment to reason and thinking for oneself, was criticism of existing ideas and institutions on the grounds of their irrationality and inhumanity.

There are many targets of Voltaire's satire in *Candide*. The satirical thread running throughout the book is a many-sided attack on the rationalism of the seventeenth-century German philosopher Gottfried Leibniz, embodied in the character of Dr. Pangloss. As one of the three leading Continental Rationalists (the other two were Descartes and Spinoza), Leibniz believed in the power of reason to understand not only the physical universe but also metaphysical realities such as God and the soul. Like the other Rationalists, Leibniz thought that the highest and surest form of reasoning was deductive reasoning, starting with first principles and logically deducing everything else from them.

An excellent example is Leibniz's proof that the universe as it is is "the best of all possible worlds" in which all that happens is "for the best"—phrases that appear frequently in *Candide* on the lips of Pangloss or Candide. Beginning with the classical Christian idea of God, Leibniz argued this way: God the Creator is omnipotent, omniscient, and perfectly good. When the omniscient God decided to create a universe God could envision an infinite number of possible universes (worlds) from which to choose. But since God is perfectly good, God could choose only the best from among all the possible universes. Since God is omnipotent, God had the power to bring into being and maintain in being and goodness the best possible universe. Therefore this universe as we have it is the best of all possible universes. It follows from this that it must be the case that a universe containing evil is better than one without evil. In *Candide* Voltaire is lampooning this abstract deductive argument by piling up example after example of the suffering and horror that are part of our actual experience of the world.

Voltaire also levels his satirical wit at the horror and folly of war—the Seven Years' War in particular, but war in general, as for example in chapters 2 and 3 on Candide's experience as a soldier for the Bulgarians. Famous for his anti-Catholic slogan "Ecrasez l'infame!" ("Crush the infamous thing!") and his lifelong criticism of the church, Voltaire in *Candide* continues his assault on organized religion. Satirizing their authoritarianism, superstitions, and moral corruption, he reminds the reader that much suffering and death has been perpetrated by religious institutions believing they were acting in the name and with the authority of God. His harsh portrayals of the Jesuits in South America and of the Muslims in Turkey are good examples of his religious satire. Significantly, the good people in *Candide* are religious heretics in the eyes of both Catholicism and Protestantism: James the Anabaptist and Martin the Manichaean. Voltaire himself greatly admired the Society of Friends or Quakers—who had been cruelly persecuted in the seventeenth century—for their religious simplicity and active good works. Look for other objects of satire in *Candide*, such as social prejudice and injustice, human pride, selfishness, and stupidity, feeling sorry for oneself, romantic love, physicians, merchants, publishers, and French and German attitudes toward each other.

The main characters in *Candide* all have significant names. *Pangloss* means "all tongue." *Candide* means white, dumb, or innocent. *Cunegonde* is the name of a minor saint in the church's calendar, but it is a harsh and ugly name to French ears. *Thunder-ten-Tronck* is meant to be one of those long, hyphenated German names that the French find unpronounceable. *Cacambo* has scatological connotations. The Argentinian Governor General has a very pretentious name, whereas the most reasonable persons in the story, James and Martin, have ordinary, straightforward names.

Central to the story of *Candide* is the imagery of gardens. In Chapter 1 we have in the baron's castle an earthly paradise, a "Garden of Eden," in which innocence is ended by the "original sin" of acquiring a certain kind of knowledge and Candide's consequent banishment. Chapters 17-18 describe the fabled land of El Dorado, an idyllic "garden of reason" in a crazy world. Finally, in Chapter 30, the protagonists dwell in another kind of garden, the garden of humankind in the real world, in which people can find a certain happiness and contentment through working and making the best they can out of life.

The three gardens embody Voltaire's "realistic optimism." While he is savagely critical of the Pollyannish optimism represented by Pangloss and Candide, he is soberly hopeful that through the growing exercise of reason people can make improvements in human life—"cultivate their gardens"—and come to recognize that their attempts to make ultimate sense of things are in a sense futile. Voltaire's outlook is a robust *humanism*, his passionate concerns and reforming activity always centered on human beings, human society, and their improvement.

QUESTIONS FOR STUDY AND REFLECTION

1. What is the importance of philosophical and cultural relativism in shaping Enlightenment thought (particularly in the early work of Montesquieu and Voltaire)?
2. Trace the development of alternatives to standard Christian belief and doctrine that developed in the Age of Reason (deism, materialism, atheism).
3. What were the main targets of Voltaire's satire in *Candide*? Give a specific example of each target (persons, ideas, institutions, events) from Voltaire's time in Europe. In what ways do his social criticisms express Enlightenment values?
4. What are the two characteristics that, according to Rousseau, humans uniquely and naturally possess? What reasons does he give for selecting them?
5. What is Rousseau's ideal of a good society with a good government? Why does he take this view?
6. Describe the social and political conditions of the *Ancien Régime* in France.
7. Examine the attitudes towards political reform held by Louis XVI; by the liberal nobility. What were the immediate causes for the outbreak of the Revolution?

SUGGESTIONS FOR FURTHER READING

Blanning, T.C.W. *The French Revolution: Class War or Culture Clash?* New York: St. Martin Press, 1997.

Cobban, Alfred, ed. *the Eighteenth Century: Europe in the Age of Enlightenment*. New York: McGraw-Hill, 1967.

Furet, Francis. *The French Revolution, 1770 - 1814*. Oxford, U.K.: Blackwell, 1996.

Gay, Peter. *The Enlightenment: An Interpretation*, 2 vols. New York: Knopf, 1966. (Norton Paperback, 1977).

_____ *The Party of Humanity: Essays in the French Enlightenment*. New York: Columbia University Press, 1970.

Hampson, Norman. *A Social History of the French Revolution*. Routledge, UK: Routledge, Chapman and Hall, 1987.

LeFebvre, George. *The Coming of the French Revolution, 1789*. Princeton: Princeton University Press, 1954.

_____ *The French Revolution*. New York: Columbia University Press, 1962-64.

Palmer, R.R. [Robert Roswell]. *Age of Democratic Revolution: A Political History of Europe and America, 1760-1800*, 2 vols. Vol I *The Challenge*, 1959. Vol II *The Struggle*, 1964. Princeton: Princeton University Press.

Roberts, J. M. *The French Revolution*. Oxford, U.K.: Oxford University Press, 1997.

Soboul, Albert. *The French Revolution 1787-1799: From the Storming of the Bastille to Napoleon*. Winchester, MA: Unwin Hyman, 1989.

Spencer, Samia, ed. *French Women and the Age of Enlightenment*. Bloomington: Indiana University Press, 1985.

---

[1] Evelyn Eatrice Hall, *Life of Volatire*, 3rd ed. New York: Putnam, 1926, p 145.

[2] Napoléon makes his career as a successful officer and later general of the French revolutionary army during the 1790s, and later turns his military victories into political victories as well, establishing France as an empire and himself as emperor in 1803.

[3] Among the most celebrated hostesses of the Enlightenment *salons* were Marie de Vichy-Chamrond, Marquise du Deffand (1697-1780); Louise-Florence d'Esclavelles, Mme D'epinay (1726-1783); and Marie Thérèse Rodet, MmeGeoffrin (1699-1777).

THE FRENCH REVOLUTION

The French Revolution looms large in the Western imagination. The Revolution abolished absolute monarchy and replaced it with republican and democratic forms of government. Rigid social divisions based on the prerogatives of birth and inheritance were replaced with notions of equality and merit. In the words of the most famous slogan of the period, the revolutionaries of 1789 created a new nation based upon the principles of "liberty, equality, and fraternity." The French Revolution is considered to be one of the founding events of the modern era.

THE PRE-REVOLUTIONARY CRISIS

The immediate cause of the French Revolution was the nation's mounting fiscal crisis. By the 1780s, France was on the brink of bankruptcy. Government spending far outpaced its income from tax revenues and other sources. While the monarchy had always spent lavishly, it was King Louis XVI's decision to support the Americans against the British in the American War of Independence that drove France to the brink of financial ruin. The French government was forced to borrow enormous sums to aid the colonists. In the years immediately following the war, France devoted nearly 50 percent of its budget to paying interest on this debt.

To help solve this problem Louis XVI and his finance minister proposed raising taxes. The clergy and the nobility, however, were legally and traditionally exempted from paying most taxes. Therefore, almost the entire tax burden fell upon the nation's poorest subjects, the peasantry. The King and his ministers knew that in order to raise revenue, they would have to target the wealthy. In 1787, Louis XVI asked the nobility and the clergy to voluntarily begin shouldering some of the tax burden.

Jean-Baptiste Regnault, "La Liberte ou la Mort"
Courtesy of Ralph Kleinhempel

Sensing weakness and desperation on the part of the King, the nobility and clergy insisted that only the Estates General—a meeting of representatives from all three estates—could authorize new taxes. The Estates General had not met in 175 years. To call it would have been an open acknowledgement of weakness on the part of Louis XVI. Yet, the situation was grave and drastic measures were necessary. The King ultimately gave in to the demands, calling for a meeting of the Estates General to begin on May 4, 1789.

While the nation was occupied with electing representatives to the Estates General, poor weather was plaguing the country. The fall harvest of 1787 was a disaster. Thunderstorms and hail produced widespread crop damage. Throughout France bread prices rose and peasants faced starvation. As representatives gathered in Versailles for the meeting of the Estates General, riots spread throughout the countryside. Over the next several months the fiscal problems gripping the nation mutated in to political and social crises, making the French Revolution all but inevitable.

THE MODERATE PHASE, 1789–1791

As an historical event, the Revolution is best understood as occurring in two phases: the moderate phase, 1789–1791, during which France went from being ruled by an absolute monarchy to a constitutional monarchy; and the radical phase, 1792–1794, characterized by war abroad and unprecedented violence at home.

The Estates General immediately bogged down on disagreements over format and procedure. The nobility insisted that the three estates each meet separately and vote as individual bodies. Since the nobility and clergy often were natural allies, this format would have made the third estate a permanent minority. Representatives of the third estate adamantly opposed this arrangement. In a nation comprised of 100,000 clergy, 400,000 nobles, and twenty five million peasants, urban workers, artisans, doctors, lawyers, and merchants, the representatives of the third estate demanded equality with the other two estates. Abbé Emmanuel-Joseph Sieyès summed up the position of the third estate with three questions: "What is the Third Estate?—*everything*. What has it been until now in the political order?—*nothing*. What does it seek?—To be *something*."

On June 7, 1789, the representatives of the third estate took a revolutionary step. Locked out of their meeting hall (either by accident or design), deputies reconvened at a nearby tennis court and declared themselves the National Assembly, the legitimate representative ruling body of the nation. Members of the third estate invited representatives from the nobility and clergy to join them and vowed not to disband until a constitution for the nation had been written. This event became known as the Tennis Court Oath.

The King responded in two ways. He ordered the first and second estates to join the new National Assembly. Yet, at the same time he massed troops around Paris and fired his reform-minded finance minister. To many in Paris it looked as if the King were going to call a halt to the activity of the National Assembly.

The reaction in Paris to this aggressive move was predictable. Already agitated by high bread prices—by July 1789 a working-class Parisian spent eighty percent of his income on bread—the common people of Paris began to arm themselves and to attack places where either weapons or food were stored. Three days of extreme violence in the city culminated with the storming of the Bastille.

On July 14, 1789 an armed mob marched on the Bastille, a fortress turned into a royal prison located in the heart of working-class Paris. The crowd stormed the Bastille and hacked its commander to death, gleefully displaying his head on a pike. The fall of the Bastille was of minor military or strategic significance, but was an important symbolic victory. In the minds of many, the Bastille represented the worst excesses of absolute monarchy. With its fall, the Old Regime came to a symbolic end and the French Revolution began.

That summer, spurred by high bread prices, food shortages, and the fear of starvation, the violent revolt that started in Paris quickly spread to the rural areas. Peasants blamed their tenuous situation on the nobility. The result was widespread rioting, looting, and destruction of nobles' property. In Versailles, the National Assembly focused on a way to quell the violence. It's solution was to end all legal distinctions between nobles and commoners. On the night of August 4, 1789 representatives of the nobility renounced all claims to special rights and privileges.

Three weeks later, on August 26, the Assembly ratified the Declaration of Rights of Man and Citizen. The "Declaration" offered a clear and bold statement of Enlightenment principles: "Men are born free and remain free and equal in rights." In its seventeen articles, the "Declaration" articulated a vision of the nation that valued equality, individual rights, and a government that can exist only with the consent of the governed.

Louis XVI, however, was reluctant to approve the "Declaration." On October 5, 1789, six thousand Parisian men and women marched to Versailles in protest of high bread prices. Shortly after, the crowd was joined by twenty thousand armed militia sympathetic to their cause. The crowd seized the King and Queen, and forced them to return to Paris. Once in Paris, the King was forced to accept the reforms.

With the King and Queen virtual prisoners in the Tuileries Palace in Paris, deputies to the Assembly—now called the Constituent Assembly—set about to write a constitution for the nation. Two years later, on September 1791, the Assembly completed its work. The new constitution remade the face of France. First, and perhaps most importantly, absolute monarchy was abolished, transforming Louis XVI into a constitutional monarch. The Assembly created a legislature as an equal branch of government with the monarchy. Landowning men were granted suffrage. All officials were elected; no offices could be bought, sold, or inherited. Second, the Catholic Church became legally subordinate to the state. The Church's vast tracts of land were seized and sold off to the highest bidders. For the first time, Catholics, Protestants, non-Christians, and non-believers stood equal before the law.

By the end of 1791, the revolutionaries were satisfied with their accomplishments. France had a constitution, the power of the monarchy was severely curtailed, and all citizens were equal in the eyes of the law. Yet, revolutions can take on a dynamic and a logic all their own. The years 1792 to 1794 would see the French Revolution move in unanticipated and often undesirable ways.

THE RADICAL PHASE, 1792–1794

By 1792, sentiment about the Revolution had broken into two opposing camps. On one side were those who wanted to press on with revolutionary reforms. On the other side were the counterrevolutionary forces. This second group included French aristocrats who had fled the country shortly after the fall of the Bastille, and disgruntled clergy and peasants who were disturbed by the revolutionary actions taken against the Church. Louis XVI was also secretly among this group.

On June 20, 1791, the royal family, in disguise, escaped the Tuileries Palace in Paris. Their plan was to flee the city, raise a counterrevolutionary force, and overturn the Revolution. They were thwarted, however, when the King was arrested in the city of Varennes and forcibly returned to Paris. The "flight to Varennes," as the episode came to be known, exposed a schism among the revolutionaries: the moderate elements still believed the King had a role to play in the government, while the radicals viewed him as a traitor and an enemy of the state.

As war approached, the moderate position became untenable. The French Queen, Marie Antoinette, was the daughter of the King of Austria. In April, 1792, the King of Austria, in league with Prussia, sent troops into France to free the French royal family and to bring the Revolution to an end. By the summer of 1792, Austrian-Prussian forces had penetrated deep into French territory. The commander of the approaching forces warned the French that if the King and Queen were harmed, Paris would be destroyed. Under the threat of foreign invasion, the National Convention (the new parliament) suspended the constitution, outlawed the monarchy and declared France a republic. New elections were held based on universal manhood suffrage. A governing body was created to write a new constitution. However, the Revolution was about to enter a new and more violent phase.

By September, 1792, with enemy forces on the outskirts of the city, Parisians resorted to mob violence. Crowds indiscriminately attacked anyone suspected of being in league with the enemy forces. Over one thousand people were killed, their bodies mutilated and put on display. In December, 1792, Louis XVI was placed on trial, and the following month he was beheaded as an enemy of the French people. Marie Antoinette was guillotined in October, 1793.

While the French forces successfully counterattacked and drove the enemy troops steadily towards the border, the political life of France fell increasingly under the authority of the most radical elements of the National Convention. In June, 1793, twenty-nine moderate members of the Convention were arrested without warning. Dissent became intolerable. Under the leadership of Maximilian Robespierre (1758–1794), a provincial lawyer, the twelve-member Committee of Public Safety was established to guide the war effort and run the nation. Under the leadership of the Committee, the Reign of Terror was instituted throughout France.

The Terror began as a military dictatorship with intent to preserve the new republic during a time of war. By 1793 the majority of European nations favored putting down the Revolution. Robespierre and the Committee believed that the new republic must be saved at all costs. The Reign of Terror was instituted to punish the enemies of the republic, both foreign and domestic. However, it quickly degenerated into a brutal and frenzied search for dissenters of any kind. Around the nation, thousands were hauled before revolutionary tribunals: the verdicts were either acquittal or death. The Committee also turned on its own allies. Groups such as the radical Parisian *sans-culottes* ("without britches"), who had supported revolutionary activity from the outset, faced the guillotine. Unsure of whom the Committee might turn on next, the National Convention finally moved against Robespierre. He and other members of the Committee were arrested. On July 28, 1794, having sentenced nearly 40,000 of his fellow-Frenchmen to death, Robespierre himself was guillotined.

With the death of Robespierre and the dismantling of the Committee of Public Safety, Revolutionary leadership fell once again into the hands of more moderate elements. Yet, the nation still faced many problems. The war against united Europe still raged, the nation had yet to recover from the Terror, and the initial problem that triggered the revolution—the failing economy—had not been solved. These were the problems Napoleon Bonaparte would face in his rise to power.

NAPOLEON BONAPARTE (1769–1821)

RISE TO POWER

Napoleon Bonaparte's rise to power is one of the most remarkable stories in the history of the Western world. He was born in 1769 to a poor family on the island of Corsica, spoke French with an Italian accent, and was imprisoned for a time during the French Revolution. Yet, by 1800, Napoleon was the ruler of France and considered to be one of the greatest military leaders of all time.

Napoleon owed his meteoric rise to power to the French Revolution. In the pre-revolutionary French army of the Old Regime, Napoleon's background would have prevented him from rising in the ranks of the officer corps. The Revolution did away with that system, however, opening career advancement to talent and merit. Under the system created during the Revolution, Napoleon was able to begin his military career as an artillery officer.

While the Revolution gave Napoleon his start in the French army, the French Revolutionary wars provided him the chance to demonstrate his tremendous skill as a military leader. In 1792, the majority of European nations joined forces to crush the Revolution. Napoleon promptly distinguished himself on the battlefield, and in 1796, at the age of twenty-six, he was given command of French forces in Italy. Two months after taking command, Napoleon had successfully beaten back Austrian forces and conquered the Kingdom of Piedmont.

Following his victories in Italy, Napoleon gained command of French forces in Egypt. His goal was to extend French hegemony throughout the middle east. After a year of fierce campaigns against the combined forces of the Egyptians, Turks, and British, Napoleon abandoned his troops and secretly made his way back to France.

Upon his return to Paris in 1799, Napoleon staged a *coup d'état* against the revolutionary leadership of the Directory. The moderate Directory, in power since 1795, was weak, and faced stiff opposition from both radical and conservative elements in the government. The Directory was no match against the popular general. On November 10, 1799, Napoleon assumed the newly-created title of "First Consul." He quickly consolidated power, strengthening his grip on France. In 1802, he proclaimed himself "First Consul for life" and on December 2, 1804, in the Cathedral of Notre Dame, Napoleon crowned himself "Emperor of the French."

IMPERIAL RULE

Once in power would Napoleon advance or betray the principles of the French Revolution? Ultimately, he did both. His primary task was to restore order and stability to a country shaken by a decade of revolutionary upheaval and violence. To do so, he curtailed many of the political liberties the French had enjoyed since 1789. Under Napoleon's rule it was illegal to criticize the government. Freedom of the press was severely restricted. The number of newspapers in Paris fell from seventy-four to four. The remaining few were simply mouthpieces of the government. Napoleon also censored artistic and theatrical productions, and closed political clubs around the nation.

Yet, Napoleon also institutionalized many of the Revolution's central tenets. He eliminated distinctions between nobles and commoners, and kept professions open to talent and merit. His greatest domestic achievement was the creation of a civil code of law called the *Code Napoléon*. The Code created a uniform system of justice that applied to all French citizens regardless of social or regional differences. These legal reforms protected property rights, equalized the tax burden, kept the Church subordinate to the state, guaranteed religious freedom, and granted civil rights to Jews. The civil law code also destroyed the last vestiges of feudalism by outlawing seignorial courts and abolishing serfdom.

In addition to the Code, Napoleon helped transform France into a modern, centralized, bureaucratic state. In order to facilitate trade, commerce, and communication, Napoleon ordered the construction and repairing of canals, bridges, and roadways, the standardization of a system of weights and measures, and the creation of the Bank of France. He also created France's *lycées*, a school system which placed education under centralized state authority.

THE NAPOLEONIC EMPIRE

With his dominance secure at home, Napoleon turned his sights abroad. Between the years 1803 and 1810, no one could match Napoleon's brilliance on the battlefield or the sheer might of his *Grande Armée*. After seven years of continual warfare, France controlled the majority of continental Europe. Only Britain and Russia escaped Napoleon's grasp.

Once in control of a foreign territory, Napoleon imposed France's legal and social system on the nation. The *Code Napoléon* became the law of the land, nobility and all vestiges of feudalism were abolished, the church lost its authority in matters of state and education, people were granted the freedom to choose their religion and professions, and internal trading tariffs were removed. Napoleon's policy of reorganizing conquered lands transformed European states into modern, secularized, bureaucratic nations.

Despite being the ruler of a vast empire, Napoleon remained unsatisfied. His goal was nothing short of complete domination of Europe. Napoleon believed the way to bring Britain to its knees was to conquer its sole remaining ally and trading partner: Russia. On June 22, 1812, Napoleon led an army of 614,000 men and 250,000 horses across the Neman river on to Russian soil. Napoleon described the invasion as "the most difficult enterprise I have ever attempted." It would ultimately lead to his demise.

Russian forces retreated eastward in the face of Napoleon's army. After a brutal battle at Borodino, where seventy-five thousand men were killed, Napoleon finally entered the city of Moscow only to find it abandoned and in flames. Within a week virtually the entire city had been burned to the ground by retreating Russian forces. For lack of adequate food supplies, Napoleon and his troops were forced to retreat in the dead of winter. By the time he re-crossed the Neman river, Napoleon had only 10,000 soldiers remaining.

Napoleon's empire could not survive the destruction of the *Grande Armée*. In October, 1813, Prussian, Swedish, Russian, and Austrian forces met France's army outside the city of Leipzig. European coalition forces pushed Napoleon and his troops back to Paris. He abdicated the throne and went into exile on the island of Elba, off the Italian coast.

Louis XVIII, younger brother of the executed Louis XVI, was restored to the throne of France. However, Napoleon was not finished. In March, 1815, he escaped from exile and returned to Paris where he was greeted by a hero's welcome. Louis XVIII fled the country, and the period known as the Hundred Days began. Raising a new army, Napoleon moved against a multi-national European force located in Belgium. In June, 1815, Napoleon was finally defeated at the Battle of Waterloo. This time, allied forces sent Napoleon to the remote St. Helena island in the South Atlantic Ocean where he spent the last six years of his life.

After Napoleon's final exile, European rulers met in Vienna to draw up a peace settlement, and to undo the consequences of Napoleonic rule. The leaders at the Congress of Vienna (1814–1815) sought to restore a balance of power among European nations, and to stamp out the ideas of the French Revolution. European monarchs viewed the principles of "liberty, equality, and fraternity," as a direct threat to their reigns. The Congress was only a moderate success. The leaders did manage to prevent another full-scale European war until 1914. However, they were much less successful in containing the ideals of the French Revolution. Indeed, revolutions would become a regular feature of European life in the nineteenth century, erupting around the continent in 1830, 1848, and 1870.

Europe in 1815. Redrawn from *A History of World Societies,* Fifth Edition, by John P. McKay, Bennett D. Hill, John Buckler, and Patricia Buckley Ebrey, (2000) Houghton Mifflin Co.

TIMELINE OF EVENTS

1765

(February): Stamp Act passed by Parliament

1772

Boston Tea Party; coercive Acts passed by Parliament

1774

First Continental Congress in Philadelphia

1775–83

War for Independence

1776

(January): Thomas Paine, *Common Sense*; (May): Congress asks each of thirteen colonies to draw up state constitutions; (June): Virginia delegation to Second Continental Congress introduces resolution for independence; Jefferson composes Declaration of Independence (adopted 4 July)

1777

(November): Congress adopts Articles of Confederation

1783–89

Confederation

1783

Treaty of Paris

1787–88

(May, 1787): Congress calls for convention to revise the Articles of Confederation; (September, 1787): U. S. Constitution agreed upon and signed; (October 1787–March 1788): 85 *Federalist* letters appear in New York newspapers.

CHAPTER FOUR

BUILDING AN AMERICAN REPUBLIC: 1765–1788

THE FEDERALIST PAPERS, DECLARATION OF INDEPENDENCE, U.S. CONSTITUTION, AND AN *ANTIFEDERALIST* RESPONSE

INTRODUCTION

In the midst of a bloody War for Independence from Great Britain (1775–83), the members of the Second Continental Congress faced a gantlet of formidable challenges. Militarily, Congress had to raise, train, and feed a Continental Army to defeat the world's strongest military power. Congress also had to find a way to pay for a war that was growing more expensive by the hour. And as royal authority collapsed during the Revolution, members of Congress had to come up with legal and, more importantly, popular ways to govern the citizens of states, counties and towns who had until recently been subjects of the king of Great Britain. With an eye to each of these problems, Congress in May 1776 called on each colony to form a state government and draw up written state constitutions based on "the authority of the people."

This idea that "the people"—not kings—were sovereign reflected a political philosophy called republicanism, a complex and fluid body of ideas with origins in classical antiquity, Renaissance Italy, and early modern England. Essentially, republicanism suggested that "self-government" by the people themselves (or by their elected representatives) better insured individual freedom and happiness than rule by kings or aristocrats. One central tenet of republicanism held that governments should operate only with the consent of the governed. Another, which grew out of "country" British politicians' opposition to the king's powerful supporters in London, involved a deep suspicion of any strong,

centralized authority. Finally, republicanism required a virtuous, public-minded and, above all, *independent* citizenry—without one, republics were doomed to failure. As classical theorists like Plato and Aristotle wrote, once citizens abandoned self-sacrifice for individual gain, republics crumbled into monarchies, oligarchies (rule by a powerful few) or, worse still, anarchy (rule by the mob).

Any reasonably educated eighteenth century person knew that republics were fragile and prone to spectacular failure. In the ancient world, Athenian democracy was short-lived, while Rome's once-stable republic had collapsed into empire. Europe's three surviving republics (Switzerland, the Netherlands, and Venice) were on the whole anti-democratic and corrupt societies that did little to inspire republican thinkers. What made eighteenth century Americans believe that they could be different—that they could "fix" the problems inherent in history's failed republics? And what did it mean to say, as the ex-colonists did time and again, that "the people" are sovereign? Finally, who were "the people?"

Between 1765 and 1789, British colonists and Americans fought a War for Independence against the world's most powerful nation, adopted governments built on popular rule, joined together in a Confederation based on the absolute sovereignty of each new state, then threw aside this union in favor of our current "federal" system. They also debated questions of power, sovereignty, citizenship, republicanism and happiness at great length. These debates will form the backdrop for this chapter's discussion of Jefferson's Declaration of Independence, the U.S. Constitution, essays written by James Madison, Alexander Hamilton and John Jay to defend it, and George Mason's essay critiquing it. Yet to understand these arguments, it will be necessary to return, briefly, to the political, economic and social conditions that preceded them: the imperial crisis with Great Britain (1765-1775), the War for Independence (1775-1783) and the Confederation (or "first republic" 1783-1789). This prelude will help explain the competing—and contrasting—visions Americans held for a truly revolutionary democratic and republican society.

THE IMPERIAL CRISIS

A dramatic series of crises destroyed Great Britain's empire in North America between 1765 and 1775. In the process, Englishmen in the colonies conducted a spirited debate among themselves over the legitimacy of the King and Parliament's authority over them.

When twenty-two-year-old George III inherited the British throne from his grandfather in 1760, the country was in the midst of a world war. Although it had important European components, the war (variously named "The Seven Year's War" or "The French and Indian War") could justifiably be called "the war for North America." When the French accepted defeat, they ceded to the British all of North America east of the Mississippi except the port of New Orleans. Great Britain's North American subjects were ecstatic: for generations the French and their Indian allies had raided British settlements on the frontier. With the Peace of Paris in 1763, most colonists foresaw a long period of prosperity. They took pride in their new king and status as Englishmen. Most colonists believed the English system of government—a "balance" of monarchy (represented by the king), aristocracy (represented by the House of Lords), and democracy (represented by the House of Commons)—was the most perfect ever put into practice. Certainly it was the most stable. The year 1763 was without a doubt the high water mark of Britain's empire in the Americas.

From a financial perspective, however, things were not so rosy for England. During the war the national debt had nearly doubled, and more than half of the empire's annual revenues went to pay the interest on the debt. Added to this was the financial

necessity of garrisoning all of Britain's New World conquests. Advisors recommended leaving at least twenty battalions (10,000 men) behind in North America, concentrating in Canada, Florida, and Indian country. This would surely add to Britain's tax burden, even though Englishmen were already among the most heavily-taxed people on earth. Who should pay for the defense of the Atlantic colonies? The answer was simple to members of Parliament: the settlers themselves, since they were the people who benefited most directly from the soldiers' presence.

The British government thus began a series of policies aimed at forcing the colonists to pay for their own defense, as well as giving the government in London more direct control over its North American possessions. Each of these policies was viewed (by growing numbers of recalcitrant colonists) as an illegitimate abuse of royal power that subjugated an underrepresented population. The most important of these policies was the Stamp Act, passed by Parliament in February 1765. The Stamp Act imposed a tax on colonial documents like deeds, wills, licenses, newspapers, pamphlets, and ships' bills of lading—and required that a special "stamp" be embossed on the documents proving that the tax had been paid. But unlike previous taxes that regulated trade, the Stamp Tax's sole purpose was raising money for the British government (making it a "direct" tax). When they first heard of the plans for the tax, all thirteen colonial assemblies petitioned Parliament to reject the Stamp Act as "taxation without representation." The British Prime Minister replied that the colonists were already "virtually" represented in Parliament, since members of the House of Commons represented all Englishmen, wherever they happened to be. The Maryland lawyer Daniel Dulany ridiculed this concept in a popular pamphlet, arguing that no member of Parliament paid the duties they imposed on the colonies. Already some British subjects were questioning the sovereignty of royal authority.

Organized colonial resistance to the Stamp Act began as soon as ships arrived in April 1765 with news of its passage. Leading the charge was a twenty-nine-year-old lawyer and member of the Virginia House of Burgesses named Patrick Henry. Henry introduced a series of resolutions in May 1765 that argued that the popularly-elected Virginia assembly alone possessed the right to tax Virginians. Even though his more radical resolutions never passed, newspapers in other colonies printed each of Henry's resolves, implying that Virginia's assembly had endorsed all seven measures. Nine colonies sent delegates to a special Stamp Act Congress in New York to protest the law, although the body was careful to underscore its loyalty to the king.

More radical opposition was manufactured by a group of angry settlers called the Sons of Liberty, led by the Boston brewer Samuel Adams. Adams engineered large street demonstrations that often turned into angry crowd actions aimed at royal authority. In one incident, a crowd ransacked the stately mansion owned by Lt. Gov. Thomas Hutchinson, leaving only the exterior walls standing. Similar actions took place in other colonies, and in twelve of thirteen the royal "stamp master" was forced to resign before he even took office. With no one to distribute the stamps, the act could not be enforced. In March 1766, Parliament repealed the Stamp Act, while reaffirming its power to legislate—and to tax—the colonies "in all cases whatsoever."

Six years later, in response to the Boston Tea Party (where angry Bostonians destroyed 342 chests of British tea to protest another tax), Parliament passed the Coercive Acts, designed to punish the colony of Massachusetts into submission. The Coercive Acts spread alarm throughout the colonies, proving that the crown was willing to impose military rule and suspend local governments. In response, every colony but Georgia sent delegates to Philadelphia in 1774 for a meeting of the First Continental Congress. Delegates were a "who's who" of the Revolutionary generation, including George Washington and Patrick Henry from Virginia, and Samuel and John Adams from Massachusetts. The Congress passed a declaration of rights ("we ask only for peace, liberty and security… we wish no diminution of royal prerogatives, we demand no new rights") that were far from radical—yet to Great Britain, the colonists had crossed another line. Although they consented to royal authority in general, they insisted on their right to revoke this consent at any time they saw fit. At stake was the very legitimacy of royal government.

REVOLUTION AND INDEPENDENCE

Before Congress had a chance to reconvene, war began in Massachusetts in 1775. The British planned a surprise, nighttime attack on a suspected ammunition storage site in Concord, Massachusetts, but were confronted with seventy armed colonists on the green in Lexington. A skirmish followed on the Old North Bridge in nearby Concord. This first battle of the Revolution demonstrated the extent of the disagreement between Britain and her colonies. The British governor and military commander of Massachusetts believed he was merely using prudent military force to quash a needling domestic insurrection. The rebels—who were beginning to call themselves "patriots"—believed they were defending their rights and liberties, as well as their homes, from an abusive power bent on subjugating them.

One month after the fighting began on Lexington Green, a Second Continental Congress assembled in Philadelphia to raise and supply an army and negotiate some kind of reconciliation with Great Britain. Yet as the war continued and hopes for an amicable settlement with England faded, more and more delegates began to weigh a risky—even treasonous—option: independence. In January 1776 advocates of independence received a boost by a sensational pamphlet called *Common Sense*. Written by a radical English printer and recent immigrant named Thomas Paine, *Common Sense* put into everyday language what two years before would have seemed treasonous: the need to end the colonies' relationship with Britain once and for all and establish a republic. Instead of stressing the links the colonies shared with England in the reserved tone used by most pamphleteers, Paine mocked as "degenerate" Britain's balanced government of monarchy, aristocracy, and democracy. The colonies, he stated matter-of-factly, could do far better by abolishing aristocratic trappings altogether and adopting a republican government. Rulers, to the republican Paine, were only representatives of the people and their laws: "the King of America … doth not make havoc of mankind like the Royal Brute of Britain … in America THE LAW IS KING … there ought to be no other." Paine's pamphlet sold more than 150,000 copies, was reprinted in numerous newspapers, and read aloud in countless taverns and public squares. Independence moved from a radical claim in December 1775 to a matter of "common sense" by late spring 1776.

On June 7, 1776 the Virginia delegation to the Second Continental Congress introduced a resolu-

Great Seal of the United States on the US Dollar Bill.
Courtesy of Letraset Phototone.

tion calling for independence. More moderate delegates seeking a reconciliation with Britain commanded enough support to delay a vote until July, but Congress agreed to appoint a committee consisting of John Adams, Benjamin Franklin, and Thomas Jefferson to prepare a declaration that would justify American independence to the world. The thirty-four-year-old Jefferson was chosen to draft the measure. In addition to a laundry list of grievances against George III, Jefferson's declaration held that the following were "self-evident truths": "that all men are created equal; that they are endowed by their Creator with certain inalienable rights; that among these are life, liberty and the pursuit of happiness." The last clause was derived from the writings of John Locke, who held that life, liberty and property were the rights of all men. By substituting the

word "happiness" for "property" Jefferson was making two things clear: first, that private property was considered, for many, a prerequisite for happiness; second, that the framers were steeped in the ideology of "classical republicanism." Derived from thinkers and political philosophers as varied as Plato, Aristotle, Cicero, Machiavelli, Harrington and Locke, classical republican theory posited that governments exist to promote the "happiness" of the people. Jefferson put it slightly differently in the declaration: "[T]o secure these rights, governments are instituted among men, deriving their just powers from the consent of the governed; that whenever any form of government becomes destructive of these ends, it is the right of the people to alter or to abolish it, and to institute new government." Risking execution for treason if captured, the delegates in Philadelphia voted to accept Jefferson's declaration.

After the delegates to the Second Continental Congress declared the colonies independent from Great Britain, they realized the need for a written document to specify the body's powers, the authority that granted them, and how it would govern. Responsibility for drawing up this written plan fell to John Dickinson of Pennsylvania, who had a reputation as a moderate and a conciliator. Dickinson's original draft of the Articles of Confederation gave Congress the power to conduct foreign relations, prosecute wars, regulate trade, borrow money, settle disputes between the various states, and administer unsettled lands in the west. The last two almost sank Dickinson's document, since colonies like Virginia and Massachusetts wanted to keep their old claims (which often fixed western boundaries at the Mississippi or even farther west) intact. After a year and a half of haggling (and waging the War of Independence), Congress finally adopted a modified Articles of Confederation in November 1777.

The differences between the Articles and Dickinson's original draft were obvious: gone were Congress' powers to oversee western territories and issue bills of credit. In their place was a loose plan of confederation, where states retained all powers and rights not explicitly delegated to Congress. There were no provisions for a national system of courts or a national executive. Each state delegation had a single vote, with seven votes (a simple majority) needed for routine action; nine votes to declare war; and thirteen votes *plus* consent of the thirteen state legislatures to amend or approve the Articles. This last provision was clearly intended to protect single states from domination by the others, and avoid any potential attempt by the government to tyrannize its states or citizens. But this fear of tyranny had a strong downside: a very weak central government, with no powers to tax, no executive, and little continuity between legislative sessions. After the conclusion of the Revolutionary War, these deliberate brakes on government power would hobble the new nation.

CONFEDERATION

For a decade after independence, the states were all-powerful and "sovereign." Except for a few functions (like declaring war and peace) explicitly granted to Congress, states commanded authority over their citizens, who tended to think of themselves as Virginians or Pennsylvanians rather than Americans. Following an order by Congress to draw up written state constitutions based on "the authority of the people," states produced various documents to lay out the rights, obligations, and liberties of their governments and citizens. Each state constitution rested on the belief that the government operates only with the consent of the governed, a central tenet of republicanism.

The cornerstone of a healthy republic, theorists stressed, was the independent, virtuous citizen. Ideally this citizen was a property holder (so no landlord or creditor could influence his vote or thinking) and placed more weight on the good of the commonwealth than on personal gain. And since republics were fragile enough as it was, their citizens should be close-knit and homogeneous people. Therefore many political thinkers argued that large, heterogeneous republics were prone to failure. To newly-minted American constitutional theorists like John Adams, the most "virtuous" government was one that abandoned the "balanced" government of England in favor of one based on "separation of powers": a legislature, an executive armed with veto power, and a judiciary independent of both. This system, Adams believed, would avoid the problems inherent in legislative bodies such as making "arbitrary laws for their own interest, [executing] all laws arbitrarily for their own interest, and [adjudging] all controversies in their own favor." Yet some critics of Adams' theories worried about a legislature that could then *create* its own constitution. These concerns led to a truly innovative idea: the constitutional convention. Constitutional conventions would be called into existence for one purpose only (drafting a constitution), and then disband, embodying "popular sovereignty" in pristine form.

For Virginia's constitution, a respected planter named George Mason drafted a declaration (or "bill") of rights that was adopted before the constitution itself. It affirmed the right to life, liberty, property, and the pursuit of happiness, while condemning all forms of hereditary privilege, guaranteeing trial by jury, extolling religious toleration, and calling for frequent turnover in office. Massachusetts' influential constitution, following Mason, also began with a bill of rights. But Massachusetts conventioners added a strong, popularly-elected governor with a qualified veto and submitted the document to the citizens themselves for approval. In 1780, they did. Other states followed Massachusetts' example.

THE CHALLENGES OF INDEPENDENCE

Following a military strategy that kept the small Continental Army intact while escalating the costs of a British victory, General George Washington was able to sustain the revolutionary war effort through nearly constant struggles in Congress and on the battlefield. After a difficult campaign near Yorktown in Virginia, the British general Cornwallis surrendered an army of 8,000 men. News of the surrender brought down the British government in March 1782, yielding a new ministry willing to grant America's independence in exchange for peace. John Adams and the New Yorker John Jay opened secret negotiations with the British soon thereafter that produced the Treaty of Paris in February 1783. The war was over, but the new nation's economy was in shambles. Each state nursed considerable war debts. Revolutionary war soldiers hadn't been paid. And serious weaknesses in the Articles of Confederation could no longer be ignored.

First and foremost, Congress had no authority to impose taxes. And since states had their own debts, most declined to fund the government. The economic recession and high state taxes pressed especially hard on debtors, who sought relief in politics. In Massachusetts, the absence of any legislation to protect debtors' farms and property from seizure led to a serious armed rebellion in 1786-87. Under the leadership of Daniel Shays, a debtor and former

Engraving: George Washington presides over the 1787 Constitutional Convention in Philadelphia. Courtesy of the Free Library of Philadelphia.

Revolutionary War captain, an organized "army" closed courts by force to stop the government from foreclosing on farms and auctioning property for back taxes owed. The governor, supported by merchants from the eastern part of the state, put down Shays' rebellion with state militia and a call to Congress for additional troops. But the Shaysites proved how unequally the fruits of revolutionary victory (and the costs of war) were being shared. Leaders in most colonies were deeply shaken by the rebellion, noting that the nearly-bankrupt Congress was impotent to put down future outbreaks. Nationalist politicians—a growing faction con-

cerned about the republic as a whole more than its individual states—were convinced that the only way to save the new nation was to strengthen the central government, and soon.

Who were the "nationalists"? Mostly officials, diplomats and military officers who had served in or with the Continental Congress, and had shed overarching loyalties to their home states. They included men like George Washington, Benjamin Franklin, John Adams and John Jay. They were joined by younger, energetic leaders like James Madison, Jefferson's neighbor from Virginia and Alexander Hamilton, a New York lawyer with mysterious origins in the West

Indies. By 1786 the nationalists were worried that rebellions like Shays' would extinguish the republican experiment. "What a triumph for the advocates of despotism," wrote Washington, "to find that we are incapable of governing ourselves." Washington's view held sway in Congress, which called for a convention in May 1787 to revise the Articles of Confederation "adequate to the exigencies of government and the preservation of the Union."

THE PHILADELPHIA CONVENTION

The fifty-five delegates who arrived in Philadelphia to amend the confederation were hardly a cross section of American society. As slaveholders, merchants, lawyers and financiers—none of the delegates were artisans, tenants, or backcountry settlers and only one was a yeoman farmer—they favored a stronger central government and supported creditors' property rights. Some delegates were well-known patriots from the Revolutionary era, including George Washington (elected president of the convention) and Benjamin Franklin. Thomas Paine was in Europe, as were Thomas Jefferson and John Adams who were there as American ministers. Samuel Adams was not chosen as a delegate by the state legislature, while Patrick Henry was—but Henry refused to attend saying he favored limited government and "smelt a rat." James Madison was sent by Virginia, and Alexander Hamilton by New York.

After selecting Washington as presiding officer, the delegates voted to close off the proceedings and deliberate only in secret. They decided each state would have one vote (identical to the rules of the Confederation) and that a majority of states would decide any single issue. Lastly, they decided to take up the so-called "Virginia Plan," conveniently compiled in advance by Madison.

JAMES MADISON AND THE VIRGINIA PLAN

James Madison was born in Orange County, Virginia in 1751. Slight and bookish, he left home to attend Princeton (then called the College of New Jersey), where he excelled in languages, history and political theory. He had served in the Continental Congress, participated in framing the Virginia Constitution of 1776, and was a leader in the Virginia assembly, where he developed a low regard for state political leaders, who he accused of "narrow ambition" and a dangerous lack of republican virtue.

Madison spent the winter months of 1786-7 studying the defects of Greek and European confederacies and drafting his Virginia Plan, a scheme for a truly national government and strong national union. The overriding goals of Madison's plan were an attempt to ensure government by men of high republican character while eliminating factional disputes, which he called "vices of the political system." To achieve this, he eclipsed state sovereignty in favor of the "supremacy of national authority": a new central government that had the power to overturn state laws. Madison outlined a government with three "layers": a lower house elected by voters, an upper house elected by members of the lower house, and an executive and judiciary chosen by both upper and lower houses. Delegates from the larger states loved the Virginia Plan. Since the lower house was based on population, it guaranteed the power of states like Virginia and Massachusetts; conversely, low-population states that had equal representation under the Articles of Confederation would be dominated. They offered their own alternative, known as the New Jersey Plan. Under this outline, Congress would be given the power to tax and make binding requisitions on the states—but each state would keep just one vote in the unicameral legislature. It looked a lot like the model proposed by Thomas Paine in *Common Sense*. Perhaps the only thing keeping the delegates going as the summer turned sultry was the knowledge that whatever plan they adopted would have to be approved by the voters.

In the last week of July, Connecticut delegates suggested a compromise between the Virginia and New Jersey plans. One house of a bicameral Congress would have "state equality" while the other was based on "proportional representation." Terms for representatives were laid out: two years for members of the lower house, six for senators, and four for a new executive chosen indirectly by an "electoral college." Each state was left to itself as to how it would choose electors, with the number totaling a state's total representatives in the House and Senate. This was just one of the methods the framers hit upon for giving states a prominent role in the new constitutional structure while removing much power to the new, central government.

The "Great Compromise" over representation left just one issue to fight over: slavery. Slavery was never a prominent issue in the convention, but it revealed

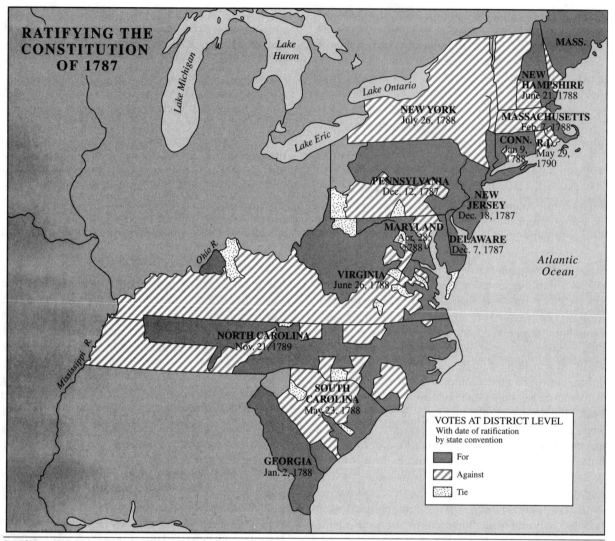

Ratifying the Constitution of 1787. Redrawn from *America's History*, Fourth Edition, Volume 1: To 1877, by James A. Henretta, David Brody, Susan Ware, and Marilynn S. Johnson, (2000), Bedford/St. Martin's Press.

that important differences between regions existed at the end of the eighteenth century. The New Yorker Gouverneur Morris spoke for many northern delegates when he attacked the institution as nefarious, and George Mason (himself a wealthy slaveholder) bitterly attacked the international slave trade. Representatives from South Carolina and Georgia, which still depended on the flow of imported slave labor, threatened to walk out of the convention if Mason's measure was passed. The Constitution thus prohibited Congress from legislating against the slave trade until 1808. Delegates also agreed to a fugitive slave clause that would help slaveholders reclaim "servants" (the word slavery does not appear in the Constitution) who escaped to other states. Finally, southern states were given a boost in Congressional representation—and their share of the tax burden—when the convention agreed to count each slave as three-fifths of a free person. While this opened up slaveholders to higher taxes, it turned into a political windfall, as the "three-fifths rule" allowed Southerners a larger share of federal power than their northern counterparts.

The final issue to hammer out was the scope of national power. Each delegate had arrived in Philadelphia prepared to add to Congress' power, but the final draft of the Constitution went farther than that. The result was a central government that had broad powers to tax, regulate commerce, and provide for military defense, as well as the authority to make any law "necessary and proper" to implement the other powers—an elastic clause indeed. The Constitution also guaranteed that federal laws and treaties would be the "supreme" law of the land and that the United States would honor the Confederation's existing debt. This amounted to a huge giveaway to the nation's creditors and a huge disappointment to debtors like the ones who followed Daniel Shays. Finally, over the eloquent objection of delegate George Mason, delegates voted not to include a bill of rights. Still, thirty-nine of the remaining forty-two delegates signed the document and sent it to "the people" for ratification—or defeat. But there would be no direct, popular referendum on the Constitution; instead, each state would elect a special convention to vote up or down on the new system of government. Unlike a legislature, the special conventions would disband after the vote.

RATIFICATION

With surprisingly little debate, the convention specified that the Constitution would go into effect as soon as it was ratified by special conventions in nine of the thirteen states. This clause was especially revolutionary considering that any amendment of the Articles of Confederation clearly required unanimous approval of all thirteen states. Rhode Island, and perhaps two or three other state legislatures would likely have voted the new covenant down. Each of the delegates was thus fully cognizant of what he hoped to accomplish: a peaceful, but illegal, overthrow of the Confederation's legal and political order. If all the states approved, of course, the legal issues would die away, and the government would rest squarely on the republican foundation of popular (not state) sovereignty. But first, the Constitution had to be ratified; its defenders would need to marshal all their powers of persuasion to make it happen.

Those in favor of the Constitution began the debate over ratification with some advantages. First, they seized the initiative by calling themselves Federalists, a monicker that masked their pursuit of a strong central government with a name that instead suggested a decentralized system. The name stuck, as did their term for their opponents: Antifederalists. There was little doubt who had the better name. Second, they began a brilliant, coordinated campaign of lectures, pamphlets and newspaper articles to justify the new Constitution. The opposition, made up mostly of localists who had little or no reputation beyond their home states, was caught completely off guard.

Federalists and their Congressional allies also took charge of the calendar. Congress submitted the Constitution to the states on September 28, 1787 and the first ratifying conventions were called for December. By New Year's Day 1788 Delaware, Pennsylvania and New Jersey had ratified the document. Connecticut followed on January 2. Excepting Pennsylvania, three of the first four states to ratify were small states, which surprised some commentators. But once the issue of representation in Congress was settled, small states stood to gain much from a stronger central government, including an end to the system of paying import duties to other *states* like New York and Pennsylvania. Small states also realized early on that they could not survive on their own as independent states, as a big state like Virginia or Massachusetts likely could have.

In Massachusetts the convention delegates debated furiously before the Federalists won 187-168. Antifederalists had demanded a host of conditional amendments, as well as taking up George Mason's stand for a bill of rights. To achieve their narrow victory, Massachusetts Federalists promised to support a bill of rights by amendment after the Constitution went into effect. Ratification came easily in Maryland and South Carolina in the spring of 1788, but there was increasing evidence that the Federalists had peaked. The Rhode Island legislature voted overwhelmingly against summoning a ratifying convention at all. And in the next group of states to call conventions—North Carolina, Virginia, New Hampshire and New York—initial majorities opposed the Constitution.

THE ANTIFEDERALIST CRITIQUE

Caught off guard in the fall of 1787, Antifederalists soon pulled together and became better at stating their case. By the summer of 1788, their arguments began to take hold. Eloquent voices took up the Antifederalist cause, including Virginians George Mason, Richard Henry Lee and Patrick Henry; New Yorkers George Clinton and Melancton Smith; and Mercy Otis Warren and James Winthrop of Massachusetts. Despite the patrician tinge of these leaders, Antifederalists came from more diverse backgrounds than the Federalists, who tended to be well-educated, wealthy, and lawyers. As a result, many Antifederalists believed the new Constitutional order was a giant power grab by society's elite: "these lawyers and men of learning and monied men expect to be managers of the Constitution," wrote a Massachusetts farmer. "[They intend to] get all the power and all the money into their own hands and then they will swallow up all us little folks . . . just like the whale swallowed up Jonah." Others argued that, in order to survive, republics had to remain small—more like city states than a 1,500 mile-wide swath of a continent. James Winthrop declared that "no extensive empire can be governed on republican principles." Moreover, Antifederalists worried that the new government outlined in the Constitution would be too far away from most people to be trusted with its new, broad powers. With the House of Representatives divided up into 30,000-person districts, few citizens would know their elected officials, most of whom would undoubtedly come from the wealthiest families. Antifederalists preferred a nation of closely-knit but independent states tied together only for defense and trade purposes. Finally, Antifederalists saw in the Constitution the outlines of a new type of aristocracy, one that could legally impose heavy taxes and other burdens on distant, subjugated citizens. In sum, Antifederalists' version of republicanism was slightly different than their Federalist opponents'. While the Federalists stressed the need for society's elite—educated men, creditors, the wealthy—to lead the new government, the Antifederalists were far more concerned with centralized power and the potential for the creation of a new aristocracy. Both sides claimed to be the true spokesmen for true republican values.

HAMILTON AND *THE FEDERALIST*

New York Antifederalists like Governor George Clinton and Melancton Smith adopted Mason's rhetoric and arguments for opposing the federal compact, adding more of their own. Smith was espe-cially eloquent in calling for a government run by "a representative body, composed principally of respectable yeomanry . . . the best possible security to liberty" as opposed to a Congress composed of wealthy men from giant districts. Eight states had already ratified the Constitution when New York's convention got underway, but a clear vote *against* the compact in any one of four key states—New York and Virginia chief among them—could derail the entire enterprise. New York was especially vital for several reasons. New York City was rapidly becoming the commercial and cultural center of the new nation, set to eclipse Philadelphia and Boston in the early years of the coming century. It was the seat of Congress under the Articles of Confederation, located strategically on the eastern seaboard, and associated neither with New England nor with Virginia. Finally, it was the home of Governor Clinton, whose outspokenness against the Constitution made the Federalists' job there even more pivotal.

It was clearly with these facts in mind that Alexander Hamilton, the leader of the ratification forces in the state, turned his formidable intellect to the task of securing the document's passage. His plan centered on a series of thorough, persuasive and thoughtful essays, published in the popular press, that would explain and justify the proposed Constitution. Hamilton knew he was speaking to a rather small audience—those influential men who made up New York's Constitutional Convention or held sway over them. Still, he hoped the essays would reach those key figures, and serve as an up-to-the-minute debate primer for speakers in the conventions in Virginia and New York. Even with his unrivaled skills in debate and rhetoric Hamilton would not be able to complete this task on his own, and he was extremely fortunate to find two extreme-ly able allies in John Jay and James Madison. Jay (1745–1829) was far more influential than the thirty-three-year-old Hamilton, having distinguished himself as a lawyer, the author of New York's Constitution of 1777 (an important source for the delegates in Philadelphia), a member of the team to negotiate peace with Britain in 1783, and the Secretary of Foreign Affairs under the Articles of Confederation. Madison, already talked about as the "father" of the Constitution, was in New York City as a member of Congress and agreed to take on a large

THE

FEDERALIST:

ADDRESSED TO THE

PEOPLE OF THE STATE OF NEW-YORK.

───────────────────────

NUMBER I.

Introduction.

AFTER an unequivocal experience of the ineffi-cacy of the subsisting federal government, you are called upon to deliberate on a new constitution for the United States of America. The subject speaks its own importance; comprehending in its consequences, nothing less than the existence of the UNION, the safety and welfare of the parts of which it is com-posed, the fate of an empire, in many respects, the most interesting in the world. It has been frequently remarked, that it seems to have been reserved to the people of this country, by their conduct and example, to decide the important question, whether societies of men are really capable or not, of establishing good government from reflection and choice, or whether they are forever destined to depend, for their political constitutions, on accident and force. If there be any truth in the remark, the crisis, at which we are arrived, may with propriety be regarded as the æra in which

A   that

───────────────────────────────

Cover of the Federalist. Courtesy of the Library of Congress.

share of the essays. "Publius," the pseudonymous author of the *Federalist* whose name in Latin trans-lates as "the public voice" was born.

Although he had worthy allies, Hamilton was Publius' prime mover. He wrote fifty-one of the eighty-five public letters, and kept the project going long after Jay became ill and Madison returned to Virginia when Congress recessed. Hamilton's biogra-phy was perhaps the most colorful of all the founders. He was born in 1757 on the island of Nevis, in the British West Indies, the illegitimate son of an itinerant Scottish merchant and a planter's daughter. The boy was clearly bright, and a Presbyterian clergyman provided Hamilton with a basic education and cast about for other proprietors to support the young man's higher education. He arrived in New York City in 1772 bearing letters of introduction from some of the Caribbean's most

influential merchants and eventually attended King's College (later Columbia). He rose quickly through the ranks in the Revolution, eventually becoming a lieutenant-colonel and General Washington's trusted aide-de-camp. When he married into one of New York's most wealthy and prominent families, Hamilton's rise from obscurity was complete: he was elected to Congress, established a successful law practice, and became a delegate to the Constitutional Convention in Philadelphia.

The Federalist was the most comprehensive body of political thought produced by the founding generation. Day after day essays by Publius appeared in the New York papers (reprinted nationwide) defending the need for a strong government to con-duct foreign affairs but pointing out that centralized authority did not necessarily mean domestic tyranny. Why? Because the Constitution rested on "mixed government" (a President, bicameral legislature, and independent judiciary) that "checked" as well as "balanced" each branch.

"Publius" took Antifederalist arguments against the Constitution quite seriously, and attempted to rebut them point by point. But he also took great pains to pick apart the failings of the Articles of Confederation, devoting seven entire essays to the subject. At the heart of the Federalist critique was the notion that, in Hamilton's words, because "men are ambitious, vindictive, and rapacious," the trick was to suppress these tendencies by never allowing any one group or faction to dominate all the others. In *Federalist No. 6* ("Concerning Dangers from War Between the States"), Hamilton deals at length on the weakness and wickedness of human nature, and foresees "frequent and violent contests" among the confederated states unless a strong union is created. He points to festering and competing revolts in North Carolina, Pennsylvania and Massachusetts (Shays' Rebellion) as potentially fatal to a young republic, unless "a FIRM Union" is established as a barrier against domestic faction and insurrection. According to Hamilton, although both state and cen-tral governments necessarily exercise direct authori-ty over their citizens, the latter must be supreme.

Madison took up similar points in *Federalist No. 10*, his most influential installment of the series and one of the most significant American contributions to the theory of representative government. In this letter Madison challenges two thousand years of accepted wisdom about republics, namely that only small ones could remain stable and survive to avoid the twin pitfalls of anarchy and monarchy. Turning conventional thought on its head, Madison suggested that the immense size of the United States would make it far more stable than a smaller one, since "factions" could not easily gain power, overwhelm the public good, and trample on the rights of minorities. Since factions were, unfortunately, the product and price of liberty and thus inevitable, it was the goal of good government to control them, not suppress them outright. Madison's solution was to "extend the sphere…and you take in a greater variety of parties and interests; you make it less probable that a majority of the whole will have a common motive to invade the rights of other citizens." Finally, Madison suggested that in a large republic, each representative would be chosen by enough citizens that elections would be "more likely to center on men who possess the most attractive merit and the most diffusive and established characters." In other words, the new government would draw on the talents of the best-educated, wisest and most virtuous citizens—a hallmark of classical republicanism. Other essays, most notably *Federalist No. 51*, carried on Madison's brilliant argument.

Supreme Court Justices still cite Publius as an authority in their opinions about constitutional questions, and many members of Congress toted dog-eared copies of *The Federalist* along during the impeachment proceedings that rocked Washington

in 1998. But it was political hard-ball that won the day for the Federalists in New York's ratifying convention, including the threat that New York City would secede from the state and ratify the Constitution on its own. New York's delegates approved the Constitution by a vote of 30-27 in July 1788, and Madison himself guided the Federalists to victory in Virginia (despite the eloquence of Patrick Henry) in June. With the addition of New Hampshire, eleven states entered the new federal compact. North Carolina rejected the Constitution in 1788 but ratified in November 1789 after the first U.S. Congress drafted a Masonian Bill of Rights; Rhode Island voted seven times against even calling a constitutional convention, but finally summoned one that ratified the document in May 1790.

It was official *and* legal: sovereignty had been removed from the King, then from government in general, and bestowed squarely on the shoulders of "the people," who then empowered different branches and levels of government through separate constitutions. There was now a strong central government, reversing the autonomy won by the individual states during the Revolution. Creditors and merchants also tended to reclaim power temporarily gained by debtors, yeomen, artisans, and ordinary citizens. Finally, a single political system—enshrined in a concise, written document—bound the concerns and interests of groups as diverse as Philadelphia blacksmiths, Virginia planters, Providence merchants and Nantucket whalemen.

GUIDE TO THE PRIMARY SOURCE READINGS

The Declaration of Independence, the U.S. Constitution, Federalist Papers 6, 10 & 51, and an Anti-Federalist article

The Declaration of Independence is one of those important documents that are so familiar they are unfamiliar: apart from a few well-worn phrases, few people have actually read carefully what it says. It is a bold statement, combining a list of specific grievances against the mother country with an undergirding rationale and a rhetoric based on Enlightenment political philosophy. Notice, first, that the opening paragraph addresses itself to the entire "civilized world": "…a decent respect to the opinions of mankind requires that they should declare the causes which impel them to the separation." The truth was, however, that the purpose of the Declaration was much more to explain and justify separation from Britain to the colonists themselves. Up to that point the war had been largely a New England affair and probably most people in the thirteen colonies were not yet inclined to separate from Britain. A sizeable number, the "Tories," remained loyal to the mother country and were often persecuted and sometimes forced into exile. To declare formally that the thirteen colonies were independent of Britain at such an early stage in the conflict was an extremely daring act engineered by a handful of men chosen by a handful of men in the various colonies. For the Declaration to be titled

"The unanimous declaration of the thirteen United States of America" much more expressed a kind of wild hope or supreme presumption than a reality.

The political philosophy enshrined in the first two paragraphs bears the clear influence of John Locke and Locke-inspired ideas. We read in the first paragraph of "the laws of nature and of nature's God." The famous lines that open the second paragraph are very Lockean. The "self-evident" truths are truths about the state of nature and natural rights, which Jefferson claims are intuitively obvious to anyone rightly using his or her reason. "Unalienable rights" are simply natural rights: those universal rights humans possess in the state of nature or just by virtue of being human, and which therefore cannot legitimately be "alienated" or taken away by governments.

When Jefferson then turns from the state of nature to civil society he again follows the tradition initiated by Locke. Humans leave the state of nature and form governments in order "to secure these [natural] rights," and all legitimate governments rest on the social contract, "deriving their just powers from the consent of the governed." Jefferson also follows Locke's doctrine of the "right of revolution": the right to "alter or abolish" any government that no longer protects rights or expresses consent. Like Locke, Jefferson is at least formally cautionary about the right of revolution, saying that "governments long established should not be changed for light and transient causes." He goes on, however, to argue that the British government has offended so egregiously against its colonial subjects that "it is their right, it is their duty, to throw off such government." Then follows the list of specific grievances.

The specific grievances listed in the Declaration refer to the various impositions upon the colonists by the British government, some of which we mentioned in the introductory paragraphs such as the quartering of troops, monopolizing trade, and above all many violations of the colonists' rights and privileges as British subjects. Notice, in the last of the "He" grievances, the reference to "the merciless Indian savages" and their barbarous methods of warfare. We are abruptly confronted here with the prevailing attitudes of Euro-Americans in 1776 and for at least another hundred years toward the native peoples of the continent. This stands in sharp and revealing juxtaposition with the noble sentiments enshrined in Jefferson's Lockean language of universal human rights.

The Declaration concludes by rehearsing all the ways in which the thirteen colonies have properly and peacefully sought redress of their grievances, to no avail. In the final paragraph Jefferson calls the signers "the representatives of the United States of America." At that stage, for the members of the Second Continental Congress to call themselves "representatives" acting "in the name and by the authority" of thirteen "united" colonies or states, was more wishful thinking than fact. Observe, finally, that the Declaration declares that "these united colonies are, and of right ought to be, free and independent states." Historically the word "state" has referred to a sovereign political and geographical entity in its own right, not to a subordinate region or unit. While the thirteen states were declared "united," they were each regarded as a "free and independent" state. This loosely-defined unity among sovereign states was not only a problem throughout the war, but after the war threatened the very existence of the new republic.

THE U. S. CONSTITUTION

As with the Declaration of Independence, people often have a vague idea of some part of the Constitution but little real knowledge of what it says. This unit is your opportunity to familiarize or re-familiarize yourself with its specific contents. The *Preamble* sets forth the purposes for which the Constitution is written. What are they? How do you think the convention delegates would have justified their presumptuous-sounding beginning, "We the people of the United States. . . ."?

As you read through the Constitution, notice how the government as structured by the framers is for the most part not directly responsive to the will of the electorate at large. Except for election to the House of Representatives, offices are filled by election from various much smaller representative bodies or by appointment. For example, the two Senators from each state were originally elected by their state legislatures (Article I, Section 3). The President is still elected, not directly by the people, but by electors appointed by state legislatures, their number the total of the Senators and Representatives from that state (Art. II, Sec. 1). And of course justices of the Supreme Court and all other federal judges are appointed (for life) by the President, "with the advice and consent of the Senate" (Art. II, Sec. 2; Art. III, Sec. 1).

The main structure of the Constitution embodies the three branches of the national government created by the Constitutional Convention: Article I describes the legislative, Article II the executive, and Article III the judicial. Notice how this threefold separation of powers has the effect of "checking and balancing" the others. As you read through the Constitution it is important to get a clear idea of what the specific duties and powers of each branch of government are, and how each provides a check on the other two. Where, for example, do all tax bills have to originate? Who has the power to declare war? What constitutes treason, and what is the punishment?

Article I, Section 10 and Article IV spell out the relative powers of the states in relation to the national government. Article V describes the process for amending the Constitution. Article VI enshrines the Constitution as "the supreme law of the land." Article VII stipulates that the Constitution will be ratified by the conventions of nine of the thirteen states, and says that at the time of signing it has been unanimously approved by the delegates of the (twelve) states present on September 17.

The Bill of Rights is of course the first ten amendments to the Constitution. They were somewhat neglected until after the Civil War and the crucially important Fourteenth Amendment (1868), which made citizens of former slaves and prohibited states from improperly depriving any citizen of "life, liberty, or property" or denying that person equal protection of the laws. Since then the Bill of Rights has played a fundamental role as a charter document of American rights and liberties. Familiarize yourself with the first ten amendments, noting for example the various freedoms catalogued in the First Amendment, the wording of the right to bear arms in the Second, and the various legal protections afforded citizens in Amendments 4-8. In recent years the Ninth and Tenth Amendments, which stipulate that "the people" have other rights than those specified in the Constitution and that any powers not specifically delegated to the national government or prohibited to the states reside in the states or in the people, have been frequently invoked in Supreme Court cases and by Republican politicians and state governors. These first ten amendments continue to play a vital role in U.S. law, from lower courts to the Supreme Court, and some of them continue to be passionately debated as to their meaning.

Since the Bill of Rights was ratified there have been only sixteen amendments to the Constitution. The framers made the amendment process a difficult one in order to make sure that changing the Constitution would not be taken lightly and would have to have substantial support in the states and the Congress. Some of the later amendments are milestones in American history: the Thirteenth, Fourteenth, and Fifteenth Amendments (1865–1870) abolishing slavery and establishing the full rights of citizenship for African-Americans (rights which it took another hundred years to begin fully to realize); the Sixteenth Amendment (1913), which authorized a federal income tax; Amendment 18 (1919), the short-lived attempt to prohibit alcoholic beverages throughout the nation that reflected the end of an era of evangelical Protestant hegemony and temperance crusades (it was repealed by Amendment 21 in 1933); the Nineteenth Amendment (1920), granting women the right to vote after seventy-two years of struggle; Amendment 24 (1964), the "voting rights" amendment, which struck down the poll taxes that had been used in the South for decades to prevent African-Americans from voting; and the Twenty-Sixth Amendment (1971), lowering the voting age from 21 to 18.

THE *FEDERALIST* PAPERS

Now let us briefly highlight some main points of the three papers you are reading. In No. 6 Hamilton argues that the Articles of Confederation will not work and that a stronger central government is required. The weakness of the Articles is that every state is a sovereign republic, neighboring states are the most likely enemies, and therefore there will continue to be nothing but strife and disunity. Appealing to history, he argues against the assumption that republics, unlike monarchies, will not war against one another, showing that republics have behaved as badly as monarchies.

Papers No. 10 and 51, both by Madison, are two of the key *Federalist* papers. The theme is factions: what they are, how they arise, and how their influence can best be reduced by the political arrangements laid down in the Constitution. You need to be clear about how Madison defines factions. Factions, he says, are endemic to human society, rooted in human nature and especially in private property. The challenge is how to secure the public good and protect individual rights against factions, while preserving "popular government" and the liberty that allows factions to flourish. Notice that Madison rejects removing the cause, private property itself, because that would infringe upon a fundamental liberty, nor does he envision the possibility of distributing property more equitably. Instead he argues that the solution is to put checks on the worst consequences of private property and the factions to which it gives rise. Of particular interest is Madison's discussion of minority and majority factions, where he argues that the chief threat comes from majority factions. This is his approach to what the French commentator on American democracy, Alexis De Tocqueville, later called the "tyranny of the majority." Direct democracy is unsatisfactory as a solution. Republican government, and especially a large federal republic such as is created by the Constitution, is the best solution because by its system of representation, its checks and balances, and its division of power between the central government and the states it will tend to diffuse and neutralize factions. In the light of Madison's discussion, did the federal structure set up by the Constitution manage to deal effectively with the glaring anomaly of slavery in a nation that defined itself in terms of human rights and liberties?

In Paper No. 51 Madison really explains the Constitution itself, focusing on the division of the branches of the national government and the checks and balances on power that provides. The "federal principle" he presents as the key to creating and preserving a viable republic was a new idea in the eighteenth century, which Madison discusses in terms of the difference between "simple" and "compound" republics. The famous lines beginning "If men were angels, no government would be necessary" deal with the crucial need of government, not only to control the governed, but to control itself.

"OBJECTIONS TO THE CONSTITUTION OF GOVERNMENT FORMED BY THE CONVENTION"

Perhaps the most eloquent Antifederalist was the Virginian George Mason. A judge and a statesman, Mason was born in 1725 and became an early and vocal opponent of Britain's colonial tax policies. In 1774 he wrote the "Fairfax Resolves," which outlined the legal grounds for the colonists' opposition to the Boston Port Act. More important, he authored Virginia's Declaration of Rights in 1776, which became a model for the bills of rights in most state constitutions and inspired Jefferson's draft of the Declaration of Independence. The Virginia Legislature selected Mason as one of the delegates to the Philadelphia Convention in 1787, and according to Madison's meticulous notes, he was one of the five most frequent speakers there. He was easily one of the most influential delegates in a body full of early American luminaries. Yet Mason decided in the last two weeks of the convention not to sign the document, and became the Constitution's most active and eloquent critic.

He explained his reasons for opposing the Constitution in writing and in great detail, allowing his critique to be published in November 1787. First and foremost, he wrote, the document lacked a written declaration of rights including liberty of conscience in religious matters, freedom of the press, and the right to trial by jury. This conspicuous absence, he suggested, nullified the declarations in various state constitutions, since one could conceivably possess the right of assembly in one state and not in another. He attacked the Constitution's provisions one by one. The House of Representatives was a "Shadow only of Representation . . . the Laws will therefore be generally made by Men little concern'd in, and unacquainted with their Effects and Consequences." The power of the federal judiciary would eclipse and therefore destroy the state judiciaries, rendering justice unattainable, "enabling the Rich to oppress and Ruin the Poor." Lacking a constitutional "council," Mason warned that the President—too powerful already—would be swayed by "Minions and Favorites or . . . become a tool of the Senate."

Many of Mason's objections were on the basis of republicanism: he thought the document "built in" measures to corrupt even virtuous men. He feared the new, powerful central government could easily fall into the hands of an oppressive aristocracy or even become a monarchy if a tyrannical chief executive, legally in control of the military, decided to remain in office. Yet he also pointed to problems of constitutionalism, including a mixing between the separate branches of government. For example, the Vice President was also President of the Senate, "dangerously blending the executive and legislative powers." Finally, Mason pointed out a real flaw in the Constitution: that it could not serve as a permanent compromise between "sections": by requiring a bare majority to make commercial laws, "the five Southern states (whose produce and Circumstances are totally different from that of the eight Northern and Eastern states) will be ruined." During the nineteenth century, disagreements over the Constitution and whether slavery would spread into new, western territory would tear the country apart.

QUESTIONS FOR STUDY AND DISCUSSION

1. What were the main issues and events that led to the American Revolution?
2. What parallels are there between Locke's political ideas and those of the Declaration of Independence? What arguments does Jefferson use in the Declaration to show the necessity of declaring independence from Britain?
3. Why was the Constitutional Convention called, what sort of people participated, and how did they deviate from their original purpose?
4. What is republicanism? Do present-day Americans still adhere to this ideology?
5. How representative were the men who drafted the U.S. Constitution?
6. What was Madison's role in the Constitutional Convention?
7. What sort of government did the Constitution create? What did it say about slaves and Native Americans?
8. What is the Bill of Rights, and why was it written? Discuss its importance kin U.S. history.
9. What does Madison mean by "Factions" in *Federalist* No. 10? What do they show about human nature, and what is the remedy for factions?
10. What were some of the differences between Federalists and Antifederalists? Describe their visions of America's future.

SUGGESTIONS FOR FURTHER READING

Akhil Reed Amar. *The Bill of Rights: Creation and Reconstruction*. New Haven: Yale U. Press, 1998.

Richard R. Beeman, Stephen Botein, Edward C. Carter, II eds. *Beyond Confederation: Origins of the Constitution and American National Identity*. Chapel Hill: North Carolina Press, 1987

Cornell, Saul. *The Other Founders: Antifederalism and the Dissenting Tradition in America*. Omohundro Institute of Early American History and Culture: North Carolina, 1999.

Countryman, Edward, ed. *What did the Constitution Mean to Early Americans?* Boston: Bedford/St. Martin's Press, 1999.

Kammen, Michael G. *A Machine that Would Go By Itself: The Constitution in American Culture*. New York: A. A. Knopf, 1986.

McDonald, Forrest. *Novus Ordo Seculorum: The Intellectual Origins of the Constitution*. University of Kansas Press: Lawrence, KS, 1985.

Edmund S. Moran. *Inventing the People: The Rise of Popular Sovereignty in England and America*. New York: Norton Press, 1988.

Herpert Storing. *The Antifederalists* (1985).

Wood, Gordon S. *The Creation of the American Republic*. New York: Norton Press, 1972.

_____. *The Radicalism of the American Revolution*. New York: A.A. Knopf, 1991.

BIOGRAPHIES

Foner, Eric. *Tom Paine*. New York: Oxford U. Press, 1976.

McCoy, Drew. *Last of the Fathers*. New York: Cambridge U. Press, 1989.

McDonald, Forrest. *Alexander Hamilton: A Biography*. New York: Norton, 1979.

Main, Jackson Turner. *The Antifederalists: Critics of the Constitution*. Chapel Hill, Institute of Early American History & Culture: University of North Carolina Press, 1961.

THE DECLARATION OF INDEPENDENCE

When, in the course of human events, it becomes necessary for one people to dissolve the political bands which have connected them with another, and to assume, among the powers of the earth, the separate and equal station to which the laws of nature and of nature's God entitle them, a decent respect to the opinions of mankind requires that they should declare the causes which impel them to the separation.

We hold these truths to be self-evident:—That all men are created equal; that they are endowed by their Creator with certain unalienable rights, that among these are life, liberty and the pursuit of happiness. That, to secure these rights, governments are instituted among men, deriving their just powers from the consent of the governed, that whenever any form of government becomes destructive of these ends, it is the right of the people to alter or to abolish it, and to institute new governments, laying its foundation on such principles and organizing its powers in such form, as to them shall seem most likely to effect their safety and happiness. Prudence, indeed, will dictate, that governments long established should not be changed for light and transient causes; and accordingly all experience hath shown that mankind are more disposed to suffer, while evils are sufferable, than to right themselves by abolishing the forms to which they are accustomed. But when a long train of abuses and usurpations, pursuing invariably the same object, evinces a design to reduce them under absolute despotism, it is their right, it is their duty, to throw off such government, and to provide new guards for their future security. Such has been the patient sufferance of these colonies; and such is now the necessity which constrains them to alter their former systems of government. The history of the present King of Great Britain is a history of repeated injuries and usurpations, all having in direct object the establishment of an absolute tyranny over these states. To prove this, let facts be submitted to a candid world.

He has refused his assent to laws, the most wholesome and necessary for the public good.

He has forbidden his governors to pass laws of immediate and pressing importance, unless suspended in their operation till his assent should be obtained; and when so suspended, he has utterly neglected to attend to them.

He has refused to pass other laws for the accommodation of large districts of people, unless those people would relinquish the right of representation in the legislature, a right inestimable to them and formidable to tyrants only.

He has called together legislative bodies at places unusual, uncomfortable, and distant from the depository of their public records, for the sole purpose of fatiguing them into compliance with his measures.

He has dissolved representative houses repeatedly, for opposing with manly firmness his invasions on the rights of the people.

He has refused for a long time, after such dissolutions, to cause others to be elected, whereby the legislative powers, incapable of annihilation, have returned to the people at large for their exercise; the State remaining in the meantime, exposed to all the dangers of invasion from without, and convulsions within.

He has endeavored to prevent the population of these States; for that purpose obstructing the laws for the naturalization of foreigners; refusing to pass others to encourage their migration hither, and raising the conditions of new appropriations of lands.

He has obstructed the administration of justice, by refusing his assent to laws for establishing judiciary powers.

He has made judges dependent on his will alone for the tenure of their offices, and the amount and payment of their salaries.

He has erected a multitude of new offices, and sent hither swarms of officers to harass our people and eat out their substance.

He has kept among us, in times of peace, standing armies, without the consent of our legislature.

He has affected to render the military independent of, and superior to, the civil power.

He has combined with others to subject us to a jurisdiction foreign to our constitutions, and unacknowledged by our laws; giving his assent to their acts of pretended legislation:

For quartering large bodies of armed troops among us;

For protecting them, by a mock trial, from punishment for any murders which they should commit on the inhabitants of these States;

For cutting off our trade with all parts of the world;

For imposing taxes on us without our consent;

For depriving us, in many cases, of the benefits of trial by jury;

For transporting us beyond seas, to be tried for pretended offenses;

For abolishing the free system of English laws on a neighboring province, establishing therein an arbitrary government, and enlarging its boundaries so as to render it at once an example and fit instrument for introducing the same absolute rule into these colonies;

For taking away our charters, abolishing our most valuable laws, and altering, fundamentally, the forms of our governments;

For suspending our own legislatures, and declaring themselves invested with power to legislate for us in all cases whatsoever.

He has abdicated government here, by declaring us out of his protection, and waging war against us.

He has plundered our seas, ravaged our coasts, burned our towns, and destroyed the lives of our people.

He is at this time transporting large armies of foreign mercenaries to complete the works of death, desolation and tyranny, already begun with circumstances of cruelty and perfidy scarcely paralleled in the most barbarous ages, and totally unworthy the head of a civilized nation.

He has constrained our fellow citizens taken captive on the high seas, to bear arms against their country, to become the executioners of their friends and brethren, or to fall themselves by their hands.

He has excited domestic insurrections among us, and has endeavored to bring on the inhabitants of our frontiers, the merciless Indian savages, whose known rule of warfare, is an undistinguished destruction of all ages, sexes and conditions.

In every stage of these oppressions we have petitioned for redress in the most humble terms; our repeated petitions have been answered only by repeated injury. A prince, whose character is thus marked by every act which may define a tyrant, is unfit to be the ruler of a free people.

Nor have we been wanting in attention to our British brethren. We have warned them from time to time of attempts by their legislature to extend an unwarrantable jurisdiction over us. We have reminded them of the circumstances of our emigration and settlement here. We have appealed to their native justice and magnanimity; and we have conjured them, by the ties of our common kindred, to disavow these usurpations, which, would inevitably interrupt our connections and correspondence. They, too, have been deaf to the voice of justice and of consanguinity. We must, therefore, acquiesce in the necessity, which denounces our separation, and hold them, as we hold the rest of mankind, enemies in war, in peace friends.

We, therefore, the representatives of the United States of America, in General Congress assembled, appealing to the Supreme Judge of the world for the rectitude of our intentions, do, in the name and by the authority of the good people of these colonies, solemnly publish and declare, that these united colonies are, and of right ought to be, free and independent states, that they are absolved from all allegiance to the British Crown, and that all political connection between them and the state of Great Britain, is and ought to be totally dissolved; and that as free and independent states, they have full power to levy war, conclude peace, contract alliances, establish commerce, and to do all other acts and things which independent states may of right do. And for the support of this declaration, with a firm reliance on the protection of Divine Providence, we mutually pledge to each other our lives, our fortunes and our sacred honor.

THE CONSTITUTION OF THE UNITED STATES

We the people of the United States, in order to form a more perfect union, establish justice, insure domestic tranquillity, provide for the common defense, promote the general welfare, and secure the blessings of liberty to ourselves and our posterity, do ordain and establish this Constitution for the United States of America.

ARTICLE I

Section 1

All legislative powers herein granted shall be vested in a Congress of the United States, which shall consist of a Senate and House of Representatives.

Section 2

The House of Representatives shall be composed of members chosen every second year by the people of the several states, and the electors in each state shall have the qualifications requisite for electors of the most numerous branch of the state legislature.

No person shall be a Representative who shall not have attained to the age of twenty-five years, and been seven years a citizen of the United States, and who shall not, when elected, be an inhabitant of that state in which he shall be chosen.

Representatives and direct taxes shall be apportioned among the several states which may be included within this union, according to their respective numbers, which shall be determined by adding to the whole number of free persons, including those bound to service for a term of years, and excluding Indians not taxed, three-fifths of all other persons. The actual enumeration shall be made within three years after the first meeting of the Congress of the United States, and within every subsequent term of ten years, in such manner as they shall by law direct. The number of Representatives shall not exceed one for every thirty thousand, but each state shall have at least one Representative; and until such enumeration shall be made, the State of New Hampshire shall be entitled to choose three; Massachusetts, eight; Rhode Island and Providence Plantation one; Connecticut, five; New York, six; New Jersey, four; Pennsylvania, eight; Delaware, one; Maryland, six; Virginia, ten; North Carolina, five; South Carolina, five; and Georgia, three.

When vacancies happen in the representation from any state, the executive authority thereof shall issue writs of election to fill such vacancies.

The House of Representatives shall choose their Speaker and other officers; and shall have the sole power of impeachment.

Section 3

The Senate of the United States shall be composed of two Senators from each state, chosen by the legislature thereof, for six years; and each Senator shall have one vote.

Immediately after they shall be assembled in consequence of the first election, they shall be divided as equally as may be into three classes. The seats of the Senators of the first class shall be vacated at the expiration of the second year, of the second class at the expiration of the fourth year; and of the third class at the expiration of the sixth year, so that one-third may be chosen every second year; and if vacancies happen by resignation, or otherwise, during the recess of the legislature of any state, the executive thereof may make temporary appointments until the next meeting of the legislature, which shall then fill such vacancies.

No person shall be a Senator who shall not have attained to the age of thirty years, and been nine years a citizen of the United States, and who shall not, when elected, be an inhabitant of that state for which he shall be chosen.

The Vice President of the United States shall be President of the Senate, but shall have no vote, unless they be equally divided.

The Senate shall choose their other officers, and also a President pro Tempore, in the absence of the Vice President, or when he shall exercise the office of President of the United States.

The Senate shall have the sole power to try all impeachments. When sitting for that purpose, they shall be on oath or affirmation. When the President of the United States is tried, the Chief Justice shall preside: and no person shall be convicted without the concurrence of two-thirds of the members present.

Judgment in cases of impeachment shall not extend further than to removal from office, and disqualification to hold and enjoy any office of honor, trust or profit under the United States; but the party convicted shall nevertheless be liable and subject to indictment, trial, judgment and punishment, according to law.

Section 4

The times, places and manner of holding elections for Senators and Representatives, shall be prescribed in each state by the legislature thereof; but the Congress may at any time by law make or alter such regulations, except as to the places of choosing Senators.

The Congress shall assemble at least once in every year, and such meeting shall be on the first Monday in December, unless they shall by law appoint a different day.

Section 5

Each house shall be the judge of the elections, returns and qualifications of its own members, and a majority of each shall constitute a quorum to do business; but a smaller number may adjourn from day to day, and may be authorized to compel the attendance of absent members, in such manner, and under such penalties as each house may provide.

Each house may determine the rules of its proceedings, punish its members for disorderly behavior, and, with the concurrence of two-thirds, expel a member.

Each house shall keep a journal of its proceedings, and from time to time publish the same, excepting such parts as may in their judgment require secrecy; and the yeas and nays of the members of either house on any question shall, at the desire of one-fifth of those present, be entered on the journal.

Neither house, during the session of Congress, shall, without the consent of the other, adjourn for more than three days, nor to any other place than that in which the two houses shall be sitting.

Section 6

The Senators and Representatives shall receive a compensation for their services, to be ascertained by law, and paid out of the Treasury of the United States. They shall in all cases, except treason, felony and breach of the peace, be privileged from arrest during their attendance at the session of their respective houses, and in going to and returning from the same; and for any speech or debate in either house, they shall not be questioned in any other place.

No Senator or Representative shall, during the time for which he was elected, be appointed to any civil office under the authority of the United States, which shall have been created, or the emoluments whereof shall have been increased during such time; and no person holding any office under the United States, shall be a member of either house during his continuance in office.

Section 7

All bills for raising revenue shall originate in the House of Representatives; but the Senate may propose or concur with amendments as on other bills.

Every bill which shall have passed the House of Representatives and the Senate, shall, before it become a law, be presented to the President of the United States; if he approve he shall sign it, but if not, he shall return it, with his objections to that house in which it shall have originated, who shall enter the objections at large on their journal, and proceed to reconsider it. If after such reconsideration two-thirds of that house shall agree to pass the bill, it shall be sent, together with the objections, to the other house, by which it shall likewise be reconsidered, and if approved by two-thirds of that house, it shall become a law. But in all such cases the votes of both houses shall be determined by yeas and nays, and the names of the persons voting for and against the bill shall be entered on the journal of each house respectively. If any bill shall not be returned by the President within ten days (Sundays excepted) after it shall have been presented to him, the same shall be a law, in like manner if he had signed it, unless the Congress by their adjournment prevent its return, in which case it shall not be a law.

Every order, resolution, or vote to which the concurrence of the Senate and House of Representatives may be necessary (except on a question of adjournment) shall be presented to the President of the United States; and before the same shall take effect, shall be approved by him, or being disapproved by him, shall be repassed by two-thirds of the Senate and House of Representatives, according to the rules and limitations prescribed in the case of a bill.

Section 8

The Congress shall have power:

To lay and collect taxes, duties, imposts and excises, to pay the debts and provide for the common defense and general welfare of the United States; but all duties, imposts and excises shall be uniform throughout the United States;

To borrow money on the credit of the United States;

To regulate commerce with foreign nations, and among the several states, and with the Indian tribes;

To establish an uniform rule of naturalization, and uniform laws on the subject of bankruptcies throughout the United States;

To coin money, regulate the value thereof, and of foreign coin, and fix the standard of weights and measures;

To provide for the punishment of counterfeiting the securities and current coin of the United States;

To establish post offices and post roads;

To promote the progress of science and useful arts, by securing for limited times to authors and inventors the exclusive right to their respective writings and discoveries;

To constitute tribunals inferior to the Supreme Court;

To define and punish piracies and felonies committed on the high seas, and offenses against the law of nations;

To declare war, grant letters of marque and reprisal, and make rules concerning captures on land and water;

To raise and support armies, but no appropriation of money to that use shall be for a longer term than two years;

To provide and maintain a navy;

To make rules for the government and regulation of the land and naval forces;

To provide for calling forth the militia to execute the laws of the union, suppress insurrections and repel invasions;

To provide for organizing, arming, and disciplining the militia, and for governing such part of them as may be employed in the service of the United States, reserving to the states respectively, the appointment of the officers, and the authority of training the militia according to the discipline prescribed by Congress;

To exercise exclusive legislation in all cases whatsoever, over such district (not exceeding ten miles square) as may, by cession of particular states, and the acceptance of Congress, become the seat of the government of the United States, and to exercise like authority over all places purchased by the consent of the legislature of the state in which the same shall be, for the erection of forts, magazines, arsenals, dockyards and other needful buildings; And

To make all laws which shall be necessary and proper for carrying into execution the foregoing powers, and all other powers vested by this Constitution in the government of the United States, or in any department or officer thereof.

Section 9

The migration or importation of such persons as any of the states now existing shall think proper to admit, shall not be prohibited by the Congress prior to the year one thousand eight hundred and eight, but a tax or duty may be imposed on such importation, not exceeding ten dollars for each person.

The privilege of the writ of habeas corpus shall not be suspended unless when in cases of rebellion or invasion the public safety may require it.

No bill of attainder or ex post facto law shall be passed.

No capitation, or other direct, tax shall be laid, unless in proportion to the census or enumeration hereinbefore directed to be taken.

No tax or duty shall be laid on articles exported from any state.

No preference shall be given by any regulation of commerce or revenue to the ports of one state over those of another: nor shall vessels bound to, or from, one state, be obliged to enter, clear, or pay duties in another.

No money shall be drawn from the Treasury, but in consequence of appropriations made by law; and a regular statement and account of the receipts and expenditures of all public money shall be published from time to time.

No title of nobility shall be granted by the United States; and no person holding any office of profit or trust under them, shall, without the consent of the Congress, accept of any present, emolument, office, or title, of any kind whatever, from any King, Prince, or foreign state.

Section 10

No state shall enter into any treaty, alliance, or confederation; grant letters of marque and reprisal; coin money; emit bills of credit; make any thing but gold and silver coin a tender in payment of debts; pass any bill of attainder, ex post facto law, or law impairing the obligation of contracts, or grant any title of nobility.

No state shall, without the consent of the Congress, lay any imposts or duties on imports or exports, except what may be absolutely necessary for executing its inspection laws: and the net produce of all duties and imposts, laid by any state on imports or exports, shall be for the use of the Treasury of the United States; and all such laws shall be subject to the revision and control of the Congress.

No state shall, without the consent of Congress, lay any duty of tonnage, keep troops, or ships of war in time of peace, enter into any agreement or compact with another state, or with a foreign power, or engage in war, unless actually invaded, or in such imminent danger as will not admit of delay.

ARTICLE II

Section 1

The executive power shall be vested in a President of the United States of America. He shall hold his office during the term of four years, and, together with the Vice President, chosen for the same term, be elected, as follows:

Each state shall appoint, in such manner, as the legislature thereof may direct, a number of electors, equal to the whole number of Senators and Representatives to which the state may be entitled in the Congress: but no Senator or Representative, or person holding an office of trust or profit under the United States, shall be appointed an elector.

The electors shall meet in their respective states and vote by ballot for two persons, of whom one at least shall not be an inhabitant of the same state with themselves. And they shall make a list of all the persons voted for, and of the number of votes for each; which list they shall sign and certify, and transmit sealed to the seat of the government of the United States, directed to the President of the Senate. The President of the Senate shall, in the presence of the Senate and House of Representatives, open all the certificates, and the votes shall then be counted. The person having the greatest number of votes shall be the President, if such number be a majority of the whole number of electors appointed; and if there be more than one who have such majority, and have an equal number of votes, then the House shall immediately choose by ballot one of them for President; and if no person have a majority, then from the five highest on the list the said house shall in like manner choose the President. But in choosing the President, the vote shall be taken by states, the representation from each state having one vote; a quorum for this purpose shall consist of a member or members from two-thirds of the states, and a majority of all the states shall be necessary to a choice. In every case, after the choice of the President, the person having the greatest number of votes of the electors shall be the Vice President. But if there should remain two or more who have equal votes, the Senate shall choose from them by ballot the Vice President.

The Congress may determine the time of choosing the electors, and the day on which they shall give their votes; which day shall be the same throughout the United States.

No person except a natural born citizen, or a citizen of the United States, at the time of the adoption of this Constitution, shall be eligible to the office of President; neither shall any person be eligible to that office who shall not have attained to the age of thirty-five years, and been fourteen years a resident within the United States.

In case of the removal of the President from office, or of his death, resignation, or inability to discharge the powers and duties of the said Office, the same shall devolve on the Vice President, and the Congress may by law provide for the case of removal, death, resignation or inability, both of the President and Vice President, declaring what officer shall then act as President; and such officer shall act accordingly until the disability be removed, or a President shall be elected.

The President shall, at stated times, receive for his services a compensation which shall neither be increased nor diminished during the period for which he shall have been elected and he shall not receive within that period any other emolument from the United States, or any of them.

Before he enter on the execution of his office, he shall take the following oath or affirmation.— "I do solemnly swear (or affirm) that I will faithfully execute the office of President of the United States, and will, to the best of my ability, preserve, protect and defend the Constitution of the United States."

Section 2

The President shall be commander in chief of the Army and Navy of the United States, and of the militia of the several states, when called into the actual service of the United States; he may require the opinion, in writing, of the principal officer in each of the executive departments, upon any subject relating to the duties of their respective offices, and he shall have power to grant reprieves and pardons for offenses against the United States, except in cases of impeachment.

He shall have power, by and with the advice and consent of the Senate, to make treaties, provided two-thirds of the Senators present concur; and he shall nominate, and by and with the advice and consent of the Senate, shall appoint ambassadors, other public ministers and consuls, judges of the Supreme Court, and all other officers of the United States, whose appointments are not herein otherwise provided for, and which shall be established by law: but the Congress may by law vest the appointment of such inferior officers, as they

think proper, in the President alone, in the courts of law, or in the heads of departments.

The President shall have power to fill up all vacancies that may happen during the recess of the Senate, by granting commissions which shall expire at the end of their next session.

Section 3

He shall from time to time give to the Congress information of the state of the union, and recommend to their consideration such measures as he shall judge necessary and expedient; he may, on extraordinary occasions, convene both houses, or either of them, and in case of disagreement between them, with respect to the time of adjournment, he may adjourn them to such time as he shall think proper; he shall receive ambassadors and other public ministers; he shall take care that the laws be faithfully executed, and shall commission all the officers of the United States.

Section 4

The President, Vice President and all civil officers of the United States, shall be removed from office on impeachment for, and conviction of, treason, bribery, or other high crimes and misdemeanors.

ARTICLE III

Section 1

The judicial power of the United States shall be vested in one supreme court, and in such inferior courts as the Congress may from time to time ordain and establish. The judges, both of the Supreme and inferior courts, shall hold their offices during good behavior, and shall, at stated times, receive for their services, a compensation, which shall not be diminished during their continuance in office.

Section 2

The judicial power shall extend to all cases, in law and equity, arising under this Constitution, the laws of the United States, and treaties made, or which shall be made, under their authority; to all cases affecting ambassadors, other public ministers and consuls; to all cases of admiralty and maritime jurisdiction; to controversies to which the United States shall be a party; to controversies between two or more states, between a state and citizens of another state, between citizens of different states, between citizens of the same state claiming lands under grants of different states, and between a state, or the citizens thereof, and foreign states, citizens or subjects.

In all cases affecting ambassadors, other public ministers and consuls, and those in which a state shall be party, the Supreme Court shall have original jurisdiction. In all the other cases before mentioned, the Supreme Court shall have appellate jurisdiction, both as to law and fact, with such exceptions, and under such regulations as the Congress shall make.

The trial of all crimes, except in cases of impeachment, shall be by jury; and such trial shall be held in the state where the said crimes shall have been committed; but when not committed within any state, the trial shall be at such place or places as the Congress may by law have directed.

Section 3

Treason against the United States, shall consist only in levying war against them, or in adhering to their enemies, giving them aid and comfort. No person shall be convicted of treason unless on the testimony of two witnesses to the same overt act, or on confession in open court.

The Congress shall have power to declare the punishment of treason, but no attainder of treason shall work corruption of blood, or forfeiture except during the life of the person attainted.

ARTICLE IV

Section 1

Full faith and credit shall be given in each state to the public acts, records, and judicial proceedings of every other state. And the Congress may by general laws prescribe the manner in which such acts, records and proceedings shall be proved, and the effect thereof.

Section 2

The citizens of each state shall be entitled to all privileges and immunities of citizens in the several states.

A person charged in any state with treason, felony, or other crime, who shall flee from justice, and be found in another state, shall, on demand of the executive authority of the state from which he fled, be delivered up, to be removed to the state having jurisdiction of the crime.

No person held to service or labor in one state, under the laws thereof, escaping into another, shall, in consequence of any law or regulation therein, be discharged from such service or labor, but shall be delivered up on claim of the party to whom such service or labor may be due.

Section 3

New states may be admitted by the Congress into this union; but no new state shall be formed or erected within the jurisdiction of any other state; nor any state be formed by the junction of two or more states, or parts of states, without the consent of the legislatures of the states concerned as well as of the Congress.

The Congress shall have power to dispose of and make all needful rules and regulations respecting the territory or other property belonging to the United States; and nothing in this Constitution shall be so construed as to prejudice any claims of the United States, or of any particular state.

Section 4

The United States shall guarantee to every state in this union a republican form of government, and shall protect each of them against invasion; and on application of the legislature, or of the executive (when the legislature cannot be convened) against domestic violence.

ARTICLE V

The Congress, whenever two-thirds of both houses shall deem it necessary, shall propose amendments to this Constitution, or, on the application of the legislatures of two-thirds of the several states, shall call a convention for proposing amendments, which, in either case, shall be valid to all intents and purposes, as part of this Constitution, when ratified by the legislatures of three-fourths of the several states, or by conventions in three-fourths thereof, as the one or the other mode of ratification may be proposed by the Congress; provided that no amendment which may be made prior to the year one thousand eight hundred and eight shall in any manner affect the first and fourth clauses in the ninth section of the first article; and that no state, without its consent, shall be deprived of its equal suffrage in theSenate.

ARTICLE VI

All debts contracted and engagements entered into, before the adoption of this Constitution, shall be as valid against the United States under this Constitution, as under the Confederation.

This Constitution, and the laws of the United States which shall be made in pursuance thereof; and all treaties made, or which shall be made, under the authority of the United States, shall be the supreme law of the land; and the judges in every state shall be bound thereby, any thing in the Constitution or laws of any state to the contrary notwithstanding.

The Senators and Representatives before mentioned, and the members of the several state legislatures, and all executive and judicial officers, both of the United States and of the several states, shall be bound by oath or affirmation, to support this Constitution; but no religious test shall ever be required as a qualification to any office or public trust under the United States.

ARTICLE VII

The ratification of the conventions of nine states, shall be sufficient for the establishment of this Constitution between the states so ratifying the same.

Done in convention by the unanimous consent of the states present the seventeenth day of September in the year of our Lord one thousand seven hundred and eighty-seven and of the Independence of the United States of America the twelfth. In witness whereof we have hereunto subscribed our names.

(Here follow the signatures of thirty-nine persons representing twelve states, headed by the name of George Washington, president of the convention.)

AMENDMENTS TO THE CONSTITUTION

ARTICLE I (1791)

Congress shall make no law respecting an establishment of religion, or prohibiting the free exercise thereof; or abridging the freedom of speech, or of the press; or the right of the people peaceably to assemble, and to petition the government for a redress of grievances.

ARTICLE II (1791)

A well regulated militia, being necessary to the security of a free state, the right of the people to keep and bear arms, shall not be infringed.

ARTICLE III (1791)

No soldier shall, in time of peace be quartered in any house, without the consent of the owner, nor in time of war, but in manner to be prescribed by law.

ARTICLE IV (1791)

The right of the people to be secure in their persons, houses, papers and effects, against unreasonable searches and seizures, shall not be violated, and no warrants shall issue, but upon probable cause, supported by oath or affirmation, and particularly describing the place to be searched, and the persons or things to be seized.

ARTICLE V (1791)

No person shall be held to answer for a capital, or otherwise infamous crime, unless on a presentment or indictment of a grand jury, except in cases arising in the land or naval forces, or in the militia, when in actual service in time of war or public danger; nor shall any person be subject for the same offense to be twice put in jeopardy of life or limb; nor shall be compelled in any criminal case to be a witness against himself, nor be deprived of life, liberty, or property, without due process of law; nor shall private property be taken for public use without just compensation.

ARTICLE VI (1791)

In all criminal prosecutions, the accused shall enjoy the right to a speedy and public trial, by an impartial jury of the state and district wherein the crime shall have been committed, which district shall have been previously ascertained by law, and to be informed of the nature and cause of the accusation; to be confronted with the witnesses against him; to have compulsory process for obtaining witnesses in his favor, and to have the assistance of counsel for his defense.

ARTICLE VII (1791)

In suits at common law, where the value in controversy shall exceed twenty dollars, the right of trial by jury shall be preserved, and no act tried by a jury shall be otherwise reexamined in any court of the United States, than according to the rules of the common law.

ARTICLE VIII (1791)

Excessive bail shall not be required, nor excessive fines imposed, nor cruel and unusual punishments inflicted.

ARTICLE IX (1791)

The enumeration in the Constitution of certain rights shall not be construed to deny or disparage others retained by the people.

ARTICLE X (1791)

The powers not delegated to the United States by the Constitution, nor prohibited by it to the states, are reserved to the states respectively, or to the people.

ARTICLE XI (1798)

The judicial power of the United States shall not be construed to extend to any suit in law or equity, commenced or prosecuted against one of the United States by citizens of another state, or by citizens or subjects of any foreign state.

ARTICLE XII (1804)

The electors shall meet in their respective states and vote by ballot for President and Vice President, one of whom, at least shall not be an inhabitant of the same state with themselves; they shall name in their ballots the person voted for as President, and in distinct ballots, the person voted for as Vice President, and they shall make distinct lists of all persons voted for as President, and of all persons voted for as Vice President, and of the number of votes for each, which lists they shall sign and certify, and transmit sealed to the seat of the government of the United States, directed to the President of the Senate,—The President of the Senate shall, in the presence of the Senate and House of Representatives, open all the certificates and the votes shall then be counted;—The person having the greatest number of votes for President, shall be the President, if such number be a majority of the whole number of electors appointed; and if no person have such majority then from the persons having the highest numbers not exceeding three on the list of those voted for as President, the House of Representatives shall choose immediately, by ballot, the President. But in choosing the President, the votes shall be taken by states, the representation from each state having one vote; a quorum for this purpose shall consist of a member or members from two-thirds of the states, and a majority of all the states shall be necessary to a choice. And if the House of Representatives shall not choose a President whenever the right of choice shall devolve upon them, before the fourth day of March next following, then the Vice President shall act as President, as in the case of the death or other constitutional disability of the President.

The person having the greatest number of votes as Vice President, shall be the Vice President, if such number be a majority of the whole number of electors appointed, and if no person have a majority, then from the two highest numbers on the list, the Senate shall choose the Vice President; a quorum for the purpose shall consist of two-thirds of the whole number of Senators, and a majority of the whole number shall be necessary to a choice. But no person constitutionally ineligible to the office of President shall be eligible to that of Vice President of the United States.

ARTICLE XIII (1865)

Section 1

Neither slavery nor involuntary servitude, except as a punishment for crime whereof the party shall have been duly convicted, shall exist within the United States, or any place subject to their jurisdiction.

Section 2

Congress shall have power to enforce this article by appropriate legislation.

ARTICLE XIV (1868)

Section 1

All persons born or naturalized in the United States and subject to the jurisdiction thereof, are citizens of the United States and of the state wherein they reside. No state shall make or enforce any law which shall abridge the privileges or immunities of citizens of the United States; nor shall any state deprive any person of life, liberty, or property, without due process of law; nor deny to any person within its jurisdiction the equal protection of the laws.

Section 2

Representatives shall be apportioned among the several states according to their respective numbers, counting the whole number of persons in each state, excluding Indians not taxed. But when the right to vote at any election for the choice of electors for President and Vice President of the United States, Representatives in Congress, the executive and judicial officers of a state, or the members of the legislature thereof, is denied to any of the male inhabitants of such state, being twenty-one years of age, and citizens of the United States, or in any way abridged, except for participation in rebellion or other crime, the basis of representation therein shall be reduced in the proportion which the number of such male citizens shall bear to the whole number of male citizens twenty-one years of age in such state.

Section 3

No person shall be a Senator or Representative in Congress, or elector of President and Vice President, or hold any office, civil or military, under the United States, or under any state, who, having previously taken an oath, as a member of Congress, or as an officer of the United States, or as a member of any state legislature, or as an executive or judicial officer of any state, to support the Constitution of the United States, shall have engaged in insurrection or rebellion against the same, or given aid or comfort to the enemies thereof. But Congress may by a vote of two-thirds of each house, remove such disability.

Section 4

The validity of the public debt of the United States, authorized by law, including debts incurred for payment of pensions and bounties for services in suppressing insurrection or rebellion, shall not be questioned. But neither the United States nor any state shall assume or pay any debt or obligation incurred in aid of insurrection or rebellion against the United States, or any claim for the loss or emancipation of any slave; but all such debts, obligations and claims shall be held illegal and void.

Section 5

The Congress shall have power to enforce, by appropriate legislation, the provisions of this article.

ARTICLE XV (1870)

Section 1

The right of citizens of the United States to vote shall not be denied or abridged by the United States or by any state on account of race, color, or previous condition of servitude.

Section 2

The Congress shall have power to enforce this article by appropriate legislation.

ARTICLE XVI (1913)

The Congress shall have power to lay and collect taxes on incomes, from whatever source derived, without apportionment among the several states, and without regard to any census or enumeration.

ARTICLE XVII (1913)

Section 1

The Senate of the United States shall be composed of two Senators from each state, elected by the people thereof, for six years; and each Senator shall have one vote. The electors in each state shall have the qualifications requisite for electors of the most numerous branch of the state legislatures.

Section 2

When vacancies happen in the representation of any state in the Senate, the executive authority of such state shall issue writs of election to fill such vacancies: *Provided,* That the legislature of any state may empower the executive thereof to make temporary appointments until the people fill the vacancies by election as the legislature may direct.

Section 3

This amendment shall not be so construed as to affect the election or term of any Senator chosen before it becomes valid as part of the Constitution.

ARTICLE XVIII (1919)

Section 1

After one year from the ratification of this article the manufacture, sale, or transportation of intoxicating liquors within, the importation thereof into, or the exportation thereof from the United States and all territory subject to the jurisdiction thereof for beverage purposes is hereby prohibited.

Section 2

The Congress and the several states shall have concurrent power to enforce this article by appropriate legislation.

Section 3

This article shall be inoperative unless it shall have been ratified as an amendment to the Constitution by the legislatures of the several states, as provided in the Constitution, within seven years from the date of the submission hereof to the states by the Congress.

ARTICLE XIX (1920)

Section 1

The right of citizens of the United States to vote shall not be denied or abridged by the United States or by any state on account of sex.

Section 2

Congress shall have power to enforce this article by appropriate legislation.

ARTICLE XX (1933)

Section 1

The terms of the President and Vice President shall end at noon on the 20th day of January, and the terms of Senators and Representatives at noon on the 3d day of January, of the years in which such terms would have ended if this article had not been ratified; and the terms of their successors shall then begin.

Section 2

The Congress shall assemble at least once in every year and such meeting shall begin at noon on the 3d day of January, unless they shall by law appoint a different day.

Section 3

If, at the time fixed for the beginning of the term of the president, the President-elect shall have died, the Vice President-elect shall become President. If a President shall not have been chosen before the time fixed for the beginning of his term, or if the President-elect shall have failed to qualify, then the Vice President-elect shall act as President until a President shall have qualified; and the Congress may by law provide for the case wherein neither a President-elect nor Vice President-elect shall have qualified, declaring who shall then act as President, or the manner in which one who is to act shall be selected, and such person shall act accordingly until a President or Vice President shall have qualified.

Section 4

The Congress may by law provide for the case of the death of any of the persons from whom the House of Representatives may choose a President whenever the right of choice shall have devolved upon them, and for the case of the death of any of the persons from whom the Senate may choose a Vice President whenever the right of choice shall have devolved upon them.

Section 5

Sections 1 and 2 shall take effect on the 15th day of October following the ratification of this article.

Section 6

This article shall be inoperative unless it shall have been ratified as an amendment to the Constitution by the legislatures of three-fourths of the several states within seven years from the date of its

submission.

ARTICLE XXI (1933)

Section 1

The eighteenth article of amendment to the Constitution of the United States is hereby repealed.

Section 2

The transportation or importation into any state, territory, or possession of the United States for delivery or use therein of intoxicating liquors, in violation of the laws thereof, is hereby prohibited.

Section 3

This article shall be inoperative unless it shall have been ratified as an amendment to the Constitution by conventions in the several states, as provided in the Constitution, within seven years from the date of the submission hereof to the states by the Congress.

ARTICLE XXII (1951)

Section 1

No person shall be elected to the office of the President more than twice, and no person who has held the office of President, or acted as President, for more than two years of a term to which some other person was elected President shall be elected to the office of the President more than once.

But this article shall not apply to any person holding the office of President when this article was proposed by the Congress, and shall not prevent any person who may be holding the office of President, or acting as President, during the term within which this article becomes operative from holding the office of President or acting as President during the remainder of such term.

Section 2

This article shall be inoperative unless it shall have been ratified as an amendment to the Constitution by the legislatures of three-fourths of the several states within seven years from the date of its submission to the states by the Congress.

ARTICLE XXIII (1961)

Section 1

The district constituting the seat of government of the United States shall appoint in such manner as the Congress may direct:

A number of electors of President and Vice President equal to the whole number of Senators and Representatives in Congress to which the district would be entitled if it were a state, but in no event more than the least populous state; they shall be in addition to those appointed by the states, but they shall be considered, for the purposes of the election of President and Vice President, to be electors appointed by a state; and they shall meet in the district and perform such duties as provided by the twelfth article of amendment.

Section 2

The Congress shall have power to enforce this article by appropriate legislation.

ARTICLE XXIV (1964)

Section 1

The right of citizens of the United States to vote in any primary or other election for President or Vice President, for electors for President or Vice President, or for Senator or Representative in Congress, shall not be denied or abridged by the United States or any state by reason of failure to pay any poll tax or other tax.

Section 2

The Congress shall have power to enforce this article by appropriate legislation.

ARTICLE XXV (1967)

Section 1

In case of the removal of the President from office or of his death or resignation, the Vice President shall become President.

Section 2

Whenever there is a vacancy in the office of the Vice President, the President shall nominate a Vice President who shall take office upon confirmation by a majority vote of both houses of Congress.

Section 3

Whenever the President transmit to the President pro Tempore of the Senate and the Speaker of the House of Representatives his written declaration that he is unable to discharge the powers and duties of his office, and until he transmits to them a written declaration to the contrary, such powers and duties shall be discharged by the Vice President as Acting President.

Section 4

Whenever the Vice President and a majority of either the principal officers of the executive departments or of such other body as Congress may by law provide, transmit to the President pro Tempore of the Senate and the Speaker of the House of Representatives their written declaration that the President is unable to discharge the powers and duties of his office, the Vice President shall immediately assume the powers and duties of the office as Acting President.

Thereafter, when the President transmits to the President pro Tempore of the Senate and the Speaker of the House of Representatives his written declaration that no inability exists, he shall resume the powers and duties of his office unless the Vice President and a majority of either the principal officers of the executive department or of such other body as Congress may by law provide, transmit within four days to the President pro Tempore of the Senate and the Speaker of the House of Representatives their written declaration that the President is unable to discharge the powers and duties of his office. Thereupon Congress shall decide the issue, assembling within forty- eight hours for that purpose if not in session. If the Congress, within twenty-one days after receipt of the latter written declaration, or, if Congress is not in session within twenty-one days after Congress is required to assemble, determines by two-thirds vote of both houses that the President is unable to discharge the powers and duties of his office, the Vice President shall continue to discharge the same as Acting President; otherwise, the President shall resume the powers and duties of his office.

ARTICLE XXVI (1971)

Section 1

The right of citizens of the United States, who are eighteen years of age or older, to vote shall not be denied or abridged by the United States or by any state on account of age.

Section 2

The Congress shall have power to enforce this article by appropriate legislation.

FOR THE INDEPENDENT JOURNAL
THE FEDERALIST NO. 6
(HAMILTON)

To the People of the State of New York:

The three last numbers of this paper have been dedicated to an enumeration of the dangers to which we should be exposed, in a state of disunion, from the arms and arts of foreign nations. I shall now proceed to delineate dangers of a different and, perhaps, still more alarming kind—those which will in all probability flow from dissensions between the States themselves, and from domestic factions and convulsions. These have been already in some instances slightly anticipated; but they deserve a more particular and more full investigation.

A man must be far gone in Utopian speculations who can seriously doubt that, if these States should either be wholly disunited, or only united in partial confederacies, the subdivisions into which they might be thrown would have frequent and violent contests with each other. To presume a want of motives for such contests as an argument against their existence, would be to forget that men are ambitious, vindictive, and rapacious. To look for a continuation of harmony between a number of independent, unconnected sovereignties in the same neighborhood, would be to disregard the uniform course of human events, and to set at defiance the accumulated experience of ages.

The causes of hostility among nations are innumerable. There are some which have a general and almost constant operation upon the collective bodies of society. Of this description are the love of power or the desire of pre-eminence and dominion—the jealousy of power, or the desire of equality and safety. There are others which have a more circumscribed though an equally operative influence within their spheres. Such are the rivalships and competitions of commerce between commercial nations. And there are others, not less numerous than either of the former, which take their origin entirely in private passions; in the attachments, enmities, interests, hopes, and fears of leading individuals in the communities of which they are members. Men of this class, whether the favorites of a king or of a people, have in too many instances abused the confidence they possessed; and assuming the pretext of some public motive, have not scrupled to sacrifice the national tranquility to personal advantage or personal gratification.

The celebrated Pericles, in compliance with the resentment of a prostitute, at the expense of much of the blood and treasure of his countrymen, attacked, vanquished, and destroyed the city of the *Samnians.* The same man, stimulated by private pique against the *Megarensians,* another nation of Greece, or to avoid a prosecution with which he was threatened as an accomplice in a supposed theft of the statuary of Phidias, or to get rid of the accusations prepared to be brought against him for dissipating the funds of the state in the purchase of popularity, or from a combination of all these causes, was the primitive author of that famous and fatal war, distinguished in the Grecian annals by the name of the *Peloponnesian* war; which, after various vicissitudes, intermissions, and renewals, terminated in the ruin of the Athenian commonwealth.

The ambitious cardinal, who was prime minister to Henry VIII, permitting his vanity to aspire to the triple crown, entertained hopes of succeeding in the acquisition of that splendid prize by the influence of the Emperor Charles V. To secure the favor and interest of this enterprising and powerful monarch, he precipitated England into a war with France, contrary to the plainest dictates of policy, and at the hazard of the safety and independence, as well of the kingdom over which he presided by his counsels, as of Europe in general. For if there ever was a sovereign who bid fair to realize the project of universal monarchy, it was the Emperor Charles V, of whose intrigues Wolsey was at once the instrument and the dupe.

The influence which the bigotry of one female, the petulance of another, and the cabals of a third, had in the contemporary policy, ferments, and pactfications, of a considerable part of Europe, are topics that have been too often descanted upon not to be generally known.

To multiply examples of the agency of personal considerations in the production of great national events, either foreign or domestic, according to their direction, would be an unnecessary waste of time. Those who have but a superficial acquaintance with the sources from which they are to be drawn, will themselves recollect a variety of instances; and those who have a tolerable knowledge of human nature will not stand in need of such lights, to form their opinion either of the reality or extent of that agency. Perhaps, however, a reference, tending to illustrate the general principle, may with propriety be made to a case which has lately happened among ourselves. If Shays had not been a *desperate debtor,* it is much to be doubted whether Massachusetts would have been plunged into a civil war.

But notwithstanding the concurring testimony of experience, in this particular, there are still to be found visionary or designing men, who stand ready to advocate the paradox of perpetual peace between the States, though dismembered and alienated from each other. The genius of republics (say they) is pacific; the spirit of commerce has a tendency to soften the manners of men, and to extinguish those inflammable humors which have so often kindled into wars. Commercial republics, like ours, will never be disposed to waste themselves in ruinous contentions with each other. They will be governed by mutual interest, and will cultivate a spirit of mutual amity and concord.

Is it not (we may ask these projectors in politics) the true interest of all nations to cultivate the same benevolent and philosophic spirit? If this be their true interest, have they in fact pursued it? Has it not, on the contrary, invariably been found that momentary passions, and immediate interests, have a more active and imperious control over human conduct than general or remote considerations of policy, utility, or justice? Have republics in practice been less addicted to war than monarchies? Are not the former administered by *men* as well as the latter? Are there not aversions, predilections, rivalships, and desires of unjust acquisitions, that affect nations as well as kings? Are not popular assemblies frequently subject to the impulses of rage, resentment, jealousy, avarice, and of other irregular and violent propensities? Is it not well known that their determinations are often governed by a few individuals in whom they place confidence, and are, of course, liable to be tinctured by the passions and views of those individuals? Has commerce hitherto done any thing more than change the objects of war? Is not the love of wealth as domineering and enterprising a passion as that of power or glory? Have there not been as many wars founded upon commercial motives since that has become the prevailing system of nations, as were before occasioned by the cupidity of territory or dominion? Has not the spirit of commerce, in many instances, administered new incentives to the appetite, both for the one and for the other? Let experience, the least fallible guide of human opinions, be appealed to for an answer to these inquiries.

Sparta, Athens, Rome, and Carthage were all republics; two of them, Athens and Carthage, of the commercial kind. Yet were they as often engaged in wars, offensive and defensive, as the neighboring monarchies of the same times. Sparta was little better than a well-regulated camp; and Rome was never sated of carnage and conquest.

Carthage, though a commercial republic, was the aggressor in the very war that ended in her destruction. Hannibal had carried her arms into the heart of Italy and to the gates of Rome, before Scipio, in turn, gave him an overthrow in the territories of Carthage, and made a conquest of the commonwealth.

Venice, in later times, figured more than once in wars of ambition, till, becoming an object to the other Italian states, Pope Julius II found means to accomplish that formidable league, which gave deadly blow to the power and pride of this haughty republic.

The provinces of Holland, till they were overwhelmed in debts and taxes, took a leading and conspicuous part in the wars of Europe. They had furious contests with England for the dominion of the sea, and were among the most persevering and most implacable of the opponents of Louis XIV.

In the government of Britain the representatives of the people compose one branch of the national legislature. Commerce has been for ages the predominant pursuit of that country. Few nations, nevertheless, have been more frequently engaged in war; and the wars in which that kingdom has been engaged have, in numerous instances, proceeded from the people.

There have been, if I may so express it, almost as many popular as royal wars. The cries of the nation and the importunities of their representatives have, upon various occasions, dragged their monarchs into war, or continued them in it, contrary to their inclinations, and sometimes contrary to the real interests of the state. In that memorable struggle for superiority between the rival houses of Austria and Bourbon, which so long kept Europe in a flame, it is well known that the antipathies of the English against the French, seconding the ambition, or rather the avarice, of a favorite leader, protracted the war beyond the limits marked out by sound policy, and for a considerable time in opposition to the views of the court.

The wars of these two last mentioned nations have in a great measure grown out of commercial considerations—the desire of supplanting and the fear of being supplanted, either in particular branches of traffic or in the general advantages of trade and navigation.

From this summary of what has taken place in other countries, whose situations have borne the nearest resemblance to our own, what reason can we have to confide in those reveries which would seduce us into an expectation of peace and cordiality between the members of the recent confederacy, in a state of separation? Have we not already seen enough of the fallacy and extravagance of those idle theories which have amused us with promises of an exemption from the imperfections, weaknesses, and evils incident to society in every shape? Is it not time to awake from the deceitful dream of a golden age, and to adopt as a practical maxim for

the direction of our political conduct that we, as well as the other inhabitants of the globe, are yet remote from the happy empire of perfect wisdom and perfect virtue?

Let the point of extreme depression to which our national dignity and credit have sunk, let the inconveniences felt everywhere from a lax and ill administration of government, let the revolt of a part of the State of North Carolina, the late menacing disturbances in Pennsylvania, and the actual insurrections and rebellions in Massachusetts, declare—!

So far is the general sense of mankind from corresponding with the tenets of those who endeavor to lull asleep our apprehensions of discord and hostility between the States, in the event of disunion, that it has from long observation of the progress of society become a sort of axiom in politics, that vicinity, or nearness of situation, constitutes nations' natural enemies. An intelligent writer expresses himself on this subject to this effect: "NEIGHBORING NATIONS [says he] are naturally enemies of each other, unless their common weakness forces them to league in CONFEDERATIVE REPUBLIC, and their constitution prevents the differences that neighborhood occasions, extinguishing that secret jealousy which disposes all states to aggrandize themselves at the expense of their neighbors." This passage, at the same time, points out the EVIL and suggests the REMEDY.

THE FEDERALIST NO. 10
(MADISON)

Among the numerous advantages promised by a well-constructed Union, none deserves to be more accurately developed than its tendency to break and control the violence of faction. The friend of popular governments never finds himself so much alarmed for their character and fate as when he contemplates their propensity to this dangerous vice. He will not fail, therefore, to set a due value on any plan which, without violating the principles to which he is attached, provides a proper cure for it. The instability, injustice, and confusion introduced into the public councils have, in truth, been the mortal diseases under which popular governments have everywhere perished, as they continue to be

the favorite and fruitful topics from which the adversaries to liberty derive their most specious declamations. The valuable improvements made by the American constitutions on the popular models, both ancient and modern, cannot certainly be too much admired; but it would be an unwarrantable partiality, to contend that they have as effectually obviated the danger on this side, as was wished and expected. Complaints are everywhere heard from our most considerate and virtuous citizens, equally the friends of public and private faith and of public and personal liberty, that our governments are too unstable, that the public good is disregarded in the conflicts of rival parties, and that measures are too often decided, not according to the rules of justice and the rights of the minor party, but by the superior force of an interested and overbearing majority. However anxiously we may wish that these complaints had no foundation, the evidence of known facts will not permit us to deny that they are in some degree true. It will be found, indeed, on a candid review of our situation, that some of the distresses under which we labor have been erroneously charged on the operation of our governments; but it will be found, at the same time, that other causes will not alone account for many of our heaviest misfortunes; and, particularly, for that prevailing and increasing distrust of public engagements and alarm for private rights, which are echoed from one end of the continent to the other. These must be chiefly, if not wholly, effects of the unsteadiness and injustice with which a factious spirit has tainted our public administration.

By a faction, I understand a number of citizens, whether amounting to a majority or minority of the whole, who are united and actuated by some common impulse of passion, or of interest, adverse to the rights of other citizens, or to the permanent and aggregate interests of the community.

There are two methods of curing the mischiefs of faction: the one, by removing its causes; the other, by controlling its effects.

There are again two methods of removing the causes of faction: the one, by destroying the liberty which is essential to its existence; the other, by giving to every citizen the same opinions, the same passions, and the same interests.

It could never be more truly said than of the first remedy that it was worse than the disease. Liberty is to faction what air is to fire, an aliment without which it instantly expires. But it could not be a less folly to abolish liberty, which is essential to political life, because it nourishes faction, than it would be to wish the annihilation of air, which is essential to animal life, because it imparts to fire its destructive agency.

The second expedient is as impracticable as the first would be unwise. As long as the reason of man continues fallible, and he is at liberty to exercise it, different opinions will be formed. As long as the connection subsists between his reason and his self-love, his opinions and his passions will have a reciprocal influence on each other, and the former

will be objects to which the latter will attach themselves. The diversity in the faculties of men, from which the rights of property originate, is not less an insuperable obstacle to a uniformity of interests. The protection of these faculties is the first object of government. From the protection of different and unequal faculties of acquiring property, the possession of different degrees and kinds of property immediately results; and from the influence of these on the sentiments and views of the respective proprietors, ensues a division of the society into different interests and parties.

The latent causes of faction are thus sown in the nature of man; and we see them everywhere brought into different degrees of activity, according to the different circumstances of civil society. A zeal for different opinions concerning religion, concerning government, and many other points, as well of speculation as of practice; an attachment to different leaders ambitiously contending for preeminence and power; or to persons of other descriptions whose fortunes have been interesting to the human passions, have, in turn, divided mankind into parties, inflamed them with mutual animosity, and rendered them much more disposed to vex and oppress each other than to cooperate for their common good. So strong is this propensity of mankind to fall into mutual animosities, that where no substantial occasion presents itself, the most frivolous and fanciful distinctions have been sufficient to kindle their unfriendly passions and excite their most violent conflicts. But the most common and durable source of factions has been the various and unequal distribution of property. Those who hold and those who are without property have ever formed distinct interests in society. Those who are creditors, and those who are debtors, fall under a like discrimination. A landed interest, a manufacturing interest, a mercantile interest, a moneyed interest, with many lesser interests, grow up of necessity in civilized nations, and divide them into different classes, actuated by different sentiments and views. The regulation of these various and interfering interests forms the principal task of modern legislation, and involves the spirit of party and faction in the necessary and ordinary operations of the government.

No man is allowed to be a judge in his own cause, because his interest would certainly bias his judgment, and, not improbably, corrupt his integrity.

With equal, nay with greater reason, a body of men are unfit to be both judges and parties at the same time; yet what are many of the most important acts of legislation, but so many judicial determinations, not indeed concerning the rights of single persons, but concerning the rights of large bodies of citizens? And what are the different classes of legislators but advocates and parties to the causes which they determine? Is a law proposed concerning private debts? It is a question to which the creditors are parties on one side and the debtors on the other. Justice ought to hold the balance between them. Yet the parties are, and must be, themselves the judges; and the most numerous party, or, in other words, the most powerful faction must be expected to prevail. Shall domestic manufacturers be encouraged, and in what degree, by restrictions on foreign manufacturers? these questions which would be differently decided by the landed and the manufacturing classes, and probably by neither with a sole regard to justice and the public good. The apportionment of taxes on the various descriptions of property is an act which seems to require the most exact impartiality; yet there is, perhaps, no legislative act in which greater opportunity and temptation are given to a predominant party to trample on the rules of justice. Every shilling with which they overburden the inferior number is a shilling saved to their own pockets.

It is in vain to say that enlightened statesmen will be able to adjust these clashing interests and render them all subservient to the public good. Enlightened statesmen will not always be at the helm. Nor, in many cases, can such an adjustment be made at all without taking into view indirect and remote considerations, which will rarely prevail over the immediate interest which one party may find in disregarding the rights of another or the good of the whole.

The inference to which we are brought is, that the *causes* of faction cannot be removed, and that relief is only to be sought in the means of controlling its *effects*.

If a faction consists of less than a majority, relief is supplied by the republican principle, which enables the majority to defeat its sinister views by regular vote. It may clog the administration, it may convulse the society; but it will be unable to execute and mask its violence under the forms of the *Constitution*. When a majority is included in a faction, the form of popular government, on the other hand, enables it to sacrifice to its ruling passion or interest both the public good and the rights of other citizens. To secure the public good and private rights against the danger of such a faction, and at the same time to preserve the spirit and the form of popular government, is then the great object to which our inquiries are directed. Let me add that it is the great desideratum by which alone this form of government can be rescued from the opprobrium under which it has so long labored, and be recommended to the esteem and adoption of mankind.

By what means is this object attainable? Evidently by one of two only. Either the existence of the same passion or interest in a majority at the same time must be prevented, or the majority, having such coexistent passion or interest, must be rendered, by their number and local situation, unable to concert and carry into effect schemes of oppression. If the impulse and the opportunity be suffered to coincide, we well know that neither moral nor religious motives can be relied on as an adequate control. They are not found to be such on the injustice and violence of individuals, and lose their efficacy in proportion to the number combined together, that is, in proportion as their efficacy becomes needful.

From this view of the subject it may be concluded that a pure democracy, by which I mean a society consisting of a small number of citizens, who assemble and administer the government in person, can admit of no cure for the mischiefs of faction. A common passion or interest will, in almost every case, be felt by a majority of the whole; a communication and concert results from the form of government itself; and there is nothing to check the inducements to sacrifice the weaker party or an obnoxious individual. Hence it is that such democracies have ever been spectacles of turbulence and contention; have ever been found incompatible with personal security or the rights of property; and have in general been as short in their lives as they have been violent in their deaths. Theoretic politicians, who have patronized this species of government, have erroneously supposed that by reducing mankind to a perfect equality in their political rights, they would, at the same time be perfectly equalized and assimilated in their possessions, their opinions, and their passions.

A republic, by which I mean a government in which the scheme of representation takes place, opens a different prospect and promises the cure for which we are seeking. Let us examine the points in which it varies from pure democracy, and we shall comprehend both the nature of the cure and the efficacy which it must derive from the Union.

The two great points of difference between a democracy and a republic are: first, the delegation of the government, in the latter, to a small number of citizens elected by the rest; secondly, the greater number of citizens, and greater sphere of country over which the latter may be extended.

The effect of the first difference is, on the one hand, to refine and enlarge the public views, by passing them through the medium of a chosen body of citizens, whose wisdom may best discern the true interest of their country, and whose patriotism and love of justice will be least likely to sacrifice it to temporary or partial considerations. Under such a regulation, it may well happen that the public voice, pronounced by the representatives of the people, will be more consonant to the public good than if pronounced by the people themselves, convened for the purpose. On the other hand, the effect may be inverted. Men of factious tempers, of local prejudices, or of sinister designs, may, by intrigue, by corruption, or by other means, first obtain the suffrages, and then betray the interests of the people. The question resulting is, whether small or extensive republics are more favorable to the election of proper guardians of the public weal; and it is clearly decided in favor of the latter by two obvious considerations:

In the first place, it is to be remarked that however small the republic may be, the representatives must be raised to a certain number, in order to guard against the cabals of a few; and that, however large it may be, they must be limited to a certain number, in order to guard against the confusion of a multitude. Hence, the number of representatives in the two cases not being in proportion to that of the two constituents, and being proportionally greater in the small republic, it follows that, if the proportion of fit characters be not less in the large than in the small republic, the former will present a greater option, and consequently a greater probability of a fit choice.

In the next place, as each representative will be chosen by a greater number of citizens in the large than in the small republic, it will be more difficult for unworthy candidates to practise with success the vicious arts by which elections are too often carried; and the suffrages of the people being more free, will be more likely to center on men who possess the most attractive merit and the most diffusive and established characters.

It must be confessed that in this, as in most other cases, there is a mean, on both sides of which inconveniences will be found to lie. By enlarging too much the number of electors, you render the representative too little acquainted with all their local circumstances and lesser interests; as by reducing it too much, you render him unduly attached to these, and too little fit to comprehend and pursue great and national objects. The federal Constitution forms a happy combination in this respect; the great and aggregate interests being referred to the national, the local and particular to the State legislatures.

The other point of difference is the greater number of citizens and extent of territory which may be brought within the compass of republican than of democratic government; and it is this circumstance principally which renders factious combinations less to be dreaded in the former than in the latter. The smaller the society, the fewer probably will be the distinct parties and interests composing it; the fewer the distinct parties and interests, the more frequently will a majority be found of the same party; and the smaller the number of individuals composing a majority, and the smaller the compass within which they are placed, the more easily will they concert and execute their plans of oppression. Extend the sphere, and you take in a greater variety of parties and interests; you make it less probable that a majority of the whole will have a common motive to invade the rights of other citizens; or if such a common motive exists, it will be more difficult for all who feel it to discover their own strength and to act in unison with each other. Besides other impediments, it may be remarked that, where there is a consciousness of unjust or dishonorable purposes, communication is always checked by distrust in proportion to the number whose concurrence is necessary.

Hence, it clearly appears, that the same advantage which a republic has over a democracy, in controlling the effects of faction, is enjoyed by a large over a small republic—is enjoyed by the Union over the States composing it. Does this advantage consist in the substitution of representatives whose enlightened views and virtuous sentiments render them superior to local prejudices and to schemes of injustice? It will not be denied that the representation of the Union will be most likely to possess these requisite endowments. Does it consist in the greater security afforded by a greater variety of parties, against the event of any one party being able to outnumber and oppress the rest? In an equal degree does the increased variety of parties comprised within the Union, increase this security. Does it, in fine, consist in the greater obstacles opposed to the concert and accomplishment of the secret wishes of an unjust and interested majority? Here again, the extent of the Union gives it the most palpable advantage.

The influence of factious leaders may kindle a flame within their particular States, but will be unable to spread a general conflagration through the other States. A religious sect may degenerate into a political faction in a part of the Confederacy; but the variety of sects dispersed over the entire face of it must secure the national councils against any danger from that source. A rage for paper money, for an abolition of debts, for an equal division of property, or for any other improper or wicked project, will be less apt to pervade the whole body of the Union than a particular member of it; in the same proportion as such a malady is more likely to taint a particular county or district than an entire State.

In the extent and proper structure of the Union, therefore, we behold a republican remedy for the diseases most incident to republican government. And according to the degree of pleasure and pride we feel in being republicans ought to be our zeal in cherishing the spirit and supporting the character of Federalists.

PUBLIUS

THE FEDERALIST NO. 51
(MADISON)

To the People of the State of New York:

To what expedient, then, shall we finally resort, for maintaining in practice the necessary partition of power among the several departments, as laid down in the *Constitution?* The only answer that can be given is, that as all these exterior provisions are found to be inadequate, the defect must be supplied, by so contriving the interior structure of the government as that its several constituent parts may, by their mutual relations, be the means of keeping each other in their proper places. Without presuming to undertake a full development of this important idea, I will hazard a few general observations, which may perhaps place it in a clearer light, and enable us to form a more correct judgment of the principles and structure of the government planned by the convention.

In order to lay a due foundation for that separate and distinct exercise of the different powers of government, which to a certain extent is admitted on all hands to be essential to the preservation of liberty, it is evident that each department should have a will of its own; and consequently should be so constituted that the members of each should have as little agency as possible in the appointment of the members. Were this principle rigorously adhered to, it would require that all the appointments for the supreme executive, legislative, and judiciary magistracies should be drawn from the same fountain of authority, the people, through channels having no communication whatever with one another. Perhaps such a plan of constructing the several departments would be less difficult in practice than it may in contemplation appear. Some difficulties, however, and some additional expense would attend the execution of it. Some deviations, therefore, from the principle must be admitted. In the constitution of the judiciary department in particular, it might be inexpedient to insist rigorously on the principle: first, because peculiar qualifications being essential in the members, the primary consideration ought to be to select that mode of choice which best secures these qualifications; secondly, because the permanent tenure by which the appointments are held in that department, must soon destroy all sense of dependence on the authority confering them.

It is equally evident, that the members of each department should be as little dependent as possible on those of the others, for the emoluments annexed to their offices. Were the executive magistrate, or the judges, not independent of the legislature in this particular, their independence in every other would be merely nominal.

But the great security against a gradual concentration of the several powers in the same department, consists in giving to those who administer each department the necessary constitutional means and personal motives to resist encroachments of the others. The provision for defense must in this, as in all other cases, be made commensurate to the danger of attack. Ambition must be made to counteract ambition. The interest of the man must be connected with the constitutional rights of the place. It may be a reflection on human nature, that such devices should be necessary to control the abuses of government. But what is government itself, but the greatest of all reflections on human nature? If men were angels, no government would be necessary. If angels were to govern men, neither external nor internal controls on government would be necessary. In framing a government which is to be administered by men over men, the great difficulty lies in this: you must first enable the government to control the governed; and in the next place oblige it to control itself. A dependence on the people is, no doubt, the primary control on the government; but experience has taught mankind the necessity of auxiliary precautions.

This policy of supplying, by opposite and rival interests, the defect of better motives, might be traced through the whole system of human affairs, private as well as public. We see it particularly displayed in all the subordinate distributions of power, where the constant aim is to divide and arrange the several offices in such a manner as that each may be a check on the other—that the private interest of every individual may be a sentinel over the public rights. These inventions of prudence cannot be less requisite in the distribution of the supreme powers of the State.

But it is not possible to give to each department an equal power of self-defense. In republican government, the Legislative authority necessarily predominates. The remedy for this inconveniency is to divide the legislature into different branches; and to render them, by different modes of election and different principles of action, as little connected with each other as the nature of their common functions and their common dependence on the society will admit. It may even be necessary to guard against dangerous encroachments by still further precautions. As the weight of the legislative authority requires that it should be thus divided, the weakness of the executive may require, on the other hand, that it should be fortified. An absolute negative on the legislature appears, at first view, to be the natural defense with which the executive magistrate should be armed. But perhaps it would be neither altogether safe nor alone sufficient. On ordinary occasions it might not be exerted with the requisite firmness, and on extraordinary occasions it might be perfidiously abused. May not this defect of an absolute negative be supplied by some qualified connection between this weaker department and the weaker branch of the stronger department, by which the latter may be led to support the constitutional rights of the former, without being too much detached from the rights of its own department?

If the principles on which these observations are founded be just, as I persuade myself they are, and they be applied as a criterion to the several State constitutions, and to the federal Constitution, it will be found that if the latter does not perfectly correspond with them, the former are infinitely less able to bear such a test.

There are, moreover, two considerations particularly applicable to the federal system of America, which place that system in a very interesting point of view.

First. In a single republic, all the power surrendered by the people is submitted to the administration of a single government; and the usurpations are guarded against by a division of the government into distinct and separate departments. In the compound republic of America, the power surrendered by the people is first divided between two distinct governments, and then the portion allotted to each subdivided among distinct and separate departments. Hence a double security arises to the rights of the people. The different governments will control each other, at the same time that each will be controlled by itself.

Second. It is of great importance in a republic not only to guard the society against the oppression of its rulers, but to guard one part of the society against the injustice of the other part. Different interests necessarily exist in different classes of citizens. If a majority be united by a common interest, the rights of the minority will be insecure. There are but two methods of providing against this evil: the one by creating a will in the community independent of the majority—that is, of the society itself; the other, by comprehending in the society so many separate descriptions of citizens as will render an unjust combination of a majority of the whole very improbable, if not impracticable. The first method prevails in all governments possessing an hereditary or self- appointed authority. This, at best, is but a precarious security; because a power independent of the society may as well espouse the unjust views of the major, as the rightful interests of the minor party, and may possibly be turned against both parties. The second method will be exemplified in the federal republic of the United States. Whilst all authority in it will be derived from and dependent on the society, the society itself will be broken into so many parts, interests and classes of citizens, that the rights of individuals, or of the minority, will be in little danger from interested combinations of the majority. In a free government the security for civil rights must be the same as that for religious rights. It consists in the one case in the multiplicity of interests, and in the other in the multiplicity of sects. The degree of security in both cases will depend on the number of interests and sects; and this may be presumed to depend on the extent of country and number of people comprehended under the same government. This view of the subject must particularly recommend a proper federal system to all the sincere and considerate friends of republican government, since it shows that in exact proportion as the territory of the Union may be formed into more circumscribed Confederacies, or States, oppressive combinations of a majority will be facilitated; the best security, under the republican forms, for the rights of every class of citizens, will be diminished; and consequently the stability and independence of some member of the government, the only other security, must be proportionally increased. Justice is the end of government. It is the end of civil society. It ever

has been and ever will be pursued until it be obtained, or until liberty be lost in the pursuit. In a society under the forms of which the stronger faction can readily unite and oppress the weaker, anarchy may as truly be said to reign as in a state of nature, where the weaker individual is not secured against the violence of the stronger; and as, in the latter state, even the stronger individuals are prompted, by the uncertainty of their condition, to submit to a government which may protect the weak as well as themselves; so, in the former state, will the more powerful factions or parties be gradually induced, by a like motive, to wish for a government which will protect all parties, the weaker as well as the more powerful. It can be little doubted that if the State of Rhode Island was separated from the Confederacy and left to itself, the insecurity of rights under the popular form of government within such narrow limits would be displayed by such reiterated oppressions of factious majorities that some power altogether independent of the people would soon be called for by the voice of the very factions whose misrule had proved the necessity of it. In the extended republic of the United States, and among the great variety of interests, parties, and sects which it embraces, a coalition of a majority of the whole society could seldom take place on any other prinicples than those of justice and the general good; whilst there being thus less danger to a minor from the will of a major party, there must be less pretext, also, to provide for the security of the former, by introducing into the government a will not dependent on the latter, or in other words, a will independent of the society itself. It is no less certain than it is important, notwithstanding the contrary opinions which have been entertained, that the larger the society, provided it lie within a practical sphere, the more duly capable it will be of self-government. And happily for the *republican cause,* the practicable sphere may be carried to a very great extent, by a judicious modification and mixture of the *federal principle.*

PUBLIUS

GEORGE MASON:
"OBJECTIONS TO THE CONSTITUTION OF GOVERNMENT FORMED BY THE CONVENTION," NOVEMBER 1787

There is no Declaration of Rights; and the Laws of the general Government being paramount to the Laws and Constitutions of the several States, the Declaration of Rights in the separate States are no Security. Nor are the people secured even in the Enjoyment of the Benefits of the common-Law: which stands here upon no other Foundation than its having been adopted by the respective Acts forming the Constitutions of the several States.

In the House of Representatives there is not the Substance, but the Shadow only of Representation; which can never produce proper Information in the Legislature, or inspire Confidence in the People: the Laws will therefore be generally made by Men little concern'd in, and unacquainted with their Effects and Consequences.*

The Senate have the Power of altering all Money-Bills, and of originating Appropriations of Money and the Sallerys of the Officers of their own Appointment in Conjunction with the President of the United States; altho' they are not the Representatives of the People, or amenable to them.

These with their other great Powers (vizt. their Power in the Appointment of Ambassadors and all public Officers, in making Treaties, and in trying all Impeachments) their Influence upon and Connection with the supreme Executive from these Causes, their Duration of Office, and their being a constant existing Body almost continually sitting, joined with their being one compleat Branch of the Legislature, will destroy any Balance in the Government, and enable them to accomplish what Usurpations they please upon the Rights and Libertys of the People.

The Judiciary of the United States is so constructed and extended, as to absorb and destroy the Judiciarys of the several States; thereby rendering Law as tedious[,] intricate and expensive, and Justice as unattainable, by a great part of the Community, as in England, and enabling the Rich to oppress and ruin the Poor.

The President of the United States has no constitutional Council (a thing unknown in any safe and regular Government); he will therefore be unsupported by proper Information and Advice; and will generally be directed by Minions and Favourites—or He will become a Tool to the Senate—or a Council of State will grow out of the principal Officers of the great Departments; the worst and most dangerous of all Ingredients for such a Council, in a free Country; for they may be induced to join in any dangerous or oppressive Measures, to shelter themselves, and prevent an Inquiry into their own Misconduct in Office; whereas had a constitutional Council been formed (as was proposed) of six Members; vizt. two from the Eastern, two from the Middle, and two from the Southern States, to be appointed by Vote of the States in the House of Representatives, with the same Duration and Rotation of Office as the Senate, the Executive wou'd always have had safe and proper Information and Advice, the President of such a Council might have acted as Vice President of the United States, pro tempore, upon any Vacancy or Disability of the chief Magistrate; and long continued Sessions of the Senate wou'd in a great Measure have been prevented.

From this fatal Defect of a constitutional Council has arisen the improper Power of the Senate, in the Appointment of public Officers, and the alarming Dependence and Connection between that Branch of the Legislature, and the supreme Executive.

Hence also sprung that unnecessary and dangerous Officer, the Vice President; who for want of other Employment, is made President of the Senate; thereby dangerously blending the executive and legislative Powers; besides always giving to some one of the States an unnecessary and unjust Pre-eminence over the others.

The President of the United States has the unrestrained Power of granting Pardon for Treason;

which may be sometimes exercised to screen from Punishment those whom he had secretly instigated to commit the Crime, and thereby prevent a Discovery of his own Guilt.

By declaring all Treaties supreme Laws of the Land, the Executive and the Senate have in many Cases, an exclusive Power of Legislation; which might have been avoided by proper Distinctions with Respect to Treaties, and requiring the Assent of the House of Representatives, where it cou'd be done with Safety.

By requiring only a Majority to make all commercial and navigation Laws, the five Southern States (whose Produce and Circumstances are totally different from that of the eight Northern and Eastern States) will be ruined; for such rigid and premature Regulations may be made, as will enable the Merchants of the Northern and Eastern States not only to demand an exorbitant Freight, but to monopolize the Purchase of the Commodities at their own Price, for many years: to the great Injury of the landed Interest, and Impoverishment of the People: and the Danger is the greater, as the Gain on one Side will be in Proportion to the Loss on the other. Whereas requiring two thirds of the members present in both Houses wou'd have produced mutual moderation, promoted the general Interest, and removed an insuperable Objection to the Adoption of the Government.

Under their own Construction of the general Clause at the End of the enumerated powers the Congress may grant Monopolies in Trade and Commerce, constitute new Crimes, inflict unusual and severe Punishments, and extend their Power as far as they shall think proper; so that the State Legislatures have no Security for the Powers now presumed to remain to them; or the People for their Rights.

There is no Declaration of any kind for preserving the Liberty of the Press, the Tryal by Jury in civil Causes; nor against the Danger of standing Armys in time of Peace.

The State Legislatures are restrained from laying Export Duties on their own Produce.

The general Legislature is restrained from prohibiting the further Importation of Slaves for twenty odd Years; tho' such Importations render the United States weaker, more vulnerable, and less capable of Defence.

Both the general Legislature and the State Legislatures are expressly prohibited making ex post facto Laws; tho' there never was, or can be a Legislature but must and will make such Laws, when necessity and the public Safety require them; which will hereafter be a Breach of all the Constitutions in the Union, and afford precedents for other Innovations.

This Government will commence in a moderate Aristocracy; it is at present impossible to foresee whether it will, in its Operation, produce a Monarchy, or a corrupt oppressive Aristocracy; it will most probably vibrate some Years between the two, and then terminate in the one or the other.

---

*This Objection has been in some Degree lessened by an Amendment, often before refused, and at last made by an Erasure, after the Engrossment upon Parchment, of the word *forty*, and inserting *thirty*, in the 3d Clause of the 2d Section of the 1st Article.

LIFE OF JOHN STUART MILL

1806
Born: son of Benthamite philosopher James Mill (1773–1832)

1809-18
Educated from age three by his father in classical languages and literatures

1823–58
Employed as clerk with the British East India Company

1826
Stricken with severe six-month mental crisis

1831
Meets Harriet Taylor (1807–58), a married woman destined to be his wife

1851
Marries Taylor shortly after her husband's death

1858
Death of Harriet Taylor Mill

1859
On Liberty

1860
The Subjection of Women

1861
Utilitarianism

1873
Autobiography; Mill's Death

1874
Three Essays on Religion published posthumously

CHAPTER FIVE

THE EMERGENCE OF LIBERALISM: JOHN STUART MILL

If we had to pinpoint one era during which the modern world was born, we might well choose the second half of the eighteenth century. The American and French Revolutions, molded by the political thought of John Locke and others, brought basic changes in both political thought and practice that would radically change traditional assumptions and beliefs about human institutions and human nature itself. If in the twentieth century we can take for granted the concept of human rights and equal opportunity, if we prefer representative democracy as a form of government, if we reject social and religious hierarchies based on tradition and birth, if, in short, we hear a good deal about the "rise of liberalism" during the last 200 years, it is because of the far-reaching political, industrial, *and* humanitarian revolutions that occurred in the late eighteenth and early nineteenth century, particularly in Great Britain, France, and the United States, revolutions whose effects are pivotal in our own times.

THE EMERGENCE OF LIBERALISM

Enlightenment political ideas and their embodiment in the American and French Revolutions, combined with the burgeoning power of industrial capitalism and the middle class, gave rise to the *liberal* tradition in political philosophy and practice between about 1770 and 1832. Though liberalism spread throughout Europe, Britain was its home. Britain had a strong parliamentary tradition, had nurtured the thought of John Locke, Thomas Paine, and Mary Wollstonecraft, as well as the poetry of Lord Byron and Percy Bysshe Shelley; and, as the home of the Industrial Revolution, had dealt earlier than other nations with the challenges of industrial capitalism. Britain also nurtured the "Philosophical Radicals," the Utilitarians, who played a key role in

advancing liberal thought, and from within whose ranks would emerge John Stuart Mill, the greatest apologist for liberalism of modern times.

What is "liberalism" in politics? "Liberal" derives from the Latin *liber*, meaning "free," particularly in the sense of being "freeborn" rather than a slave. Some uses of the word "liberal" derive from qualities such as generosity, believed ideally to mark the person who was not only freeborn but highborn—a member of the nobility. Thus we speak still of someone giving "liberally" to charities. The phrase "liberal arts," which appears on thousands of university graduates' diplomas, is used to describe academic study generous in its breadth of subjects: history, philosophy, literature and languages as well as physics, biology, mathematics, psychology, anthropology, sociology, and others. Such an education, at one time suitable only for the freest persons in society—those of high social rank—is now available to all who seek it.

With the emergence of modern political thought in the seventeenth and eighteenth centuries, notably the thought of John Locke (1632-1704), the word "liberal" came to mean those political philosophies that affirmed basic individual rights, above all individual liberty, and government founded on and representative of the consent of the governed—government, in Abraham Lincoln's later resonant phrase, of, by, and for the people.

In late eighteenth and early nineteenth century Europe, *conservatives*, those who wished to strengthen the foundations of traditional society, believed in several things: 1) the importance of community over individual rights; 2) the primacy of the traditional social hierarchy led by a landed aristocracy; 3) the state as rooted in history and tradition; 4) human beings as inherently flawed and therefore in need of stable social structures and the habit of obedience to hereditary authority (social, political, and religious). By contrast, *liberals* espoused contrasting ideas: 1) enhancing individual freedom over government, social, and religious controls; 2) the primacy of rational principles such as natural rights and social contract as a basis of the state; 3) individual status as based on personal achievement rather than on birth; 4) human beings as, if not always reasonable, at least "capable of reason," and therefore capable of responsible choice in matters both public and personal. Edmund Burke's *Reflections on the Revolution in France* (1791) is the classic statement of the conservative view within the framework of parliamentary democracy. Thomas Paine, who participated in both the American and the French Revolutions, expressed the liberal outlook in answering Burke in *Rights of Man* (1792), and with such success that he (Paine) was burned in effigy in the streets of London.

Liberalism found its chief support among the rapidly growing middle classes. Among the practical commitments of the early liberals were positions particularly favorable to those classes. This early liberalism is usually called **classical liberalism**, which sought mainly seven ends: 1) minimal government; 2) maximal individual freedom of action and expression; 3) advancement of education; 4) the sanctity of property rights; 5) individual rights guaranteed by written constitutions; 6) freely elected parliaments with power distributed among the branches of government; and 7) extension of voting rights to the middle classes.

Two tenets of classical liberalism reveal that its commitment to expansion of liberty did not extend to the working classes: its espousal of *laissez-faire* economic theory and its distrust of popular democracy. The liberals initially opposed reforms designed to alleviate poverty and improve working conditions in mines and factories, arguing that this was interfering with the "natural" law of supply and demand and with the freedom of owners. Over time, some liberals modified their views, influenced by more "radical" liberals such as the Utilitarians and John Stuart Mill, who argued that government should improve the condition of working people through universal education and the alleviation of poverty and bad working conditions. The Utilitarians argued that such active measures were

needed precisely to enhance individual liberty—the liberty of working-class individuals.

As one might expect, classical liberals also distrusted popular democracy. They did so because they found incompatible with one another the Enlightenment ideals of liberty and equality. They believed the working class's zeal for equality would destroy individual freedom and produce a willingness, perhaps an eagerness, to accept even dictatorial rule. Liberals had before them the lamentable example of what had happened to the original aims of the French Revolution in 1792–3, when the radical Jacobins, whose strength lay in the volatile Parisian working classes (the *sans-culottes*), seized control and instituted the Reign of Terror, resulting in some 20,000 deaths. Classical liberals believed that political power should rest with reliable men of education and property.

It is important to see that in nineteenth-century Europe, as in the French Revolution, two kinds of revolution were going on, often in conflict with one another: a middle-class revolution, represented by classical liberalism, and a working-class revolution, which manifested itself mainly in popular protests, political revolution, and an organized labor movement. Throughout the century an increasing willingness on the part of middle-class reformers to recognize the needs of workers combined with the growing power of workers movements to bring the goals of both groups more closely together.

Present-day "conservatives" in the U. S. are partly heirs of the classical liberal tradition, believing in less government, a less-regulated market, and more individual liberty and responsibility. They are divided, however, over social and moral issues such as the family, education, gender roles, reproductive rights, sexual orientation, crime and punishment, and the role of religion in public life. These heirs of Edmund Burke want to conserve, partly through legislation and public sanctions, certain values they believe are both right and widely affirmed. Modern-day U.S. "liberals" tend to believe that the individual liberty conservatives espouse with regard to government and the market should apply as well to moral and social issues. They advocate minimal government interference in lifestyle choices and individual behavior that does not harm others, and resist efforts to "legislate morality." In this "libertarian" stance on moral and social issues and practices (though not in their general view of the role of government and the market) they stand in the tradition formulated by John Stuart Mill and Harriet Taylor in *On Liberty*.

UTILITARIANISM

A key figure in British radical liberalism was Jeremy Bentham (1748-1832), the founder of British **Utilitarianism.** Bentham was a very influential British philosopher with revolutionary ideas who wrote extensively on ethics and law. There gathered around him a circle of intellectuals and reformers that included James Mill (1773-1836), the father of John Stuart Mill and second only to Bentham in his importance for the early Utilitarian movement. The Bentham circle called themselves the "Philosophic Radicals." Among the things that set these radical liberals apart from other liberals was their belief that government must play an active role in insuring justice and alleviating human distress. This conviction arose from their philosophy, called Utilitarianism.

Deeply imbued with the Enlightenment's commitment to applying reason and science to all aspects of life, Utilitarianism was a moral and political theory based on what its adherents considered to be scientific observation of human nature and behavior. Humans, they believed, are motivated by their desires, above all by the desire for pleasure or happiness and avoidance of pain. Based on what they believed to be the psychological fact that for humans pleasure or happiness is the highest good (the chief thing desired), the Utilitarians reasoned that pleasure or happiness *ought* to be the highest good. The test of whether or not an action is right or wrong is whether it will tend to produce pleasure or pain.

The theory that humans are mainly motivated by the desire for pleasure or happiness is called **psychological hedonism**. Moral philosophies that say that humans *ought* to pursue happiness or pleasure as the highest moral good are forms of **ethical hedonism**.

From the principle that happiness or pleasure not only is but ought to be the highest human good, Bentham developed the famous **principle of utility:** "that principle which approves or disapproves of every action whatsoever, according to the tendency which it appears to have to augment or diminish the happiness of the party whose interest is in question."[1] The "party whose interest is in question" may

be an individual or a group; in the latter case it may be an entire society. Each person desires to maximize his or her own happiness, and the happiness of a community of people is simply the aggregate or the sum of the happiness of the individuals who comprise it. Thus the highest good in its universal expression is **the greatest happiness of the greatest number of persons.** This principle provides the goal of Utilitarian efforts in the social and political arena. The Utilitarians tried to figure out what human behaviors and legislative actions are the most *useful*, the most effective, in reducing human unhappiness and contributing to the widest possible general happiness. Utility, from the Latin word *utilis* meaning "useful," is simply another term for usefulness.

Bentham believed that the differences among pleasures were purely *quantitative* and could even be measured. He developed what he called the *hedonic calculus*, a scheme for calculating the likely effects in pleasures or pains of a particular moral or social decision. As an adult, in his classic defense of the principle of utility entitled *Utilitarianism* (1861), John Stuart Mill departed from Bentham by arguing that there are clearly *qualitative* and not merely quantitative differences among pleasures: "It is quite compatible with the principle of utility to recognise the fact, that some kinds of pleasure are more desirable and valuable than others."[2] In this connection he famously remarked that it is "better to be Socrates dissatisfied than a fool satisfied."[3] The lasting pleasures of the mind or spirit, exemplified by Socrates, are qualitatively superior to the transient, mindless pursuit of physical pleasure. Even Socrates' dissatisfaction (which was an inevitable aspect of his enduring devotion to reasoned, critical discussion) is preferable in the scale of values to the blind, fleeting pleasures of the fool.

As a political and legal theory, Utilitarianism involved careful, objective analysis of social issues, and the search for solutions based on the principle of utility. Trying to be truly scientific, Bentham and his followers rejected any appeal to divine will, to tradition, or even to the idea of natural rights, as unscientific. The Utilitarians were thoroughly secular, not only rejecting organized Christianity and its beliefs but regarding religion as generally harmful in its effects on people's lives. They believed that society could and should be reformed solely in accordance

Portrait of John Stuart Mill. Courtesy of the Library of Congress.

with people's observed nature, needs, and desires. This gave them what they considered an entirely rational basis for political, legal, and social reform.

John Stuart Mill (1806–1873), the most influential British philosopher of the nineteenth century, was at the center of the rise of radical liberalism. The chief inheritor of the ideas of the entire Utilitarian circle of thinkers (including Jeremy Bentham and James Mill), Mill transformed the concept of Utilitarianism. *On Liberty*, which Mill co-authored with Harriet Taylor (a long-time companion whom he eventually married), is one of the most influential writings of the liberal tradition, and is frequently invoked in debates on the limits of individual freedom and human rights. If John Locke created the idea that men by nature have a decisive role to play in their political governance, John Stuart Mill and Harriet Taylor created the idea that men, and women, have a determinative role to play in their personal governance.

Mill was the product of an extraordinary education. His father took complete charge of young John's instruction, working out a program of study founded on Utilitarian psychological principles. John

never attended school or university, but received from his father a classical education virtually complete by age twelve, when the precocious young scholar had the equivalent of a university degree in classics. Mill was reading Greek at age three and had read six of Plato's dialogues before his eighth birthday in 1814, which he celebrated by beginning the study of Latin. From Greek and Latin, Mill moved on to logic, mathematics, and political economy (combining what we now call political science and economics). Not just a prodigious learner but a teacher as well, while still in his teens John tutored his younger siblings some three hours each day.

James Mill excluded religious instruction from the education of his young genius. He did so because as a doctrinaire Utilitarian he believed religion fostered irrationality and immorality. John would become a stern critic of many Christian beliefs and practices throughout his writings, including *On Liberty*; but like many of his skeptical contemporaries, he deeply admired Jesus as a moral teacher at the same time that he rejected the supernatural events surrounding Jesus' ministry. In 1823, at age 16, Mill organized a debating society to serve as a forum for discussion of Utilitarian ideas. By his twentieth birthday Mill had published more than fifty articles and reviews in various journals, and was deeply involved in political and social reform. At about this same time, Mill joined the British East India Company as a mere clerk; he eventually rose to the station of Head Examiner of India Correspondence. This lifetime of administrative work provided the security he needed to carry on his study, writing, and reforming activities.

A crisis and recovery. But Mill's efforts of intellect and reform came at a personal cost. In 1826, the emerging twenty-year old philosopher found himself deeply depressed, the result he believed of an upbringing that had emphasized intellectual development at the expense of both emotional and aesthetic experience. After nearly six months of deep gloom and virtual mental paralysis, Mill began to recover, in part through his reading of an eighteenth-century French writer, Jean-François Marmontel, whose memoirs, Mill later said, released his feelings and led him "to adopt a theory of life, very unlike that on which [he] had before acted:

> I never, indeed, wavered in the conviction that happiness is the test of

all rules of conduct, and the end of life. But I now thought that this end was only to be attained by not making it the direct end. Those only are happy ... who have their minds fixed on some object other than their own happiness; on the happiness of others, on the improvement of mankind, even on some art or pursuit, followed not as a means, but as itself an ideal end .... This theory now became the basis of my philosophy of life. [4]

Mill's insight—that one does not achieve happiness by aiming for happiness—is another example of his departure from the central Utilitarian assumption that humans act mainly out of self-interest, pursue happiness, and seek to avoid pain. Though Mill always affirmed the principle of utility as the chief *criterion* for evaluating moral and social behavior and the goal of human life, he now developed a radically different psychology of human *motivation* that led him to reinterpret, some would say to reject, Utilitarianism in favor of a broader humanism.

A related result of Mill's recovery from deep mental distress was the realization that the full development of the inner life of the individual is just as important to human well-being as the improvement of society. This growing insight was to be of fundamental importance to his entire conception of individual freedom in *On Liberty*, some two decades later. Furthermore, he was coming to understand that individual development could not be one-sidedly intellectual, as his own had been; individual growth had to involve the nurturing of all sides of the person in a balanced and harmonious way. In particular, he wrote, "cultivation of the feelings became one of the cardinal points in my ethical and philosophical creed." [5]

Mill's reading of Marmontel led to further literary study, now among the British Romantic poets and essayists, particularly William Wordsworth and Thomas Carlyle, both near-contemporaries. In Wordsworth he found a lover of the beauties of nature—trees, flowers, mountains, rivers and streams. But he found something more as well, something like a religious feeling free of religious dogma:

Portrait of Harriet Taylor Mill. Courtesy of the National Portrait Gallery, London.

What made Wordsworth's poems a medicine for my state of mind, was that they expressed, not mere outward beauty, but states of feeling, and of thought coloured by feeling. ... In them I seemed to draw from a source of inward joy, of sympathetic and imaginative pleasure, which could be shared in by all human beings.... [6]

In Carlyle Mill found both a mentor and a friend, and this so in spite of their differing political views, the Scots Carlyle being deeply traditional and conservative in both his religion and his politics. It is a tribute to Mill's breadth of intellectual sympathy that he loved "the wonderful [poetic] power" of Carlyle's language at the same time that he disagreed with much that he found in Carlyle's philosophy. [7]

Mill's turn to literary art probably played a part in discovering the love of his life, Harriet Taylor, with whom he enjoyed a long and intimate friendship and whom he eventually married. They met in 1831 when he was twenty-five and single and she twenty-three and married with children. Harriet remained married until her husband's death in 1849. The friendship was conducted it seems with complete propriety, and Mill knew and admired her husband; but some persons in London circles regarded their long "courtship" as nothing less than scandalous. Harriet and John married in 1851, and Harriet's daughter, Helen Taylor, became both John's consolation and active co-worker after Harriet's sudden death in 1858.

GUIDE TO THE READING: *ON LIBERTY*

Harriet Taylor's influence on Mill certainly exceeded Wordsworth's and Carlyle's; it approached only that of James Mill, John's first teacher and mentor. By Mill's own account Harriet reshaped both his life and his thinking. His praise of her intellect and character in the *Autobiography* is so extravagant that some readers have thought him blinded by his devotion to her and have discounted her influence on his thought. More recently, however, scholars examining the matter from a feminist historical perspective have argued that we can take Mill at his word, particularly in the case of *On Liberty*, which Mill said "belongs to her as much as to me." Harriet Taylor died when they were finishing with its writing, and Mill published it a year after her death as a memorial to her, though—it must be noted—without her name on the title page.[8]

Mill and Taylor characterized their treatise on individual liberty as "a kind of philosophic text-book of a single truth, which the changes progressively taking place in modern society tend to bring out into ever stronger relief: the importance, to man and society, of a large variety in types of character, and of giving full freedom to human nature to expand itself in innumerable and conflicting directions."[9] Such expansion of human potential, they argued, can be achieved only by enlarging and protecting individual liberty of opinion and action: "The only purpose for which power can be rightfully exercised over any member of a civilized community, against his will, is to prevent harm to others. His own good, either physical or moral, is not a sufficient warrant."[10]

Mill and Taylor divided their argument in the book into a) **liberty of thought and speech**, and b) **liberty of action**, which included developing one's own potentialities in one's own way and freely associating with other individuals for various purposes. "Of the Liberty of Thought and Discussion" is the longest chapter of the book. In it Taylor and Mill develop four arguments for complete freedom of expression: 1) All human beliefs, however true we may believe them to be, are fallible, and by suppressing some ideas we may be suppressing what turns out to be true. 2) Even if we are almost certain that some beliefs are false, they may contain some truth (and the most widely held beliefs usually contain some error), and it is only in the free conflict of beliefs that we can correct errors all around. 3) Even if we are sure that certain beliefs are true, unless they are repeatedly challenged and tested we will come to accept them simply as dogmas or prejudices and not know their rational basis. 4) If widely-held beliefs simply become dogmas to which we give formal assent, they will cease to be meaningful in our lives as individuals or societies.

Taylor and Mill acknowledged the influence of the French political thinker Alexis de Tocqueville on the ideas of *On Liberty*. In *Democracy in America*, based on his travels in America in the 1830s, de Tocqueville was taken by the young republic's enthusiastic commitment to democracy—not just to the democratic process of representation and legislation, but more fundamentally to the principle of equality. De Tocqueville believed democracy was the political order of the future, and saw in the United States democracy's chief harbinger. However, the perceptive Frenchman observed something else: a distinct *tension* between democracy as a principle of political equality, and democracy as a principle of individual liberty enshrined in Jefferson's Declaration of Independence and the Bill of Rights. Democracy as equality, he argued, is ever in danger of enforcing abject conformity, mediocrity, leveling out everyone, reducing all to the lowest common denominator, suppressing dissent in thought and act. On the other hand, individual liberty requires respect for individual differences of ability, of opinion, and lifestyle, and willingness to allow these differences to flourish.

De Tocqueville spoke memorably of the "tyranny of the majority," a phrase Mill would used in *On Liberty* to describe a new form of tyranny made possible by the emergence of democracy since 1775: the imposition on all by force of public opinion, and even by force of law, of the view and values of the majority. But what if the majority was wrong, unjust, or vulgar in its views? What made de Tocqueville's view so penetrating was its exposure of the tyranny of the majority as both a tyranny of ideas and beliefs and a tyranny of laws and institutions created at the behest of the majority. In words that might or might not astonish us today, de Tocqueville wrote of 1830s America: "I know of no country in which there is so little independence of mind and real freedom of discussion as in America . . . freedom of opinion does not exist in America."[11] In the enthusiasm for democratic equality in the U.S. of the Jacksonian Era, de Tocqueville saw a disturbing tendency toward conformity and a willingness to silence dissent and individuality. These observations—coupled no doubt with Mill's and Taylor's very recent experience of public disapproval of their unconventional liaison—informed their insistence in *On Liberty* on the role of individual freedom of opinion and behavior in achieving both individual and public well-being.

Mill's and Taylor's argument for the broadest possible interpretation of individual liberty was rooted in Mill's enlarged, humanized version of the principle of utility. In *On Liberty*, as in *Utilitarianism*, two years later, he defined happiness as the individual well-being that results from the fullest development of each person's unique possibilities, the fullest pursuit of his or her interests and abilities. In this view, Mill is closer to Aristotle's holistic idea of what constitutes human happiness than he is to Bentham's calculations of pleasures and pains. In *On Liberty*, Mill and Taylor argue that maximum individual freedom is necessary to individual happiness in the most complete sense, and that a society that permits its citizens the most varied scope for individual growth is the most stable form of society.

Mill and Taylor were particularly concerned about freedom of development and what we might call "lifestyle," as they reveal in the chapter titled "Of Individuality, as One of the Elements of Well-Being":

> It is not by wearing down into uniformity all that is individual in themselves, but by cultivating it and calling it forth, within the limits imposed by the rights and interests of others, that human beings become a noble and beautiful object of contemplation; . . . by the same process human life also becomes rich, diversified, and animating, furnishing more abundant aliment to high thoughts and elevating feelings, and strengthening the tie which binds every individual to the [human] race by making the race infinitely better worth belonging to. In proportion to the development of his individuality, each person becomes more valuable to himself, and is, therefore, capable of being more valuable to others.[12]

This individual and social ideal cannot be realized, Taylor and Mill argue, in a society whose laws and public opinion discriminate against minority groups and lifestyles and seek to enforce the beliefs of the majority. In American history the heavy-handed Puritan attempts to build a "godly society" in New England, the treatment by Euro-Americans of African- and Native-Americans throughout our history, discrimination by the Protestant majority first against Catholics and then against Jews since the early nineteenth century, the McCarthy anti-Communist purges of the 1950s, and in our time the regular attempts to suppress certain books and viewpoints in public schools, are just a few examples of the sorts of "majority tyranny" against which *On Liberty* inveighs.

Every democratic system wrestles again and again with the deep tension between individual rights on the one hand, and the commitment to equality of rights and opportunity on the other, between personal freedom and the public good. *On Liberty*'s argument has been very influential in the U. S. and Britain, but it has not gone unchallenged. Continuing an argument that begins in the 1790s, with Edmund Burke's opposition to the French Revolution, there are those who argue that what Mill and Taylor call a "very simple principle" of maximum personal liberty is just that—too abstractly simple a response to a complex question, ignoring or underestimating many genuine difficulties connected with day-to-day social and political life.[13] Others believe that *On Liberty* still speaks persuasively, and remains timely in its protest against discrimination, censorship, conformity, and suppression.

Given Mill's powerful commitment to personal liberty in the face of disapproving public opinion, it is no surprise that among leading British Victorian thinkers, female and male, he was one of the most outspoken feminists: an active advocate for full rights and equality for women from his teenage years. His friendship and marriage to Harriet Taylor, involving as he said the co-authoring of *On Liberty*, deepened his commitment to equal rights for women. Harriet Taylor was herself an active feminist, and the primary author of the article "Enfranchisement of Women" that appeared anonymously in 1851 in *The Westminster Review*. Many contemporary readers thought the article was by Mill. Some ten years later, shortly after the death of Harriet Taylor, Mill drafted a book he titled *The Subjection of Women*. He published it in 1869 as a tribute to Taylor and her influence on his thought. In it, Mill—like Mary Wollstonecraft in the 1790s, Thomas Hardy in the 1890s, and Virginia Woolf in the 1920s—argues that marriage as understood and defined in British law was servitude if not slavery for women.[14] In the 1860s this was indeed the case, for in Britain, the Continent, and the U. S. marriage was "civil death" for women. Wives had no existence in civil law; they were represented entirely by their husbands, who possessed sole legal right to their wives' body, property, earnings, and children. Women could not vote and were effectively barred from careers in business and the professions. Mill argued, on sound utilitarian grounds and out of the depth of his experience with the brilliant Harriet Taylor, that the subjection of more than half the population was an enormous waste of intelligence and talent, and that women would be happier if free to develop their individual promise to the uttermost. He applied to women as well as to men the same arguments Taylor and he had advanced for maximum personal liberty in *On Liberty*. Like Wollstonecraft in the 1790s, like Hardy in the 1890s, and like Woolf in the 1920s, Mill believed that women must be free to choose their personal futures with as much freedom as men and with full rights as citizens; and that in order to do so they must have access to the best education available.

In 1865, Mill was elected to the British House of Commons, where he served for three years. He represented the Radical Party and pressed for liberal reforms, including women's suffrage. In 1868, he retired to Avignon, France, where he and Harriet had spent some of their happiest days together, and where she was buried. He died in 1873.

QUESTIONS FOR STUDY AND REFLECTION

1. What were the effects on Mill's thought of the "mental crisis" he experienced as a young man? In what ways did Harriet Taylor influence him, and how did her influence relate to the literary influences he opened himself to after his mental crisis?
2. What are Mill's and Taylor's main arguments for individual liberty in *On Liberty*? Describe what they (and Alexis de Tocqueville) mean by the phrase "the tyranny of the majority." Is there such a tyranny to be found in the U. S. of the twenty-first century?
3. Summarize Mill's arguments for equal rights for women in *The Subjection of Women* as discussed above. Do you find his arguments sound?
4. How does Mill's Philosophy of Utility differ from Bentham's and James Mill's?
5. What is "classical liberalism" of the nineteenth century, and how does it differ from twenty-first century liberalism?

SUGGESTIONS FOR FURTHER READING

Bullock, Alan and Maurice Shocken, eds. *The Liberal Tradition from Fox to Keynes*. NY: NYU Pr., 1957.
Himmelfarb, Gertrude. *The Idea of Poverty: England in the Early Industrial Age*. NY: Knopf, 1983.
_____. *On Looking Into the Abyss: Untimely Thoughts on Culture and Society*. NY: Knopf, 1994.
MacCoby, Simon. *The English Radical Tradition, 1763-1914*. London: N. Kaye, 1952.
Mill, John Stuart. *Autobiography*. Ed. & Intro., J. M. Robson. London: Penguin, 1989.
_____. *Utilitarianism, On Liberty, Essay on Bentham; together with selected writings of Jeremy Bentham and John Austin*. Ed. & Intro., Mary Warnock. Cleveland: World Publ., 1962.
_____. and Harriet Taylor Mill. *Essays on Sex Equality*. Ed. & Intro., Alice S. Rossi. Chgo: U. Chgo. Pr., 1970.
de Ruggiero, Guido. *The History of European Liberalism*. Tr. R. G. Collingwood. Gloucester, MA: P. Smith, 1981.
Spadafora, David. *The Idea of Progress in 18th Century Britain*. New Haven: Yale UP, 1990.
de Tocqueville, Alexis. *Democracy in America*. Ed., R. D. Heffner. NY: NAL, 1956.

[1] Jeremy Bentham, *An Introduction to the Principles of Morals and Legislation*, chapter I–V, in John Stuart Mill, *Utilitarianism, On Liberty, Essay on Bentham*, edited and with an introduction by Mary Warnock. Cleveland: the World Publishing Company, 1962. 33.

[2] John Stuart Mill, *Utilitarianism*, ibid., 259.

[3] Ibid., 260

[4] *Autobiography*. J.M. Robson, ed. London: Penguin, 1989, 44.

[5] Ibid., 118.

[6] Ibid., 121.

[7] Ibid., 138–39.

[8] That Mill in 1859 did not provide Taylor's name as co-author is probably best understood as a concession to lingering public disapproval of their relationship over the previous decade, as well as to contemporary skepticism toward women's involvement in serious intellectual work. It must be remembered that Taylor and Mill published *On Liberty* in 1859, the same year in which Mary Ann Evans published the novel *Adam Bede* under the male pseudonym George Eliot. Evans chose this course because she understood British distaste for "serious" fiction by women.

[9] *Autobiography*, 189.

[10] *On Liberty*. E. Rapaport, ed. Indianapolis: Hackett, 1978), 9.

[11] *Democracy in America*. R. D. Heffner, ed. NY: NAL, 1956, 117, 119.

[12] *On Liberty*. 60.

[13] See e.g., Gertrude Himmelfarb, "Liberty: 'One Very Simple Principle'," in *On Looking Into the Abyss: Untimely Thoughts on Culture and Society*. NY: Knopf, 1994, 74–106.

[14] In this regard, see Wollstonecraft, *A Vindication of the Rights of Woman* (1792).

LIFE OF MARY SHELLEY

1789 French Revolution begins.

1791 Luigi Galvani postulates the existence of "animal electricity."

1792 Mary Wollstonecraft's *A Vindication of the Rights of Woman* is published.

1793 England declares war on France; war continues until 1815. William Godwin's *An Enquiry Concerning Political Justice* is published.

1794 Fanny Imlay, illegitimate child of Mary Wollstonecraft and the American Industrialist Gilbert Imlay, is born 25 August.

1797 Marriage of William Godwin and Mary Wollstonecraft, 29 March. Mary Wollstonecraft Godwin born 30 August; Mary Wollstonecraft dies 10 September from puerperal infection resulting from improper post delivery medical treatment. Godwin adopts Fanny Imlay.

1800 Alessandro Volta develops the first electric battery.

1801 Godwin marries Mary Jane Clairmont, a widowed mother of two, Charles and Jane (later known as Claire).

1806 Mary hears Coleridge recite "The Rime of the Ancient Mariner," a work that will considerably influence *Frankenstein*.

1812 Mary meets Percy Bysshe Shelley and his wife Harriet at Godwin's house.

1814 Mary meets Shelley again in London and elopes with him to France and Switzerland, accompanied by Claire Clairmont. They return to London later this year.

1815 On 22 February, Mary gives birth to a premature baby girl, Clara, who dies 6 March. Napoleon is defeated at Waterloo.

1816 A son, William, is born to Mary and Percy Shelley on 29 January. Percy, Mary, William, and Claire join Lord Byron and his physician, John William Polidori, in Switzerland in May. The group spends several days and nights together in the Villa Diodati at Coligny. *Frankenstein* begun. Fanny Imlay kills herself. Harriet Shelley drowns herself. Mary and Percy marry in London on 30 December.

1817 The Shelleys move to Marlow. Mary makes corrections on and transcribes the manuscript of *Frankenstein* during April and apparently completes it in May. After being rejected by two publishers, *Frankenstein* is accepted in August. The Shelley's third child, named Clara after their first daughter, is born 2 September. Mary's *History of a Six Weeks' Tour*, based on her travels with Shelley, is published in December.

1818 *Frankenstein; or The Modern Prometheus* is published anonymously in March. One-year-old Clara dies in Venice in September.

1819 Three-year-old William dies of malaria in Rome on 7 June. Percy and Mary's only child to survive to adulthood, Percy Florence, is born on 12 November in Florence.

1822 Mary suffers a miscarriage, which almost costs her her life, on 16 June. Percy Shelley drowns in a shipwreck on 8 July.

1823 Mary and Percy Florence return to England in August. The first dramatic adaptations of *Frankenstein* are performed in London, and the second edition of the novel is published during July and August. Mary publishes *Valperga*.

1826 *The Last Man* is published in February.

1830 *Perkin Warbeck* published.

1831 A revised edition of *Frankenstein* is published. It remains the most commonly read version of the novel.

1835 *Lodore* published.

1836 William Godwin dies on 7 April.

1837 *Falkner* published.

1844 *Rambles in Germany and Italy*, inspired by trips with Percy Florence, is published.

1851 On 1 February, Mary Shelley dies from a brain tumor.

CHAPTER SIX

MARY SHELLEY'S *FRANKENSTEIN*: CULTURAL CONSCIOUSNESS AND LITERARY CRITIQUE

INTRODUCTION

Mary Shelley's *Frankenstein* (1818) is a story that most people "know" without having actually read the novel. As William St. Clair explains, "Frankenstein and his monster continue to live largely independently of books."[1] Those who have not cracked the binding of this almost two-hundred-year-old text have most likely encountered the creature and his creator in its creative transformations into films, television shows, cartoons, Halloween costumes—even General Mills' Franken Berry cereal. Though it seems odd to work backwards from the breakfast table to find the origins of this literary and pop culture phenomenon, tracking the genesis of Frankenstein leads back to a young woman challenged to write a ghost story. In her 1831 "Author's Introduction" to the novel, Mary Shelley claims that she wanted to create a story to "make the reader dread to look around, to curdle the blood, and quicken the beatings of the heart."[2] Critics Ellen Moers and Judith Spector claim that what Mary Shelley created in Frankenstein was the first Science Fiction novel. While the novel may bridge Gothic/Romantic and Science Fiction genres, one thing about *Frankenstein* is certain: it is the most enduring novel ever written by a teenager.

BACKGROUND TO A CLASSIC

Mary Shelley's *Frankenstein* is an influential expression of the **Romantic movement** that flourished at the end of the eighteenth and during the first half of the nineteenth centuries throughout Europe in the visual arts, music, literature, philosophy, theology, and political thought. A "founding father" of the Romantic movement was Jean-Jacques Rousseau (1712–78), who through his writings on politics and education became one of the most influential thinkers of modern Europe. Among the well-known figures of Romanticism are the writers Johann Wolfgang von Goethe, Germaine de Staël, and Ralph Waldo Emerson; the composers Ludwig von Beethoven, Franz Schubert, and Frédéric Chopin; and the painters J. M. W. Turner, Caspar David Friedrich, and Eugene Delacroix. Mary Shelley's world was of course the England of the great Romantic poets, including William Wordsworth, Samuel Taylor Coleridge, her husband Percy Shelley, their friend Lord Byron, and John Keats.

The Romantics carried forward the Enlightenment's celebration of individual freedom and commitment to remaking society, but critiqued and transformed these ideals. Above all the Romantics criticized the rationalism of the Enlightenment thinkers and activists—what they believed to be their overemphasis on reason and neglect of other vital aspects of human life. Because the Romantics sought to be more holistic about human life, they regarded feeling, intuition, and imagination as sources of knowledge that were just as important and valid as reason. This emphasis led the various Romantic artists and thinkers in many new directions.

Generally speaking, Romanticism rejected the restraints on and rules governing form and style in literature, art, and music that had dominated the Neo-Classicism of the Age of Reason. The Romantics sought to break free of these constraints and experiment with new forms. Wordsworth influentially expressed this new outlook in the Preface to his *Lyrical Ballads*,

Beethoven in forsaking elegance for passion and exploring new musical forms in works like the choral movement of his Ninth Symphony, and Turner in prefiguring the Impressionists with seascapes that were stunning studies of light and color.

The Romantic emphasis on individual freedom as passionate self-expression often exhibited in moral and social unconventionality has almost become a stereotype of Romanticism. We need look no further for real-life examples than Mary and Percy Shelley and their circle of friends, including the "scandalous" Lord Byron, and the stereotype found enduring expression in Puccini's opera *La Bohème*, with its "Bohemian" starving artists and "free love." But in the case of some of the Romantics the commitment to passionate individual self-expression and unconventionality manifested itself in thought and art that went hand-in-hand with a generally conventional and even respectable life, as in the cases of Wordsworth and Emerson.

Romantic novels, poems, and paintings portrayed idealized themes and characters. The poet Wordsworth idealized nature in poems such as "Tintern Abbey," and the French painter Géricault the nobility of human suffering and endurance in the face of tragedy in his *Medusa*. In *Frankenstein* Mary Shelley gives us two characters, Elizabeth and Clerval, who represent a certain Romantic ideal of what a woman and a man should be and can strike the modern reader as simply "too good to be true."

Wordsworth's idealization of the gentle English countryside, Mary Shelley's descriptions of the majestic and untamed beauties of the Alps, Henry David Thoreau's account of his time at Walden Pond, and the German painter Caspar David Friedrich's dramatic portrayal of a single human being confronting the vastness of nature in *The Wanderer above the Mists*—all are expressions of Romanticism's new attitude toward nature and the human place in nature. The Romantics emphasized nature, not like the Scientific Revolution as a great machine, but as an organic process, a totality of which humans are one expression and the foundation of human rootedness and renewal. There was a new interest in wild rather than cultivated nature, and a contrasting of the freedom bestowed by nature with the stifling conventions and artificialities of human society. Some of the Romantics used their art to decry the Industrial Revolution, which had begun in the mid-eighteenth

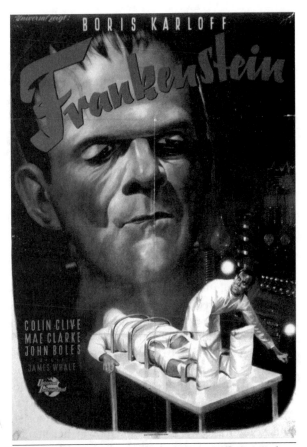

Bruno Rehak, Frankenstein movie poster. Reprinted, by permission of AKG London Ltd.

century and by the nineteenth had begun to sully the countryside with factories and smokestacks and cause people to crowd into the cities. There is no better example than the poet William Blake, who wrote of the "dark Satanic mills." Others, like Mary Shelley, raised serious questions about the steady march and growing dominance of science and its technological applications, and presciently anticipated the great moral dilemmas that would result for our time with our power to alter human nature itself.

Among some of the Romantics, protest against developments of the time in Europe expressed itself in a nostalgia for the past, above all the Middle Ages. Novels such as Sir Walter Scott's *Ivanhoe*, the paintings of the Pre-Raphaelite Brotherhood, and the Gothic revival in architecture express a longing for the Middle Ages as a time of Christian unity, elevated religious art and architecture, the chivalry of knighthood, close-knit human community, and pre-industrial rusticity.

Finally, some of the Romantics had a taste for the exotic, the bizarre, and the forbidden, which was an aspect of the emphasis on individual self-expression and the protest against conventionality. Coleridge's opium-induced poem "Kubla Khan," Delacroix's romanticized portrayals as a European of Moroccan Muslim culture (an ethnocentric attitude now called "Orientalism"), and the poet Baudelaire's dark explorations of the self in *Les Fleurs du Mal* (*Flowers of Evil*)—all reflect this side of Romanticism. And of course there is no more famous example of the Romantic interest in the strange and the forbidden than Mary Shelley's creation of Victor Frankenstein and his monster.

AUTHOR: MARY SHELLEY

In the 1831 introduction, Mary Shelley comments, "I shall thus give a general answer to the question so very frequently asked me—how I, then a young girl, came to think of and to dilate upon so very hideous an idea."[3] During the thirteen years between the novel's 1818 publication and 1831 revision, readers continually asked how her young mind produced such an intriguingly dark text. Yet, considering she was the only child of the feminist writer Mary Wollstonecraft and the political theorist, philosopher, and writer William Godwin, her literary inclination was destined by her lineage. The young Mary Wollstonecraft Godwin was the "fruit of the most famous radical literary marriage of eighteenth-century England," and knowing the weight of her genealogy, she understood the inevitable route to her life as a writer: "It is not singular that, as the daughter of two persons of distinguished literary celebrity, I should very early in life have thought of writing."[4]

Her famous parents afforded her access to a literary life, but it was a life without her mother. Just days after the birth of Mary Wollstonecraft Godwin, Mary Wollstonecraft died of puerperal infection, leaving behind Mary, her three-year-old daughter Fanny Imlay (Wollstonecraft's illegitimate child with the American businessman and gambler, Gilbert Imlay), and husband William Godwin, who was so despondent that he could write no more than the date and time of Wollstonecraft's passing in his journal.[5] With the death of Mary Wollstonecraft, the author of *A Vindication of the Rights of Woman* (1792), the late eighteenth century lost "the most ardent advocate of her times for the education and development of female capacities."

Mary Wollstonecraft Godwin lost her mother, but this did not keep her from knowing her mother through her mother's writing. She always kept her mother's work with her, reading and rereading her journals and political writings, most often while at her mother's grave in St. Pancras Churchyard.[6]

After her mother's death, Mary did, however, have her equally famous father (and his words) there to guide her. Godwin's *An Enquiry Concerning the Nature of Political Justice* (1793) critiqued marriage, organized religion, and centralized government and "earned this peace-loving and unrevolutionary man his reputation as the father of anarchism."[7] William Godwin, after Wollstonecraft's death, was left without his intellectual partner and left to care for his infant daughter Mary and the toddler, Fanny Imlay (whom he called Fanny Godwin). Neither of Godwin's daughters was formally educated; however, both had access to Godwin's "excellent library of English authors" as well as to their father's literary acquaintances.[8] Among her father's literary guests was Samuel Taylor Coleridge. Mary heard Coleridge recite "The Rime of the Ancient Mariner," and "the image of the tormented, isolated mariner would haunt her own fiction, even as Coleridge's verses reverberate through Frankenstein." Clearly, Mary Godwin's exposure to some of the literary giants of her day influenced her own creativity.

Her affection for her father also shaped her life. Without a mother, Mary was cared for by wet nurses and governesses, but "during her first four years, she became intensely attached to her father [. . .] whom she worshipped" possibly because of anxiety over the absence of a mother. Though he was rather distant from his daughter and did not provide her formal education, Godwin did give her a rich "intellectual experience," because he saw her as the "child most suited to carry on his work as a writer and thinker."[9]

Although he provided the stimulation his daughter needed to grow intellectually, he knew that this would not be enough to completely "mold" her properly, and within a year of Wollstonecraft's death in 1801, he took a new wife, Mary Jane Clairmont, a widow "with a six-year-old son Charles and a four-year-old daughter Jane." This new situation, while it provided a "family" for her, also created lifelong strife for Mary Godwin. Hating her stepmother as a rival for Godwin's affection, and constantly feeling pestered by her stepsister Jane, "Mary Godwin cast herself in the role of Cinderella, deprived by her wicked stepmother of both motherly love and fatherly understanding. And her fairy-tale has some basis in fact."[10]

In what can be called an "exile" (one strongly endorsed by Mrs. Godwin), Mary was sent away to spend part of her youth in Scotland at the home of one of Godwin's acquaintances, William Baxter. Some mark this as the beginning of William Godwin's "rejection" of Mary, and interestingly, the beginning of her imaginative life. In the 1831 "Introduction," Mary Shelley explains:

> I lived principally in the country as a girl and passed a considerable time in Scotland. I made occasional visits to the more picturesque parts, but my habitual residence was on the blank and dreary northern shores of the Tay, near Dundee. Blank and dreary on retrospection I call them; they were not so to me then. They were the aerie of freedom and the pleasant region where unheeded I could commune with the creatures of my fancy. I wrote then, but in a most common-place style. It was beneath the trees of the grounds belonging to our house, or on the bleak sides of the woodless mountains near, that my true compositions, the airy flights of my imagination, were born and fostered.[11]

If it was in this Scottish landscape that the "creatures" of her fancy were born out of her engagement with the natural environment, the Baxters gave Mary her first experience of a truly loving close-knit family; and her experiences in Scotland reinforced her idealized desire for a loving environment for herself. Upon returning to England in 1812 for a visit, she first encountered the man who would become her husband.

While Mary was in Scotland, Percy Bysshe Shelley, a twenty-one year old poet and political radical who had been expelled from Oxford for writing *The Necessity of Atheism*, had become a part of the Godwin household. Because of Godwin's revolutionary politics, Shelley was one of Godwin's most devoted disciples.[12] Mary Godwin was fifteen when she first met Shelley, who at this time in his life was

Portrait of Mary Shelley.

still content with his wife, Harriet. It was not until the spring of 1814 that Percy Shelley, now disenchanted with his ill-matched spouse, truly noticed Mary. Their mutual attraction was only strengthened by their shared admiration for Mary's parents' writings and politics, and Percy Shelley declared his love for Mary at Wollstonecraft's grave. However, when William Godwin discovered their romantic relationship, he forbade them to meet, seeing their situation as "criminal" since Percy was a married man with children. This condemnation contradicts Godwin's published views on marriage, and Percy and Mary used both Wollstonecraft's and Godwin's radical philosophies to legitimize their actions.[13] Godwin advocated "free sexual relations between consenting men and women" and had in his own life lived with Wollstonecraft before they were married.[14] Yet, his condemnation of Mary and Percy's relationship began a three-and-a-half year silence between Mary and her father. He refused to see or write to her while she was with Percy (though Godwin did rely on them financially), and Godwin broke his silence only after Mary and Percy were legally able to wed.

When Percy and Mary eloped in 1814, taking Mary's stepsister Jane Claire Clairmont with them, they embarked on the travels that helped Mary create her first notable publication, a travelogue titled *History of A Six Weeks Tour*. Looking to her mother's journals, Mary fashioned her text by similarly recording the sublime beauty of the natural scenery of France, Germany, Switzerland, Holland, and especially the landscape around Lake Geneva. This time was both turbulent and productive. It was productive in that Mary was writing and reading constantly, encouraged by Percy, but turbulent because Mary gave birth, two months prematurely, to a daughter, Clara, who died less than a month later. Her journals record her painful emotions at the loss of her first child: "Still think about my little baby—'tis hard, indeed, for a mother to lose a child [....] Dream that my little baby came to life again; that it had only been cold, and that we had rubbed it before the fire, and it lived. Awake and find no baby."[15] Mary soon became pregnant again and gave birth to a son, William, named for her distant father whom she still adored. Despite Godwin's continued silence, Mary was happy during this brief moment, as she had a healthy son. During this time, Claire aggressively sought the affections of the most popular writer of the day, Lord Byron, and Claire's connection to Byron led to one of the most important summers in literary history.

CREATION AND THE SUMMER OF 1816
Feeling confident in her relationship with Shelley and doting over a new son, Mary herself, intrigued by the famous Byron, agreed to accompany Percy and Claire to Geneva to help Claire in her pursuit of Byron. In the summer of 1816, Percy, Mary, Claire, Byron, and Byron's physician, Dr. John William Polidori, spent time together on the banks of Lake Geneva. Because of bad weather, much of their time was spent inside the Villa Diodati reading and discussing the most influential and intriguing topics of the day. Her 1831 "Author's Introduction" explains that the group had been reading ghost stories, and Byron proposed that they should each write one.[16] But this atmosphere was charged by more than ghost stories. As Mary Shelley explains:

> Many and long were the conversations between Lord Byron and Shelley to which I was a devout but nearly

silent listener. During one of these, various philosophical doctrines were discussed, and among others the nature of the principle of life, and whether there was any probability of its ever being discovered and communicated. They talked of the experiments of Dr. [Erasmus] Darwin [...] who preserved a piece of vermicelli in a glass case till by some extraordinary means it began to move with voluntary motion. Not thus, after all, life would be given. Perhaps a corpse would be reanimated; galvanism had given token of such things: perhaps the component parts of a creature might be manufactured, brought together, and endued with vital warmth. [17]

Mary, still haunted by the death of her first child (and her dream of bringing it back to life by rubbing it in front of the fire), had another haunting vision: a waking dream of a "pale student of unhallowed arts kneeling beside the thing he had put together." [18] In her dream she saw "the hideous phantasm of a man stretched out, and then, on the working of some powerful engine, show signs of life and stir with an uneasy, half-vital motion."[19] Influenced by her intelligent and engaging company, by a bit too much laudanum (opium distilled in alcohol), her own desire to understand these "principles of life," and her own anxieties and feelings of loss, the ghost story Mary created from Byron's prompt and from her own waking dream became the "most famous dream in literary history."[20] If this summer of 1816 was important to literary history, it is also one that has captivated contemporary movie audiences as well. No fewer than three contemporary major motion pictures have been made based on events at the Villa Diodati that summer by Lake Geneva, and each film strives to recreate the intellectually and erotically charged atmosphere that these writers created (Ken Russell's 1987 *Gothic* is a standout among the other film versions: 1988's *Haunted Summer* and *Rowing With The Wind*). That these films exist indicates that much like those nineteenth century readers who asked the young author how she thought of such a story, contemporary filmmakers seek answers about the environment that, and the woman who, created this myth, this Frankenstein.

The summer of 1816 guided Mary Godwin to create the novel that would make her one of the most notable writers of the last two centuries, but the rest of 1816 was marked with the suicides of Mary's half-sister, Fanny Imlay Godwin, and Harriet Shelley, Percy's legal wife and mother of two of his children. Harriet's death allowed Mary and Percy to wed legally on 30 December 1816, and Mary ended this tumultuous year with a new name and a strained reconciliation with her father, who witnessed the wedding.

The next few years proved equally tumultuous. Mary Shelley gave birth to another daughter in 1817 who died a year later, and in the summer of 1819, their three-year-old son, William, died of malaria. In November of the same year, a son, Percy Florence, was born and was their only child to survive into adulthood. Mary Shelley's companion at Lake Geneva in 1816, Dr. John William Polidori, inexplicably committed suicide in 1821. In 1822, Mary suffered a miscarriage and almost bled to death. If the last few years had not been difficult enough, in July of 1822, Percy drowned at sea. At twenty-four, the widowed and motherless Mary Shelley had lost several of those close to her to suicide, seen three of her children die, and almost died herself from a miscarriage. Yet, during this turbulent time, this troubled young wife produced a novel that has never gone out of print, and a story that is inextricably a part of our own cultural consciousness.

CRITICAL APPROACHES TO THE NOVEL

In 1818, the anonymously published *Frankenstein* received mixed critical reviews, but was enthusiastically received by the general public. But, while the public interest flourished over the next few decades, the critical reception of the novel continued to be mixed or negative well into the twentieth century. Were it not for two critics, M.A. Goldberg and Harold Bloom, who took the text and its author seriously, critical analysis of this novel might have stagnated. Since Goldberg (in 1959) and Bloom (in 1964) developed pivotal critical perspectives on the novel, "Frankenstein has been recognized as the ingenious, complex creation of a young woman who registered and questioned myriad influences in her cultural milieu."[21] One does not need to look much farther than the full title of the novel to see that *Frankenstein, or The Modern Prometheus* is an intertextual palimpsest of influences, both literary and scientific. Her novel was informed by the culture in which she lived and by her own voracious reading, study, and observation. That she listened intently to Shelley's and Byron's discussions of Dr. Erasmus Darwin's experiments with galvanism and reanimation indicates Mary Shelley's immersion in a culture charged with new theories and science surrounding the principles and origins of life.

These scientific theories were coupled with Mary Shelley's own knowledge of mythology, especially of Aeschylus' *Prometheus Bound*. While there are numerous versions of the myth of Prometheus, two in particular inform the novel as much as the scientific discussions she witnessed and absorbed. In one version of the myth, the Titan Prometheus took clay from the plain of Boeotia and used it to mold man into shape, and thus gave life to humankind. In another version, the one retold in Aeschylus' dramatic interpretation, Prometheus defies Zeus by stealing and giving fire to mortals to raise them up from "beasts" into beings capable of building culture. Both versions of the myth reflect themes omnipresent in *Frankenstein*: Promethean overreaching (overstepping the established boundaries between gods and humans), creation of humans, and hubris (amplified egotism). Victor Frankenstein's voice, before he has successfully animated his creation, sounds particularly Promethean when he explains:

> Life and death appeared to me ideal bounds, which I should first break through, and pour a torrent of light into our dark world. A new species would bless me as its creator and source; many happy and excellent natures would owe their being to me. No father could claim the gratitude of his child so completely as I should deserve theirs.[22]

And, especially in the latter version of the myth, Prometheus does not go unpunished for his actions of "benevolence" toward mortals: Prometheus, chained to Mount Caucasus, has his liver eaten out daily by a bird of prey, only to have the liver grow back each day so the whole gruesome process can continue. The tortured, creative and destructive figure of Prometheus was a mascot for Romantic writers like Byron, Shelley, and Mary Shelley. Harold Bloom explains:

> No Romantic writer employed the Prometheus archetype without a full awareness of its equivocal potentialities. The Prometheus of the ancients had been for the most part a spiritually reprehensible figure, though frequently a sympathetic one, in terms of both his dramatic situation and in his close alliance with mankind against the gods. But his alliance had been ruinous for man in most versions of the myth, and the Titan's benevolence toward humanity was hardly sufficient recompense for the alienation of man from heaven that he had brought about.[23]

What Bloom continues to explore in his analysis of the Promethean overreacher Victor Frankenstein and his exiled and tortured creature is the true humanness of the wretched monster: "The greatest paradox and most astonishing achievement of Mary Shelley's novel is that the monster is more human than his creator."[24] Bloom's contentions lend themselves to an explanation of one of the most intriguing readings of the novel. Victor Frankenstein's creation is decried as "the wretch," "the monster," "the creature," "the demon," but he is never given a name. Yet, many tend to call the monster "Frankenstein." Bloom's description of the monster and Victor as two halves of one self may help explain this "confusion" over the misnaming of the nameless creature:

> Frankenstein and his monster are the solipsistic and generous halves of the one self. Frankenstein is the mind and emotions turned in upon themselves, and his creature is the mind and emotions turned imaginatively outward, seeking a greater humanization through a confrontation of other selves.[25]

In this sense, then, Victor and the monster can be seen as *doppelgängers* (literally "double goers"), and the frequent misnaming of the creature as Frankenstein may be understandable, as, in this critical perspective, he is an inextricable part of his creator.

Because Mary Shelley's life is so intriguing and inescapable, some psychoanalytic critics read the novel through the critical lens of the Oedipus complex and repressed desires and Mary Shelley's own psychological life. One critic has described *Frankenstein* as a text that essentially excludes women, but that ultimately is a "parable of motherhood."[26] Claiming that the novel is a representation of Mary Shelley's search for her dead mother, this critic notes the irony of a feminist's daughter writing this "parable of motherhood entirely in terms of men."[27] However, he also claims that *Frankenstein* is clearly a "woman's book," as "Mary Shelley is the animator and progenitor of her story; if it is a retelling of Prometheus, it does so by recasting the legend in terms of conception, pregnancy, and birth."[28] That Mary Shelley herself experienced the loss of a mother, the loss of children and infants, as well as rejection by her father, makes clear how biographical and psychological critics can use her life to inform their readings of the text she created. In a novel where almost every character is motherless or orphaned, Rubenstein's claim that "motherhood" is central in *Frankenstein* without significant female characters is compelling and supportable.

In the last three decades, feminist, scientific, and cultural critiques have dominated the criticism of *Frankenstein*. Since the *Frankenstein* films have imprinted an indelible image on the public mind, it is not surprising that those who read the novel for the first time are shocked by the relatively brief creation scene. First-time readers will probably expect to read of the bubbling chemicals, the looming dark castle, the flashing and crackling of electrified laboratory equipment, the hunchbacked assistant, Igor, cranking the creature up to the roof where a lightning bolt will bring him to life, and the mad scientist who screams in a frenzy, "It's Alive! It's Alive!" These readers will be startled to find that the entire creation occurs in a single paragraph, devoid of any real specifics regarding the actual method of animation. Chapter five of *Frankenstein* opens with just three sentences, and this opening paragraph is the only description of how Victor, a young college student alone in his "filthy workshop of creation" in an upstairs apartment, brings the creature to life. It is amazing how years of cinematic tinkering have exploded these few lines into some of the most striking and unforgettable images in film history.

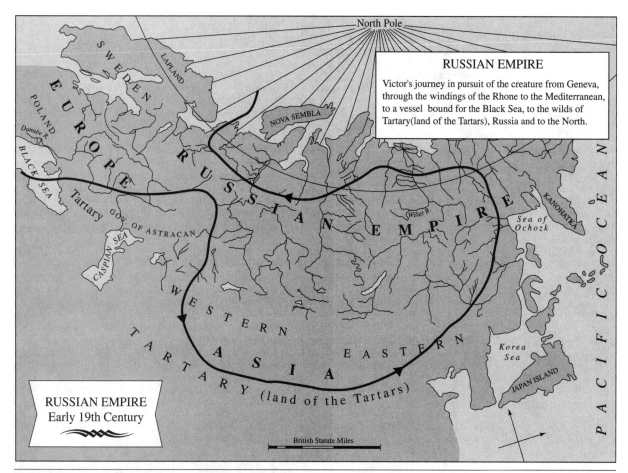

Russian Empire, Early 19th Century. Redrawn from *The Annotated Frankenstein,* by Mary Wollstonecraft Shelley, introduction and notes by Leonard Wolf (1977), Clarkson N. Potter.

Truly, Mary Shelley could not have detailed the creation scene much more than those few sentences, as this feat was obviously unknown. Having read such works as Humphry Davy's *Lectures on Chemistry* (1802) and his *Elements of Chemical Philosophy* (1812), she knew the current scientific experiments and theories of her day. Mary Shelley was aware of Luigi Galvani's 1791 publication on what he called "animal electricity" which came to be known as "galvanism" (a "natural" form of electricity—as opposed to "artificial" [i.e., static electricity]—activating "nerves and muscles when they were connected by a pile of copper and zinc plates").[29] Early in 1803, Professor Luigi Aldini put Galvani's theories to the test by performing galvanic experiments on animal and human corpses. Aldini was able to give the "appearance of re-animation" with these experiments, as witnesses saw jaws twitching, eyes open-

ing, fists clenching, but no true "life" was restored to the dead flesh. What Mary Shelley compiled in her novel was based mainly on conjecture, as neither Galvani nor Aldini truly restored or created life. It has been agreed that Mary Shelley "used a strong scientific basis for the novel and as such there is reason for calling it [. . .] the first novel of speculative fiction."[30]

Mary Shelley even employs a clever trick to keep Victor's design and animation of the creature a rightfully guarded secret. Victor, in telling his tale to Robert Walton, cleverly tells Walton that he will not reveal how he came to create the creature he now chases northward. Victor explains: "I see by your eagerness and the wonder and hope which your eyes express, my friend, that you expect to be informed of the secret with which I am acquainted; that cannot be."[31] Begging Walton to listen to his frightful tale, Victor hopes to "dash the cup" of the

The Creature and His Bride-to-Be, from James Whale's *Bride of Frankenstein* (1938) Reprinted by permission of Corbis Images.

"intoxicating draught" from Walton's lips so he may save another from the deadly quest for forbidden knowledge.[32]

Tampering with forbidden knowledge is one of the novel's most timely themes. Current culture continues, increasingly, to grapple with the moral aspects of issues like cloning, stem cell research, and genetic engineering, and *Frankenstein* reveals the intriguing, complicated, timeless, and potentially destructive power that such Faustian knowledge yields. Though science has progressed tremendously beyond nineteenth-century tenets, and medical and biological advancements have worked to improve human health and life, there are still those who balk when science comes too close to detailing and replicating secrets of the principles of life.

Mary Shelley's tale is as much about creation as it is about destruction. Guided by Professor M. Waldman's words, Victor fervently longs to "penetrate into the recesses of nature and show how she works in her hiding-places," but his route to these hiding places is dark and filthy and solitary.[33] His trips to the charnel houses, vaults, and slaughterhouses collected into the "horrors of [his] secret toil [. . .] among the unhallowed damps of the grave."[34] Simultaneously disgusted and driven by his task, Victor thinks his creation will be beautiful. While the films would have viewers believe that the mad scientist ecstatically welcomes the creature, the novel is far different. Mary Shelley's pale young student can hardly face his creation, let alone laud his animation with even a single "It's Alive!" In the novel, Victor's rejection of the creature is immediate and his judgment of the "beauty" he created leaves him sickened. Viewing his catastrophic wretch, Victor realizes only after he has bestowed life on this hideous monster that "the beauty of the dream vanished, and breathless horror and disgust filled [his] heart."[35] As the novel progresses, it is clear that creation without forethought, acceptance, and guidance leads to a spiral of destruction.

If the *Frankenstein* films give us the deranged scientist, then they also give us the stiff, monosyllabic, grunting monster devoid of the agility and mental capacity of the creature in the novel. That Mary Shelley's creature is eloquent and well-read directly contrasts with the image of Boris Karloff as the monster in director James Whale's 1931 film *Frankenstein*. Complete with green makeup (though the film was black and white), electrodes through his neck, lumbering gait, and stilted speech, Karloff's monster is the image most associated with the name "Frankenstein" even decades and dozens of films later. Again, those informed entirely by the cinema may be surprised to read Shelley's creature's well-spoken narrative as he confronts Victor, but the biggest surprise may come when the creature expresses his wish for a tranquil domestic life with a companion. Desiring a female "mate," the creature plaintively requests that Victor give him happiness, finally, by fulfilling his need for someone who will not reject him. The creature promises to "quit the neighbourhood of man," and live in the "vast wilds of South America," eating only berries and nuts (the creature is even a vegan). Oddly swayed by the creature's argument, Victor agrees to create a female, but this promise allows him the contemplative forethought he lacked in his first creative endeavor. Now fully aware of the horror of his project, Victor weighs the potential consequences of fulfilling his promise to create a female companion for the creature.[36]

If Boris Karloff solidified the cinematic image of the monster, then Elsa Lanchester, as the "bride" in director James Whale's 1935 *Bride of Frankenstein*, equally solidified the twitching and shrieking, electrified, black-and-white-Marge Simpson-haired mate for the monster. Though the cinema brought her lasting image to life, Mary Shelley never did. Based on Victor's newfound ability to reason with his "science" and fully consider the consequences of creat-

ing another being who could be even more "terrible," before animating the female creature he decides to tear her to pieces, refusing to be responsible for a creature who could, he darkly speculates, cause the destruction of the whole human race. That she could propagate "a race of devils" terrifies Victor, and, in an interesting biological possibility, removes him from the role of creator. He could have created both a male and a female of a new species, but the female creature's reproductive potential threatens his control, and he destroys her.

Combining scientific and feminist critique, one critic has claimed that Victor "substitutes solitary paternal propagation for sexual reproduction," and in so doing, "he engages in a concept of science that Mary Shelley deplores, the notion that science should manipulate and control rather than describe, understand, and revere nature."[37] Mary Shelley's own reverence for nature was informed by her literary knowledge: "A reader of Wordsworth, Mary Shelley understood nature in his terms, as a sacred all-creating mother, a living organism or ecological community with which human beings interact in mutual dependence."[38] In his manipulation of the living organism nature (not his revered understanding or mere observation), Victor not only engages dangerously in Promethean overreaching but also defies and usurps the female role when he seeks to control the powers of creation. Victor "has sought power over the female. He has 'pursued nature to her hiding places' in an attempt not only to penetrate nature and show how her hidden womb works but actually to steal or appropriate that womb."[39] But the danger in this pursuit is in labeling nature as female, since it inevitably leads to further attempts to control "her," as nature is the female Other whom the driven and manipulative scientist exploits to his own destructive ends.

Mary Shelley was one of the first to point out the risks of using gendered metaphors of the "aggressive, virile male scientist" who "captures and enslaves a fertile but passive nature," and she reinforces these dangers by not letting Victor go unpunished.[40] In the end, Victor is equally as desolate as his creature: he has lost his wife, his young brother, his good friend Clerval, and his parents, and he has seen Justine executed. Now, he has only himself and his intense, constant connection to the creature who weakens him in a dramatic, and eventually deadly, global chase. Mary Shelley leaves the reader with both Victor's

THE FAR SIDE   By GARY LARSON

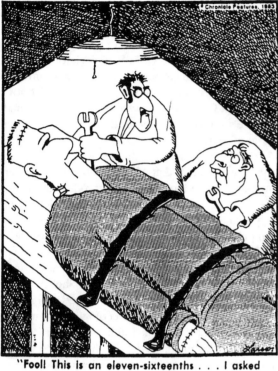

"Fool! This is an eleven-sixteenths . . . I asked for a five-eighths!"

Gary Larson, "Cartoon: "Fool!"" Courtesy of FarWorks, Inc.

and the creature's final "laments," as each seeks to justify his actions one last time. Victor perishes from exhaustion, and the creature plans to burn himself in order to destroy the evidence of his gigantic frame that could raise questions and further investigation if found by someone as curious and driven as Victor. The cycle of creation and destruction ends with the deaths of both the creator and his creation.

CREATIVE TRANSFORMATIONS AND CULTURAL CONSCIOUSNESS

If the creature burns himself up at the end of the novel, what rises from his ashes once the book is closed is an inescapable pop culture lineage of his image and character. Only five years after its publication, *Frankenstein* was already inspiring dramatic theatrical versions, and a film history began its long life with Charles Ogle's portrayal of the creature in the 1910 Edison Kinetogram. But Ogle could not have known that he would be the first "creature" in

a long line of pop culture images. From the transvestite Dr. Frank-N-Furter and his beefcake creation in the 1975 cult classic *The Rocky Horror Picture Show* to Mel Brooks' delightful crack-up *Young Frankenstein* (1975) to the downright absurd *Jesse James Meets Frankenstein's Daughter* (1966) and *Frankenhooker* (1990), the "Frankenstein" films have run the gamut from ridiculously funny to oddly perverse, but never quite accurate. Even this brief list suggests that the novel's creative transformations are limitless. Theatre and film aside, that there is a breakfast cereal named for the creature and that one can't go long without hearing some inadvertent reference to the novel and these characters, says much about how indelible these images and references are: to say that someone has "created a monster," or "created a Frankenstein," through compiling incongruous parts is a natural and idiomatic component of the English language. Almost every easy crossword puzzle contains the clue, "Frankenstein's helper." Four letters. Starts with "I" and ends in "R." Igor lives, indeed, but only outside the novel. And the doltish and stiff, green-faced monster has gleefully grunted "Trick or Treat" on late October doorsteps for years. The monster has hawked candy bars, guest-starred on *Scooby Doo*, garnered laughter on *Saturday Night Live*, and even made a brief cameo in a Universal Studios commercial (where he was, oddly, painting a vacationing woman's toenails) that aired during the 2002 Super Bowl—one of America's most expensive, coveted, and watched advertising times.

Could a nineteenth century teenager have known the influence and impact that her "ghost story" would have? Could she have known the way her characters would enter inextricably into cultural consciousness through pop culture appropriations? Could she have known that two centuries later readers would come to this novel with so much (mis)information about its characters without ever having read a single word? Probably not. Whether or not she succeeded in writing a story to "make the reader dread to look around, to curdle the blood, and quicken the beatings of the heart,"[41] Mary Shelley certainly succeeded in creating a monster we continue to pursue.

QUESTIONS FOR STUDY AND DISCUSSION
1. How might Mary Shelley's own biography inform a critical reading of Frankenstein? Are

there dangers or benefits in using biography to critique a novel?

2. Should Victor create a mate for the creature? Consider Victor's arguments for why he decides to destroy her, and consider the kind of life the creature imagines for himself and his mate. Is the creature's retaliation against Elizabeth "justified" in light of Victor's broken promise to the creature?

3. Is the novel relevant today? In what way(s)? Explain how this novel does or does not retain "meaning" for current audiences.

4. Consider the term *doppelgänger* and the characters of Victor and the creature. How are they "doubles" of each other? How are they different?

5. Considering the pop culture presence of the creature in films, commercials, cartoons, and toys, why has the image of the monster/creature lasted so long? Why is the story, or myth, of "Frankenstein" told and transformed and retold? Why have so many versions of the story strayed from the original novel?

6. Review the last chapter of the novel. Whose final "lament" is more persuasive? Is it easier to sympathize with Victor? With the creature?

SUGGESTIONS FOR FURTHER READING/VIEWING

Florescu, Radu. *In Search of Frankenstein: Exploring the Myths Behind Mary Shelley's Monster.* London: Robson, 1996.

Levine, George and U.C. Knoepflmacher, eds. *The Endurance of Frankenstein: Essays on Mary Shelley's Novel.* Berkeley: U of California P, 1979.

Mellor, Anne K. *Mary Shelley: Her Life, Her Fiction, Her Monsters.* New York: Routledge, 1988.

Seymour, Miranda. *Mary Shelley.* London: John Murray, 2000.

The True Story of Frankenstein. Narr. Roger Moore. Dir. Richard Brown. A&E Home Video. 1995.

---

[1] William St. Clair, "The Impact of *Frankenstein*," *Mary Shelley in Her Times*, ed. Betty T. Bennett and Stuart Curran (Baltimore: Johns Hopkins Pres, 2000) 54.

[2] Mary Shelley, *Frankenstein* (1831; New York: Signet, 1994) ix

[3] Ibid., viii.

[4] Anne K. Mellor, *Mary Shelley: Her Life, Her Fiction, Her Monsters* (New York: Routledge, 1988) 1; vii.

[5] Katherine C. Hill-Miller, *"My Hideous Progeny"; Mary Shelley, William Godwin, and the Father-Daughter Relationship* (Newark: U of Delaware Press, 1995) 20.

[6] Mellor, 1; 20.

[7] Miranda Seymour, *Mary Shelley* (London: John Murray, 2000, 6–7.

[8] Mellor, 11.

[9] Hill-Miller, 25.

[10] Mellor, 13.

[11] Shelley, viii.

[12] Hill-Miller, 36–37.

[13] Elisabeth Bronfen, "Rewriting the Family: Mary Shelley's 'Frankenstein' in its Biographical/Textual Context," *Frankenstein, Creation, and Monstrosity*, ed. Stephen Bann (London: Reaktion, 1994) 24.

[14] Hill-Miller, 39.

[15] Quoted in Mellor, 32.

[16] Shelley, ix.

[17] Ibid., 4

[18] Ibid., xi

[19] Ibid., 1

[20] Mellor, 37.

[21] Mary Lowes-Evans, *Frankenstein: Mary Shelley's Wedding Guest* (New York: Twayne, 1993) 16.

[22] Shelley, 52.

[23] Harold Bloom, afterword, *Frankenstein*, by Mary Shelley (1831), New York: Signet, 1994) 213–14.

[24] Ibid., 215.

[25] ibid.

[26] Marc A. Rubenstein, "'My Accursed Origin': The Search for the Mother in Frankenstein," *Studies in Romanticism* 15.2 (Spring 1976): 165.

[27] Ibid., 187.

[28] Ibid.

[29] Mellor, 104.

[30] Samuel Holmes Vasbinder, *Scientific Attitudes in Mary Shelley's Frankenstein* (Ann Arbor: UMI Research Press, 1984) 82.

[31] Shelley, 51.

[32] Ibid., 26.

[33] Ibid., 47.

[34] Ibid., 53.

[35] Ibid., 56.

[36] Ibid.,158.

[37] Mellor, 100.

[38] Ibid., 110.

[39] Ibid., 112.

[40] Ibid., 89.

[41] Ibid., ix.

LIFE OF CHARLES DARWIN

1809

Charles Darwin born to well-to-do family of a prominent physician on the same day as Abraham Lincoln; first substantial argument for evolution proposed by French biologist Jean Baptiste Lamarck

1820–33

Sir Charles Lyell, *Principles of Geology*

1831

Darwin graduates Christ's College, Cambridge, intent on career in the ministry; Darwin's Cambridge science teacher arranges for him to join H.M.S. *Beagle* for five-year voyage of exploration around the globe

1831–36

Voyage of the *Beagle*

1837

Voyage of the Beagle published

1838

Darwin reads T. R. Malthus, *Essay on the Principle of Population* (1798)

1844

Robert Chambers, *Vestiges of Creation*

1858

Darwin and Alfred Russel Wallace present joint papers on natural selection

1859

Origin of Species

1871

The Descent of Man

1882

Darwin's death

CHAPTER SEVEN

CHARLES DARWIN AND THE THEORY OF EVOLUTION

INTRODUCTION

Historians generally rank the English naturalist Charles Darwin (1809–1882) as one of the foremost thinkers in the history of science, a man who provoked a great revolution in biology with his *Origin of Species*. Many authors compare the Darwinian Revolution to the revolution produced in the physical sciences by Newton in his *Mathematical Principles of Natural Philosophy* (1687). Contrary to popular opinion, however, Darwin was not the first evolutionist, he did not invent the crucial mechanism of natural selection, nor was he the sole founder of evolutionary biology. Darwin and Darwinism nevertheless occupy a central position in modern thought.

PRE-DARWINIAN IDEAS OF EVOLUTION

Evolution refers to a process in which life first arises from non-life and basic forms then change through time into other forms. As far back as the sixth century B.C.E. some Indian philosophers, and shortly afterwards some of the early Greek philosophers, proposed evolution as a naturalistic alternative to the popular beliefs in supernatural creation, such as those found in the Hebrew Bible. But their brilliant speculations did not establish evolution on a factual, authoritative foundation. It was not until the eighteenth century in Europe that scientists slowly began to assemble bits of concrete evidence to flesh out earlier insightful guesses, although the term "speculative" still best characterized their works.

The first substantial argument for evolution was proposed by the French biologist Jean Baptiste Antoine de Monet, Chevalier de Lamarck (1744–1829), in the early nineteenth century. After a brilliant career as a botanist, during which he pub-lished a four-volume work on French flora, Lamarck turned at the age of forty-nine to invertebrate zoology, a field he established on its modern footing.

As late as 1797 Lamarck believed in the immutability or unchangeability of species, but by 1800 his views had diametrically changed, and by 1815 he had discussed his new ideas on evolution in *Philosophie Zoologique* (1809), where he stated that large changes in the environmental circumstances of animals bring about major changes in their actions. If their new needs become constant or especially long-lived, the animals then assume new *habits*, which lead to new parts and organs, all of which may be inherited after long habitual use. Over eons of time new life forms appear—they slowly evolve.

Lamarck thought life arose first from "infusoria" ("infinitely small animals with gelatinous, transparent, homogeneous and very contractile bodies") spontaneously, whenever conditions are "favorable." Once the lower forms appear, over long periods of time branching out occurs, leading toward greater and greater perfection of organisms. Humans are the end product of the entire process: "This predominant race, having acquired an absolute supremacy over all the rest, will ultimately establish a difference between itself and the most perfect animals, and indeed will leave them far behind."[1] The human lineage nevertheless is that of any animal.

Lamarck also impressed many non-evolutionists as well. When the pioneering English geologist Charles Lyell (1797–1875) discussed the issue of the existence and duration of species in his landmark textbook on geology, *Principles of Geology,* he singled out Lamarck's evolutionary arguments for refutation because they represented the best case available. Two fundamental keys to the subject of evolution were 1) the natural limits to species variation and 2) time. Lyell nevertheless concluded that God, the Author of nature would not allow species to vary beyond prescribed limits because they would perish. Besides, Lamarck had never actually seen a new organism formed. As a believer in a steady-state geological **uniformitarianism**—the view that natural laws operating today are the same ones which operated in the past—Lyell also thought the present was the key to the past: because he could not see unlimited variation (that is, evolution) at the present time, none could have occurred in the past. But Lyell also argued that vast time scales had been involved in earth's history, and that the laws of physics and chemistry had produced today's world.

The issue of time posed no serious impediments to acceptance of Lyell's argument regarding geological history. During the seventeenth and eighteenth centuries scientific thinkers had been expanding the geological time scale substantially. Georges Buffon, for example, discussed tens of thousands of years; Lamarck in 1802 assumed millions of years in earth's history. By the time Charles Lyell's *Principles of Geology* was published, Archbishop Ussher's mid-seventeenth century calculations, suggesting the earth had been created during the morning of October 23, 4004 B.C.E., were no longer universally accepted.

Once the time barrier was overcome many scientists began to suspect that adaptive species change over millions of years might be cumulative. Readers of Lyell, such as Robert Chambers (1802-1871), Herbert Spencer (1820-1903), Alfred Russel Wallace (1823-1913), and Charles Darwin, were impressed by his geological arguments proving the uniform operation of inorganic nature over millions of years, but they balked at Lyell's refusal to accept evolution of the organic world during those same eons of time. Much later, after Darwin's *Origin of Species* (1859) had appeared, Lyell himself cautiously and timidly lent support to the evolutionists.

Robert Chambers, in his anonymously published *Vestiges of Creation* (1844 et seq.), first pushed Lyell's uniformity arguments to the limit, focusing on astronomy, geology, plant, animal and even human evolution. The scientific public reacted very negatively to his suggestions, despite extensive experimental and observational evidence in *Vestiges*. Chambers even cited Charles Darwin's *Voyage of the Beagle* (1839) as one of many authorities to sup-

port his novel thesis. Unfortunately, although the argument was tight and cohesive, the evidence itself was uneven, and criticism was widespread and severe. The British biologist Thomas H. Huxley (1825-1895), later one of Darwin's main champions in Great Britain, savagely attacked the tenth and best edition of *Vestiges* in 1853. By contrast, the English poet, Alfred Lord Tennyson, was deeply influenced by Chambers and poetically alluded to *Vestiges* in his great poem *In Memoriam* (1850).[2]

Chambers described the developmental principles of *Vestiges* in this way: "*the simplest and most primitive type, under a law to which that of like production is subordinate, gave birth to the type next above it, this again produced the next higher, and so on to the very highest*, the stages of advance being in all cases very small—namely from one species only to another; so that the phenomenon has always been of a single and modest *character*."[3]

Why did progressive development occur? What was the mechanism? By 1853, in the tenth edition of *Vestiges*, Chambers hypothesized two "impulses" or natural tendencies of nature as causal mechanisms, under the "Providence" of God. Chambers otherwise relied heavily upon solid scientific arguments familiar to evolutionists today: species variation, geographical distribution of species, the geological record, embryology, vestigial organs, and natural affinities of organs. What he lacked were a high degree of scientific sophistication and judgment and scientifically acceptable examples. Chambers' tendency to tackle taboo subjects, such as the human place in nature, also met with a close-minded Victorian public.

Darwin had uncomplimentary words for *Vestiges*. He wrote to his botanist friend Joseph Dalton Hooker (1817-1911) that the anonymously published book was more of a "nine day wonder than a lasting work." Despite the admirable writing and arrangement, "his geology strikes me as bad, and his zoology far worse." But in the "Historical Sketch" to the *Origin of Species*, first appearing in 1861, Darwin remarked that the tenth edition of *Vestiges* had paved the way "for the reception of analogous views," and we must naturally assume he referred to his own or similar enlightened ideas.[4]

The co-discoverer (independently of Darwin) of natural selection, the English naturalist Alfred Russel Wallace, had been profoundly affected by Chambers' book. Wallace was a product of a growing skepticism and materialism in nineteenth-century England. Born into a relatively poor middle-class family, Wallace struggled to survive with a number of jobs, ranging from surveying to teaching school. Nothing completely satisfied his true interests: he yearned for faraway lands, exotic plants and animals, strange natives—the unknown mysteries of our planet. He was particularly mesmerized by the strong probability—to his agnostic mind—that species evolve in nature.

On December 28, 1845, Wallace wrote his friend Henry Walter Bates (1825–1892) that he thought the central thesis of *Vestiges*—progressive development—was sound; one needed only to gather more solid scientific evidence to test that hypothesis. In pursuit of that goal, Wallace proposed that he and Bates travel to the Amazon River basin for field work. To support themselves they collected specimens and sold them through an agent in England. Wallace returned home in 1852, but his ship unexpectedly sank in the Atlantic along with his collections, and he barely completed his voyage after a harrowing rescue at sea in a creaky old boat. After a short stay in England, he continued his quest in the Malay Archipelago/Indonesian region to discover why species evolve. There he brought to fruition his first public statements on evolution.

Wallace's essay "On the Law which Has Regulated the Introduction of New Species" (1855) focused on well-known published geological and geographical evidence. He concluded his essay: "*Every species has come into existence coincident in both space and time with a pre-existing closely allied species.*"[5] No real mechanism was proposed, but he had sketched out a cogent, cautious, purely scientific argument for evolution. Public acclaim for this revolutionary announcement, however, did not even register on the Richter scale. The private response was quite a different matter, for Charles Lyell, Edward Blyth (1810–1873), and Charles Darwin all read and were extremely impressed by Wallace's arguments.[6]

Wallace, unaware of the impact of his article on those key scientists, continued searching for a mechanism, a key to explaining *why* evolution occurred. The moment of enlightenment came several years later, during February 1858, on Gilolo (Halmahara) in the Moluccas Islands, when Wallace, in a feverish

Engraving from Bertarelli Collection, Charles Darwin. Courtesy of Art Resource.

state, was reflecting on human evolution. Suddenly, in a flash of delirious inspiration, he understood that the positive consequence of the struggle for existence, and the competition for the food supply, was that the best adapted, or fittest, species survived and propagated their kind. Natural selection improved the race; Lyell and others understood only the negative aspects of the process—negative selection or extinction. The creative side had escaped them. Wallace wrote up his ideas quickly upon arriving back at the island of Ternate, and sent his paper "On the Tendency of Varieties to Depart Indefinitely from the Original Type" to Charles Darwin in England on March 9, 1858. After receipt of Wallace's paper, joint publication of his paper and a selection of the discussion of natural selection from Darwin's "1844 Essay" were presented, under the sponsorship of Charles Lyell and Joseph Hooker, before the distinguished natural history organization, the Linnaean Society of London on July 1, 1858. The papers were published August 20, 1858 in the society's journal, before Wallace had a chance to approve or disapprove their decision to publish. Darwin now had a bonfire lighted under him to complete his work on species.

DARWIN'S LIFE AND THE DEVELOPMENT OF HIS IDEAS

Darwin was born of a distinguished family—his grandfather, Dr. Erasmus Darwin, was a renowned writer, physician and speculative evolutionist, and his father, Dr. Robert Darwin, enjoyed a very successful medical practice. Charles floundered in medical school at the University of Edinburgh, for he found the study of medicine distasteful. He then attended Cambridge University to provide him with a respectable career as a clergyman in the Church of England. At Cambridge Darwin befriended Professor John Stevens Henslow (1796-1861), professor of botany, who also knew "entomology, chemistry, mineralogy and geology," and Adam Sedgwick (1783-1873), who lectured on geology. They encouraged and helped develop Darwin's scientific interests. He graduated with his B.A. in January 1831, without honors and tenth in his class. He later described his formal schooling as "wasted" time.

Professor Henslow secured for Darwin a post as unpaid naturalist on the H. M. S. *Beagle*. The task with which the captain and crew were charged was to (a) take chronometric readings around the world, (b) survey the South American coastline (Patagonia, Tierra del Fuego, Chile, and Peru), (c) ascertain angles on all important geographical points, and (d) prepare geological maps. That trip from December 27, 1831 to October 2, 1836, most particularly a visit to the Galapagos Islands, transformed Darwin's life. He later wrote, "The voyage of the *Beagle* has been by far the most important event in my life and has determined my whole career."[7] By the end of the voyage he was committed to his long career in science. He gave up the idea of the ministry and later described himself in the post-*Beagle* period as a human machine for slowly grinding theories from vast stores of scientific facts.

It was the *Beagle* voyage that furnished Darwin with an educational experience that transformed his scarcely recognized potential into a keen, observant, thoughtful naturalist. Early letters sent to John Henslow at Cambridge about the *Beagle* expedition established Darwin as a scientist to be reckoned with even before his return. His reputation grew even more rapidly after his return as major works

flew from his pen. In the period between 1837 and 1845 Darwin published his *Journal of Researches into the Natural History and Geology of the Countries Visited During the Voyage of H.M.S. Beagle* (1839, 2nd ed. 1845), an account of the famous *Beagle* voyage; a pioneering book on the formation of coral reefs, *The Structure and Distribution of Coral Reefs* (1842); four definitive volumes on living and fossil barnacles; and various books on the natural history discoveries during the *Beagle* voyage, including contributions to *The Zoology of the Voyage of the H.M.S. Beagle* (3 vols., 1838-1843) and the book *Geological Observations on South America* (1846).

Upon completing his book *The Voyage of H.M.S. Beagle* in 1837, Darwin began in a series of notebooks to review the species question in light of the hypothesis of evolution. He had first read the second volume of Lyell's *Principles* (1832) during the voyage, with its forceful discussion and rejection of evolution, and this provided the view against which to test the hypothesis. These notebooks, beginning in July 1837, opened with excerpts from his grandfather Erasmus Darwin's *Zoonomia*, a speculative work on evolution that he had already read and no doubt heard discussed at home.

Darwin soon realized that if plants and animals can evolve, humanity probably does too. *Homo sapiens* may indeed be the summit of a natural process not requiring creative effort by a deity after all. But what mechanism, other than God, could drive this process? Late in September 1838 Darwin happened to read the Reverend Thomas R. Malthus' *Essay on the Principle of Population* (1798). Emphasizing the human condition, Malthus had argued that the human population when unchecked tends to increase geometrically (i.e., exponentially), while the food supply needed for survival increases only arithmetically.

From Malthus' observations Darwin (and Wallace) extrapolated these ideas to the entire animal kingdom; the entire process became crystal clear. Populations, animal and human, tend to increase geometrically; food supplies increase arithmetically; and thus populations tend to outstrip food supply. Consequently, there is a **struggle for existence**, resulting in the best adapted species surviving and propagating their race. The process is one of **natural selection**.

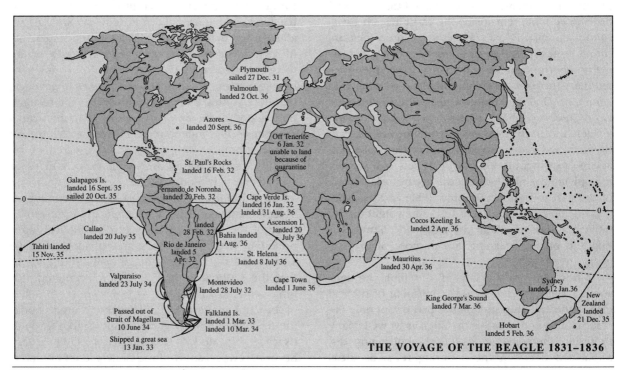

Voyage of the *Beagle* 1831–1836. Redrawn from *Darwin: A Norton Critical Edition,* Second Edition, edited by Philip Appleman, (1979), W.W. Norton & Company.

This long path led inevitably back to the origin of species, on which Darwin again began to focus full time. In late November 1859, 1,250 copies of Darwin's *On the Origin of Species by Means of Natural Selection* finally saw the light of day. A new era began in humankind's view of the origins and development of nature and of the human race.

The Voyage of the Beagle alone would have elevated Darwin to the top ranks of English naturalists, and the title page of the *Origin* displayed his credentials: "By Charles Darwin, M.A., Fellow of the Royal Geological, Linnaean, Etc. Societies; Author of 'Journal of Researches During H.M.S. Beagle's Voyage Round the World.'" The fact of Darwin's distinguished lineage and his own reputation as a naturalist were vital components of his success.

THEOLOGICAL RESPONSES TO DARWINISM IN THE NINETEENTH CENTURY

In 1896 Andrew Dickson White published a two-volume work entitled *A History of the Warfare Between Science and Theology.* Over a hundred years later it still seems to be a common assumption that the relationship between science and religion is a "warfare" or "conflict," that it is a matter of science *versus* religion. This is a vast oversimplification of a much more complex and subtle relationship, and a serious distortion of the modern history of science and of religion. The great "paradigm shifts" in the history of science—notably the Copernican theory that put the sun rather than the earth at the center of the solar system and Darwin's theory of evolution through natural selection—have always divided *both* the scientific *and* the religious communities. In response to both Copernicanism and Darwinism there were scientists who opposed and resisted the new ideas and theologians who accepted and affirmed them. In this section we will examine the range of nineteenth-century theological reactions to Darwin.

When Darwin published *The Origin of Species* in 1859, there were indeed Christians who argued that there could be no compromise: we must choose *either* the Bible (the Genesis creation stories) *or*

Darwinism—both cannot be true. Philip Gosse, a prominent naturalist, even speculated that God had distributed fossil remains on the earth in such a way as to make plausible an evolutionary interpretation, simply to test people's faith! But after 1859 a growing number of Protestant theologians accepted evolutionary theory as entirely compatible with belief in a creator God and specifically with Christianity. Paving the way for this acceptance was the growing influence of critical-historical study of the Bible in the early and mid-nineteenth century. German scholars, most of them Protestant Christians, led the way in applying the methods of ordinary historical study of the past to both the Hebrew Bible and the New Testament, shedding a great deal of new light on the biblical authors in their historical and cultural setting and on the meaning and purpose of the language they used.

Critical-historical study of the Bible brought about a reinterpretation of the meaning of biblical inspiration and authority on the part of not only liberal but also conservative theologians as well. Many Protestant theologians and biblical scholars now distinguished between the enduring religious ideas expressed in the Genesis creation stories and the ancient Israelite cosmology or worldview in which they were historically expressed. They interpreted the Genesis stories as symbolic and poetic affirmations of the dependence of the universe and human life upon God, not as literal history or science. As with earlier scientific discoveries, these Protestant scholars believed that the theory of evolution provides us with a vastly expanded and corrected knowledge of just *how* God creates and sustains the universe. This became and has remained the outlook of "mainstream," non-fundamentalist Protestant theologians and churches to the present day: faith and reason are compatible in the case of evolutionary biology as in other branches of scientific knowledge.

Something similar happened among nineteenth-century Roman Catholic thinkers. While officially the Church was slow to accept evolution, in time it acknowledged the evolution of the human body from animal ancestry but affirmed the special creation of each human soul by God. In the twentieth century there have been two important papal documents addressing evolution: Pope Pius XII's encyclical *Humani generis* in 1950, and Pope John Paul II's "Message on Evolution to the Pontifical Academy of Sciences" in 1996. Pius XII cautiously affirmed that evolutionary theory was compatible with Catholic teaching as long as it did not deny the special creation of the human soul. Building on the statements of his predecessor, John Paul went further. Referring to twentieth-century developments in evolutionary biology such as the dramatic discoveries in genetics, he said: ". . . new knowledge has led to the recognition that the theory of evolution is more than a hypothesis. It is indeed remarkable that this theory has been progressively accepted by researchers, following a series of discoveries in various fields of knowledge. The convergence, neither sought nor fabricated, of the results of work that was conducted independently is in itself a significant argument in favor of the theory."[8] With regard to biblical interpretation, Catholic scholars and theologians have always had a certain advantage over Protestants in that the Catholic outlook is church-centered, not Bible-centered: the biblical writings are the product of the Church's early life and are the Church's book; the teaching authority is the living Church through its leadership. Modern Catholic scholars fully accept historical-critical study of the Bible and do not interpret the Genesis stories literally. In their affirmation of the compatibility of faith and reason with regard to modern science, they stand squarely in the tradition of Augustine and Thomas Aquinas.

This "mainstream" approach in both Protestantism and Catholicism (also of Reform and Conservative Judaism) that arose in the nineteenth century in response to Darwin's theory may be called *theistic evolutionism*. Since then the serious intellectual debate has not been between evolutionists and "creationists," since creationism is not science, but between *theistic* evolutionists and *naturalistic* or *non-theistic* evolutionists.

Following the publication of Darwin's *Origin of Species*, a group of thinkers and writers of the Church of England wrote articles and books defending Darwinism and arguing its compatibility with Christian belief. They were among the earliest theistic evolutionists. The Anglican priest Charles Kingsley, who was also a popular novelist, championed evolution, as did theologians such as Aubrey Moore and J. R. Illingworth and the eminent poet, critic, and lay theologian Matthew Arnold. Both Moore and Illingworth were contributors to an important and controversial volume of essays entitled *Lux Mundi* ("Light of the World"; 1890). The contributors to the book, all of them Anglican clergy, were not "liberals." They were high-church Anglicans who saw themselves as standing squarely in the tradition of classical Trinitarian Christianity. Aubrey Moore made this remarkable statement in his book *Science and the Faith*: "Evolution as a theory is infinitely more Christian than the theory of 'Special Creation.' For it implies the immanence of God in nature, and the omnipresence of his creative power. Those who opposed the doctrine of evolution in defense of a 'continued intervention' of God seem to have failed to notice that a theory of occasional intervention implies as its correlative a theory of ordinary absence. . . . Anything more opposed to the language of the Bible and the Fathers can hardly be imagined. . . ."[9] Illingworth's *Lux Mundi* essay, titled "The Incarnation and Development," (1890) was a restatement of the Christian doctrine of the Incarnation (the belief that Jesus is fully God and fully a human being) in the light of the new knowledge of human origins and development from evolutionary theory. He viewed the theory of evolution as simply the latest in a centuries-old series of intellectual revolutions that the churches had assimilated, taking the best thought of every age "captive to Christ" and simply reinterpreting ancient religious truth in the light of the new scientific knowledge. Illingworth tried to show how the idea of the Incarnation, rightly understood, embraced the idea of evolution.[10]

At this point it should be observed that like most non-scientist interpreters of evolution (and even some scientists) in the nineteenth century, most theologians interpreted evolution as a progressive, purposeful development of life on earth from simple life-forms to its culmination in the human species. That is not the properly scientific theory of evolution, which simply describes change over time through natural selection without thinking of the whole process as having some ultimate direction, meaning, or goal. In other words, most people thought of evolution in positive metaphysical and moral terms—which of course made it attractive to both Christian theologians and secular humanists.

In the United States, as in Britain, a number of Christian intellectuals from liberal to orthodox endorsed evolutionary theory as true and entirely compatible with Christian teaching. On the liberal side were people such as Lyman Abbott, a prominent Congregationalist minister, writer, and editor. He wrote two books, *The Evolution of Christianity* (1892) and *Theology of an Evolutionist* (1897), in which, typically, he thought of evolution as a universal and progressive process of development in both the natural and the human orders. Among theologically conservative adherents of evolution, notable was Asa Gray, the Harvard biologist who was the main champion of Darwinism in America. Gray was a Calvinist Presbyterian and thoroughly orthodox in his Christian beliefs. James McCosh, president of Princeton Theological Seminary and a prominent Presbyterian leader, argued that God had established the initial design of the whole evolutionary process but continues to work through what appear to us to be "spontaneous" (random) changes in the process. Interestingly, as Calvinists, both Gray and McCosh had a deep sense of the struggle and tragedy of human existence and of all nature; they had no problem with the theory of natural selection, which just seemed to reinforce that dark view of an earth in the grip of original sin.

What we call "fundamentalism" did not arise until the early twentieth century. It was a new movement, and not the same thing as traditional Christian orthodoxy. Fundamentalism arose specifically as a reaction against "modernism" in all its forms: it condemned critical study of the Bible, evolutionary theory, and various other developments in modern knowledge. The movement originated in a series of pamphlets, *The Fundamentals*, published in 1909. The specific fundamentalist doctrines were a literalistic interpretation of biblical inerrancy, an emphasis on Jesus' atoning death and second coming, and the sudden conversion of the believer in accepting Jesus as personal savior. While in previous centuries Christian orthodoxy had held that the biblical writings were the fully inspired Word of God, this had not been tied to a literal interpretation of the biblical texts. In the twentieth century it has been fundamentalists, not "mainstream" orthodox Christians, who have aggressively opposed evolutionary theory with creationist views based upon a literalistic interpretation of the opening chapters of Genesis, treating them as if they were a textbook of science and history.

Summing up, we may say that the picture of Christian theological responses to Darwinism in the nineteenth century is a complex and subtle one.

Those responses ran the gamut from full acceptance, by both liberal and orthodox Christian thinkers, to complete rejection by fundamentalists. Out of the positive responses emerged the "mainstream" Protestant and Catholic affirmations of evolution in the twentieth century. In line with the Christian tradition's centuries-old confidence in the harmony between the Christian message and the advances of human knowledge, the broad Christian consensus has been what we have called "theistic evolutionism." There is a rich body of twentieth-century literature by Christian theologians who are also trained as scientists that discusses all the issues raised by evolution for Christianity and argues for the compatibility of theistic faith and full acceptance of evolution. Among the leading figures in this enterprise have been scientist-priests such as Pierre Teilhard de Chardin in France, Ian Barbour in the U.S., and Arthur Peacocke and John Polkinghorne in Britain.

At bottom, what really troubles those who reject evolution in favor of creationist theories (for which the only "evidence" is a certain kind of literalistic reading of the first chapters of Genesis) is that they believe that evolutionary theory is equivalent to atheism—or, as it is often described, *naturalism*, the belief that there is simply nature, the physical universe, and nothing more. And indeed, there are prominent evolutionary biologists, such as Richard Dawkins, who firmly believe that naturalism is true. But naturalism is not science, but a metaphysical theory or worldview based on science. To equate evolutionary theory with atheism or naturalism is simply a mistake: scientific assumptions, methods, and knowledge are compatible with a variety of views of the ultimate character of reality.

The same mistake is made on the theistic side by creationists and "intelligent design" proponents. Creationists raise questions and criticisms of aspects of evolutionary theory that have been satisfactorily answered over and over again (while offering no scientific evidence for their views), but at bottom is the fear that to accept evolution means to espouse a "godless, secular atheism": one simply cannot be a Christian or even a theist and an evolutionist. Proponents of "intelligent design," whose arguments are typically much more sophisticated than those of creationists, believe that the complexity of organic life on earth cannot be fully explained by evolutionary biology, and argue that we must posit an "intelli-gent designer" in order to provide a full explanation. The problem is that hypotheses such as an intelligent designer are simply outside the purview of science. Science is the natural explanation of natural phenomena. It is not proper scientific method to introduce into it assumptions or hypotheses from outside of nature such as an intelligent designer or God. From a philosophical or theological point of view, one may legitimately question whether evolutionary theory completely "explains," in some complete and total sense of explanation, organic life on the planet. But evolutionary biology explains what it does within the framework and limits of science. What further explanation might be called for is not within the realm of science. As a strictly scientific theory explaining the origins and development of life, Darwinism is compatible with a variety of metaphysical views, including both theism and atheism.

LITERARY RESPONSES: THE ANGUISHED AGNOSTICISM OF THOMAS HARDY

The theological implications of Darwin's science mesmerized not just nineteenth-century religious thinkers. It captured the imaginations of several of the century's leading novelists and poets as well—Alfred Lord Tennyson, Matthew Arnold, Gerard Manley Hopkins, and Algernon Charles Swinburne, among others—but most particularly Thomas Hardy (1840-1928). Hardy's long career straddled the Victorian Age. Born into a devout Church of England family of modest means, Hardy was a church musician and an experienced ecclesiastical architect before becoming the leading poet-novelist of the late Victorian Age. Like Darwin, he had been bent on a career in the Church; like Darwin, whose writings (along with Huxley's) he studied with great care, Hardy turned to a secular vocation—along with church architecture the writing of fiction and poetry of a distinctively philosophical kind. Often described as a pessimist, he is in fact a tragic realist, one of whose favorite subjects was the dilemma of all living creatures—human and non-human—fated to exist in a world without the Creator they thought they had and knew. In 1890, on the occasion of his fiftieth birthday, Hardy remarked that he had been looking for God for fifty years, but had failed to find Him, at least in an objective sense. Not surprisingly, his religious poems are frequently poems of searching and seeking.

For example, in a poem titled "In a Wood" (1887: 1896) Hardy exhibits the alarm of a woman fleeing the hustle and bustle of city-life for the peace of the countryside:

> Heart-halt and spirit-lame,
>   city-opprest
> Unto this wood I came
>   as to a nest;
> Dreaming that sylvan peace
> Offered the harrowed ease—
> Nature a soft release
>   From man's unrest.

Hardy's "harrowed" peace-seeker learns quickly that life in the woodlands offers anything but "soft release" and "ease." What she finds there is life-and-death combat among various species of plants.

> But, having entered in
>   Great growths and small
> Show them to men akin—
>   Combatants all!
> Sycamore shoulders oak,
> Bines the slim sapling yoke,
> Ivy-spun halters choke
>   Elms stout and tall.

As his notebooks reveal, Hardy was an avid reader not only of Darwin's *Origin* from the moment of its publication in 1859, but also a serious student of the religious and philosophical controversies surrounding it.[11] "In a Wood" reflects his reading of T. H. Huxley (a personal friend), most probably Huxley's influential essay "Evolution and Ethics" (1893), in which "Darwin's bulldog," as Huxley was then called, makes a moving argument for humanity's "power of bettering things" human.[12] Hardy, ever the skeptic, is having a bit of fun in this poem with Huxley's notion that men and women are caught up in the "supreme service of [their] kind." "In a Wood" exhibits a deadly competition rather than a symbiotic coexistence among the woodland plants.

Hardy's refugee from the city is no fool. She has gone to the woods in search of spiritual solace. Once there, she sees the irony of the warring plants being "to men akin," rather than the reverse (warring men being "to plants akin"); she sees as well the even keener irony of having to hightail it back to London because in London, of all places, "now and then," fellow-feeling and even kindness are to be found.

Portrait, Thomas Hardy. Courtesy of Corbis Images.

> Since, then, no grace I find
>   Taught me of trees,
> Turn I back to my kind,
>   Worthy as these.
> There at least smiles abound,
> There discourse trills around,
> There, now and then, are found
>   Life-loyalties.[13]

Better to know the smiles, conversation, and occasional life-loyalties of city-folk than the aggression of sycamores and bines (a twining shrub), and of lethal ivy-nooses that strangle tall elms.

It is also important to note what is absent from this poem—that more familiar (and controversial) analogy between human and non-human mammals, particularly between humans and apes. This was of course the implication of Darwin's *Origin* that most outraged certain of Hardy's contemporaries. On the entire vexed matter of humanity's supposed descent from the apes, Hardy was given to saying that *if* such a kinship existed, then humans had a special duty to act on it by showing kindness to animals. He especially deplored the treatment of horses, buried family pets in

formal ceremonies in a private cemetery, and cam-
paigned actively in the 1890s for humane methods of
transporting and slaughtering cattle.

As for that other implication of evolutionary science that tortured many Victorians—that a loving,
just, and merciful God had *not* created
humankind—Hardy was too much the **agnostic** (a
word invented in 1869 by his friend T. H. Huxley and
meaning literally "not-knower") to take sides. He
chose instead to frame and re-frame this momen-
tous question in poems written throughout his
career. One example is the haunting poem he titled
"Nature's Questioning" (bef. 1898). Here, Hardy's
Nature, impersonal and distant, a bit of a dullard, is
under intense interrogation from several of its creatures—"field, flock, and lonely tree"—who are asking in pointed terms how on earth they came to be:

> 'Has some Vast Imbecility,
>   Mighty to build and blend,
>   But impotent to tend,
> Framed us in jest, and left us now to
>   hazardry?
>
> 'Or come we of an automaton
>   Unconscious of our pains? . . .
>   Or are we live remains
> Of Godhead dying downwards, brain
>   and eye now gone?
>
> 'Or is it that some high plan betides,
>   As yet not understood,
>   Of evil stormed by good
> We the forlorn hope over which
>   achievement strides?'[14]

Hardy's "field, flock, and lonely tree," speaking in
unison, ask Nature, their Creator, four questions that
are in fact four metaphors of the Creator: Are You a
"Vast Imbecility"? Are You an unconscious
"Automaton"? Are You a brain-dead, eyeless
"Godhead"? Or, are You that traditional Author of
some "high" plan? The Huxleyan possibility may be
the fourth—a 'High Planner' using an altruistic
humanity as Its shock-troops in a cosmic battle with
"evil." Whichever It may be, in all four cases Its men
and women suffer, victims of "hazardry" (chance),
neglect, uncertainty, or war. One thing is certain:
each metaphor bespeaks a Creator incomprehensi-
ble to Its Creations, impervious to their suffering
and need. Semi-conscious Nature does not reply:

> . . . No answerer I . . .
>   Meanwhile the winds, and rains,
>   And earth's old glooms and pains
> Are still the same, and life and death
>   are neighbours nigh.

If by the 1890s theologians were learning to
accommodate Darwin's theory of origins, many
thoughtful persons found it impossible to reconcile
evolution with their traditional belief in a God of Love
and Justice. Neither scientist nor theologian could
speak for such people, for whom religion was a matter of lived and felt experience rather than of intellectual debate. The distress of people such as these is
heard in Hardy's poem "To Outer Nature" (bef. 1898).

> Show thee as I thought thee
> When I early sought thee,
>   Omen-scouting,
>   All undoubting
> Love alone had wrought thee—
>
> Wrought thee for my pleasure,
> Planned thee as a measure
>   For expounding
>   And resounding
> Glad things that men treasure.
>
> Of for but a moment
> Of that old endowment—
>   Light to gaily
>   See thy daily
> Iris-hued emowment!
>
> But such re-adorning
> Time forbids with scorning—
>   Makes me see things
>   Cease to be things
> They were in my morning.
>
> Fad'st thou, glow-forsaken,
> Darkness-overtaken!
>   Thy first sweetness
>   Radiance, meetness,
> None shall re-awaken.
>
> Why not sempiternal
> Thou and I? Our vernal
>   Brightness keeping,
>   Time outleaping;
> Passed the hodiernal!

This is a cry of bewilderment from the heart of a former believer, once "all-undoubting" that Nature was Love-wrought, now aware of the terrible truth that something precious—"that old endowment"—is forever gone, and gone with it the assurance there exists something that 'outleaps' time and circumstances. Belief that Nature is the creation of God now cohabits in this person's consciousness with knowledge that Nature is itself creative process. All Hardy's troubled believer can do is ask Why?

But if Hardy could imagine that God is *not* Love, and that God's Love is *not* the driving force behind Nature, honest doubter that he was, he also doubted his doubt, as in the poignant "The Impercipient (*At a Cathedral Service)*":

> That with this bright believing band
>   I have no claim to be,
> That faiths by which my comrades
>   stand
>   Seem fantasies to me,
> And mirage-mists their shining land,
>   Is a strange destiny.
>
> Why thus my soul should be con-
>   signed
>   To infelicity,
> Why always I must feel as blind
>   To sights my brethren see,
> Why joys they've found I cannot find,
>   Abides a mystery.
>
> . . . . . .
>
> Yet I would bear my shortcomings
>   With meet tranquility,
> But for the charge that blessed things
>   I'd liefer not have be.
> O, doth a bird deprived of wings
>   Go earth-bound wilfully!

Written from the point of view of all living creatures—animal and vegetable—Hardy's poetry conveys the sense that for many persons something precious, and irretrievable, was forever lost with the publication of *Origin of Species*. He never questions the authority of Darwin's science. At the same time, dubious about his own doubt, he suggests that his doubt—far from being an iconoclastic truth—may be blindness and impoverishment of the spirit. The

answer to his closing exclamatory-interrogatory question—"O doth a bird deprived of wings/Go earth-bound wilfully!"—is of course "No, such a bird comes to earth unwillingly because a bird's nature is to fly." From this point of view traditional religious belief may very well be 'percipience', even perhaps genuine wisdom. There is no evidence that Hardy ever decided; he remained open to instruction from both science and religion, and remained persistent in his questioning: "Why not sempiternal/Thou and I?". "O, doth a bird deprived of wings/Go earth-bound wilfully!"

The range of response to Darwin and the Darwinians after 1859 was as serious as it was varied: evolutionists vs creationists, theistic evolutionists vs naturalistic evolutionists, writers like Hardy exploring the feelings of men and women living, in the words of a contemporary, "between two worlds, one dead, the other powerless to be born."

SOCIAL DARWINISM

In the last decades of the nineteenth century, following the publication of Darwin's *Origin*, evolutionary ideas emphasizing natural selection came to be known as "Darwinism." Like a tidal wave, evolution swept over many areas of thought, including philosophy, economics, political theory, sociology, education, and, as we have seen, the theology and the novels and poetry of the late nineteenth and early twentieth centuries. Applied to society, what is called **Social Darwinism** rose to special prominence, although the roots of these ideas were in place decades before 1859. The general intellectual climate in the late nineteenth century was congenial to unrestricted capitalism, colonial expansionism, and opposition to voluntary social change. Social Darwinism seemed to provide "scientific" foundation to such views.

Social Darwinism is *the use of concepts of evolutionary theory as norms for interpreting human moral, social, economic, and political life*. It has expressed itself in a variety of ways, from late-nineteenth-century advocacy of *laissez faire* or unregulated capitalism to the fascism of Hitler and Mussolini. The leading Social Darwinist exponent of *laissez faire* capitalism in the nineteenth century was Darwin's British contemporary Herbert Spencer (1820–1903). Spencer tried to work out a fully scientific view of the world based on the

Thomas Henry Huxley. Corbis-Bettmann.

assumption that not only nature but also human life in both its physical and mental aspects is governed entirely by natural laws. Well before Darwin had publicly presented his theory of natural selection, Spencer in his writings used the concept of evolution. By "evolution" he meant that growth and development, governed by natural laws, was common to the physical, organic, and human worlds, and that the key to the process is the advance from the simple to the complex. Unlike Darwin and truly scientific evolutionism, Spencer interpreted evolution as inevitable progress from "lower" to "higher"—an interpretation that has been enormously influential in the nineteenth and twentieth centuries.

On the basis of his interpretation of the evolutionary process, Spencer argued that progress in the human realm meant the increase of those humans best adapted to their environment—the strongest or fittest—and the dying out of the weak or unfit. It was he, not Darwin, who introduced the phrase "the sur-

vival of the fittest." Spencer believed that this is what we see in the struggle for survival among animals in nature, and that the same holds true for the human world as part of nature. Hence he argued for minimal government regulation of human life, including efforts to alleviate poverty through poor laws, on the grounds that this interfered with the natural course of things making for human progress. Accepting the Utilitarian principle of the greatest happiness for the greatest number, Spencer disagreed with the Utilitarians such as John Stuart Mill that it could be achieved by active government involvement in areas like industrial and educational reform. Spencer believed that the industrial capitalism of his day, which exemplified the principles of the natural struggle, was the best assurance of human progress by gradually improving the standard of living for more and more people. Interfering with the free market was going against nature.

Spencer realized that his vision of a society in which government does not help the weak and needy sounded cruel, but he argued that it was "being cruel to be kind": in the long run it was kinder and better for the improvement of the human race to let the less fit perish. He did allow for private forms of assistance for those who are able and willing to help themselves but have experienced difficulties and setbacks of one sort or another. A good short summary of Spencer's social and political philosophy can be found in the essay "The Survival of the Fittest," from his book *Social Statics* (1851).

Social Darwinism of the Spencerian sort found a ready audience in the United States, which was experiencing rapid industrialization after the Civil War under the leadership of self-made "captains of industry" such as John D. Rockefeller and Andrew Carnegie. Carnegie in fact published an essay entitled "Wealth" in 1892 that became a classic American exposition of Social Darwinism. Surprisingly, after defending the unregulated market with such ideas as the "law of competition," the "law of accumulation of wealth," and the "survival of the fittest," Carnegie went on to argue just as vigorously that the great entrepreneurs who are the natural leaders of society have a moral duty to give away most of their fortune during their lifetime—not primarily to their heirs, or for social programs or higher wages for their workers, but for public works such as libraries and parks that will enrich and beautify the lives of all classes of society.

One of the leading nineteenth-century critics of Social Darwinism was Thomas Henry Huxley (1825-1895). Huxley, who was a friend of Spencer, was Darwin's most effective exponent, a creative biologist in his own right, and a man of letters who belongs (with Darwin and Spencer) among the "eminent Victorians." In essays such as "The Struggle for Existence in Human Society" (1888) and "Evolution and Ethics" (1893), Huxley emphasized that the workings of nature may often seem cruel to us, but they are in fact governed by impersonal physical laws and not by moral laws. We project onto nature our human standards, and thus imagine wolves as savage predators killing helpless deer. But of course wolves are not "immoral"; they are simply doing what wolves naturally do, and killing and eating deer is part of the natural selection process, helping to weed out the weaker members of the deer species and thus keeping its population healthy. Nature, including natural selection, is neither "moral" nor "immoral"; it is simply "amoral"—our moral standards do not apply to it.

But Huxley then went on to argue that, while natural selection applies to the human species, with the emergence of humans there is another factor just as important: our reasoning ability and our sense of right and wrong. It is inappropriate to regard wolves killing deer as immoral, whereas it is entirely proper to regard humans killing other humans as immoral. With their powers of reason, imagination, memory, language, and moral and aesthetic values, humans have in a sense "short-circuited" the slow process of natural selection and superimposed on it the rich and varied realm of human culture.

Thus we defy the "law of the survival of the fittest," assisting the biologically "weaker" members of the human species to survive and thus to reproduce and transmit their "weak" genetic traits to their offspring—and we are right to do so, argued Huxley. Similarly, the most desirable human societies are those whose institutions are designed to alleviate human suffering, mitigate the inequities among humans, and maximize the opportunities for individual and social happiness. All this flows from the highest moral values—love, compassion, mercy, pity—which are products of human culture and do not exist in the rest of nature. The task of human society, Huxley wrote, is not "the survival of the fittest" but "the fitting of as many as possible to survive."

A skeptic or—to use the term he coined, an *agnostic*—with regard to religion, Huxley regarded this opposition between the human realm of social and moral values and the rest of nature simply as a puzzling dualism arising from the evolutionary process itself. He concluded: "Social progress means a checking of the cosmic process at every step and the substitution for it of another, which may be called the ethical process; the end of which is not the survival of those who may happen to be the fittest, in respect of the whole of the conditions which obtain, but of those who are ethically the best."[15]

But the most influential social and intellectual forces of the late nineteenth and early twentieth centuries were on the side of Social Darwinism. One fateful effect of the application of Darwinism to social issues was to reinforce the traditional subordination of women with supposedly "scientific" arguments for their evolutionary inferiority as less adaptive and "fit" humans—arguments to which Darwin himself seemingly contributed. Another fateful consequence was the development of the modern concept of "race." There was a wide consensus among eminent anthropologists, paleontologists, and other researchers on the human phenomenon, that distinct races could be identified and arranged hierarchically in terms of their evolutionary progress and general fitness. Since it is human brainpower that has made possible distinctively human achievements, there were scientists, for example, who assumed a direct correlation between skull size and intelligence, collected human skulls and measured them, and not surprisingly concluded that caucasians were the most intelligent, followed by Asiatics, with blacks at the bottom. Growing European dominance of the world during the modern period was viewed as hard evidence that the white race was the "fittest." Such ideas provided a "scientific" rationalization for the aggressive imperialism and colonialism of European nations during the late nineteenth and early twentieth centuries. The "white man's burden" was to bring a higher form of religion, morality, education, politics, economics, and law to the benighted black, brown, and yellow races—and to add territory and turn a profit in the bargain. Politicians such as the German Chancellor Otto von Bismarck and the American President Theodore Roosevelt emphasized such ideas to justify their expansionist ambitions.

Darwin and Huxley. By Stephen Lahey.

GUIDE TO THE READINGS: *ORIGIN OF SPECIES*, AND "EVOLUTION AND ETHICS"

In ***The Origin of Species*** Darwin makes four claims: (1) the organic world is constantly changing. (2) The changes may be small and numerous or large and rare. (3) All living organisms have evolved from a single source (a hypothesis confirmed by genetics only in the past decade, with the discovery that all organisms contain the same molecular "dictionary"). (4) Natural selection is the mechanism for these changes.

He presents his case as a tapestry of logic, factual data, observations, citations of eminent authorities, numerous experiments, and statements asking the reader to accept Darwin's judgment and trust the veracity of his conclusions. Structurally, the book is divided into two parts: (a) the argument for an evolutionary mechanism, and (b) the case for evolution. The cornerstone of his mechanism section was the use of analogy, particularly the humanity/nature analogy, which allowed Darwin to develop a substantial step-by-step argument, moving from the known and acceptable to the unknown and unacceptable.

The subject of "Variation under Domestication," Darwin's first chapter, focused on a subject of common knowledge to the English. Cattle and pigeon breeding was widely practiced, and a vast literature had grown up which explicated a broad range of domestic variations. Lamarck had also referred to domestic varieties, and Darwin was definitely aware of those views, perhaps drawing specifically on that eminent source. In addition to citing eminent authorities repeatedly, Darwin stated that he himself bred domestic pigeons and was on excellent terms with pigeon breeders. He therefore knew the subject intimately and extensively.

Variation in nature is also evident to any ordinary observer. These differences have existed for eons of time. Furthermore, nature is boundless and extraordinarily powerful. We know on the authority of many authors that species and varieties in nature are engaged in a constant struggle for life—"Nature red in tooth and claw," as

Tennyson famously put it in *In Memoriam.* Just as humans select and shape domestic species such as dogs, pigeons and cattle to produce new varieties, so also does nature select the best adapted organisms in the struggle for life to produce new varieties, species, families, and orders. With enormous time and power at nature's disposal, it can produce various extraordinary revolutions throughout the earth.

The remainder of Darwin's book focused on the case for evolution *per se,* and involved many strategies. Darwin himself raised various difficulties with the concept, which allowed him to pre-configure the structure of his opponents' arguments. These primary difficulties and objections were the following: (1) There seems to be an absence of transitional forms of life, the existence of which would be important evidence of evolution. (2) How could certain organic beings with peculiar habits and structures originate and evolve into different creatures? How, for example, could an insectivorous quadruped be converted into a flying bat? (3) How can instinctive behavior be explained on an evolutionary model? (4) Since sterility frequently results from hybridization, how can it be explained by evolution by natural selection? Some difficulties were so grave, said Darwin, that "to this day I can never reflect on them without being staggered; but, to the best of my judgment, the greater number are only apparent, and those that are real are not, I think, fatal to my theory."[16]

Imperfections of the geological record and the geographical distribution of life were difficult although not insurmountable problems, and the facts as Darwin presented them better accorded with descent and natural selection than with the prevailing belief in the immutability of species. In general, he argued, the relationships of organisms through both time (geology) and space (geography) are best explained by evolution, working through natural selection, rather than by special creation by God, as commonly believed then.

Other pertinent subjects discussed by Darwin to support his belief in evolution by natural selection were the natural system of classification, morphology, embryology, and rudimentary (vestigial) organs—all of which had been discussed by other evolutionists. He concluded a brilliant summary of his evolutionary arguments with a powerful and poetic statement:

> It is interesting to contemplate an entangled bank, clothed with many plants of many kinds, with birds singing on the bushes, with various insects flitting about, and with worms crawling through the damp earth, and to reflect that these elaborately constructed forms, so different from each other, and dependent on each other in so complex a manner, have all been produced by laws acting around us. These laws, taken in the largest sense, being Growth with Reproduction; Inheritance which is almost implied by reproduction; Variability from the indirect and direct action of the external conditions of life, and from use and disuse; a Ratio of Increase so high as to lead to a Struggle for Life, and as a consequence to Natural Selection, entailing Divergence of Character and the Extinction of less-improved forms. Thus, from the war of nature, from famine and death, the most exalted object which we are capable of conceiving, namely, the production of the higher animals, directly follows. There is grandeur in this view of life, with its several powers, having been originally breathed into a few forms or into one; and that, whilst this planet has gone cycling on according to the fixed law of gravity, from so simple a beginning endless forms most beautiful and most wonderful have been, and are being, evolved.[17]

In none of the first six editions of *The Origin of Species* did Darwin apply all these ideas to humans, although he clearly believed that they were applicable. Even in *The Descent of Man* he hardly mentioned human evolution, although what he said is unambiguous in placing the human species squarely within the evolutionary process. Darwin's long-standing reticence on this issue reflected, not his own beliefs, but his realization that the theory of evolution was probably the most dramatic challenge ever made to human beliefs about our uniqueness and superiority.

"Evolution & Ethics." In his essay Huxley opens with some clever quips about pessimists and optimists and how good or evil the world is, concluding that it is neither as good nor as bad as it is often thought to be. That leads him to state that we ought to do what we can to improve the world, and to ask what light the theory of evolution sheds on this question.

Propounders of the "ethics of evolution"—and Huxley has in mind Social Darwinists like Herbert Spencer—speak of the evolution of moral sentiments, and he thinks their view could more accurately be called the "evolution of ethics." It is true, says Huxley, that human moral sentiments have developed evolutionarily, but we must also acknowledge that there has been an evolution of *immoral* sentiments as well. Cosmic evolution (by which he simply means evolution) can tell us how both the good and the evil tendencies in humankind have come about, but it cannot tell us how to choose between good and evil. All evolutionary theory can do is describe, not prescribe. And indeed, that is the case with all science: it explains what is, it cannot tell us what we ought to do.

The other fallacy of the "ethics of evolution," according to Huxley, is to take the evolutionary concept of "survival of the fittest" and use it as the standard for how human society should improve. However, "fittest" does not equal "best," but simply "most adaptive to the natural environment." Huxley uses as an example what might happen if the climate in the northern hemisphere were to cool sharply. The "fittest" would be lichens, diatoms or microscopic organisms such as those which give red snow its color.

Humans undoubtedly are subject to the cosmic process, and historically the strongest tend to tread on the weakest, and we see this, Huxley says, in the most primitive of societies. However, the progress of civilization consists in resisting this evolutionary "pull" and replacing it as much as possible with a morality of compassion and fairness. Human activity should be directed toward opposing the cosmic struggle for existence, rather than "ruthless self-assertion."

While it is seriously argued by some that we must base morality on the cosmic struggle (the strong survive, the weak die)—what Huxley calls "fanatical individualism"—this is in every way wrong. Our ethical course lies in combating the cosmic process, with its "struggle for existence," in every way that we can in the human realm. We must not imitate the cosmic process but fight it.

Huxley then traces the development of the realm of human culture or civilization—one in which, "by virtue of his [humankind's] intelligence, the dwarf [human] has bent the Titan [Cosmos] to his will"—leading us to the last two centuries which have seen the most rapid and remarkable change because of science and technology.

Huxley is no utopian, but he does believe that human beings—if they apply their intelligence and will—can improve society and the lot of humankind. In a statement that might indirectly be a critical reference to the Utilitarians, Huxley says that escape from pain and sorrow is not the proper object of life. Both good and evil are the possibilities that lie in our path, and we may fail in the end, but we must do what good we can while we can to make human society more humane, compassionate, and just.

> It may be that the gulfs will wash us down,
> It may be we shall touch the Happy Isles,
> . . . . but something ere the end,
> Some work of noble note may yet be done.

QUESTIONS FOR STUDY AND DISCUSSION

1. In what ways has the theory of evolution through natural selection revolutionized the understanding of nature and the human place in nature?
2. How did the writings of Thomas Malthus and Charles Lyell influence Darwin?
3. What was Alfred Russel Wallace's role in the development of evolutionary theory?
4. Define and discuss the terms "evolution" and "natural selection."
5. What were the theological responses to Darwin's and Wallace's theory in the nineteenth century? What were the issues at stake, and what were the different ways in which Christian theologians and churches dealt with the challenge of evolution?
6. How did Darwinism affect Thomas Hardy's interpretation of nature and human life in his poetry? What does it mean to speak of his "anguished agnosticism"?
7. What is Social Darwinism? How can all the following be examples of Social Darwinism: *laissez-faire* capitalism, European and American imperialism and colonialism, and Nazism?
8. What is T. H. Huxley's argument against Social Darwinism in "Evolution and Ethics"? How would you evaluate it?

SUGGESTIONS FOR FURTHER READING

Appleman, Philip, ed. *Darwin: A Norton Critical Edition*. 3rd ed. New York: W. W. Norton & Co., 2001.

Barlow, Nora, ed. *The Autobiography of Charles Darwin, 1809–1882*. New York: Harcourt Brace & Co., 1958.

Barrett, Paul H., ed. *The Collected Papers of Charles Darwin*. 2 vols. Chicago: University of Chicago Press, 1977.

Beer, Gillian. *Darwin's Plots: Evolutionary Narrative in Darwin, George Eliot, and Nineteenth-Century Fiction*. London: Routledge & Kegan Paul, 1983.

Clark, Ronald W. *The Survival of Charles Darwin*. New York: Avon Books, 1984.

Darwin, Charles. *On the Origin of Species*. Facsimile report. New York: Atheneum, 1967.

Desmond, Adrian. *Huxley: The Devil's Disciple*. New York: Viking Penguin, 1994.

Hardy, Thomas. *The New Wessex Edition of the Complete Poems of Thomas Hardy*. James Gibson, ed. London: Macmillan, 1976.

Irvine, William. *Apes, Angels, and Victorians*. Lanham, MD: University Press of America, 1983.

Lightman, Bernard. *The Origins of Agnosticism: Victorian Unbelief and the Limits of Knowledge*. Baltimore: Johns Hopkins University Press, 1987.

Livingston, James. *Modern Christian Thought: From the Enlightenment to Vatican II*. New York: Macmillan, 1971; see especially ch. 8.

McKinney, H. Lewis, editor and translator. *Lamarck to Darwin: Contributions to Evolutionary Biology, 1809–1859*. Lawrence, KS: Coronado Press, 1972.

Moore, J. R. *The Post-Darwinian Controversies: A Study of the Protestant Struggle to Come to Terms with Darwin in Great Britain and America, 1870–1900*. Cambridge: Cambridge University Press, 1981.

Wallace, Alfred Russel. *Darwinism*. London: Macmillan, 1889.

White, Andrew D. *A History of the Warfare of Science with Theology in Christendom*. 2 vols. New York: D. Appleton & Co., 1896.

Wilson, A. N. *God's Funeral*. New York: W. W. Norton & Co., 1999.

-----

[1] Lamarck, *Philosophical Zoology*, trans. Hugh Elliot (New York & London: Hafner, 1963), 171.

[2] Milton Millhauser, *Just Before Darwin: Robert Chambers and "Vestiges"*, (Middletown, CT: Wesleyan University Press, 1959), 156 ff.

[3] Robert Chambers, *Vestiges of the Natural History of Creation* (London: John Churchill, 1844), 222. Emphasis by Chambers.

[4] Millhauser, *Just Before Darwin*, chpt. 6. Also, Peter Brent, *Charles Darwin* (New York & London: W. W. Norton, 1981), 399 ff.

[5] Reprinted in McKinney, *Lamarck to Darwin*.

[6] See McKinney, *Wallace and Natural Selection* (New Haven, CT & London: Yale University Press, 1972), chpt. 7.

[7] Fredrick Burkhardt & Sydney Smith, eds. "Introduction," *The Correspondence of Charles Darwin*, Vol. I (Cambridge: Cambridge University Press, 1986), xiv.

[8] *Inside the Vatican*, January 1997, 29

[9] London, 1889, 184–5; quoted in James C. Livingston, *Modern Christian Thought: From the Enlightenment to Vatican II*, New York: Macmillan, 1971, 232.)

[10] Charles Gore, ed., *Lux Mundi: Studies in the Religion of the Incarnation*, London: John Murray, 1890, 187.

[11] Gillian Beer. *Darwin's Plots: Evolutionary Narrative in Darwin, George Eliot, and Nineteenth-Century Fiction*. London: Routledge & Kegan, 1983. See especially ch 8: "Finding a Scale for the Human: Plot and Writing in Hardy's Novels," 236–58.

[12] Thomas Henry Huxley, "Evolution and Ethics," in *Selections from the Essays*, ed. Alburey Castell. Northbrook, IL: AHM Publishing Corporation, 1948, 108.

[13] All references to Hardy's poetry are to *The New Wessex Edition of the Complete Poems of Thomas Hardy*, James Gibson, ed. London: MacMillan, 1976.

[14] Hardy claimed to have been one of the earliest "acclaimers" of Darwin's *Origins*; and on several occasions, when asked what thinkers were most important to his writing, Hardy quoted the same names: Darwin, Huxley, Spencer, Comte, Hume, Mill, and others (four evolutionists, two biologists, and two philosophers).

[15] Huxley, "Evolution and Ethics."

[16] Charles Darwin, *On the Origin of Species*. London: John Murray, 1859. 171.

[17] *Ibid.*, 489–90.

CHARLES DARWIN:
Selections from *ON THE ORIGIN OF SPECIES* and *THE DESCENT OF MAN*

ON THE ORIGIN OF SPECIES

Nothing is easier than to admit in words the truth of the universal struggle for life, or more difficult—at least I have found it so—than constantly to bear this conclusion in mind. Yet, unless it be thoroughly engrained in the mind, the whole economy of nature, with every fact on distribution, rarity, abundance, extinction, and variation, will be dimly seen or quite misunderstood. We behold the face of nature bright with gladness, we often see super-abundance of food; we do not see or we forget, that the birds which are idly singing round us mostly live on insects or seeds, and are thus constantly destroying life; or we forget how largely these songsters, or their eggs, or their nestlings, are destroyed by birds and beasts of prey; we do not always bear in mind, that though food may be now super-abundant, it is not so at all seasons of each recurring year.

* * * *

A struggle for existence inevitably follows from the high rate at which all organic beings tend to increase. Every being, which during its natural life-time produces several eggs or seeds, must suffer destruction during some period of its life, and during some season or occasional year, otherwise, on the principle of geometrical increase, its numbers would quickly become so inordinately great that no country could support the product. Hence, as more individuals are produced than can possibly survive, there must in every case be a struggle for existence, either one individual with another of the same species, or with the individuals of distinct species, or with the physical conditions of life. It is the doctrine of Malthus applied with manifold force to the whole animal and vegetable kingdoms; for in this case there can be no artificial increase of food, and no prudential restraint of marriage. Although some species may now be increasing, more or less rapidly, in numbers, all cannot do so, for the world would not hold them.

There is no exception to the rule that every organic being naturally increases at so high a rate that, if not destroyed, the earth would soon be covered by the progeny of a single pair. Even slow-breeding man has doubled in twenty-five years, and at this rate, in less than a thousand years, there would literally not be standing-room for his progeny. Linnaeus has calculated that if an annual plant produced only two seeds—and there is no plant so unproductive as this—and their seedlings next year produced two, and so on, then in twenty years there would be a million plants. The elephant is reckoned the slowest breeder of all known animals, and I have taken some pains to estimate its probable minimum rate of natural increase; it will be safest to assume that it begins breeding when thirty years old, and goes on breeding till ninety years old, bringing forth six young in the interval, and surviving till one hundred years old; if this be so, after a period of from 740 to 750 years there would be nearly nineteen million elephants alive, descended from the first pair.

But we have better evidence on this subject than mere theoretical calculations, namely, the numerous recorded cases of the astonishingly rapid increase of various animals in a state of nature, when circumstances have been favourable to them during two or three following seasons. Still more striking is the evidence from our domestic animals of many kinds which have run wild in several parts of the world; if the statements of the rate of increase of slow-breeding cattle and horses in South America, and latterly in Australia, had not been well authenticated, they would have been incredible. So it is with plants; cases could be given of introduced plants which have become common throughout whole islands in a period of less than ten years. Several of the plants, such as the cardoon and a tall thistle, which are now the commonest over the wide plains of La Plata, clothing square leagues of surface almost to the exclusion of every other plant, have been introduced from Europe; and there are plants which now range in India, as I hear from Dr. Falconer, from Cape Comorin to the Himalaya, which have been imported from America since its discovery. In such cases, and endless others could be given, no one supposes, that the fertility of the animals or plants has been suddenly and temporarily increased in any sensible degree. The obvious explanation is that the conditions of life have been highly favourable, and that there has consequently been less destruction of the old and young, and that nearly all the young have been enabled to breed. Their geometrical ratio of increase, the result of which never fails to be surprising, simply explains their extraordinarily rapid increase and wide diffusion in their new homes.

In a state of nature almost every full-grown plant annually produces seeds, and amongst animals there are very few which do not annually pair. Hence we may confidently assert, that all plants and animals are tending to increase at a geometrical ratio,—that all would rapidly stock every station in which they could anyhow exist,—and that this geometrical tendency to increase must be checked by destruction at some period of life. Our familiarity with the larger domestic animals tends, I think, to mislead us: we see no great destruction falling on them, but we do not keep in mind that thousands are annually slaughtered for food, and that in a state of nature an equal number would have somehow to be disposed of.

The only difference between organisms which annually produce eggs or seeds by the thousand, and those which produce extremely few, is, that the slow-breeders would require a few more years to people, under favourable conditions, a whole district, let it be ever so large. The condor lays a couple of eggs and the ostrich a score, and yet in the same country the condor may be the more numerous of the two; the Fulmar petrel lays but one egg, yet it is believed to be the most numerous bird in the world. One fly deposits hundreds of eggs, and another, like the hippobosca, a single one; but this difference does not determine how many individuals of the two species can be supported in a district. A large number of eggs is of some importance to those species which depend on a fluctuating amount of food, for it allows them rapidly to increase in number. But the real importance of a large number of eggs or seeds is to make up for much destruction at some period of life; and this period in the great majority of cases is an early one. If an animal can in any way protect its own eggs or young, a small number may be produced, and yet the average stock be fully kept up; but if many eggs or young are destroyed, many must be produced, or the species will become extinct. It would suffice to keep up the full number of a tree, which lived on an average for a thousand years, if a single seed were produced once in a thousand years, supposing that this seed were never destroyed, and could be ensured to germinate in a fitting place. So that, in all cases, the average number of any animal or plant depends only indirectly on the number of its eggs or seeds.

In looking at Nature, it is most necessary to keep the foregoing considerations always in mind—never to forget that every single organic being may be said to be striving to the utmost to increase in numbers; that each lives by a struggle at some period of its life; that heavy destruction inevitably falls either on the young or old, during each generation or at recurrent intervals. Lighten any check, mitigate the destruction ever so little, and the number of the species will almost instantaneously increase to any amount.

The causes which check the natural tendency of each species to increase are most obscure. Look at the most vigorous species; by as much as it swarms in numbers, by so much will it tend to increase still further. We know not exactly what the checks are even in a single instance. Nor will this surprise any one who reflects how ignorant we are on this head, even in regard to mankind, although so incomparably better known than any other animal. This subject of the checks to increase has been ably treated by several authors, and I hope in a future work to discuss it at considerable length, more especially in regard to the feral animals of South America. Here I will make only a few remarks, just to recall to the reader's mind some of the chief points. Eggs or very young animals seem generally to suffer most, but this is not invariably the case. With plants there is a vast destruction of seeds, but, from some observations which I have made it appears that the seedlings suffer most from germinating in ground already thickly stocked with other plants. Seedlings, also, are destroyed in vast numbers by various enemies; for instance, on a piece of ground three feet long and two wide, dug and cleared, and where there could be no choking from other plants, I marked all the seedlings of our native weeds as they came up, and out of 357 no less than 295 were destroyed, chiefly by slugs and insects. If turf which has long been mown, and the case would be the same with turf closely browsed by quadrupeds, be let to grow, the more vigorous plants gradually kill the less vigorous, though fully grown plants; thus out of twenty species growing on a little plot of mown turf (three feet by four) nine species perished, from the other species being allowed to grow up freely.

The amount of food for each species of course gives the extreme limit to which each can increase; but very frequently it is not the obtaining food, but the serving as prey to other animals, which determines the average number of a species. Thus, there seems to be little doubt that the stock of partridges, grouse, and hares on any large estate depends chiefly on the destruction of vermin. If not one head of game were shot during the next twenty years in England, and, at the same time, if no vermin were destroyed, there would, in all probability, be less game than at present, although hundreds of thousands of game animals are now annually shot. On the other hand, in some cases, as with the elephant, none are destroyed by beasts of prey; for even the tiger in India most rarely dares to attack a young elephant protected by its dam.

* * * *

Many cases are on record showing how complex and unexpected are the checks and relations between organic beings, which have to struggle together in the same country.

* * * *

[*I give an*] instance showing how plants and animals, remote in the scale of nature, are bound together by a web of complex relations. I shall hereafter have occasion to show that the exotic Lobelia

fulgens is never visited in my garden by insects, and consequently, from its peculiar structure, never sets a seed. Nearly all our orchidaceous plants absolutely require the visits of insects to remove their pollen-masses and thus to fertilise them. I find from experiments that humble-bees are almost indispensable to the fertilisation of the heartsease (Violo tri-color), for other bees do not visit this flower. I have also found that the visits of bees are necessary for the fertilisation of some kinds of clover; for instance, 20 heads of Dutch clover (Trifolium repens) yielded 2,290 seeds, but 20 other heads protected from bees produced not one. Again, 100 heads of red clover (T. pratense) produced 2,700 seeds, but the same number of protected heads produced not a single seed. Humble-bees alone visit red clover, as other bees cannot reach the nectar. It has been suggested that moths may fertilise the clovers; but I doubt whether they could do so in the case of red clover, from their weight not being sufficient to depress the wing petals. Hence we may infer as highly probable that, if the whole genus of humble-bees became extinct or very rare in England, the heartsease and red clover would become very rare, or wholly disappear. The number of humble-bees in any district depends in a great measure upon the number of field-mice, which destroy their combs and nests; and Col. Newman, who has long attended to the habits of humble-bees, believes that "more than two-thirds of them are thus destroyed all over England." Now the number of mice is largely dependent, as every one knows, on the number of cats; and Col. Newman says, "Near villages and small towns I have found the nests of humble-bees more numerous than elsewhere, which I attribute to the number of cats that destroy the mice." Hence it is quite credible that the presence of a feline animal in large numbers in a district might determine, through the intervention first of mice and then of bees, the frequency of certain flowers in that district!

* * * *

If under changing conditions of life organic beings present individual differences in almost every part of their structure, and this cannot be disputed; if there be, owing to their geometrical rate of increase, a severe struggle for life at some age, season, or year, and this certainly cannot be disputed; then, considering the infinite complexity of the relations of all organic beings to each other and to their conditions of life, causing an infinite diversity in structure, constitution, and habits, to be advantageous to them, it would be a most extraordinary fact if no variations had ever occurred useful to each being's own welfare, in the same manner as so many variations have occurred useful to man. But if variations useful to any organic being ever do occur, assuredly individuals thus characterised will have the best chance of being preserved in the struggle for life; and from the strong principle of inheritance, these will tend to produce offspring similarly characterised. This principle of preservation, or the survival of the fittest, I have called Natural Selection. It leads to the improvement of each creature in relation to its organic and inorganic conditions of life; and consequently, in most cases, to what must be regarded as an advance in organisation. Nevertheless, low and simple forms will long endure if well fitted for their simple conditions of life.

Natural selection, on the principle of qualities being inherited at corresponding ages, can modify the egg, seed, or young, as easily as the adult. Amongst many animals, sexual selection will have given its aid to ordinary selection, by assuring the most vigorous and best adapted males the greatest number of offspring. Sexual selection will also give characters useful to the males alone, in their struggles or rivalry with other males; and these characters will be transmitted to one sex or to both sexes, according to the form of inheritance which prevails.

Whether natural selection has really thus acted in adapting the various forms of life to their several conditions and stations, must be judged by the general tenor and balance of evidence given in the following chapters. But we have already seen how it entails extinction; and how largely extinction has acted in the world's history, geology plainly declares. Natural selection, also, leads to divergence of character; for the more organic beings diverge in structure, habits, and constitution, by so much the more can a large number be supported on the area,—of which we see proof by looking to the inhabitants of any small spot, and to the productions naturalised in foreign lands. Therefore, during the modification of the descendants of any one

species, and during the incessant struggle of all species to increase in numbers, the more diversified the descendants become, the better will be their chance of success in the battle for life. Thus the small differences distinguishing varieties of the same species, steadily tend to increase, till they equal the greater differences between species of the same genus, or even of distinct genera.

We have seen that it is the common, the widely-diffused and widely ranging species, belonging to the larger genera within its class, which vary most; and these tend to transmit to their modified offspring that superiority which now makes them dominant in their own countries. Natural selection, as has just been remarked, leads to divergence of character and to much extinction of the less improved and intermediate forms of life. On these principles, the nature of the affinities, and the generally well-defined distinctions between the innumerable organic beings in each class throughout the world, may be explained. It is a truly wonderful fact—the wonder of which we are apt to overlook from familiarity—that all animals and all plants throughout all time and space should be related to each other in groups, subordinate to groups, in the manner which we everywhere behold—namely, varieties of the same species most closely related, species of the same genus less closely and unequally related, forming sections and sub-genera, species of distinct genera much less closely related, and genera related in different degrees, forming sub-families, families, orders, sub-classes and classes. The several subordinate groups in any class cannot be ranked in a single file, but seem clustered round points, and these round other points, and so on in almost endless cycles. If species had been independently created, no explanation would have been possible of this kind of classification; but it is explained through inheritance and the complex action of natural selection, entailing extinction and divergence of character. . . .

The affinities of all beings of the same class have sometimes been represented by a great tree. I believe this simile largely speaks the truth. The green and budding twigs may represent existing species; and those produced during former years may represent the long succession of extinct species. At each period of growth all the growing twigs have tried to branch out on all sides, and to overtop and kill the surrounding twigs and branches, in the same manner as species and groups of species have at all times overmastered other species in the great battle for life. The limbs divided into great branches, and these into lesser and lesser branches, were themselves once, when the tree was young, budding twigs; and this connection of the former and present buds by ramifying branches may well represent the classification of all extinct and living species in groups subordinate to groups. Of the many twigs which flourished when the tree was a mere bush, only two or three, now grown into great branches, yet survive and bear the other brandies; so with the species which lived during long-past geological periods, very few have left living and modified descendants. From the first growth of the tree, many a limb has decayed and dropped off; and these fallen branches of various sizes may represent those whole orders, families, and genera which have now no living representatives, and which are known to us only in a fossil state. As we here and there see a thin straggling branch springing from a fork low down in a tree, and which by some chance has been favoured and is still alive on its summit, so we occasionally see an animal like the Ornithorhynchus or Lepidosiren, which in some small degree connects by its affinities two large branches of life, and which has apparently been saved from fatal competition by having inhabited a protected station. As buds give rise by growth to fresh buds, and these, if vigorous, branch out and overtop on all sides many a feebler branch, so by generation I believe it has been with the Great Tree of Life, which fills with its dead and broken branches the crust of the earth, and covers the surface with its ever-branching and beautiful ramifications.

* * * *

I have now recapitulated the facts and considerations which have thoroughly convinced me that species have been modifed, during a long course of descent. This has been effected chiefly through the natural selection of numerous successive, slight, favourable variations; aided in an important manner by the inherited effects of the use and disuse of parts; and in an unimportant manner, that is in relation to adaptive structures, whether past or present, by the direct action of external conditions, and by

variations which seem to us in our ignorance to rise spontaneously. It appears that I formerly underrated the frequency and value of these latter forms of variation, as leading to permanent modifications of structure independently of natural selection. But as my conclusions have lately been much misrepresented, and it has been stated that I attribute the modification of species exclusively to natural selection, I may be permitted to remark that in the first edition of this work, and subsequently, I placed in a most conspicuous position—namely, at the close of the Introduction—the following words: "I am convinced that natural selection has been the main but not the exclusive means of modification." This has been of no avail. Great is the power of steady misrepresentation; but the history of science shows that fortunately this power does not long endure.

It can hardly be supposed that a false theory would explain, in so satisfactory a manner as does the theory of natural selection, the several large classes of facts above specified. It has recently been objected that this is an unsafe method of arguing; but it is a method used in judging of the common events of life, and has often been used by the greatest natural philosophers. The undulatory theory of light has thus been arrived at, and the belief in the revolution of the earth on its own axis was until lately supported by hardly any direct evidence. It is no valid objection that science as yet throws no light on the far higher problem of the essence or origin of life. Who can explain what is the essence of the attraction of gravity? No one now objects to following out the results consequent on this unknown element of attraction; notwithstanding that Leibnitz formerly accused Newton of introducing "occult qualities and miracles into philosophy."

I see no good reason why the views given in this volume should shock the religious feelings of any one. It is satisfactory, as showing how transient such impressions are, to remember that the greatest discovery ever made by man, namely, the law of the attraction of gravity, was also attacked by Leibnitz, "as subversive of natural, and inferentially of revealed, religion." A celebrated author and divine has written to me that "he has gradually learnt to see that it is just as noble a conception of the Deity to believe that He created a few original forms capable of self-development into other and needful forms, as to believe that He required a fresh act of creation to supply the voids caused by the action of His Laws."

Why, it may be asked, until recently did nearly all the most eminent living naturalists and geologists disbelieve in the mutability of species? It cannot be asserted that organic beings in a state of nature are subject to no variation; it cannot be proved that the amount of variation in the course of long ages is a limited quantity; no clear distinction has been, or can be, drawn between species and well-marked varieties. It cannot be maintained that species when intercrossed are invariably sterile, and varieties invariably fertile; or that sterility is a special endowment and sign of creation. The belief that species were immutable productions was almost unavoidable as long as the history of the world was thought to be of short duration; and now that we have acquired some idea of the lapse of time, we are too apt to assume, without proof that the geological record is so perfect that it would have afforded us plain evidence of the mutation of the species, if they had undergone mutation.

But the chief cause of our natural unwillingness to admit that one species has given birth to other and distinct species, is that we are always slow in admitting great changes of which we do not see the steps. The difficulty is the same as that felt by many geologists, when Lyell first insisted that long lines of inland cliffs had been formed, and great valleys excavated, by the agencies which we see still at work. The mind cannot possibly grasp the full meaning of the term of even a million years; it cannot add up and perceive the full effects of many slight variations, accumulated during an almost infinite number of generations.

Although I am fully convinced of the truth of the views given in this volume under the form of an abstract, I by no means expect to convince experienced naturalists whose minds are stocked with a multitude of facts all viewed, during a long course of years, from a point of view directly opposite to mine. It is so easy to hide our ignorance under such expressions as the "plan of creation," "unity of design," &c., and to think that we give an explanation when we only restate a fact. Any one whose disposition leads him to attach more weight to unexplained difficulties than to the explanation of a certain number of facts will certainly reject the theory. A few naturalists, endowed with much flex-

ibility of mind, and who have already begun to doubt the immutability of species, may be influenced by this volume; but I look with confidence to the future,—to young and rising naturalists, who will be able to view both sides of the question with impartiality. Whoever is led to believe that species are mutable will do good service by conscientiously expressing his conviction; for thus only can the load of prejudice by which this subject is overwhelmed be removed.

Several eminent naturalists have of late published their belief that a multitude of reputed species in each genus are not real species; but that other species are real, that is, have been independently created. This seems to me a strange conclusion to arrive at. They admit that a multitude of forms, which till lately they themselves thought were special creations, and which are still thus looked at by the majority of naturalists, and which consequently have all the external characteristic features of the species,—they admit that these have been produced by variation, but they refuse to extend the same view to other and slightly different forms. Nevertheless they do not pretend that they can define, or even conjecture, which are the created forms of life, and which are produced by secondary laws. They admit variation as a *vera causa* in one case, they arbitrarily reject it in another, without assigning any distinction in the two cases. The day will come when this will be given as a curious illustration of the blindness of preconceived opinion. These authors seem no more startled at a miraculous act of creation than at an ordinary birth. But do they really believe that at innumerable periods in the earth's history certain elemental atoms have been commanded suddenly to flash into living tissues? Do they believe that at each supposed act of creation one individual or many were produced? Were all the infinitely numerous kinds of animals and plants created as eggs or seed, or as full grown? And in the case of mammals, were they created bearing the false marks of nourishment from the mother's womb? Undoubtedly some of these same questions cannot be answered by those who believe in the appearance or creation of only a few forms of life, or of some one form alone. It has been maintained by several authors that it is as easy to believe in the creation of a million beings as of one; but Maupertuis' philosophical axiom "Of least action" leads the mind more willingly to admit the smaller number; and certainly we ought not to believe that innumerable beings within each great class have been created with plain, but deceptive, marks of descent from a single parent.

As a record of a former state of things, I have retained in the foregoing paragraphs, and elsewhere, several sentences which imply that naturalists believe in the separate creation of such species; and I have been much censured for having thus expressed myself. But undoubtedly this was the general belief when the first edition of the present work appeared. I formerly spoke to very many naturalists on the subject of evolution, and never once met with any sympathetic agreement. It is probable that some did then believe in evolution, but they were either silent, or expressed themselves so ambiguously that it was not easy to understand their meaning. Now things are wholly changed, and almost every naturalist admits the great principle of evolution. There are, however, some who still think that species have suddenly given birth, through quite unexplained means, to new and totally different forms: but, as I have attempted to show, weighty evidence can be opposed to the admission of great and abrupt modifications. Under a scientific point of view, and as leading to further investigation, but little advantage is gained by believing that new forms are suddenly developed in an inexplicable manner from old and widely different forms, over the old belief in the creation of species from the dust of the earth.

It may be asked how far I extend the doctrine of the modification of the species. The question is difficult to answer, because the more distinct the forms are which we consider, by so much the arguments in favour of community of descent become fewer in number and less in force. But some arguments of the greatest weight extend very far. All the members of whole classes are connected together by a chain of affinities, and all can be classed on the same principle, in groups, subordinate to groups. Fossil remains sometimes tend to fill up very wide intervals between existing orders.

Organs in a rudimentary condition plainly show that an early progenitor had the organ in a fully developed condition; and this in some cases implies an enormous amount of modification in the descendants. Throughout whole classes various structures are formed on the same pattern, and at a very early age the embryos closely resemble each other. Therefore I cannot doubt that the theory of descent with modification embraces all the members of the same great class or kingdom. I believe that animals are descended from most only four or five progenitors, and plants from an equal or lesser number.

Analogy would lead me one step farther, namely, to the belief that all animals and plants are descended from one prototype. But analogy may be a deceitful guide. Nevertheless all living things have much in common, in their chemical composition, their cellular structure, their laws of growth, and their liability to injurious influences. We see this even in so trifling a fact as that the same poison often similarly affects plants and animals; or that the poison secreted by the gall-fly produces monstrous growths on the wild rose or oak tree. With all organic beings, excepting perhaps some of the very lowest, sexual reproduction seems to be essentially similar. With all, as far as is at present known, the germinal vesicle is the same; so that all organisms start from a common origin. If we look even to the two main divisions—namely, to the animal and vegetable kingdoms—certain low forms are so intermediate in character that naturalists have disputed to which kingdom they should be referred. As Professor Asa Gray has remarked, "the spores and other reproductive bodies of many of the lower algae may claim to have first a characteristically animal, and then an unequivocally vegetable existence." Therefore, on the principle of natural selection with divergence of character, it does not seem incredible that, from such low and intermediate form, both animals and plants may have been developed; and, if we admit this, we must likewise admit that all the organic beings which have ever lived on this earth may be descended from one primordial form. But this inference is chiefly grounded on analogy, and it is immaterial whether or not it be accepted. No doubt it is possible, as Mr. G. H. Lewes has urged, that at the first commencement of life many different forms were evolved; but if so, we may conclude that only a very few have left modified descendants. For, as I have recently remarked in regard to the members of each great kingdom, such as the Vertebrata, Articulata, &c., we have distinct evidence in their embryological, homologous, and rudimentary structures, that within each kingdom all the members are descended from a single progenitor.

When the views advanced by me in this volume, and by Mr. Wallace, or when analogous views on the origin of species are generally admitted, we can dimly foresee that there will be a considerable revolution in natural history. Systematists will be able to pursue their labours as at present; but they will not be incessantly haunted by the shadowy doubt whether this or that form be a true species. This, I feel sure and I speak after experience, will be no slight relief. The endless disputes whether or not some fifty species of British brambles are good species will cease. Systematists will have only to decide (not that this will be easy) whether any form be sufficiently constant and distinct from other forms, to be capable of definition; and if definable, whether the differences be sufficiently important to deserve a specific name. This latter point will become a far more essential consideration than it is at present; for differences, however slight, between any two forms, if not blended by intermediate graduations, are looked at by most naturalists as sufficient to raise both forms to the rank of species.

Hereafter we shall be compelled to acknowledge that the only distinction between species and well-marked varieties is, that the latter are known, or believed, to be connected at the present day by intermediate graduations whereas species were formerly thus connected. Hence, without rejecting the consideration of the present existence of intermediate graduations between any two forms, we shall be led to weigh more carefully and to value higher the actual amount of difference between them. It is quite possible that forms now generally acknowledged to be merely varieties may hereafter be thought worthy of specific names; and in this case scientific and common language will come into accordance. In short, we shall have to treat species in the same manner as those naturalists treat genera, who admit that genera are merely artificial combinations made for convenience. This may not be a cheering prospect; but we shall at least be freed from the vain search for the undiscovered and undiscoverable essence of the term species.

The other and more general departments of natural history will rise greatly in interest. The terms used by naturalists, of affinity, relationship, community of type, paternity, morphology, adaptive characters, rudimentary and aborted organs, &c., will cease to be metaphorical, and will have a plain signification. When we no longer look at an organic being as a savage looks at a ship, as something wholly beyond his comprehension; when we regard every production of nature as one which has had a long history; when we contemplate every complex structure and instinct as the summing up of many contrivances, each useful to the possessor, in the same way as any great mechanical invention is the summing up of the labour, the experience, the reason, and even the blunders of numerous workmen; when we thus view each organic being, how far more interesting—I speak from experience—does the study of natural history become!

A grand and almost untrodden field of inquiry will be opened, on the causes and laws of variation, on correlation, on the effects of use and disuse, on the direct action of external conditions, and so forth. The study of domestic productions will rise immensely in value. A new variety raised by man will be a more important and interesting subject for study than one more species added to the infinitude of already recorded species. Our classifications will come to be, as far as they can be so made, genealogies; and will then truly give what may be called the plan of creation. The rules for classifying will no doubt become simpler when we have a definite object in view. We possess no pedigrees or armorial bearings; and we have to discover and trace the many diverging lines of descent in our natural genealogies, by characters of any kind which have long been inherited. Rudimentary organs will speak infallibly with respect to the nature of long-lost structures. Species and groups of species which are called aberrant, and which may fancifully be called living fossils, will aid us in forming a picture of the ancient forms of life. Embryology will often reveal to us the structure, in some degree obscured, of the prototypes of each great class.

When we can feel assured that all the individuals of the same species, and all the closely allied species of most genera, have within a not very remote period descended from one parent, and have migrated from some one birthplace; and we better know the many means of migration, then, by the light which geology now throws, and will continue to throw, on former changes of climate and of the level of the land, we shall surely be enabled to trace in an admirable manner the former migrations of the inhabitants of the whole world. Even at present, by comparing the differences between the inhabitants of the sea on the opposite sides of a continent, and the nature of the various inhabitants on that continent in relation to their apparent means of immigration, some light can be thrown on ancient geography.

The noble science of Geology loses glory from the extreme imperfection of the record. The crust of the earth with its imbedded remains must not be looked at as a well-filled museum, but as a poor collection made at hazard and at rare intervals. The accumulation of each great fossiliferous formation will be recognised as having depended on an unusual concurrence of favourable circumstances, and the blank intervals between the successive stages as having been of vast duration. But we shall be able to gauge with some security the duration of these intervals by a comparison of the preceding and succeeding organic forms. We must be cautious in attempting to correlate as strictly contemporaneous two formations, which do not include many identical species, by the general succession of the forms of life. As species are produced and exterminated by slowly acting and still existing causes, and not by miraculous acts of creation; and as the most important of all causes of organic change is one which is almost independent of altered and perhaps suddenly altered physical conditions, namely, the mutual relation of organism to organism,—the improvement of one organism entailing the improvement or the extermination of others; it follows, that the amount of organic change in the fossils of consecutive formations probably serves as a fair measure of the relative, though not actual lapse of time. A number of species, however, keeping in a body might remain for a long period unchanged, whilst within the same period several of these species by migrating into new countries and coming into competition with foreign associates, might become modified; so that we must not overrate the accuracy of organic change as a measure of time.

In the future I see open fields for far more important researches. Psychology will be securely based on the foundation already well laid by Mr. Herbert Spencer, that of the necessary acquirements of each mental power and capacity by gradation.

Much light will be thrown on the origin of man and his history.

Authors of the highest eminence seem to be fully satisfied with the view that each species has been independently created. To my mind it accords better with what we know of the laws impressed on matter by the Creator, that the production and extinction of the past and present inhabitants of the world should have been due to secondary causes, like those determining the birth and death of the individual. When I view all beings not as special creations, but as the lineal descendants of some few beings which lived long before the first bed of the Cambrian system was deposited, they seem to me to become ennobled. Judging from the past, we may safely infer that not one living species will transmit its unaltered likeness to a distant futurity. And of the species now living very few will transmit progeny of any kind to a far distant futurity; for the manner in which all organic beings are grouped, shows that the greater number of species in each genus, and all the species in many genera, have left no descendants, but have become utterly extinct. We can so far take a prophetic glance into futurity as to foretell that it will be the common and widely-spread species, belonging to the larger and dominant groups within each class, which will ultimately prevail and procreate new and dominant species. As all the living forms of life are the lineal descendants of those which lived long before the Cambrian epoch, we may feel certain that the ordinary succession by generation has never once been broken, and that no cataclysm has desolated the whole world. Hence we may look with some confidence to a secure future of great length. And as natural selection works solely by and for the good of each being, all corporeal and mental endowments will tend to progress towards perfection.

It is interesting to contemplate a tangled bank, clothed with many plants of many kinds, with birds singing on the bushes, with various insects flitting about, and with worms crawling through the damp earth, and to reflect that these elaborately constructed forms, so different from each other, and dependent upon each other in so complex a manner, have all been produced by laws acting around us. These laws, taken in the largest sense, being Growth with Reproduction; Inheritance which is almost implied by reproduction; Variability from the indirect and direct action of the conditions of life, and from use and disuse: a Ratio of Increase so high as to lead to a Struggle for Life, and as a consequence to Natural Selection, entailing Divergence of Character and the Extinction of less-improved forms. Thus, from the war of nature, from famine and death, the most exalted object which we are capable of conceiving, namely, the production of the higher animals, directly follows. There is grandeur in this view of life, with its several powers, having been originally breathed by the Creator into a few forms or into one; and that, whilst this planet has gone cycling on according to the fixed law of gravity, from so simple a beginning endless forms most beautiful and most wonderful have been, and are being evolved.

THE DESCENT OF MAN

GENERAL SUMMARY AND CONCLUSION

The main conclusion arrived at in this work, and now held by many naturalists who are well competent to form a sound judgment, is that man is descended from some less highly-organized form. The grounds upon which this conclusion rests will never be shaken, for the close similarity between man and the lower animals in embryonic development, as well as in innumerable points of structure and constitution, both of high and of the most trifling importance—the rudiments which he retains, and the abnormal reversions to which he is occasionally liable—are facts which cannot be disputed. They have long been known, but until recently they told us nothing with respect to the origin of man. Now, when viewed by the light of our knowledge of the whole organic world, their meaning is unmistakable. The great principle of evolution stands up clear and firm, when these groups of facts are considered in connection with others, such as the mutual affinities of the members of the same group, their geographical distribution in past and present times, and their geological succession. It is incredible that all these facts should speak falsely. He who is not content to look, like a savage, at the phenomena of Nature as disconnected, cannot any longer believe that man is the work of a separate act of creation. He will be forced to admit that the close resemblance of the embryo of man to that, for instance, of a dog—the construction of his skull, limbs, and whole frame, independently of the uses to which the parts may be put, on the same plan with that of other mammals—the occasional reappearance of various structures, for instance, of several distinct muscles, which man does not normally possess, but which are common to the Quadrumana—and a crowd of analogous facts—all point in the plainest manner to the conclusion that man is the co-descendant with other mammals of a common progenitor.

[This] conclusion . . . that man is descended from some lowly-organised form, will, I regret to think, be highly distasteful to many persons. But there can hardly be a doubt that we are descended from barbarians. The astonishment which I felt on first seeing a party of Fuegians on a wild and broken shore will never be forgotten by me, for the reflection at once rushed into my mind—such were our ancestors. These men were absolutely naked and bedaubed with paint, their long hair was tangled, their mouths frothed with excitement, and their expression was wild, startled, and distrustful. They possessed hardly any arts, and, like wild animals, lived on what they could catch; they had no government, and were merciless to every one not of their own small tribe. He who has seen a savage in his native land will not feel much shame, if forced to acknowledge that the blood of some more humble creature flows in his veins. For my own part, I would as soon be descended from that heroic little monkey, who braved his dreaded enemy in order to save the life of his keeper; or from that old baboon, who, descending from the mountains, carried away in triumph his young comrade from a crowd of astonished dogs—as from a savage who delights to torture his enemies, offers up bloody sacrifices, practices infanticide without remorse, treats his wives like slaves, knows no decency, and is haunted by the grossest superstitions.

Man may be excused for feeling some pride at having risen, though not through his own exertions, to the very summit of the organic scale; and the fact of his having thus risen, instead of having been aboriginally placed there, may give him hopes for a still higher destiny in the distant future. But we are not here concerned with hopes or fears, only with the truth as far as our reason allows us to discover it. I have given the evidence to the best of my ability; and we must acknowledge, as it seems to me, that man with all his noble qualities, with sympathy which feels for the most debased, with benevolence which extends not only to other men but to the humblest living creature, with his godlike intellect which has penetrated into the movements and constitution of the solar system—with all these exalted powers—Man still bears in his bodily frame the indelible stamp of his lowly origin.

THOMAS HENRY HUXLEY: "EVOLUTION AND ETHICS"

(1893)

Modern thought is making a fresh start from the base whence Indian and Greek philosophy set out; and, the human mind being very much what it was six-and-twenty centuries ago, there is no ground for wonder if it presents indications of a tendency to move along the old lines to the same results.

We are more than sufficiently familiar with modern pessimism, at least as a speculation; for I cannot call to mind that any of its present votaries have sealed their faith by assuming the rags and the bowl of the mendicant Bhikku, or the wallet of the Cynic. The obstacles placed in the way of sturdy vagrancy by an unphilosophical police have, perhaps, proved too formidable for philosophical consistency. We also know modern speculative optimism, with its perfectibility of the species, reign of peace, and lion and lamb transformation scenes; but one does not hear so much of it as one did forty years ago; indeed, I imagine it is to be met with more commonly at the tables of the healthy and wealthy, than in the congregations of the wise. The majority of us, I apprehend, profess neither pessimism or optimism. We hold that the world is neither so good, nor so bad, as it conceivably might be; and, as most of us have reason, now and again, to discover that it can be. Those who have failed to experience the joys that make life worth living are, probably, in as small a minority as those who have never known the griefs that rob existence of its savor and turn its richest fruits into mere dust and ashes.

Further, I think I do not err in assuming that, however diverse their views on philosophical and religious matters, most men are agreed that the proportion of good and evil in life may be very sensibly affected by human action. I never heard anybody doubt that the evil may be thus increased, or diminished; and it would seem to follow that good must be similarly susceptible of addition or subtraction. Finally, to my knowledge, nobody professes to doubt that, so far forth as we possess a power of bettering things, it is our paramount duty to use it and to train all our intellect and energy to this supreme service of our kind.

Hence the pressing interest of the question, to what extent modern progress in natural knowledge, and, more especially, the general outcome of that progress in the doctrine of evolution, is competent to help us in a great work of helping one another?

The propounders of what are called the "ethics of evolution," when the "evolution of ethics" would usually better express the object of their speculations, adduce a number of more or less interesting facts and more or less sound arguments in favor of the origin of the moral sentiments, in the same way as other natural phenomena, by a process of evolution. I have little doubt, for my own part, that they are on the right track; but as the immoral sentiments have no less been evolved, there is, so far, as much natural sanction for the one as the other. The thief and the murderer follow nature just as much as the philanthropist. Cosmic evolution may teach us how the good and the evil tendencies of man may have come about; but, in itself, it is incompetent to furnish any better reason why what we call good is preferable to what we call evil than we had before. Some day, I doubt not, we shall arrive at an understanding of the evolution of the aesthetic faculty; but all the understanding in the world will neither increase nor diminish the force of the intuition that this is beautiful and that is ugly.

There is another fallacy which appears to me to pervade the so-called "ethics of evolution." It is the notion that because, on the whole, animals and plants have advanced in perfection of organization by means of the struggle for existence and the consequent "survival of the fittest"; therefore men in society, men as ethical beings, must look to the same process to help them towards perfection. I suspect that this fallacy has arisen out of the unfortunate ambiguity of the phrase "survival of the fittest."

"Fittest" has a connotation of "best"; and about "best" there hangs a moral flavor. In cosmic nature, however, what is "fittest" depends upon the conditions. Long since, I ventured to point out that if our hemisphere were to cool again, the survival of the fittest might bring about, in the vegetable kingdom, a population of more and more stunted and humbler and humbler organisms, until the "fittest" that survived might be nothing but lichens, diatoms, and such microscopic organisms as those which give red snow its color; while, if it became hotter, the pleasant valleys of the Thames and Isis might be uninhabitable by any animated beings save those that flourish in a tropical jungle. They, as the fittest, the best adapted to the changed conditions, would survive.

Men in society are undoubtedly subject to the cosmic process. As among other animals, multiplication goes on without cessation, and involves severe competition for the means of support. The struggle for existence tends to eliminate those less fitted to adapt themselves to the circumstances of their existence. The strongest, the most self-assertive, tend to tread down the weaker. But the influence of the cosmic process on the evolution of society is the greater the more rudimentary its civilization. Social progress means a checking of the cosmic process at every step and the substitution for it of another, which may be called the ethical process; the end of which is not the survival of those who may happen to be the fittest, in respect of the whole of the conditions which obtain, but of those who are ethically the best.

As I have already urged, the practice of that which is ethically best—what we call goodness or virtue—involves a course of conduct which, in all respects, is opposed to that which leads to success in the cosmic struggle for existence. In place of ruthless self-assertion it demands self-restraint; in place of thrusting aside, or treading down, all competitors, it requires that the individual shall not merely respect, but shall help his fellows; its influence is directed, not so much to the survival of the fittest, as to the fitting of as many as possible to survive. It repudiates the gladiatorial theory of existence. It demands that each man who enters into the enjoyment of the advantages of a polity shall be mindful of his debt to those who have laboriously constructed it; and shall take heed that no act of his

weakens the fabric in which he has been permitted to live. Laws and moral precepts are directed to the end of curbing the cosmic process and reminding the individual of his duty to the community, to the protection and influence of which he owes, if not existence itself, at least the life of something better than a brutal savage.

It is from neglect of these plain considerations that the fanatical individualism of our time attempts to apply the analogy of cosmic nature to society. Once more we have a misapplication of the stoical injunction to follow nature; the duties of the individual to the state are forgotten, and his tendencies to self-assertion are dignified by the name of rights. It is seriously debated whether the members of a community are justified in using their combined strength to constrain one of their number to contribute his share to the maintenance of it; or even to prevent him from doing his best to destroy it. The struggle for existence which has done such admirable work in cosmic nature, must, it appears, be equally beneficent in the ethical sphere. Yet if that which I have insisted upon is true; if the cosmic process has no sort of relation to moral ends; if the imitation of it by man is inconsistent with the first principles of ethics; what becomes of this surprising theory?

Let us understand, once for all, that the ethical progress of society depends, not on imitating the cosmic process, still less in running away from it, but in combating it. It may seem an audacious proposal thus to put the microcosm against the macrocosm and to set man to subdue nature to his higher ends; but I venture to think that the great intellectual difference between the ancient times with which we have been occupied and our day, lies in the solid foundation we have acquired for the hope that such an enterprise may meet with a certain measure of success.

The history of civilization details the steps by which men have succeeded in building up an artificial world within the cosmos. Fragile reed as he may be, man, as Pascal says, is a thinking reed: there lies within him a fund of energy operating intelligently and so far akin to that which pervades the universe, that it is competent to influence and modify the cosmic process. In virtue of his intelligence, the dwarf bends the Titan to his will. In every family, in every polity that has been established, the cosmic process in man has been restrained and otherwise modified by law and custom; in surrounding nature, it has been similarly influenced by the art of the shepherd, the agriculturist, the artisan. As civilization has advanced, so has the extent of this interference increased; until the organized and highly developed sciences and arts of the present day have endowed man with a command over the course of non-human nature greater than that once attributed to the magicians. The most impressive, I might say startling, of these changes have been brought about in the course of the last two centuries; while a right comprehension of the process of life and of the means of influencing its manifestations is only just dawning upon us. We do not yet see our way beyond generalities; and we are befogged by the obtrusion of false analogies and crude anticipations. But Astronomy, Physics, Chemistry, have all had to pass through similar phases, before they reached the stage at which their influence became an important factor in human affairs. Physiology, Psychology, Ethics, Political Science, must submit to the same ordeal. Yet it seems to me irrational to doubt that, at no distant period, they will work as great a revolution in the sphere of practice.

The theory of evolution encourages no millennial anticipations. If, for millions of years, our globe has taken the upward road, yet, some time, the summit will be reached and the downward route will be commenced. The most daring imagination will hardly venture upon the suggestion that the power and the intelligence of man can ever arrest the procession of the great year.

Moreover, the cosmic nature born with us and, to a large extent, necessary for our maintenance, is the outcome of millions of years of severe training, and it would be folly to imagine that a few centuries will suffice to subdue its masterfulness to purely ethical ends. Ethical nature may count upon having to reckon with a tenacious and powerful enemy

as long as the world lasts. But, on the other hand, I see no limit to the extent to which intelligence and will, guided by sound principles of investigation, and organized in common effort, may modify the conditions of existence, for a period longer than that now covered by history. And much may be done to change the nature of man himself. The intelligence which has converted the brother of the wolf into the faithful guardian of the flock ought to be able to do something towards curbing the instincts of savagery in civilized men.

But if we may permit ourselves a larger hope of abatement of the essential evil of the world than was possible to those who, in the infancy of exact knowledge, faced the problem of existence more than a score of centuries ago, I deem it an essential condition of the realization of that hope that we should cast aside the notion that the escape from pain and sorrow is the proper object of life.

We have long since emerged from the heroic childhood of our race, when good and evil could be met with the same "frolic welcome"; the attempts to escape from evil, whether Indian or Greek, have ended in flight from the battlefield; it remains to us to throw aside the youthful overconfidence and the no less youthful discouragement of nonage. We are grown men, and must play the man

strong in will
To strive, to seek, to find, and not to yield,

cherishing the good that falls in our way, and bearing the evil, in and around us, with stout hearts set on diminishing it. So far, we all may strive in one faith toward one hope:

It may be that the gulfs will wash us down,
It may be we shall touch the Happy Isles,

. . . . but something ere the end,
Some work of noble note may yet be done.

SECTION FOUR

LIFE OF KARL MARX

1818

Born in Trier, Germany

1835-41

University studies in Bonn and Berlin, Ph. D., University of Jena, 1841

1842–43

Editor of Reinishce Zeitung a liberal-democratic journal.

Suppressed by Prussian authorities

1843

Marriage to Jenny von Westphalen, moves to Paris where he meets Friedrich Engels

1847

The Poverty of Philosophy

1848

Living in Brussels. Founded the German Worker's party and active in the Communist League. Publishes *The Communist Manifesto* (with Friedrich Engels)

1849

Settles in London

1852

The 18th Brumaire of Louis Bonaparte

1859

The Critique of Political Economy

1864

International Workingmen's Association founded

1867

Volume I, *Capital* (Volumes II & III completed by Engels after Marx's death)

1883

Dies in London

CHAPTER EIGHT

THE MARXIST HERITAGE

INTRODUCTION

"A spectre is haunting Europe—the spectre of Communism." Thus began the *Communist Manifesto*, written by Karl Marx and Friedrich Engels in Brussels, Belgium, and first published in February, 1848. That spectre grew over the almost 150 years that followed to haunt not only Europe but many other parts of the world, including the United States. The Russian Revolution of 1917 created a communist state in one of the largest countries in the world. Through Soviet power and influence, the period following the end of World War II in 1945 saw communist political regimes come to power in Eastern Europe, China, Cuba, and a number of other countries around the globe. The fear of communism and its continuing spread was an often-stated motivating factor in U.S. and West European international actions, and indeed dominated U.S. foreign policy for nearly five decades. Only in 1989 did dramatic repudiations of this power take place in Eastern Europe, followed by the collapse of the communist regime in the USSR in 1991 and the subsequent break-up of the Soviet Union. This period of history is clearly part of Marx's heritage. But it is only one part.

In our part of the globe, Marxism (or Communism) has long been a "dirty word." It is an ideology against which Americans for generations believed they had to protect themselves at all costs. Indeed, this fear reached a point of hysteria in the 1950s when congressional hearings into allegedly subversive Communist activities were held—the hearings were known by the name of the senator who led them, Joseph McCarthy—that bore a disconcerting similarity to medieval witch trials. Whether the perceived threat was ever real, or exaggerated, or still exists, and whether Marx or Marxism are to blame for it is still debated.

In addition to politics, Marx has had a profound influence on other aspects of nineteenth and twentieth century life and thought. He was the driving force behind the International Working Men's Association, founded in 1864. It was largely through his efforts that the labor union movement grew and helped improve the lot of workers in the industrial world. His trenchant criticism of the evils of industrialism as found in mid-nineteenth century England played an important role in bringing about much-needed change. His materialist interpretation of history and his emphasis on the importance of economic forces in social development have influenced the methods of analysis and research of historians, political and social scientists, psychologists, philosophers, and literary critics. In the last two decades both American and European feminist theoreticians have used various aspects of Marxism as a foundation for feminist theory. His analysis of **ideology** continues to serve as a model for uncovering vested interests and penetrating below the surface of political rhetoric.

One need not be a Marxist to acknowledge Marx's positive contributions to Western civilization. Even the most adamant anti-Marxist cannot help but be influenced by his thought, for important aspects of it have been absorbed into Western culture. Jean-Paul Sartre (1905–1980), the famous French existentialist philosopher and writer of the post-World War II period, went so far as to say that Marxism remains "the philosophy of our time. We cannot go beyond it because we have not gone beyond the circumstances which engendered it." Although a clear exaggeration in one sense, in another it underlines the great influence—positive and negative—of Marx's thought both on those who follow it and on those who react against it.

BACKGROUND TO MARX'S THOUGHT

Although Marx's views may have been influential because of their seeming originality, they were not without their historical roots. In philosophy Marx is a product of the Enlightenment and shares the Enlightenment beliefs in reason and progress. He was especially influenced by the two German philosophers, Georg W. F. Hegel (1770–1831) and Ludwig Feuerbach (1804–1870). He combined and adapted Hegel's **dialectical method** and Feuerbach's **materialism**, and, applying both to history, developed his materialist conception of history. Although he never used the term, his later followers refer to his fully developed view as "**historical materialism**." Marx never wrote on the nature of reality in general later Marxists call the general doctrine of reality attributed to Marx and to his collaborator, Friedrich Engels (1820–1895), "dialectical materialism."

Marx's views of communism grew from the earlier views of the socialist thinkers François-Marie-Charles Fourier (1772–1837), Claude-Henri Saint-Simon (1760–1825), and Robert Owen (1771–1858). Even though Marx's analysis of human beings as social beings, and not economically and individualistically utility-maximizing beings turns the theories of some of his philosophical predecessors on their heads, his economic views can be traced back to the English philosophers John Locke (1632–1704) and Thomas Hobbes (1588–1679), the Scottish philosopher-economist, Adam Smith (1723–1790), and the English economist, David Ricardo (1772–1823). Marx continues their works but develops them into a new distinctive position that bears his unmistakable imprint.

The technological and social development of the nineteenth century, namely **industrial capitalism**, gave further impetus to the development of Marxist theory. Along with the language and institutions of representative democracy, the Enlightenment gave Europeans the theory and practice of capitalism, which has become the dominant mode of economic organization in the modern world. The thirteenth, fourteenth, and fifteenth centuries saw the rapid growth of cities, trade, and banking in Europe, overseas expansion by the European states, and the accompanying rise of the middle class. Over time, the new developments brought about the end of feudalism, which was the medieval social and economic system based on land, social hierarchy, and mutual obligation. The new realities of individual entrepreneurship, maximization of profit, the measuring of wealth in commodities rather than land, and the "new breed" of people involved in all these changes, were revolutionary developments that would permanently alter the world. Wedded to the Industrial Revolution that began in the mid-eighteenth century, these trends fundamentally transformed the economic, social, and political life of Europe, the United States, and, since World War II, the entire world.

Capitalism is the economic system in which most of the means of production and distribution are privately owned and operated for profit, normally under competitive conditions. Enlightenment philosophers gave us the theory and justification of capitalism. John Locke's *Second Treatise of Government* was an influential early expression. He included private property among the natural rights to be protected by government, and he argued that since the development of money the unlimited acquisition of property is fully compatible with representative government, social justice, and individual liberty. After Locke, a close connection developed, both historically and intellectually, between the political ideas of individual rights, representative government, and equality before the law and the economic ideas of the free market and the inviolability of private property. Some leading political and economic thinkers of the late eighteenth and the nineteenth centuries believed that they were simply two sides of the same coin. A number of people still do today. For those in this "Lockean" tradition, capitalism is the rational economic system, just as representative government based on human rights is the rational political system. Basic to both is the idea of individual liberty against governmental interference.

The **Industrial Revolution**, another legacy of the Enlightenment period, greatly complicated the phenomenon of capitalism. It created a new, modern form of capitalism, industrial capitalism, which seemed to some thinkers to be incompatible with human rights and representative government. Beginning in the mid-eighteenth century in Britain, the Industrial Revolution saw the replacement of hand tools by machines and power tools and the development of large-scale industrial production embodied in the factory system. By the early decades of the nineteenth century, the Industrial Revolution was bringing massive changes to Britain, and in the decades that followed it produced foundational changes in the social and economic organization of other European countries, the United States, and eventually much of the world.

Capitalist entrepreneurs organized the new technologies into new industries that could produce goods more cheaply and on a large scale. The first half of the nineteenth century witnessed the spectacular growth of what Karl Marx, using the French term, called the bourgeoisie, the propertied middle class, epitomized by the capitalist owners of the means of production and distribution of goods. They produced the factory system, which was characterized by what Marx called individual ownership and social production—that is, the actual producing of goods was done by a large force of workers with only their labor to sell.

Industrialization greatly accelerated the process of urbanization that had begun in the late Middle Ages. European societies in the late eighteenth and early nineteenth centuries were mainly agricultural; the production of wealth was land-based and the population mainly rural. With industrialization, farm workers began to leave the land to work in the new factories located in cities.

The long-term effects of the combination of capitalism and industrialization were a dramatic improvement in living standards for the great majority of people in Europe and the United States. In the short run, however, industrial capitalism created serious problems: social dislocation of individuals and families, and terrible housing, health, education, and working conditions for many. The new industrial towns and cities spawned slums, crime, and public health problems. Working conditions in the mines and factories were appalling, as *The Sadler Report* (1832), commissioned by the British Parliament, graphically revealed through interviews with workers. Men, women, and children—whole families—had to work long hours at back-breaking labor just to survive. They had only their labor to sell at subsistence wages, a phenomenon Marx examined in his analysis of "surplus value." There was typically no concern on the part of factory and mine owners about the health and safety of their workers, who often worked in dark, dangerous, disease-ridden environments. Companies provided no benefits and assumed no liability for injury or death. Workers

Centers of Revolutionary Activity 1848-1849. Redrawn from *A History of Civilization,* Eighth Edition, by Robin W. Winks, Crane Brinton, John B. Christopher, and Robert Lee Wolff, (1992), Prentice-Hall, Inc.

were expendable commodities. This was the industrial capitalism that Marx and Engels knew, the context in which they formed their ideas, the human condition that they believed must be thoroughly analyzed, then challenged at its very roots, and fundamentally changed.

MARX AND ENGELS: BIOGRAPHICAL SKETCHES

Karl Marx. Marx is a paradoxical figure. Although he was trained and received his doctorate in philosophy, his major work, *Capital,* is a classic of economic theory. Born in 1818 in Trier, Prussia, and educated at the Universities of Bonn and Berlin, he spent most of his adult life in London, England, researching and writing in the Library of the British Museum. Born to and raised in a bourgeois family, he championed the cause of the proletariat—the class of ordinary workers who, without any ownership of the means of production, had to sell their labor power in order to live. A founder and leader of the Workingman's Association, he was never a worker himself. He wrote about the advanced industrial countries, which he saw as ripe for revolution—a revolution that, if it has taken place at all, took place in Russia in 1917 and in China in 1949, when each was primarily an agricultural country.

Portrait of Karl Marx. Courtesy of the Library of Congress.

Marx was the son of Jewish parents both descended from a long line of rabbis. Heinrick Marx was prevented from practicing law because he was a Jew so he converted to the Lutheran faith (state church of Prussia) in order to facilitate social and professional acceptance in a society that discriminated against Jews. This was not uncommon among fully assimilated Jews. Karl was baptized and attended a Lutheran elementary school and later the classical Gynmasium (college preparatory high school) in Trier.

Marx attended the Universities of Bonn and Berlin. He wanted to be a poet and playwright, so he studied philosophy and literature. Berlin was at that time, the 1830s, the center of intellectual excitement in Germany, as well as the center of the "Young" or "Radical" Hegelians. Georg W. F. Hegel had died just a few years before but his ideas were kept alive with-

in this group of young students who interpreted and critiqued his ideas from a "left-wing" political, religious, or philosophical standpoint. Marx became a part of this group and, as mentioned above, was deeply influenced by Hegel's philosophy. He received the Ph.D. in philosophy from the University of Jena in 1841.

Unable to secure a teaching position because of his political ideas, the young Marx made his living as a journalist and engaged in radical political activity. In 1843 he married his childhood sweetheart, Jenny von Westphalen. They would have seven children, of whom three daughters survived to adulthood. He spent some time in Paris, where he met Friedrich Engels, had his first real involvement with the working class, and began the serious study of economics. Expelled from France in 1845, he spent a few years in Brussels, Belgium, where he founded the German Workers' Party and was active in the Communist League. Marx together with his lifelong friend, Frederick Engels, wrote the famous *Communist Manifesto*, a statement to the world of principles and goals, for the Communist Party between December 1847 and January 1848. Expelled by the Belgian government, Marx was back in Germany, in Cologne, in 1848–49. Significant revolutions for social and economic justice on the part of the working class took place throughout Europe in 1848, and Marx was a participant in this upheaval.

After being expelled from Cologne and then again from Paris, Marx and his family settled in London, a haven for political exiles and the capital city of the world's most advanced industrial, capitalist society. There he spent the rest of his life as a "stateless exile," eking out a living as a journalist for both German- and English-language publications. A man of immense learning and formidable intellectual powers, including a prodigious mastery of languages, Marx spent most of his time doing research and writing in the great Reading Room of the British Museum. He was an indefatigable and very conscientious scholar, always consulting original sources. He read, in the original languages, everything written on economics. In 1864 he helped found the International Workingmen's Association in London, which Marxists later called the First International. His main contribution to the labor movement for the rest of his life was his writings and correspondence; his economic and social theory and proposals for change became the most powerful shapers of labor and socialist movements beginning in the late nineteenth century.

The Marx family always lived close to poverty, saved from starvation by ongoing generous financial support from the affluent Engels, who was also living in England. Marx was a devoted husband and family man, loving his wife and daughters and loved by them in return. His daughters achieved prominence, together with their husbands, in the French and British socialist and labor movements. His wife's death in 1881 devastated him, and Marx himself died in 1883.

Friedrich Engels (1820–95) was, with Marx, the co-founder of modern socialism, a close friend and collaborator with Marx for many years, the editor of Marx's writings following his death, and the developer of Marx's ideas in ways that became orthodox Marxism. Engels is an important thinker in his own right, although he always deferred to Marx.

Like Marx, Engels was born into the middle-class. His father was a German textile manufacturer, a genuine capitalist entrepreneur and factory owner and, incidentally, a tyrannical Christian fanatic. As a young man doing military service in Berlin, Engels, like Marx, embraced the ideas of the Young Hegelians. Between 1842–44 he worked in the office of a spinning factory, of which his father was a co-owner, in Manchester, England. Here Engels observed industrialism at first hand, since Manchester was the manufacturing center of Britain. During this period he studied the leading economic writers such as Smith and David Ricardo, but also early socialist writings by thinkers such as Robert Owen and Charles Fourier. Engels met Marx in Paris on his way back to Germany in 1844, and the two formed a close and lasting friendship.

From 1844 to 1849, Engels was in Germany, Belgium, and France, writing and participating in revolutionary activities. He actually fought in an 1849 revolutionary uprising in Germany, escaped to England, and, like Marx, spent the rest of his life there. Unable to make a living as a writer, Engels reluctantly returned to his father's business in Manchester in 1850 so that he could help Marx financially. Upon his father's death in 1864, he became a partner in the firm, and by 1869 he had made enough to support himself and Marx and was able to sell his share of the business. Engels lived

Friedrich Engels, 1820–1895. From the Bettmann Archive.

near Marx the rest of his life, seeing him daily. Generous and fun-loving, Engels was the perfect "English gentleman." Brilliant and versatile, he was a successful businessman, a specialist on military affairs, a scientific investigator, and had, like Marx, an impressive knowledge of languages.

MARXIST THEORY

Critique of society and call for human liberation. When Marx went to the University of Berlin in 1836, the influence of Hegel, who had died five years earlier, was still strong. A group of his followers, which Marx joined and which were called the Young or Left Hegelians, rejected the content of Hegel's doctrine but adopted and adapted his dialectical method.

According to Hegel, if we penetrate deeply enough into the concepts we use, we find that one concept tends to pass over into or call forth its opposite. There is no such thing as an isolated concept; thinking is inherently relational. To take a simple example, we cannot understand the concept "light" without the concept "dark." At a more complex level, we cannot understand the behavior of a living organism without understanding what it is not: the environment with which it is in interaction. Hegel tried to show that it is only through this relational or dialectical reasoning that we can understand the structure of both human thought and the universe.

In Hegel's dialectical approach to human history, history was seen as a developing whole. One idea or state of affairs produces a reaction, an opposite idea or state of affairs. The clash of the two produces a synthesis, which in turn produces a further reaction. Even though history has periods of regression, on the whole the development of history is progressive. Historically, ideas and knowledge develop through time; and historically human freedom has increased over time. But Hegel interpreted all this as the development of human thought or consciousness. For him human history is the development of human consciousness as expressed in its institutions, and it is pushed forward through the activity of great men—what he called "world-historical" individuals such as Alexander the Great, Julius Caesar, and Napoleon. But according to Marx, this view stands history on its head. Hegel's dialectical method is the correct way to understand the nature of the historical process, but Hegel fails to see that ideas are **not** the motive force of history. Ideas are the rationalizations people develop to explain and justify their actions. Since how people live and produce determines what they think, the key to history is to be found in the material forms of production, in economic factors, rather than in ideological ones. History is also to be understood primarily in terms of societies and social movements rather than in terms of "great individuals." In this way, Marx claims to stand history back up on its feet, and he develops the materialist or economic doctrine of history.

The ultimate aim of Marx's adoption of the Left Hegelian social critique, in which religion and aristocratic government are criticized for their oppression, is the liberation of humankind from oppression, alienation, and exploitation. Oppression, alienation, and exploitation are found on many levels, the political being a clear one. Government is made by and for people. Yet it is frequently (Marx would say always) used by those in power to protect and foster

their own interests, and in the process they oppress the masses. The French revolutionary slogan of "Liberty, Equality and Fraternity" expresses values and ideals that Marx endorsed but found absent in the society of his day. Just as the remedy for religion lies not in attacking religion directly but in attacking social oppression (in relation to which religion is merely an "opium" intended to relieve the pain and suffering of such oppression), so the remedy for political oppression and alienation is to be sought not on the political surface but at its roots. Typical political revolutions simply replace one ruling and oppressive group or regime with another. Just as true religious emancipation for Marx consists in people being free from religion, so real political emancipation consists not in people being free to engage in politics but in their being free from politics.

Thus political freedom basically consists in putting an end to the domination of human beings by other human beings. This means doing away with the state as an instrument of oppression. In turn this is only possible by doing away with the source of human oppression, which Marx finds on the level of economics and in particular in the institution of private property. Private property, by which Marx means private ownership of the means of production, is the basis for the division of humankind into classes. The need to protect private property leads to the establishment of the state and to the appearance of human exploitation and alienation. Hence the emancipation of humankind requires the elimination of private property. This can be accomplished only if the oppressed masses, the working class, who "have nothing to lose but their chains" (*Communist Manifesto*) free themselves by putting an end to private property, and so to classes, exploitation, and alienation. Since Marx equates the interests of humanity in general with the interests of the workers, the triumph of the proletariat, or the mass of workers, will for the first time in history result not in the oppression of one group by another but in the end of all oppression. Through the resulting unification of all society, all its members will work for the benefit of all.

Central to Marx's view of human emancipation is his view of what it means to be a human being. The key to any being's nature, Marx tells us, is what it does. Human beings are different from other entities insofar as they alone produce the means of their own

Marx and Engels. By Stephen Lahey.

subsistence. What and how they produce determines their lives. Although some people may emphasize the intellectual accomplishments of human beings (and put emphasis on their minds, brains, or souls) for Marx these are secondary. Human beings must live before they think, and how they live determines what they think. Human beings make themselves by what they do. They are essentially social beings, who live in society and are truly human only in society. The notion of a truly individual human being, separate from society, is an abstraction. Similarly, the notion of individual human rights as rights against all others reflects a misconception about human beings. Radical individualism pretends that each person is complete, independent of all others. In fact, human beings are members of a species and become fully human only in and through society.

Marx's view may be said to be **materialistic**, because he claims that the material nature of human beings is primary, and their spiritual or intellectual attributes secondary. He denies the possibility of independently existing spirits or minds or souls.

Following Hegel, Marx's view is communitarian rather than individualistic, because he believes that individuals are and become human only in society. He is interested in liberating people, not by freeing individuals, but by freeing all of society from **oppression**, **exploitation**, and **alienation**. His view of human nature is dynamic, in that he sees what human beings are and what they are capable of becoming as a historical process. We should not mistake the nature of human beings by looking only at one period of history, for example, our own, and extrapolating from that.

In a capitalist society, property becomes all-important. People are judged by what and how much they have. Products thus come to dominate people—a state of affairs that Marx describes by saying workers are alienated from the products of their labor. The result of excessive division of labor, characteristic of assembly line production in which each person does one repetitive action, results in the workers' alienation from the labor process. Instead of labor being the means of developing one's talents and leading to an individual's all-round development, work becomes stultifying. People then work to live and live only when they do not work, for example, on weekends or vacation times. The result of capitalist competition results in the alienation of human beings from one another. Competition pits them against one another for jobs, raises, promotions, goods.

The ideal towards which Marx aims is a society in which people will live together harmoniously instead of in conflicting classes; in which people can develop their capacities through creative labor; in which people are free from domination by others, free from the domination of things, free from alienation. Such human liberation can only be achieved by changing society's basic structures (especially by abolishing private property and class divisions), and not simply by persuading, encouraging or helping individuals to change themselves.

The materialist view of history. The aim of human liberation by itself is a goal and expresses a value which Marx finds developing throughout history. Marx argues that the goal of human emancipation remains utopian, an unreachable ideal, unless it can be shown to be grounded in reality and joined with a practical plan of action that outlines how to attain it. The ideals expressed by the socialists who preceded him had always been utopian. Each of them expressed their views; a few tried social experiments; but none had any concrete plan for changing all of society. This is the basis of Marx's critique in *The Communist Manifesto* of various historical forms of socialism.

According to Marx, a dialectical and materialistic interpretation of human history shows that there have been four periods or stages of development, to be followed in the future by a fifth.

1. The first is that of **primitive communal society**. This is the period that precedes written history. In primitive communal societies property was held in common and people lived communally. Since there was no private property, there were no class divisions, no exploitation or oppression of one group by another. But all lived in great poverty, surviving as best they could.

2. As productive resources developed, as animals were domesticated and herding was introduced, the basis appeared for some to have more than others, and thus the introduction of private

property took place. This led to the next stage of human society, namely to **slave-holding societies**. People were now divided into two classes, the slaveholders, who owned property or the means of production, and the slaves, who performed the work. This division in the economic conditions, or the economic base, of society caused a division in the social superstructure that was built on it.

In general the economic base of any society consists of the **forces of production** and the **relations of production**. The forces of production consist of the means of production (or the material used for production) and the modes of production (or the manner in which production is organized and takes place). The relations of production in their legal form are ownership relations.

Clearly slaveholders and slaves do not associate together outside of the productive process. The nonproductive social interactions—those of family life, friendly associations, joint cultural activities, and the like—are built on the **economic base**. These social relations, plus social institutions (for example, the state, schools, and churches), and what Marx calls "**ideological forms**" (such as religion, philosophy, art, and law) make up the **social superstructure** built on the economic base. The slaveholders rule society and establish institutions to serve their purposes. They pass laws and establish a police force and an army to protect their property and their interests. They justify their property and the existing structures of society in the religious doctrines preached in the churches, in the philosophy taught in the schools, and in the legal theory enforced by the courts. They support and hence directly or indirectly control the art, literature, dance, and rituals of the society, which reflect and justify their interests and views. The dominant culture of any period is the culture of the ruling class.

3. As productive forces develop, slavery becomes less and less useful and slaves are gradually replaced with serfs. The change in economic production leads to the next stage of history, namely, **feudalism**. As the economic base changes, this requires corresponding changes in the superstructure. Laws, governmental institutions, philosophy, and so on, all change accordingly.

4. Feudalism in its turn gives way to the stage of **capitalism**. The change from feudalism to capitalism takes place as productive forces develop. The

Industrial Revolution is incompatible with feudal relations of production. The rise of a merchant class and the development of machine production, which replaced hand craft, led to the new capitalist stage of economic development, characterized by the rise of a class—the bourgeoisie—who came to own the factories, the farms, ships, and buildings. The cities grew. All of this economic activity led to the general overthrow of monarchy, to the rise of democracy, to changing social relations, legal institutions and structures of government, and to the rise of individualistic philosophies (such as those of Descartes, Hobbes, and Locke) which corresponded to the individualism characteristic of capitalism. Serfs gave way to industrial workers, the proletariat. As the serfs left the farms for the cities they had to sell their labor power (get jobs) in order to live, since they owned neither land nor machines. At the same time the aristocracy was replaced by the bourgeoisie, the class of those who owned the means of production.

5. Marx describes the capitalist era and the dynamics of its development in his major work, *Capital*. He finds that capitalism contains a basic opposition, the overcoming of which will lead to the development of the next stage of historical development, at which he and Engels hint in the *Manifesto*, and which he calls communism.

Marx maintains that the basic opposition of capitalism lies in the fact that while ownership relations (or the relations of production) are private, the forces of production under capitalism have become socialized. Manufacturing is a joint enterprise involving a great division of labor, with many people each performing given tasks to achieve a final product. The capitalist modes of production are thus cooperative and socialized, while the profit derived from production is appropriated by private individuals. The workers are the creators of wealth, but they receive only a portion of it. These oppositions can be overcome only by making ownership social, and thus allowing it to correspond to the social forces of production.

According to Marx, the gap between the haves and the have-nots will increase under capitalism. This is why, in the *Manifesto*, he and Engels call the *bourgeoisie*, whose activities drive this process of impoverishing the proletariat, or have-nots, "the most revolutionary class heretofore." The workers, who are the vast majority, will eventually realize that they are the real creators of social wealth and they will be forced by their deteriorating economic position to seize control of the means of production. Once they do, they will socialize the economy. By doing away with private ownership of the means of production, all people will share in the profits that were previously appropriated by the capitalist owners. The people will be working for themselves instead of for their employers. Productivity will increase and the goods produced can be equitably distributed for the benefit of all.

Since the basis of classes, namely, private property (or private ownership of the means of production), will have disappeared, classes will disappear. The social superstructure will in turn change. There will be no need for institutions to protect private property, no need for a state to enforce the exploitation of one group by another. Hence in time the state as a repressive body will be unnecessary and will wither away. The governance of people will be replaced by the administration of things.

Of course, this will not happen all at once, any more than feudalism replaced slavery or was replaced by capitalism all at once. There will initially be a transition phase from capitalism to socialism, which Marx calls the period of the **dictatorship of the proletariat**. In this period the bourgeoisie will be kept in check and the beginnings of communism established. This will lead to **socialism**, which is the first phase of communism, and which will lead eventually to the next phase, or full **communism**.

It was Engels who gave the name of **historical materialism** to Marx's view of history. It was also primarily Engels who, after Marx's death in 1883 developed the doctrine called **dialectical materialism**. According to dialectical materialism all of reality—nature, history, and human thought—is governed by **three laws of dialectics**, which are discovered through scientific investigation. These three laws are the law of the interpenetration of opposites; the law of the transition from quantity to quality; and the law of the negation of the negation.

According to the first law, all of reality is in movement, and the movement is the product of internal conflict. Thus the movement of the atom is generated by the presence of the positive and negative particles that make it up. Similarly, each idea or state of society brings forth an opposing idea or state of society, moving history on.

According to the second law, development from quantity to quality takes place as the result of incremental changes in quantity. At a certain point, called a "nodal point," a qualitative change takes place. Thus water can be heated to 211 degrees fahrenheit, at which point the addition of one more unit of heat changes water from a liquid state into a gas or steam. In social development, incremental changes in the base take place until a nodal point is reached, which we call revolution. At that point the straw that breaks the camel's back leads to the overthrow of the existing regime and the creation of a new one.

The third law, the negation of the negation, describes the movement that reconciles two conflicting states of affairs (or ideas) to produce a new state of affairs (or idea) which in its turn will generate its opposite. The reconciliation takes place by preserving the positive aspect of each of the conflicting elements, negating the negative elements, and combining the positive elements into a higher form. Thus primitive communal society was communal—its positive aspect—but poor—its negative aspect. Class society was divided into classes—its negative aspect—but it developed wealth—its positive aspect. Communist society will combine the community of the first with the wealth of the second to produce a society superior to both of its predecessors.

The analysis of capitalism. According to Marx, the key question to answer if one is to understand capitalism and its historical place is: Where does profit come from? Marx begins his analysis with a study of commodities—items that because of their use value are actually exchanged, and thus have exchange value. The general rule in a barter system is that equals are exchanged for equals. If this were not so, what one would gain as a seller one would lose as a buyer. But for exchanges to take place one must be able to determine equivalent values. There must be some common denominator, something common to all commodities, by which their respective exchange values can be determined. The only common element of all commodities is that they are all the products of human labor. This leads to Marx's **labor theory of value**, which he adopts and adapts from Locke, Smith, and others, who, in turn, borrowed elements of it from medieval economic theory.

In Marx's theory, the value of any commodity is determined by the average socially necessary labor time needed to produce it. Providing the result is of equal quality, a product is not worth more if a slow worker produces it rather than a fast worker. Hence the measure of the value of a product is the average socially necessary time needed to produce it. Since machines increase what a worker is able to produce in a given amount of time, a machine-made product incorporates less labor time (even when we include the labor time necessary to produce the machine) than a hand-made product. Hence the value (and so the cost) of the product decreases. The great virtue of capitalism is that through the development of productive forces (e.g., machines and assembly-line production), a great variety of goods gradually became plentiful and affordable to the masses. Capitalism was thus progressive with respect to feudalism, and it was a necessary stage in the history of humankind's development.

Nonetheless, Marx asks: Where does profit come from? He argues that since equals are traded for equals even in a money economy, profit can only come from not paying the real value for something. According to his analysis, this something turns out to be the common element of all commodities, namely, human labor. By paying workers less than the value they produce, the entrepreneur is able to sell commodities at their real value and still make a profit. Profit is the "**surplus value**" the worker contributes to the product for which he or she is not paid. Surplus value is the difference between the amount of labor that is needed to produce a product and the cost of maintaining that labor. The productive nature of labor means that it always produces more than is required to sustain it, and the entrepreneur, by paying less for labor than labor produces, is able to capture this difference as profit.

Since entrepreneurs wish to maximize their profits, they wish to have workers work as many hours as possible for as low wages as possible. By contrast, workers wish to work as short a time as possible for as high a wage as possible. But owners of the means of production are in the stronger position since the workers need work and wages in order to live. If the supply of workers is greater than the demand—if there is unemployment—workers are willing to work for lower wages than otherwise. Hence unemployment and the resulting "reserve army of the unemployed" is to the owners' advantage. There is a level, however, below which wages cannot fall without adversely affecting the owners, and that is the level necessary to sustain a family. If wages fall below this subsistence level, the workers cannot support themselves or produce their replacements. If the primary wage earner—typically the male in Marx's day—is paid less than subsistence, his wife will be forced to work. Since her wage is supplementary, women could be hired for less than men. The final stage of exploitation is reached when the joint wages of husband and wife fail to reach the subsistence level, and the children must be sent to work as well, at wages even less than those paid women.

This scenario might sound extreme to many Americans, but the situation that Marx described was the one that actually existed in England at the time he was writing. The British government investigated the situation of workers, and a resulting government document called *The Sadler Report* (1832) detailed the atrocious working conditions in British factories, including the fact of child labor, with children sometimes chained to their machines so they would not wander. Marx did not make up these facts, but sought to devise a theory that would account for and explain them. Only with such a theory could he hope to understand the dynamics of the system, understand where the system was going, and devise a program to help the workers improve their position and preserve the positive aspects of capitalism while ridding it of its exploitation, inequality, oppression, and misery.

In his view the tendency of capitalism, if unchecked, would force the workers into greater and greater poverty. He believed they would eventually be forced by their conditions to revolt, to seize the means of production from the hands of the capitalists, to socialize ownership, and to end society's exploitation. Once they unfettered society's productive forces, they would produce an abundance of goods that would be available to all and that would enable all to have what they need. The entrepreneurs would not willingly give up their special position and would use the police and the army to protect their vested interests. A violent revolution by the workers would probably be necessary to move society into its next stage. Since the economic base in the highly industrialized societies is adequate to support a society with enough goods to satisfy the basic needs of all, Marx expected the revolution leading to socialism to take place first in the highly industrialized countries, such as Germany or England. Other

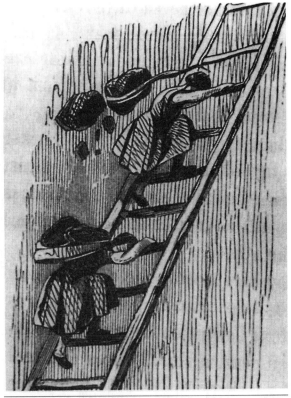

Girls haul up ladders in Scottish coal mine in an 1843 print. The Library of Congress.

countries would follow until the world had moved into the age of socialism.

Superstructure, ideology, and the analysis of ideological forms. Ultimately, according to Marx, the economic base of a society determines its social superstructure. But this determination is neither direct nor simple. The superstructure can also influence and affect the base. Through legislation, for example, a government may for a time succeed in preventing the development of the productive forces of a society. A government would be interested in doing so especially if it foresaw that the continuing development of productive forces would threaten its position. But neither law nor government regulations nor any other aspects of the superstructure can preserve slavery or feudalism indefinitely. Ultimately the productive forces win out. The same, Marx holds, will be true of capitalism.

The superstructure can help promote the development of productive forces. Once they have been developed in one society, the progressive government of a less developed society can help hasten

James Woelfel at Karl Marx's grave, Highgate Cemetery, London. Photo by Sarah Trulove.

its own society's productive development. It can import or copy the first society's inventions, techniques, or technological innovation. Marx tells us that one society can learn from another. But it cannot leap over stages and pass, for instance, from feudalism to capitalism simply by legislating a new social order. It must first build its economic base. Thus, different societies will move into socialism at different rates and at different times.

Although the base determines the superstructure, the different parts of the superstructure mutually affect one another. Developments in religion, or in philosophy, or in art, for instance, each influence the other areas. Moreover, there is carryover in each of these areas from one historical period to the next, and in each successive period we may find remnants of the previous period. Thus, Greek philosophy influenced medieval philosophy and the latter influenced modern philosophy. The same is true of art, and today we can appreciate Greek, Renaissance, and early modern art, although there are clearly differences among them. In general, the influence from

one period to the next is in logical development or form, while the content is determined by the prevailing economic conditions of the time. Thus Aristotle and Plato both justified slavery because they lived in slave-holding societies. Their philosophies influenced the form and nature of the problems discussed and the logical development of the views of later philosophers; but once slavery was no longer profitable, later philosophers no longer justified it. This substantive change in moral outlook came about not by abstract logical discussion, but as a result of changing economic reality.

For Marx, **ideology** is in general a systematically distorted view of reality. It arises from seeing reality from a skewed, one-sided perspective. For example, members of the class of slave-holders see reality from their vantage point and tend to justify their position and vested interests. They teach their children to view the world from that point of view, which appears to those who grow up with it as natural, normal, and correct. Although ideology is **false consciousness**, this does not imply self-deception or maliciousness. Defenders of class dominance may well be sincere in their defense of existing institutions, themselves believing what they preach to others.

The ruled have different interests from the rulers and hence develop their own ideology. But it is usually suppressed. Since the rulers dominate the society, it is their point of view that is taught in the schools, preached from the pulpit, printed in the books, developed in philosophy, expressed in law. Since the dominant view is taught as well to the ruled, it tends to mollify them and it induces them to accept their condition as natural, appropriate, and justified. To some extent the rulers succeed in convincing the masses of the legitimacy of the rules under which they live.

Marx thus provides us with a technique for analyzing political statements, social institutions, literature, art, philosophy, religion, and all other ideological forms or other aspects of the superstructure. None of them should be accepted at face value, any more than we accept at face value individuals' appraisals of themselves.

Marx's view of ideology is related to classes: according to him, individuals have ideologies as members of a class. It is possible, though rare, for members of one class to identify with another class and to adopt its point of view. Thus Marx, born into a bourgeois family, came to identify with the proletariat and became its articulate spokesman. Although Marx believed that workers would be forced by their circumstances to revolt, he also believed that theory was necessary to guide their actions. He saw his task as raising the consciousness of the workers, helping them see their true situation, and so facilitating their taking appropriate and successful action when the material conditions were ripe.

The Doctrine of Communism. Communism was for Marx the next state of society to be achieved, the movement by which it could be achieved, and the doctrine that was to guide the movement. Communism, as we saw, could not be achieved all at once in any society and would not be achieved simultaneously in all societies. Capitalism was a necessary precondition for the development of communism. Only after capitalism had developed the productive forces of society was communism possible.

During the transition stage between capitalism and communism, the period of the revolutionary dictatorship of the proletariat, the proletariat would seize the means of production, take over the factories, and remove the ruling class from its position of power. The proletariat would exercise its dictatorship over the bourgeoisie, which it would control in order to prevent a counter-revolution. This phase would give way to the first phase of communism, which Marx called "socialism," and which he characterized by the slogan "From each according to his ability, to each according to his work." Everyone would be required to work, but rewards would be differential and proportional to what one produced. Great gaps between the have and have-nots would be eliminated, as would classes and class structures. In this period, inequalities, although reduced, would still exist, but exploitation would be eliminated. As people gained control of society and of their lives, alienation would disappear. People's views would begin to change to express their real conditions of life and the socialization of ownership.

Eventually the phase of full communism would be reached. Marx characterized this phase by the slogan "From each according to his ability, to each according to his need." All would contribute what they could and all would receive what they required. To make this possible the society must have achieved great development of its productive forces, yielding a great outpouring of the goods necessary to satisfy people's needs. When alienation, the domination of some people by others, classes, exploitation, and private ownership of the means of production have all disappeared, the need for the existence of the state itself would disappear. Exactly how the society would be run, and how distribution would be achieved, Marx does not say. But since the people would have achieved freedom, they would be free to decide these questions for themselves. No one would or could decide for them and impose that decision upon them.

Marx's heritage is multifaceted. In capitalist countries, his influence on the labor union movement improved the lot of the workers. In Germany, conditions seemed ripe for revolution when the German Social Democratic Party adopted Marxism as its official doctrine, but the anticipated revolution never occurred. Instead a revolution took place in Russia, a country mired in stage three, not the appropriate "jumping off point" which Marx had specified. The leader of that revolution, V. I. Lenin, recast Marxism into a form that justified the revolution of October 1917. This new "**Marxism-Leninism**" spread to other areas of the globe, most particularly to China in 1949. Lenin's early death in 1924 brought to power the infamous Josef Stalin, who initiated further, far-reaching changes to Marxist doctrine and revolutionary practice. In China, another variation of Marxism-Leninism was known as Maoism, named after the leader of the Communist revolution there in 1949.

As it grew over the course of the twentieth century, the spectre of communism gathered a host of differing ethnic and religious groups under its Marxist-Leninist banner. The question we must now ask ourselves is whether the conflicts that have arisen as a result of the break-up of the Communist world have been brought about because of centuries-old unresolved religious and national/ethnic differences, or because of the failure of the social-political system that held these disparate groups together over the past several decades. Have we returned to our starting point with the failure of another revolution? And if so, is there another synthesis to be made? Western Marxists, many of them in universities in the U.S. and Europe, have developed new interpretations and applications of Marxist theory in the light of the newer movements for human liberation. They continue to reject the identification of Marxism with the Soviet Union and China and they see Marx's analysis of the economic base and social superstructure, ideology, and the roots of exploitation as lasting contributions. Marx has strongly influenced the Western tradition and continues to do so for better or for worse, positively and negatively. While his views do not have to be accepted, they cannot be ignored by anyone interested in understanding the contemporary world.

GUIDE TO THE READINGS: *THE COMMUNIST MANIFESTO*

A reader of *The Communist Manifesto* should keep two things in mind: first, the *Manifesto* is an early presentation of Marxist ideas (before the publication of Darwin's *Origin of Species* in 1859, for example, which Marx and Engels believed was a crucial scientific underpinning of their dialectical interpretation of nature and history); and second, the *Manifesto* is a summary statement of the principles of a political party to the public at large and a call to action, not a careful, comprehensive, scholarly treatise (although a great deal of research and reflection lies behind it).

Part I, "Bourgeois and Proletarians," briefly presents Marx's and Engel's analysis of history, based on their theory that the dynamic of history is generated by economic life and the class struggle that results and focusing on the modern struggle between bourgeoisie and proletariat. This section contains perhaps the most analytically, rhetorically, and prophetically powerful description ever written of the nature and history of capitalism and its revolutionary character. With profound and prescient insight Marx describes the spirit of capitalism in terms that are clearly still applicable in our highly technologized and globalized world. Part II, "Proletarians and Communists," announces the specifics of the program of the Communist Party and argues why it is the only party through which the proletariat can be emancipated. Part III, "Socialist and Communist Literature," offers a short history and critique of the various forms of socialist thought that have emerged since the Middle Ages. Marx and Engels differentiated their socialism from other forms by arguing that it was truly "scientific"—based on universal laws derived from historical facts—while previous forms of socialism were merely "utopian"—often expressing good intentions but not based in reality.

QUESTIONS FOR STUDY AND DISCUSSION

1. Explain the relation of classes and private property.
2. According to Marx, what does human liberation consist of? How can it be achieved?
3. What is the materialist view of history?
4. According to Marx, where does profit come from? Is Marx's labor theory of value satisfactory as an economic theory? Discuss.
5. What is the relation of the economic base of society to the social superstructure? Explain what each consists of.
6. Are Marx's views ideological (according to his conception of ideology)? Discuss.
7. What are the three laws of dialectics?

SUGGESTIONS FOR FURTHER READING

Berlin, Isaiah. *Karl Marx*. 4th ed. Oxford: Oxford University Press, 1978.

Guettel, Charnie. *Marxism and Feminism*. Toronto: The Hunter Rose Company, 1974.

Hook, Sidney. *Marx and the Marxists*. Reprinted: Melbourne, FL: Krieger, 1982.

Kolakowski, Leszek. *Main Currents of Marxism*. 3 vols. Translated by P. S. Falla. Oxford: Clarendon Press, 1978.

Körner, Stephan. Kant. New York: Penguin Books, 1982.

McLellan, David. *The Thought of Karl Marx: An Introduction*, New York: Harper Torchbooks, 1974.

Moore, John H. ed. *Legacies of the Collapse of Marxism*, Fairfax, VA: George Mason University Press, 1994.

Tucker, Robert C., ed. *The Marx-Engels Reader*. 2nd ed. New York: W. W. Norton, 1978.

_____. *Philosophy and Myth in Karl Marx*. 2nd ed. New York: Cambridge University Press, 1972.

Wolfe, Bertram D. *Marxism: 100 Years in the Life of a Doctrine*. Reprinted: Boulder, CO: Westview, 1985.

_____. *Three Who Made a Revolution: A Biographical History*. 4th ed. revised. Reprinted: Briarcliff, NY: Stein & Day, 1984.

LIFE OF W.E.B. DU BOIS

1868

Born in Great Barrington, MA

1888

B.A. from Fisk University

1890

B.A. from Harvard, Ph. D., 1896

Dis. *The Suppression of the African slave Trade to the United States, 1638-1870*

1896–1897

Assistant instructor in sociology, University of Pennsylvania

1899

The Philadelphia Negro: A Sociological Study

1900

Introduced to Pan-Africanism. Attends Congresses in 1919 (Paris), 1921 (Brussels and London), 1923 (London and Lisbon, 1927 (New York) and 1945 (Manchester, England)

1903

The Souls of Black Folk

1905

Launches Niagra Movement

1909

Founding of NAACP, serves as director of publicity and research and editor of *The Crisis* until 1934. Returns to serve from 1944–48

1934–1944:

On the faculty of Atlanta University, GA. Publishes *Black Reconstruction in America,* 1860-1889, (1935)

Post WW II

Du Bois active in ban the bomb and peace movements

1947

The World and Africa: An Inquiry into the Part Which Africa Has Played in World History

1950

Runs on the socialist ticket for U.S. Senate from New York

1951

Caught up in the McCarthy witchhunt against communists, Du Bois charged with being and agent for a foreign power. Acquitted

1958-59

Travels in Russia and China

1961

Joins the Communist Party, moves to Ghana, Africa

1963

Dies in Ghana

CHAPTER NINE

W. E. B. DU BOIS

SLAVERY IN THE UNITED STATES

Probably no nation on earth better illustrates the contradictions of western thought and history over the past two centuries than the United States. The fledgling country began as an experiment in enlightened thinking, a bold attempt to remove Locke's assertions of natural-born equality and the classical traditions of self-government from the realms of theory and memory and put them into actual practice. Within a century and a half of its founding, the United States had grown from a collection of English-speaking colonies huddled on the eastern coast of North America into a global empire, spanning not only the breadth of its home continent, but the far reaches of Alaska, the Caribbean and the Pacific Islands. Indeed, for many people living today, the nation's amazingly rapid rise to power and wealth, with institutions that serve as models for democracy worldwide, marks it as one of Western civilization's outstanding accomplishments.

If this is so, then the story of America's national expansion also exposes the inherent flaws of unrestrained growth, and perhaps even of democracy itself. When the federal government of the United States was established, more people were excluded from citizenship within its body politic than were included. Women were denied the right to vote, as were Native Americans, and for that matter, most white males, since the majority of states imposed property qualifications that gave full political rights only to men of wealth. As the United States conquered new territory in the nineteenth century, more dark-skinned peoples joined the nation—western Indians, Hispanics, Asians—all of them contributing to the rich diversity of languages, religions and customs that makes America a unique place. The challenge of the American experience has been to reconcile abstract theories about democracy and equality for all with the actual realization of those values as the country has grown to absorb more peoples under its banner than the founders of the republic ever intended or even thought possible. Meeting that challenge has been a process of conflict, so much so that it is fair to say that the American Revolution still has not ended. Women, racial minorities, Jews, and working-class Euro-Americans have fought long, hard struggles to complete those promises that the revolutionaries of 1776 left unfulfilled. African Americans often have been in the forefront of that revolution, first in their efforts to eradicate slavery and later in their campaigns for equal civic and social rights.

The black experience in America has its roots in slavery. White Americans were not alone in their use of slave labor, nor were they the first to try it. Human slavery dates back to ancient times; the Greeks and Romans held slaves, as did Native Americans and Africans themselves. What made the American version of slavery unique was its scope and racially based nature. Whereas most ancient cultures saw a slave owner holding only a handful of slaves, mostly as household servants, slavery as practiced in the United States resulted in huge plantations where hundreds of persons worked in bondage to produce agricultural commodities like tobacco and cotton. Greco-Roman law recognized the slave's legal status as a human being, but in the American version, slaves enjoyed no legal rights and could be bought, sold, or even killed in most cases by their owners, who regarded them as property and nothing more. The first African slaves arrived in Virginia as early as 1619, and within two centuries the United States had become the largest slave-owning country in the western hemisphere. The profits that slave labor generated allowed for the emergence in the South of a genteel class of political and economic leaders who used their power and influence in the state and federal governments to thwart any suggestion that slavery should be reformed or abolished, or that black rights should be recognized in any way.

Although few people of European descent believed blacks to be their racial equals, there had always been many western thinkers and reformers who thought slavery an abomination and committed themselves to ending it. England especially, influenced by political liberalism, saw the rise of a vigorous **abolitionist** movement. During the course of the nineteenth century, England applied economic pressure against slave owning countries in the Caribbean and Latin America—an ironic policy, since England simultaneously pursued racist and imperialist policies in its own African and Indian colonies. The role of blacks themselves in ending slavery should not be forgotten. Violent slave rebellions were common occurrences, and the refusal of slaves to remain shackled, combined with international sanctions, encouraged the gradual end of legal slavery in Cuba, Brazil and other countries throughout the world.

In the United States, abolitionism never attained a power comparable to that of its equivalent in England, but its chief proponents did contribute to a shift of public opinion, at least in the North. Slavery had developed along regional lines; plantation agriculture and its slave system dominated the South, whereas northern states became more reliant on capitalist wage labor. Abolitionists like Frederick Douglass, a former slave himself, and Harriet Beecher Stowe held northern whites spellbound relating the horrors of the South's "peculiar institution." The election of Abraham Lincoln in 1860 brought to the presidency a candidate who opposed the expansion of slavery into newly-acquired western territories, leading to the secession of the southern states and the Civil War. This great conflict, which ultimately cost the lives of more than half a million Americans, had a number of complex causes, division over the slavery issue being only one of them. But a major consequence of the war was the end of legalized slavery. On January 1, 1863, Lincoln's "emancipation proclamation" freed all slaves then living in states held by the Confederacy. Lincoln's decision had less to do with humanitarianism than with military necessity,

because he hoped to encourage black freedmen to abandon their plantations and flock to Union army lines. Thousands of slaves already had done this, but after emancipation, black men enlisted in the United States Army in such numbers that they comprised ten percent of its manpower during the last two years of the war, thus tipping the scales in the North's favor. By mid-1865, the Confederacy lay defeated, and a new era of opportunities seemed to await four million African Americans.

So began the period known as **Reconstruction** from 1865 to 1877, when Northern politicians debated the best means to re-incorporate the southern states into the federal government and what assistance to provide the recently-freed former slaves. By 1870, Congress had approved and the states had ratified three constitutional amendments (the 13th, 14th, and 15th) that outlawed slavery and granted to freedmen (only males) the full rights of citizenship, including suffrage. Congress also established the Freedmen's Bureau, which helped to build black schools, translated legal documents for the illiterate, and provided a number of services to help blacks with the transition to freedom. But the commitment of northern whites to black advancement had definite limits. Most believed that emancipation meant blacks now had a fair place at the starting line when it came to competing for economic and social progress, unaware of or apathetic toward the ways in which slavery's legacies continued to cripple the chances blacks had for better lives. Since most blacks had few skills other than as agricultural workers, many returned to their old plantations to work as sharecroppers, renters who farmed land they did not own and paid their landlords in crops or cash after the harvest. Sharecropping became an oppressive system in which blacks (and often poor whites) remained in perpetual debt to landowners. Freedmen also lived in terror of the Ku Klux Klan, a secret society of former Confederates who terrorized blacks into submission through violence, burning schools and churches, and scaring freedmen away from voting places. Until 1877, the Union Army, which still maintained several regiments in the South, kept much of white southerners' hostility toward black rights in check. This changed, however, with the disputed presidential election of 1876. The Republican candidate, Rutherford B. Hayes, despite having lost the popular vote, was given the electoral

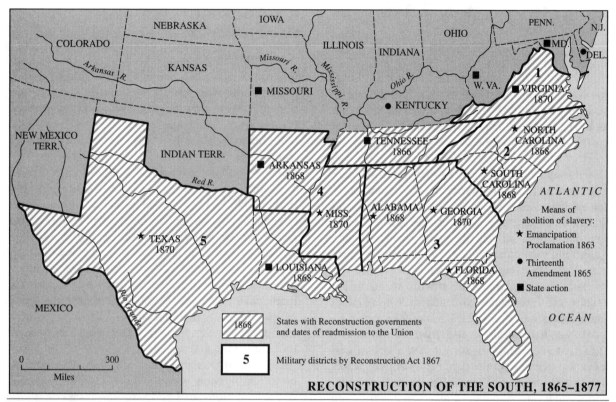

Reconstruction of the South, 1865-1877. Redrawn from *These United States: The Questions of Our Past,* Fourth Edition, Combined Edition, by Irwin Unger, Prentice-Hall, Inc.

votes needed to win the presidency by the opposing, southern-based Democratic party. In return, Hayes agreed to remove all remaining Union troops from the South.

The official end of Reconstruction reversed many of the gains that African Americans had begun to realize. Abandoned by their northern protectors, blacks now faced an onslaught of discriminatory laws designed to revoke their status as free people by circumventing the thirteenth, fourteenth and fifteenth amendments. Southern states passed a number of initiatives in the late 1800s known as "Jim Crow laws" that stripped away black political rights. Along with poll taxes and grandfather clauses that excluded most blacks from voting, other measures mandated social segregation by forcing blacks to ride in separate street cars and eat in separate restaurants, refusing them service in theatres, schools and hospitals defined as "white," along with a host of other laws that prevented interracial mingling. African American lead-

ers looked to the federal government in the hope that such laws would be ruled unconstitutional, but in the 1896 Plessy v. Ferguson case, the United States Supreme Court decided that the establishment of "separate but equal" facilities remained a prerogative of the state governments. Racial violence against blacks rose dramatically; between 1865 and 1945, more than five thousand African American men—approximately sixty per year—were lynched by white mobs. Lynching even became a grotesque form of public entertainment in the South, where white families would sometimes travel for miles to watch such events and occasionally even took souvenirs from the victim's corpse afterwards. As of 1900, blacks had won their legal freedom and a number of "paper rights" but little else, constituting an inferior social caste in a nation whose official ideology denied the existence of natural-born inequalities. African Americans would use a dual approach in trying to improve their situation, combining certain Western ideas with their own African-based culture and spiritual beliefs.

AMERICAN RACISM

Even in the twenty-first century, foreign observers often are struck by the persistence of racism in the United States. The pattern is an old one; in the 1830s, the French traveler Alexis de Tocqueville remarked on the amazing degree of egalitarian belief among white Americans, where men of the lower classes—unlike workers in Europe—acknowledged no social superiors, but then expressed outrage at the idea of black equality with whites. Historians and philosophers have puzzled over this paradox. Some have been quick to describe slavery and racism as exceptions, minor aberrations in an otherwise unbroken trend toward equality and democracy, while others claim that the competing strands of racism and equality are interrelated and in fact were defined simultaneously. The historian Edmund Morgan, in his book *American Slavery, American Freedom*, contends that acceptance of slavery and a consequent belief in black inferiority by the United States' founders made possible their beliefs about equality within the white race. As of the late eighteenth century, terms such as "equality" and "democracy" were as yet radical notions. American revolutionaries employed these terms conservatively, using them only to undermine the authority of monarchy and aristocratic privilege, not to assert a universal belief in the equality of all humankind. From the country's inception, "white" equality and freedom was necessarily qualified by, and even dependent on, the justified exploitation of those who were non-white, and subsequently, non-free.

Through the course of the nineteenth century, "whiteness" increasingly became a criterion for "Americanness." The 1790 Naturalization Act, which provided the legal means for foreign immigrants to become citizens, limited citizenship status only to men of the white race, deliberately excluding Indians and blacks. The framers of this act probably expected that future migrants would come mostly from England. With the advent of the Industrial Revolution, however, the United States would attract immigrants from all of Europe, and all would eventually qualify for membership in the new republic, provided they could legitimately claim themselves to be "white." In this manner, terms such as "white"

and "black," which carried no particular meaning or conveyed no special privilege in Europe and Africa, came to hold great significance in America.

The belief that human beings are easily divisible into categories called "races" received initial support from the physical and social sciences. In a corruption of Charles Darwin's biological theories about evolution, the doctrine of "racial darwinism" held that human races evolve at different speeds, and that some races such as Africans bear a closer resemblance to humanity's primate ancestors than others. The eugenics movement, led by then-respectable thinkers like Lothrop Stoddard and Madison Grant, taught that human races can be arranged hierarchically with the white race at the peak. If whites wished to continue their ascendancy, warned the eugenists, they must refrain from mixing or interbreeding with inferior races. Ideas like these lent intellectual credence not only to the Jim Crow laws of the United States, but also to the imperialistic expansion of Western countries into Africa, Asia, India and other dark-skinned regions. Today, scientists generally concur that "race" is not a category of biological science, while revelations of the horrors of the Nazi Holocaust and the later advances of the civil rights movement have—for the most part—repudiated racism as a way of thinking. But prior to the Second World War, racism offered a worldview that most whites found appealing, since it explained differences in technology and culture between diverse peoples and affirmed Western civilization's own sense of global superiority.

Such were the ideas that African Americans had to confront on their road toward freedom and justice. Contrary to slave owners' opinions that blacks had no culture other than what they learned from whites, the first slaves brought from Africa a cosmology based on spirituality and animism, and these beliefs sustained them and their descendants through centuries of bondage. Unlike the rationalistic western view, which sees a dichotomy between body and soul, traditional African religions taught the totality of human beings and their oneness with spirit and nature. When slaves awoke at dawn and declared, "I journeyed to Africa last night," they described not a simple dream, but a metaphysical projection in which the soul travels through the universe during the body's sleeping hours. Enslavement represented a limited, temporary condition, never able to constrain the person's true essence. Over time, slave culture combined native African beliefs with Western Christianity to produce a syncretistic "African American" religion that borrowed selectively from Judeo-Christian traditions. The story of Moses leading his people out of slavery in Egypt, as told in the Book of Exodus, became a favorite in the slave cabins, immortalized in songs and prayers. Despite their hardships, slaves formed vibrant communities on the larger plantations, holding frequent celebrations, marrying and raising families, and developing communication networks in order to keep in touch with loved ones. Children separated from their parents by a sale would often be adopted by a relative or raised by the community, leading to a concept of "family" as one rooted in extended kinship or race rather than in a nuclear household.

Like white society, African American society developed its own internal structure. When the Civil War began, nearly half a million free blacks lived in the United States, having acquired their freedom through manumission or self-purchase. Mostly concentrated in urban areas, they formed the core of what became a black elite after emancipation, providing the leadership skills necessary to open and manage black schools, businesses, churches, newspapers and other institutions. During Reconstruction, when blacks still enjoyed the right to vote, some African Americans won elected positions in state and federal governments. From this growing black middle class came the "race leaders" who experimented with various ways of combating discrimination and violence. The author and journalist Ida B. Wells, for example, led a decades-long battle to end southern lynchings. Others believed that the future of the black race lay in its complete separation from whites. Colonization advocates like Henry Turner and Benjamin Singleton raised money to establish all-black communities, either in the American West or in Africa. Although thousands of African Americans did depart the South in the late 1800s, the majority did not relocate to northern and western cities until the twentieth century. In the meantime, most blacks and southern whites lived segregated but parallel lives in towns and rural hinterlands, neither group affording the luxury of complete isolation from the other.

The mutual destiny of whites and blacks in rebuilding the southern economy became a major

Booker T. Washington. Photo from Boston Photo News Company.

theme in the teachings of Booker T. Washington, undoubtedly the most significant African American leader at the turn of the twentieth century. Born a slave in Virginia in 1856, Washington received his education at the Hampton Institute, became a teacher, and in 1881 opened the Tuskegee Institute in Alabama. In keeping with the principles he learned at Hampton, Washington—who considered himself a realist—placed little emphasis on classical education; his curriculum offered little in the way of history, sociology or any of the humanities and social sciences. Instead, Tuskegee taught "practical" skills commensurate with the types of work that blacks would be likely to find: carpentry, mechanics, agriculture, domestic service, and others relevant for specific trades. Washington's educational goals emanated from his larger vision for the future of the black race. Historians have characterized his approach as "accommodationist," meaning he believed that blacks of his time should adapt to the realities of segregation. Rather than confront whites' racism and attempt to compete with them on their terms, blacks should practice racial uplift from within, elevating themselves through proficiency in farming and other artisan labor so they could become economically independent. Washington offered an approach to black advancement that appeared non-threatening to white interests, summarized in his speech to the Atlanta Exposition in 1895: "In all things that are purely social we can be as separate as the five fingers, yet one as the hand in all things essential to mutual progress." Leaders of both races responded positively to his message, donating huge sums of money to Tuskegee and other black schools based on the Tuskegee model. Through his control of various newspapers and businesses and his ability to earn the trust of whites, Washington ruled African American society by the early 1900s nearly as a dictator, obtaining and deciding black appointments to government and academic positions and raising funds for black causes.

Yet not all African Americans endorsed Washington's leadership. Northern, middle-class blacks like W.E.B. Du Bois rebuked his emphasis on trade and agricultural work at a time when the United States was becoming more urban and factory labor was replacing skilled craftsmanship. As Du Bois would write in *The Souls of Black Folk*, Washington had taught his people to set their sights too low, striving to become farmers and servants when they could be competing in the professions. Other black reformers believed that Washington had sacrificed his moral authority in accepting the Jim Crow laws and in not publicly condemning lynchings. Few people knew at the time that Washington had worked anonymously to try to establish anti-lynching laws; a genuine Machiavellian, he could present an accommodating image to whites while keeping his true convictions private. But the critique of Washington's approach has merit, especially when seen within its limits as a class-based philosophy rather than a race-based one. Washington knew personally the experience of slavery, having come from a rural southern setting where the immediate daily problems of blacks involved economic needs rather than social acceptance by whites. As more African Americans gained formal education, entered the middle class, and settled in urban areas, new approaches to civil rights that would address their needs inevitably formed. Although racial solidarity has been a strong and continuing feature of black history, black society has developed such a diversity of classes, sub-cultures, and perspectives that it is impossible for the views of any one African American to represent them all.

Thus the publication of Du Bois' *Souls of Black Folk* in 1903 occurred in the midst of an oppressive racial era, and at a time when some blacks were preparing to wrest control of the leadership of black society from the powerful "Wizard of Tuskegee." Both the author and the work are revolutionary in two ways: Du Bois dared to challenge the dominant racism of the time by asserting the dignity of black culture, and he also challenged the nation's foremost black spokesperson, Booker T. Washington, by advocating a new direction and a new set of goals for African Americans. Du Bois' approach gradually supplanted Washington's. Civil rights leaders such as Martin Luther King, Jr. and Jesse Jackson have tended to focus more on the attainment of political rights and the end of discriminatory social practices than on racial uplift and economic autonomy. The twentieth century also witnessed an increase in black nationalism, evident in the success of men like Marcus Garvey and Malcolm X, who taught blacks to embrace their African cultural heritage. The collapse of imperialist empires after the Second World War drew increased attention to the plight of peoples and nations of color on a global scale, so that African Americans discovered common interests with native Africans, Indians, Latinos and others who have endured the affects of racism. Likewise, white scholars and reformers have discovered in the writings of Du Bois and his successors a useful corrective to once unquestioned claims about universal progress, as well as the usefulness of incorporating minority perspectives in any discussion about the Western tradition and its significance.

DU BOIS' LIFE

Through a life that spanned nearly a century, William Edward Burghardt Du Bois served as the leading intellectual champion for a civil rights revolution, even though his privileged background made him a rather unrepresentative candidate to speak for black society. Born in 1868 in Great Barrington, Massachusetts, Du Bois was descended from free blacks of French and Haitian ancestry. Unlike his ideological rival Washington, neither Du Bois nor his parents had personal experience with slavery. William's childhood in liberal New England was spent among abolitionists, middle-class African Americans like his own family, and whites sympathetic to black rights. Few people of any race in the late nineteenth century had the educational opportunities that Du Bois had as a young man, having graduated from Fisk University, later obtaining a Ph.D. from Harvard, and then studying history and sociology in Berlin, Germany on a postdoctoral fellowship. By the age of thirty, Du Bois was already an internationally-known scholar; his dissertation on the Atlantic slave trade and his first major study on the black community in Philadelphia marked him as a promising young authority on social and racial issues. As one who had traveled and read extensively, Du Bois learned to approach the subject of race on a comparative and historical basis, fascinated and curious about the relative freedom and acceptance that he as a black man enjoyed in Europe as compared to the oppression of his home country.

Du Bois' musings on the peculiar dilemma of race in the United States became more personal and urgent because of two crises in 1899. While teaching at Atlanta University, Du Bois was shocked by the ghastly murder of a local black farmer named Sam Hose. Two thousand screaming whites gathered on the outskirts of Atlanta, Georgia to lynch Hose and burn and mutilate his body. Du Bois, of course, had always known of such incidents, but, having been raised in the North, he had been relatively sheltered from the extremes of violence and bigotry that southern blacks faced daily. After passing a storefront where the murdered Hose's knuckles were prominently displayed, Du Bois wrote that he "could not be a calm, cool, and detached scientist" any longer. The second event, only a month later, shook him more deeply; when his two-year old son, Burghardt Jr., contracted diptheria and died because of inadequate treatment created by Atlanta's segregated system of medical care. Du Bois would deal with Burghardt's death and his family's own private grief in *The Souls of Black Folk* four years later. These tragedies moved Du Bois from the role of objective scholar to passionate reformer; like Karl Marx, his subsequent intellectual activity would not be simply studying society and culture, but making sharp recommendations for changing it in order to achieve justice.

W.E.B. Du Bois. The Library of Congress.

For several months, Du Bois traveled the rural South, interviewing former slaves, studying sharecropping, and recording black prayers and songs, all as part of his research for *Souls of Black Folk*. Its publication in 1903 further established Du Bois as one of the premier writers of his time. It was also during this period that his ideas about civil rights and black advancement crystallized into a coherent philosophy that he called "the Talented Tenth." From his study of ancient civilizations and the dominant Hegelian theory of history with which he became enamored during his studies in Germany, Du Bois believed that all races and peoples advance through the leadership of an elite corps within their ranks that comprises perhaps ten percent of the whole; hence the term "talented tenth." Given the proper encouragement and opportunity, this talented corps of businessmen, statesmen, academics, journalists and other professionals would lead the black race to greatness. This particular part of Du Bois' thinking provided his major source of contention with Booker Washington, whose educational goals Du Bois believed would lead African Americans into a

March on Washington. August 28, 1963. From
Associated Press/World Wide Photos.

permanent state of mediocrity rather than allowing
the brightest individuals to reach their potential. In
order for this small class of elites to progress, legal
and social barriers based on race would have to be
eliminated, thus demanding a confrontation with
white racism.

Between 1903 and 1910, Du Bois spoke for the
growing cadre of black professionals who considered
themselves "talented tenth" material, men and
women who grew more vocal in their criticism of
and disappointment with Washington's leadership.
Recognizing his competition, Washington shrewdly
offered Du Bois a teaching position at Tuskegee, probably in an effort to co-opt the radical young professor,
but Du Bois with equal shrewdness refused the offer.
Du Bois relocated to New York and became active in
the growing Niagara Movement, the first serious
attempt since Reconstruction to organize African
Americans in defense of their civil rights. From this
movement* came the founding of the **National
Association for the Advancement of Colored
People.** The NAACP embraced the same constituents who had led the abolitionist movement—

middle-class blacks and northern white liberals—and
in fact employed much of that earlier movement's
rhetoric and tactics. Through the twentieth century,
the NAACP worked for the basic realization of Du
Bois' philosophy, raising money for black institutions,
issuing legal challenges to discriminatory state and
federal laws, and educating the white public about
the harms of racism. It would be an NAACP victory in
the 1954 U.S. Supreme Court case, Brown v. Board of
Education of Topeka, Kansas, that launched a new
stage of minority activism led by Martin Luther King,
Jr. and others. Du Bois abandoned his teaching career
to lend his strength and talents to the NAACP when
he became editor of the organization's newspaper,
The Crisis, which reported on the black community's
fight against Jim Crow, lynchings, and other racial
problems. As editor of *The Crisis* and as a distinguished scholar and orator, Du Bois created a body of
ideas that lent themselves well to the growing civil
rights revolution, just as Rousseau and Voltaire had
done for the French Revolution and Locke for the
American Revolution centuries earlier.

Born shortly after the end of slavery and living
into the tumultuous 1960s, Du Bois witnessed many
changes that caused him to expand, and at times to
reassess, his thinking. African participation in the
two world wars, and the frustrations that global conflict imposed on Western imperialism, energized Du
Bois to help mobilize the **Pan-African movement**.
Through a series of international conferences beginning in the 1920s, Pan-Africanism tried to accomplish on a global scale what the NAACP had done on
a national one: mobilize people of African descent
the world over to liberate Africa from colonialism. As
Du Bois came to see the plight of African Americans
as part of a larger pattern of oppression by white
countries, he moved surprisingly in the direction of
a man whose ideas he had once disdained, namely
Booker T. Washington. More and more in his later
years, Du Bois grew convinced that economic deprivation, rather than segregation and prejudice, was
the chief obstacle to black progress. The Great
Depression of the 1930s only solidified this belief. As
his insistence that racial problems be studied within
an economic and global context increased, Du Bois
found himself at odds with the directors of the
NAACP, who limited their efforts to political and
legal rights for black Americans only. Citing personality and ideological differences, Du Bois resigned

from *The Crisis* in 1934. Concern with economic inequalities also led to his growing attraction to Marxism; during the early Cold War, when Americans endured persecution for expressing pro-Communist sympathies, Du Bois openly wrote of the advantages that Soviet Russia and Communist China had brought to people of color, wondering aloud if Marx's theories about capitalism and class revolution held some solutions for black advancement.

Despite the excellent health that he enjoyed into his nineties, Du Bois' last years were unhappy ones. Many of his former friends and colleagues had abandoned him during his dalliance with communism. Although he approved of Martin Luther King, Jr.'s Southern Christian Leadership Conference (about which Du Bois, a longtime agnostic, remained skeptical, since he had long discounted the significance of organized religion) Du Bois grew pessimistic about the prospect of black equality in the United States. Forsaking his American citizenship, he and his second wife moved to the newly independent African nation of Ghana during the last year of his life, and there he died on the night of August 27, 1963—the eve of the Great March on Washington and the delivery of King's famous "I Have a Dream" speech from the steps of the Lincoln Memorial.

It is difficult to classify Du Bois intellectually, because over the course of his long life, he experimented with every known idea or philosophy that had a chance of bettering the lives of people of color. He is best remembered as the author of *The Souls of Black Folk*, his most significant if not most representative work. Therefore, students are quick to categorize him as "the black author," as if his blackness says all that is relevant about him. In fact, Du Bois—like his writings, like most people—is complex. Although he consciously represented himself as a racial spokesperson for all African Americans, his class background also informs his thinking. Du Bois' critics often described him as an elitist, whose advocacy of "talented tenth" leadership and emphasis on obtaining theoretical rights over economic self-sufficiency helps upper- and middle-class minorities like himself more than the poor and uneducated. Today, most African American leaders concede that ending racial discrimination has not been enough and that the black community's problems of poverty and unemployment demand new solutions for which the Du Boisian model of civil rights provides little guidance. An overview of his major book nevertheless reveals many of the important themes that black leaders have employed over the last century in ending Jim Crow and establishing a genuine "African American" identity.

GUIDE TO THE READINGS

The Souls of Black Folk stands as Du Bois' masterpiece for the way in which it addresses questions of culture and sociology through an artistic, almost poetic writing style commonly used more in literature than in social science. As a student at Fisk University, Du Bois taught black children in rural Tennessee, observing firsthand the conditions of southern blacks at the start of the Jim Crow era. These observations, combined with his later research, form the bulk of the text's subject matter. Rather than produce an analytical study, Du Bois used unforgettable descriptions of people he had known through his travels to expose the poverty and scarcity of opportunities for African Americans. The book consists of fourteen independent essays that explore interrelated topics: education, spirituality, white-black relations, psychology, economics, and so on. Most of the characters he describes are authentic; in some cases, such as in the chapter "Of the Coming of John," Du Bois creates fictional personages whom he uses as representatives of the black personality. This literary technique was used by many reform writers of his day, including Upton Sinclair and Willa Cather.

The framework of *duality* provides a useful way to interpret this text. In trying to link the internal conflicts that African Americans experience on a daily basis to larger racial trends, Du Bois employed the concept of dualism first on a personal, psychological level, and then on a grand social one. His first use of personal duality begins in Chapter One, "Of Our Spiritual Strivings," which he opens with the question "How does it feel to be a problem?" Unlike whites, who are considered the "normal" race of America and so can sometimes afford to think in color-blind terms, blacks can never forget their minority status, as they are reminded of it constantly by laws and customs. Consequently, they face psychological choices between multiple identities, part of what philosophers call "existential angst." For Du Bois, these choices break down to a dichotomous tension between race and nationality. Despite the oppression they have faced here, African Americans historically have been patriotic people, proud and supportive of their country's democratic and liberal traditions. Du Bois acknowledges this when he writes, "He [the black man] would not Africanize America, for America has too much to teach the world and Africa,"[1] and later, "there are today no truer exponents of the pure human spirit of the Declaration of Independence than the American Negroes."[2] Yet at the same time, none would "bleach his Negro soul in a flood of white Americanism, for he knows that Negro blood has a message for the world. He simply wishes to make it possible for a man to be both a Negro and an American . . . ."[3] Herein lies the key to what Du Bois claims as the central challenge for minority peoples: the reconciliation of these apparently conflicting drives, one toward full equality in a modern republic, and the other toward preservation of a glorious black culture. When he writes, "One ever feels his two-ness—an American, a Negro; two souls, two thoughts, two unreconciled strivings; . . . The history of the American Negro is the history of this strife . . . ,"[4] Du Bois suggests that equality at the price of assimilation and loss of ethnic heritage would be disastrous, not only for blacks but for the American experiment at large.

Following his use of duality to describe the "double consciousness" of the black psyche, Du Bois broadens the concept in Chapter Two, "Of the Dawn of Freedom." This chapter opens with what is perhaps his most memorable and quoted statement: "The problem of the twentieth century is the problem of the color line—the relation of the darker to the lighter races of men in Asia and Africa, in America and the islands of the sea."[5] Writing this when the twentieth century was only three years old, Du Bois acted here as a prophet rather than a historian. It is odd that he introduces an idea of such global relevance in a chapter devoted to the origins of the Freedmen's Bureau. His phrase "the color line" becomes clearer in his later writings on imperialism and Pan-Africanism, although its inclusion in *The Souls of Black Folk* is significant in that he sees America's racial problems as an awful harbinger of things to come. "The color line" describes the stark separation between blacks and whites that typified American society in 1903. Du Bois predicted that as the United States and other Western countries would expand in future decades, the color line would be expanded also. As Chinese, Filipinos, Hispanics, native Africans and others would endure similar systems of racial oppression that African Americans already had suffered for centuries, racism and racial warfare would overshadow all other problems. From a contemporary perspective, one may well conclude Du Bois was right, considering the twentieth century's nightmares of racial and ethnic genocide. Occasionally, as in Chapter Eleven, Du Bois uses the term "the Veil" synonymously with "the color line," again referring to the stark inequalities between whites and nonwhites.

Du Bois devotes most of the second chapter to a history of the Freedmen's Bureau. Here, he uses a traditional narrative approach to offer an interpretation of the Bureau and Reconstruction that for its time was highly controversial. History is far from an exact science, though it would be easier for students and teachers if it were; historians constantly debate the meanings and causes of certain events, and often their interpretations are employed, or in some cases even created, to affirm and legitimize certain political or social points of view. One hundred years ago, whites sympathetic to slavery and the southern cause dominated much of the historical writing on the Civil War and Reconstruction periods. In these interpretations, the Freedmen's Bureau was presented as an oppressive institution that elevated uneducated freedmen over whites, while Reconstruction itself was described as a failed social experiment in black equality. "Of the Dawn of Freedom" may be read as Du Bois' rebuttal to this overly negative appraisal by white historians. He emphasizes the Bureau's establishment of free black schools, peasant ownership of land, and suffrage rights that—had they been consistently enforced—would have hastened the freedmen toward equal citizenship. Most importantly, Du Bois explains the financial constraints under which the Bureau worked, suggesting that Reconstruction policies did not so much fail to produce black progress as they were not allowed to succeed, given their imposed limits.

Chapter Three contains Du Bois' assessment of Washington's leadership, the essay that helped to launch the Niagara Movement and that remains today a classic criticism of the racial uplift model. In a fair and even-handed manner, Du Bois gives Washington his proper due, complimenting him and the Tuskegee Institute for their many positive accomplishments. Drawing on his considerable knowledge of history, Du Bois then attacks with scathing language the older man's call for submission and his emphasis on material gains: "In the history of all other races and peoples the doctrine preached at such crises has been that manly self-respect is worth more than lands and houses, and that a people who voluntarily surrender such respect, or cease striving for it, are not worth civilizing."[6] By refusing to resist bigoted measures that revoke political rights, African Americans not only suffer "civic death," but they lose whatever power they hold to protect the very trade skills and small businesses that Washington would have them acquire. Furthermore, in refusing to support higher education for blacks, Washington fails to acknowledge that the very instructors who have made industrial-technical schools like Tuskegee successful in the first place were themselves graduates of upper-level black universities. Some of Du Bois' "talented tenth" ideas are evident here, as when he asks "Is it possible . . . that nine millions of men can make effective progress in economic lines if . . . allowed only the most meager chance for developing their exceptional men?" Essentially, Du Bois' critique amounts to a moral argument, claiming that any advances that blacks might attain under accommodationism would be meaningless if they willingly concede their most fundamental right to political equality. By evoking the Declaration of Independence in his closing paragraph, he even contextualizes his ideas within the larger tradition of revolutionary resistance revered by black and white Americans alike.

Du Bois elaborates on his ideas for black progress in chapters four through nine, in which he develops several interesting and original themes. First, his criticism of industrial training schools rests mostly on his perception that such institutions prepare blacks to be little more than workers in a large capitalist machine. Contrary to Washington's assertion that cultivation of practical skills will lead to racial autonomy, Du Bois believes that an educational system that limits blacks to manual labor only increases their economic dependence on white employers, essentially replacing the old system of legal slavery with a new type of wage slavery. Although he speaks primarily about African Americans' situation, his declared purpose for higher education as a tool for social change remains relevant for all persons, especially a century later: "The function of the university is not simply to teach breadwinning, . . ."[8] and later, "The foundations of knowledge in this race, as in others, must be sunk deep in the college and university if we would build a solid, permanent structure."[9] Du Bois also expands his economic and social appraisal of the postwar South in these chapters. In his descriptions of the Black Belt of Georgia and the nuances of sharecropping, he fills his text with personal vignettes of various individuals, both to personalize the subject matter and to establish his authenticity as a northern-born black man writing about southern conditions. Despite his emphasis on political advancement, Du Bois reveals his deep concern for the South's economic progress. Frequently, his writings show frustration with capitalism and Americans' obsession with money, a frustration that grew in later decades as Du Bois gradually embraced the cause of radical socialism.

The final chapters, ten through fourteen, are devoted to a discussion of the importance of religion in African-American life. Although Du Bois did not personally practice an organized faith, he understood its significance; in fact, the epigraph for each essay contains the bars of black spirituals, and he points to the "sorrow songs" in the concluding chapter as a vibrant illustration of black culture. Some scholars hold *The Souls of Black Folk* as a literary predecessor to the Harlem Renaissance of the 1920s, when black music, art, and literature flourished and made in-roads into white culture. Du Bois links the sadness and "blues" of the slavery and Jim Crow experiences to African Americans' spiritual and musical expressions, anticipating the many contributions that blacks have make to American culture: "Our song, our toil, our cheer, and warning have been given to this nation in blood-brotherhood. Are not these gifts worth the giving? Is not this work and striving? Would America have been America without her Negro people?"[10] Du Bois' own personal sorrow song appears in Chapter Eleven, perhaps the most moving essay of the book, titled "Of the Passing of the First-Born." Here the reader is privileged to see Du Bois' mournful lament for his deceased infant son, Burghardt Jr. Du Bois poignantly describes a father's love for the eldest child, love filled with hope and potential, looking forward to a life of pride in his offspring's accomplishments. Yet "the Veil" of American racism intrudes even on this most basic emotion, for soon his boy dies, deprived of adequate medical care, and Du Bois is left to await the day when the color line has no further power to separate parents from children: "Sleep then, child, sleep till I sleep and waken to a baby voice and the ceaseless patter of little feet—above the Veil."[11]

Published in the early twentieth century when the literacy rate among African Americans was rising dramatically, *The Souls of Black Folk* became a popular bestseller, read by whites as well as blacks. Since 1903, the book has been translated into numerous languages and today is commonly assigned in college courses on race and African American history. Many of Du Bois' other writings have gained international acclaim, read by school-children as far away as China and Africa. As an early and prominent example of what later generations would call "black pride" literature, his text not only prepared the way for authors such as James Baldwin and Toni Morrison, but has helped to stimulate similar genres for other minority groups, for example, Latinos and Native Americans, which combine cultural descriptions and analyses with critiques of American society. For students being introduced to the Western canon, *Souls of Black Folk* delivers a haunting expose of the potential for racism and unrestrained capitalism to thwart democracy and equality, and of the ways in which people denied access to the traditional means of power can resist those tendencies.

QUESTIONS FOR STUDY AND DISCUSSION
1. Describe the legal and economic barriers to black advancement at the turn of the twentieth century.
2. Compare and contrast the approaches of Booker T. Washington and W. E. B. Du Bois in their efforts to gain equal rights for African Americans. Whose approach do you think has prevailed today? What advantages and disadvantages has that approach brought?
3. Analyze Du Bois' usage of the term "the Veil." Does this concept explain the full nature of inequality in the United States? How does his class background combine with his racial identity to inform his ideas?
4. Du Bois claimed in 1903 that the problem of the twentieth century is the problem of the color line. Reviewing the history of the twentieth century from the present, do you think this prediction was accurate?
5. How does Du Bois both challenge and continue the ideas of earlier Western thinkers?

SUGGESTIONS FOR FURTHER READING
W. E. B. Du Bois. *Black Reconstruction in America*. New York: Maxwell Macmillan International, [1935], 1992.

_____. *The World and Africa: An Inquiry into the Part Which Africa has Played in World History* (enl. ed., with new writings on Africa, 1955-1961). New York, International Publishers, 1965.

John Hope Franklin and Alfred A. Moss, Jr. *From Slavery to Freedom: A History of African Americans*, 8th ed. New York: A.A Knopf, 2000.

David Levering Lewis. *W.E.B. Du Bois: Biography of a Race, 1868-1919* (New York: Henry Holt and Company, 1993).

_____. *W.E.B. Du Bois: The Fight for Equality and the American Century*. New York: Henry Holt and Company, 2000.

August Meier. *Negro Thought in America, 1880-1915*. Ann Arbor: University of Michigan Press, 1988.

Washington, Booker T. Up From Slavery. William L. Andrews, editor. Oxford and New York: Oxford University Press, 1995.

---

[1] Du Bois, W. E. B. *The Souls of Black Folk*. New York: Dover Publications, In. 1994, 3.

[2] Ibid., 7.

[3] Ibid., 3.

[4] Ibid., 2.

[5] Ibid., 9.

[6] Ibid., 30.

[7] Ibid., 31.

[8] Ibid., 52.

[9] Ibid., 66.

[10] Ibid., 163.

[11] Ibid., 131.

LIFE OF FYODOR DOSTOEVSKY

1815
End of Napoleonic Wars

1821
Dostoevsky's birth in Moscow

1825–55
Rule of Tsar Nicholas I

1838–40
Trains as a military engineer in St. Petersburg

1844
Resigns military commission to devote himself to writing

1846
Publishes first novel, *Poor Folk*, followed by *The Double*

1847
Active in intellectual circles, joins Petrashevsky Circle

1849
Members of Petrashevsky Circle arrested, condemned to death, "reprieved" at last moment

1850–59
Period of imprisonment and exile in Siberia

1853–56
Crimean War

1855–1881
Rule of Tsar Alexander II

1860
Returns to St. Petersburg

1861
Emancipation of the serfs

1862–64
Travels in Europe

1864
First wife dies; publishes *Notes from Underground*

1865
Marries Anna Grigorievna Snitkina

1866
Crime and Punishment

1867–1871
Traveling—and gambling—in Europe

1869
The Idiot

1872
The Possessed

1881
Dies in St. Petersburg; *The Brothers Karamazov* published

CHAPTER TEN

RUSSIA AND THE WEST: FYODOR DOSTOEVSKY

INTRODUCTION

There is a question that quickly arises when we examine Russian history, and remains a major problem of interpreting Russian culture and society today. An important version of the problem appears in Dostoevsky's *Notes from Underground*: is Russia Eastern or Western or something different from either? For contemporary application, the question can be simply: why do the Russians behave the way they do? Why do they, at least on the surface, seem more distinct from Americans than most other Europeans? Why do they seem plagued by tumultuous upheavals, such as in 1917 or in more recent years? Where are they going? In *Notes from Underground* these questions frame an interpretation of the meaning of the West as well as an interpretation of the nature of human beings.

Geographically, Russia is at the eastern edge of what is considered "Western." This geography has marked the social and cultural development of Russia. For example, many of the major intellectual movements in Western civilization—the Renaissance, Reformation, and Enlightenment—barely touched Russia or arrived much later. This absence or at least lag has produced a sort of schizophrenic character in Russia, never knowing whether it wants to be Western or uniquely Russian, and its modern history is marked by a tug-of-war between these two perspectives. Travelers to Russia at all times have emphasized this duality of character, this identity problem, and Russians themselves have discussed and written at length trying to define who they are. For example, St. Petersburg, the capital of the Russian Empire from the beginning of the eighteenth century until the Bolshevik Revolution of 1917, appears to the observer as quite Western, but almost deliberately and superficially so. Today it is often compared to Vienna or Venice, perhaps the most European and least "Americanized" cities in Europe. On the other hand, Moscow, the capital before 1700, and again since 1918, is usually perceived as Eastern, "exotic," even Oriental. (Strangely, too, in the twentieth century Moscow has added a measure of American but still non-European atmosphere). Much of Russian cultural history can thus be treated as a tale of two cities, reflecting the strikingly different characters of Moscow and St. Petersburg and expressing a perpetual identity crisis or national split personality.

HISTORY AND CULTURE

The first thousand years or so of Russian history can be told as essentially a story of these two countervailing European and non-European influences. During the first important period of Russian political and cultural development, from roughly 860 to 1200, the peoples inhabiting the forests of Eastern Europe were subject to outside influences, but more from North and South than from East or West. The Varangians (Vikings or Scandinavians) came from the Baltic in search of wealth and adventure and to provide military and political leadership, but they were quickly absorbed by the more numerous Slavs. Arriving from the South were merchants, craftsmen, and priests from one of the highest civilizations of that time, Byzantium or the Eastern Roman Empire.

With the common interests of Scandinavians and Greeks to serve, a flourishing trade route prospered through the territory of what became known as Rus. Byzantine influences naturally dominated the art and architecture, and in 988, by the initiative of Grand Prince Vladimir, one of whose wives was Greek, Rus formally adopted Christianity from the Greek Orthodox Church. A Greek alphabet, adapted for

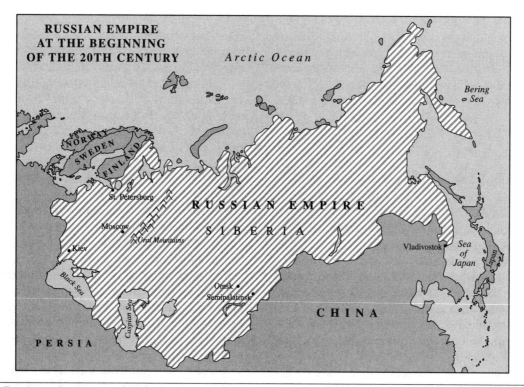

Russian Empire at Beginning of 20th Century.

Slavs and known as "Cyrilic," provided a written language for the inhabitants. Territorial expansion and developments in building, culture, and commercial wealth reached its zenith in the eleventh century, by which time Rus had established important links with Western Europe. After that, internal political weakness, the decline of the trade route, and powerful new external enemies led to the end of this first East Slavic polity. The population, although somewhat dislocated, would retain much of its early culture as new political centers emerged farther north.

The interim between the decline of Rus and the rise of Muscovy is often referred to as the Mongol or Tatar "yoke," with its connotation of oppression and submission. The great Mongol invasion of Europe in the thirteenth century was actually the culmination of a series of incursions by nomadic Turkish peoples, the last and most numerous of whom were the Tatars. They raided and plundered the Russian cities, controlled the mostly treeless expanse north of the Black and Caspian Seas known as the steppe, and thus cut off the Slavs from Byzantium and the Black Sea. With their superior military ability and greater cohesion and organization, the Tatars dominated the

remaining Slavic cities, requiring regular payments of tribute, but they left undisturbed most Slavic customs and institutions such as the Church. In the North, the Teutonic and Livonian orders of German-speaking knights moving eastward pushed the Slavs back from the Baltic. Grand Prince Alexander Nevsky stopped this German tide in 1242—with Tatar assistance—thus becoming a great Russian hero in defeating foreign invasion.

The debate over the extent of "Oriental" or Turkic influences upon Russia has continued ever since this episode, with some arguing that Turkic influences played a major role in the development of Muscovite absolutism (or Oriental despotism) that later may have influenced Communist totalitarianism; others credit the period of 1250–1500 for the emergence of a distinctive "Russian" civilization. Most important, especially for students of Western civilization, Russia was isolated and separated for several centuries from Western Europe, so that vital foundations of modern Western history—the Renaissance, the Reformation, and the Scientific Revolution—were practically unknown in Russia. Very little by way of institutions and ideas came from the West between 1250 and 1650.

By the middle of the seventeenth century, the military needs of a Russian state that was forced to contest with powers to the west (Poland) the north (Sweden) and the south (the Ottoman Empire) over long, poorly defined land frontiers brought increased contact with Western Europe, especially with Britain and Holland. A settlement of foreign craftsmen and advisors was established near Moscow. These new residents strove to modernize the Russian army, and in the process incidentally helped shape the adolescent mind of an heir to the throne named Peter.

Peter the Great (1672-1725) was a giant of a man, physically and mentally. While apparently able to beat, outrun, and outdrink any of his subjects, Peter possessed an enormous energy, ambition, and curiosity about the world around him. He believed that the way to enhance Russian—and his own—stature and power was by borrowing extensively from the West, especially from its military technology and governmental institutions. Such borrowing meant reform (some would say revolution) on a large scale. Peter therefore set about responding, rather unsystematically and haphazardly, to the needs of war by weakening and destroying the existing Russian forms and customs and political elites and replacing them with Western models.

At the time of his death in 1725, Peter had left much undone and numerous unresolved contradictions. While building bridges to the most "modern" parliamentary countries of Europe (England and Holland), he nevertheless strengthened absolutism in Russia. Emphasizing technology and training with the founding of mathematical schools and the Academy of Sciences, he failed to establish any universities to support humanistic traditions. While shackling the upper classes to serve the state, he also increased the burdens on the peasant masses. In promoting a more permanent base for Westernization, he built a new "Western" capital, St. Petersburg. But when he had his own son killed for opposing him, and then married a servant woman, he left his own Romanov dynasty shattered and vulnerable. What Peter did leave behind was a partially remolded generation of political and military officials and a veneer of Western civilization over an otherwise undisturbed traditional and Orthodox Christian population, thus initiating a cultural gulf in Russian society that would be a crucial factor in its further unfold-

ing. Peter's open windows to the West might have been subsequently boarded up, except for three things: (1) his having made Russia a great military power in Europe and a part of the European system of alliances and balance of power; (2) the striking successes of Russia's first scholars of arts and sciences; and (3) the somewhat accidental ascendancy of a remarkably brilliant and ambitious German woman to the Russian throne.

Whereas Peter was a roughly self-made Westerner, Catherine the Great (1729-1796) was Western by birth and upbringing. Married to Peter's nephew, whose brief period of rule she helped shorten, her reign (1762-96) more than expanded upon the work of Peter; it was nurtured by one of the most intellectually stimulating and productive periods of world history—the Enlightenment—and by economic prosperity—the Commercial Revolution. While Catherine fostered extensive contacts with the West, thorough "westernization" was something else. Although she seriously considered legal and governmental reforms for Russia, especially early in her reign, little was really accomplished. The nobility was partially emancipated from service obligations to the state and became more Western in dress, language (French) and custom, but the peasantry remained mired in servile conditions and restricted in movement both physically and socially. Her most "enlightened" subjects were eventually silenced by an official censorship that was inspired by fears of the radical turn that the Enlightenment was taking in the French Revolution. A contradictory duality of liberal Westernization and Russian autocratic repression was in uneasy coexistence in Russia by the end of the eighteenth century.

The contradictory tendencies in Russian society and politics under Peter and Catherine were reinforced and magnified by the epoch of the Napoleonic Wars (1796-1815) in which Russia played a major role. Because of a much more intimate involvement with Europe and because of the impact of Napoleon's political and economic reforms and military ambitions, more and more of the Russian elite came in contact with Western European cultures. By the time of the restoration of peace at the Congress of Vienna in 1815, the Russian empire had expanded into westernized Finland, incorporated more of Poland, and even extended over Alaska and into Northern California. Diplomatic relations were established for the first time with the

A Russian peasant village at the turn of the 20th century. The Library of Congress.

United States in 1809, and Russia benevolently attempted to mediate peace in the War of 1812. These new contacts with the West and the shock of the invasion of Russia by Napoleon's army of over 600,000 in 1812, followed by the occupation and destruction of Moscow, emphasized the backwardness of Russia and its military vulnerability. A large part of the Russian army followed Napoleon's retreat from Moscow back into Western Europe. Its commander, Tsar Alexander I, became the "Savior of Europe," and Russia, in a situation resembling the conclusion of World War II, became the leading military power on the continent. Many of the Russian elite who served as officers, however, could easily observe for themselves the contrast between military power on the one hand and social inequality and backwardness in Russia on the other.

The influx of European influences continued after the war as Russians, in greater numbers than ever before, traveled to the West, many to study at German universities. Similarly, West Europeans and Americans came to Russia to seek fortunes or out of curiosity. Some of them became tutors to noble families or joined the staffs of the several new universities that were founded in the first half of the nineteenth centu-

ry. The combination of greater exposure to the West, new romantic ideals, and an underemployed officer corps for a large standing army produced Russia's first serious movement for substantial political reform and change from outside the monarchy itself.

Known as **Decembrists** for their failed military revolt in December, 1825 following the November death of Tsar Alexander I, these radical and liberal reformers advocated a variety of institutional reforms. Their various and often conflicting ideas were largely imported from the West. Some advocated a military *coup d'etat* to produce a strong centralized government that would resemble the Directory after the French Revolution and that would carry out sweeping economic and social reforms. Others wanted a looser and more federal constitutional arrangement, similar to that of the United States. The Decembrist revolt, being poorly planned and executed, was doomed to an early defeat. Many of the leaders were arrested and sent into Siberian exile, and five were hanged. The rebels became martyrs for the continuing cause of social justice and an inspiration to the liberals and radicals who followed, but they also inspired conservatives who questioned their goals and methods.

After the Decembrist revolt, the two main currents of Russian thought that developed among the intelligentsia in and around the universities in St. Petersburg and Moscow in the 1830s and 1840s were the **Slavophiles** and the **Westernizers**. With German writers such as Kant, Goethe, Schiller, and Herder serving as guides to both sides, many of the growing numbers of this intelligentsia delved deeper into the extreme romanticism and idealism of the age. The Slavophiles were influenced especially by the mystical system of Friedrich Schelling. Through the latter's writings, they gained a sense of continuity and wholeness set in motion by national forces. By studying German Romanticism the educated elite sought to solve the riddles of Russia's past and to erect a framework for their search for national identity. It might be said that Russia, having missed the Renaissance and Reformation, and only in a cursory way partaken of the Enlightenment, now absorbed Western Romanticism "whole-hog."

The intellectuals who gathered in the debating circles of Moscow and St. Petersburg also studied the ideas of Hegel and French utopian socialists. In their search for vitality and wholeness in Russian history, they consequently discovered the peasant village and observed what they believed to be its collectivist, socialist character (*obshchina*) miraculously preserved over hundreds of years. This collectivism involved periodic redistribution of land among families and cooperation in work methods and in fulfilling financial responsibilities. The Slavophiles and the Westernizers both stressed the importance of Russia's collectivist past in this *obshchina*, but the Slavophiles believed that it was being threatened by destructive Western influences and by the administrative policies of the Russian government.

The **Slavophiles**, moreover, emphasized the distinctiveness of Russian history and national character, the superior spiritual qualities of the Russian Orthodox Church, and even the advantages of Russian autocracy itself in an idealized patriarchal form. According to them, the central problem of Russia was nefarious Western influences, especially beginning with the reign of Peter the Great, which had produced an alien bureaucratic structure and diverted the autocracy from its true role as the upholder and protector of Russian institutions. Ironically, they thought that by following German romantic models, Russia could rediscover its real

past and purify itself of Western aberrations. The Slavophiles were basically conservative in thought, but their criticism of the government and advocacy of reform naturally provoked the opposition of official Russia. Not surprisingly, their center of activity was the old capital, Moscow.

Although they agreed with the Slavophiles on the importance to Russia of the Russian peasant collectivism, the **Westernizers** believed in the compatibility of this institution with Western notions of an idealized and harmonious life for humankind in socialist communities. As with the French socialists, they saw no role for the church in this society and believed the state must continue to modernize along Western lines to eliminate barbarism and inefficiency. They advocated the elimination of autocracy and the establishment of socialistic self-government. Their anti-religious posture clearly separated them from the Slavophiles. To most of the Westernizers, moreover, Peter the Great was a hero who had gallantly pushed Russia toward its inevitable Western destiny. The problem was that many of his successors, out of a sense of self-preservation, had resisted further Western reforms.

DOSTOEVSKY'S LIFE

Fyodor Dostoevsky was born in Moscow in 1821, the son of a staff physician at a Moscow hospital. Educated to be a military engineer in St. Petersburg, he disliked school and his chosen profession and loved literature instead. We find echoes of his student days in Part II of *Notes from Underground*. Dostoevsky resigned his military commission in 1844 to devote himself to writing. He published his first novel, *Poor Folk*, in 1846, a book that was highly praised by the leading Russian literary critics. The same year he published *The Double*, a story about a government clerk who is haunted and finally driven mad by a man who is his exact double. Here Dostoevsky took a familiar theme from Gothic romance novels—the *Doppelgänger* or "double-goer"—and turned it into a brilliant psychological study. As ignored and neglected as *Poor Folk* had been praised, *The Double* only came to be appreciated much later.

Although always basically religious and conservative, as a young man Dostoevsky was for a time caught up in the revolutionary ideas and activities that were engaging the younger Russian intelligentsia and that we have outlined above. In 1847 he

Fyodor Dostoevsky by Pete Vasilij. Corbis-Bettmann.

became a member of the mildly subversive Petrashevsky Circle, and in 1849 its members were arrested by the tsar's police. Dostoevsky was imprisoned for eight months and then sentenced to death. The sentence was literally commuted at the last moment, when he thought he was about to be executed. It was actually a hoax—the government had never intended to execute the Petrashevsky Circle but only wanted to scare them to death—but Dostoevsky never forgot the experience.

Dostoevsky spent eight years in Siberia, where political prisoners were often sent, the last four in the Siberian army. He used the time in Siberia to do much reading and thinking, and this period was very important in shaping his mature work. Dostoevsky returned to St. Petersburg in 1859 with a wife, Maria Issaeva, a widow whom he had met and married in Siberia, and her son Pasha. The years 1860–65 were an extremely difficult period for Dostoevsky, and at the same time the crucible out of which his most important work emerged. The marriage was an

unhappy one. Mother and son were not in good health, and Dostoevsky always had money problems trying to support a family entirely by writing and editing and then undermining his own efforts with compulsive gambling. He himself suffered from epilepsy. In 1861 he published *Memoirs from the House of the Dead*, his reminiscences of his time in Siberia, where he had been deeply impressed by the dignity, decency, and faith of many of his fellow prisoners. In 1862–63 Dostoevsky traveled to Western Europe to get away from his creditors, restore his health, and gamble. He was critical of what he saw: a civilization dominated by rationalism and possessive individualism (capitalism). In 1864 both his wife and his brother died. Out of all this unhappiness came *Notes from Underground* (1864) the first of Dostoevsky's five great novels.

Things began to improve somewhat for Dostoevsky in 1865, when he married a second time to Anna Grigorievna Snitkina, a practical, well-balanced woman who provided him with the stability and solidity his life needed. In 1866 he published *Crime and Punishment*, his profound exploration of the themes of crime, guilt, and redemption through the portrayal of the student Raskolnikov. From 1867 to 1871 the Dostoevskys lived in Western Europe. They continued to have serious money problems, and Dostoevsky continued to gamble. (He published his powerful story, "The Gambler," in 1866; it is still used by the organization that helps compulsive gamblers, Gamblers Anonymous.) While in Europe, Dostoevsky wrote his novel *The Idiot*, published in 1869, which portrayed a modern Christ-figure, Prince Myshkin. *The Possessed* followed in 1872, a story based on an actual event. A radical Russian revolutionary named Nechaev had a member of his group murdered in 1869 because he would not obey Nechaev without question. Dostoevsky saw Nechaev and his moral code as the inevitable end result of liberalism and socialism. During the 1870s, Dostoevsky became increasingly active in social and political causes from a conservative, Slavophile, and Russian Orthodox perspective.

Dostoevsky is often seen as the quintessential Russian writer, an embodiment of the "Russian soul." He was an eloquent voice of Slavophilism and a challenging critic of important aspects of modern Western civilization: secularism, rationalism, possessive individualism, and socialism. In him we can see clearly and articulately portrayed the clash between traditional Russian and modern Western values. His influence on Western thought and literature has been important, and his novels are part of our cultural heritage. Along with Sören Kierkegaard and Friedrich Nietzsche, Dostoevsky is also seen as one of the three nineteenth-century pioneers of **existentialism**.

As a writer Dostoevsky was a brilliant explorer of the human psyche, exposing our inner contradictions, the role of the unconscious, and the fundamental role of desire and will in human life. Nietzsche acknowledged his own indebtedness to Dostoevsky in *Twilight of the Idols*, and Freud likewise recognized him as a profoundly astute investigator of the mind. Another aspect of Dostoevsky's genius is the "polyphony" of his writings, which is to say, his ability to speak in many voices. His characters embody alternative and conflicting ideas and ideals in a convincing way. For all his devotion to the Christianity of the Russian Orthodox Church, Dostoevsky experienced to the full the range of alternative views of things, which he represents in his characters in a realistic way.

Dostoevsky definitely has a message, however, which is that faith in Christ alone gives meaning to these crazy lives of ours. He expressed this through the Christianity of ordinary Russian people—Russian Orthodoxy in its popular form—such as the peasants he had known during his imprisonment in Siberia. But Dostoevsky is too complex, too good a writer, simply to "preach" to the reader. Instead, in the later novels he tries to show the consequences of ways of life not based on faith: Underground Man's paralysis of will, Raskolnikov's belief in his superiority, Nechaev's authoritarian socialism, and Ivan Karamazov's atheism.

GUIDE TO THE READINGS

Notes from Underground is the first of Dostoevsky's five great novels and the first presentation of themes that would dominate the later novels. It takes the form of a "confession" (the title he originally gave it) by a forty-year-old civil servant. In Part One the nameless narrator introduces himself and his outlook on life. In Part Two, by way of illustrating what kind of man he is, he tells a story about himself at age twenty-four, intruding unwanted on a party held by former schoolmates and ending up with a prostitute who takes seriously his half-cynical, half-genuine urgings that she reform her life.

The context for *Notes* was the Westernizer-Slavophile controversy. The story is a direct response to a novel published in 1863 entitled *What is to be Done?* by the revolutionary writer Nikolai Chernyshevky. Chernyshevky's novel occupies a place in modern Russian literature roughly comparable to Harriet Beecher Stowe's *Uncle Tom's Cabin* in America. (Like many literate Russians, Vladimir Lenin, the chief founder of the Soviet Union, read the book as a boy and later gave one of his own books the same title). Chernyshevsky was a utilitarian, feminist, pre-Marxist radical socialist. He believed strongly in the persuasive power of reason, in science, education, and social reform. Chernyshevsky blended Western and Russian ideas, envisioning a utopian society patterned somewhat after the Russian peasant communes. The basic problems in Russia, he believed, were patriarchalism and social hierarchy. Gradual reform was not enough; revolution was necessary. One of the two main characters in the novel, Vera Pavlovna, has a series of dreams that are utopian visions of the future and that provide the theme of the novel: through education and a radical egalitarian restructuring of society, individual humans will come to know what is truly good and in their actual self-interest, and they will act on the fact that their true self-interest and the good of society as a whole coincide.

Dostoevsky's *Notes from Underground* is a direct parody of Chernyshevsky's book. He lifts passages, ideas, and images (such as the "Palace of Crystal") straight from the book. The powerful arguments against Enlightenment rationalism and socialism in Part I are directed against Chernyshevsky's views. Part I, in fact, contains a brilliant attack by Underground Man (who is here speaking for Dostoevsky himself) on the assumptions of the Enlightenment that humans are rational beings who always choose what they believe to be good but err through ignorance and simply need a properly just society and the right education to choose what is truly good. The middle sections of Part I are among the most trenchant attacks on Western rationalism and utopian social schemes ever written. Underground Man's understanding of human nature and his criticism of prevailing assumptions about the role of reason make this a key text in the development of existentialism.

Photo: Crystal Palace, London, England. Courtesy of AP/Wide World Photos.

While not readily apparent, Dostoevsky's conservative Christian viewpoint underlies *Notes*. The original title of the book, recall, was "Confession." In a letter to his brother in March of 1864, after the first part of the book was published, Dostoevsky wrote: "It would have been better not to publish the penultimate chapter at all (the main one, where the essential thought is expressed) than to publish it the way it is, i.e. with its forced sentences and internal contradictions. But what is to be done? The censors are swine; they passed the parts where I ridiculed everything and sometimes blasphemed for show, but they cut the part where I deduced from all this the need for belief and for Christ."[1] This statement also reminds us of the literary censorship that existed in Dostoevsky's Russia: writers were not free to say whatever they pleased.

You may find Underground Man, the narrator of *Notes*, a puzzling and repulsive character, but there is much to learn from him about ourselves. Underground Man longs for the "highest and best," the "sublime and the beautiful," but is always dragged down by his worst self. He is spiteful out of sheer boredom, he needs to dominate but takes both pleasure and outrage in being humiliated, he is unable to love, he is isolated from "real life" and wrapped up in literature and dreams. Underground Man, however, knows what he is; he is ruthlessly honest with himself and the reader, and he is deeply insightful about the inner conflicts of the human soul generally—much more so than the great majority of people. Yet for all his clarity of vision about what is wrong with him, he lacks the will to seek forgiveness, healing, and redemption through faith. Underground Man gives us many hints that he is not only miserably unhappy but also longs for something that transcends the self-conflict and ugliness of his situation—the true "highest and best." For Dostoevsky, he is a person who clearly needs the forgiveness and redemption that only Christian faith can bring, but he lacks the will to seek it.

Dostoevsky spells out his religious message the most explicitly at the very end of the novel. Consider carefully the concluding remarks of Underground Man, and notice how he shifts from "I" to "we." Notice also his "sermon" to Lisa in the brothel. The part on marriage is a traditionally Christian picture of a good marriage.

Dostoevsky's message, here and in the other later novels, is that humanism, of whatever form, is doomed to defeat and despair. By "humanism" he means secular humanism, which he interprets as all the ways, beginning with the Enlightenment, in which humans have replaced God with themselves. The grand rational schemes of the Enlightenment—science, capitalism, revolution, democracy, socialism—all come to grief on the rocks of our very flawed human nature. But so, in *Notes*, do all forms of romantic intellectualism, escapism, and individualism, as represented by Underground Man.

As the reader begins *Notes from Underground*, he or she should think about the title and the layers of meaning it has in the story. Underground Man, the nameless narrator, calls himself an "anti-hero." What does that mean? How old is he at the time he tells the story, and how old was he when he had the experiences he describes in Part II? While the reader may find Underground Man a very strange and unpleasant character, it is worthwhile to pay close attention to his account of his childhood in Part II and what he says at the very end of the book. Is it possible to pity him? Is Underground Man crazy? neurotic? ruthlessly honest? Sigmund Freud argued that everyone is neurotic to some degree, and that "normal" people learn much about themselves from people who are more extreme in their feelings and behavior.

Dostoevsky's Underground Man stands as the defiant anti-hero of a challenge to reason. The novel can therefore also be interpreted as an existentialist inquiry that is the culmination of a century of debate over rationalism and romanticism and, in Russia, over Westernism and Slavophilism. From a position of self-imposed social exile (isolated in his "hole" under the floor, as he puts it), Underground Man preaches the conviction and fear that human beings can't explain anything by reasoning and consequently it is useless to reason. This emotional conclusion is based on two considerations: the nature of being human and the nature of reason.

Concerning the first of these considerations, the Underground Man asserts that human reason "reason, gentlemen, is a fine thing, that is unquestionable, but reason is only reason and satisfies only man's reasoning capacity, while wanting is a manifestation of the whole of life—that is, the whole of human life, including reason and various little itches."[2] For the Underground Man, as well as apparently for Dostoevsky, human nature is multifaceted and resistant to simple rational characterizations of itself. Reason is merely a single aspect of human nature that at times can be and even must be ignored as we engage with the world and live with others.

According to Underground Man, "free and unfettered choice," not reason, is what supremely characterizes human existence. To concentrate on the rational aspects of human existence is appropriate, therefore, only when they are seen within the broader perspective of human will or volition. The use of rational methods to pursue an understanding of reality is itself an act of the will. The use and validity of reason is a result of a free choice and tied to a willful commitment made by a human being. If someone disputes another's use of reasons in a particular context, or attempts to do so in all contexts, like the Underground Man, then that conflict is best seen as a clash of wills, not as rational misunderstandings. For if a person chooses not to let reason influence his or her decisions and actions, then a rational argument that attempts to persuade him or her to change his or her mind will certainly have little force. Thus, when the Underground Man says humans can be explained by reason he is asserting the importance of human choice in rational investigations and the need to see that explanations depend not only on the dictates of reason, but also on the willful human decision and choice to use reason. Consequently it is useless to reason if one does not acknowledge the dependence of rational methods on human volition, for the human subject's choice to use rational methods is an inherent part—indeed, the starting point—of rational inquiry.

Concerning the second aspect of the Underground Man's considerations, the nature of reason, he says that when reason is left wholly to itself it proves unable to provide a ground or starting point for human action. "I exercise thinking, and, consequently, for me every primary cause immediately drags with it yet another, still more primary one, and so on ad infinitum."[3] The faculty of reason, he asserts, has the remarkable quality of always being able to reflect on and analyze its own methods and nature. When we have reached a conclusion by rational methods, it is perfectly appropriate, if not rationally necessary, to investigate the rational worth of the methods used to reach that particular conclusion. The axioms, methods, and hypotheses of an inquiry are always open to rational scrutiny. The Underground Man finds that rational, self-reflective inquiry is unable to check or terminate itself, and so produces an unending process of reflection.

Therefore, nothing can be explained through reason because the grounds for any explanation can always be rationally investigated and the grounds of that investigation can then themselves be rationally scrutinized, and so on, interminably. Final and complete explanation, which for the Underground Man means rational explanation, is impossible, and thus reason is useless (if the goal is fully rational explanation, that is, complete and final answers) because rational inquiry yields only various forms of relative explanations and critical questions.

At this point there are obvious objections: Isn't there something rather quixotic or contradictory in the Underground Man's challenge to and rejection of reason? Don't reason and logic have an objective force independent of human desires? It does not seem that the Underground Man or anyone else can question the value of reason without already using it and accepting its basic legitimacy. To refute reason requires the use of reason. The Underground Man, in fact, takes note of this very point when he has an imaginary dialogue partner object, "you can't rebel: it's two times two is four! Nature doesn't ask your permission; it doesn't care about your wishes, or whether you like its laws or not. You're obliged to accept it as it is, and consequently all its results as well."[4] One must, it seems, use reason to challenge the validity of reason. That fact in itself seems to show its invulnerability to subjective, willful rejection.

This criticism of the Underground Man and of Dostoevsky's existentialist position is, however, a misunderstanding of the strength of the claim the Underground Man makes. In reply to this criticism, the Underground Man simply remarks, "what do I care about the laws of nature and arithmetic if for some reason these laws and two times two is four are not to my liking?"[5] The human subject is perfectly capable, according to the Underground Man, of rejecting reason and its implications, regardless of the fact that an argument to that effect presupposes the canons of rationality. Hence the Underground Man does not argue that the human subject refutes or rationally disputes the necessity and laws of reason, but says simply that she or he can choose not to give priority in a particular context, or in her or his life in general, to such necessity and laws. The Underground Man is an example of a person who chooses not to allow reason to play the leading role in his life. And this is what the text shows, not what it argues.

In this presentation of the Underground Man, Dostoevsky shows his existentialist leanings, for it is here that he forcefully exhibits the primacy of the human subject over objective laws. Human beings can freely reject the choice and demands of reason in favor of other subjective choices, for example, choosing to follow or be governed by one's feelings, or by principles of religious faith. (Whether humans should choose reason as a guide for action is still, of course, an appropriate question.) By not choosing to accept the demands of reason, an individual brings rational debate about the implications of the rejected use of reason to an end. To try rationally to debate about the particular implications of a rational way of life with someone who has rejected the importance of reason as a means of deciding how to act, is fruitless and without meaning, since the very methods required to convince the person have already been disputed or rejected.

Dostoevsky, however, does not leave the question here. The existential gap between subjective choice and objective justification and reason finds its most dramatic expression in Dostoevsky's novel *The Brothers Karamazov* (1881) which was undoubtedly Dostoevsky's greatest novel, and which is generally regarded as one of the masterpieces of world literature (Freud ranked it with *Oedipus the King* and *Hamlet*.) To understand Dostoevsky's final posing of the question that he first raises in *Notes*, we must turn briefly to the episode in the chapter of *The Brothers Karamazov* entitled "The Grand Inquisitor." Particularly in this and the preceding chapters, *The Brothers Karamazov* has been characterized as containing the most powerful presentation of the problem of evil in modern literature. Ivan Karamazov, one of the four brothers in the novel, searingly argues the case against God in a tavern conversation with Alyosha, his younger brother. The suffering and death of children are for Ivan the ultimate challenge to the reality and goodness of God, since children are innocent and cannot be said to "deserve" punishment in the form of suffering. Ivan tells harrowing stories of gratuitous cruelty to children by adults, and concludes that if that is the price to be paid for believing that the universe is governed by a God of love, he respectfully "returns the ticket."

Alyosha, the religious believer who is deeply troubled by Ivan's arguments, appeals to the figure of Jesus, in whom Christians believe God is most fully revealed as suffering our sin and dying our death to forgive us our sins and overcome our pain and death. Ivan's response is to tell a story about Jesus' anonymous return to the city of Seville in Spain during the sixteenth century, the time of the Reformation and the Spanish Inquisition. The Grand Inquisitor is a Roman Catholic cardinal who is in charge of the Inquisition—rooting out and punishing all forms of heresy.

Here the conflict between freedom and reason that appears in *Notes from Underground* is most vividly developed. The supreme believer in reason and rationally governed action, the Grand Inquisitor, is brought face to face with the preeminent believer in human freedom and subjective existence, Jesus. One of the most interesting aspects of this meeting is that it is not a debate or rational argument; rather it is a long soliloquy. Jesus remains silent throughout the entire encounter, while the Inquisitor relates what is has contemplated in silence for the past ninety years. Why does Dostoevsky present Jesus in such a way? Why does he not allow him to answer the demeaning criticisms made by the Inquisitor? The answers to these questions center on the crucial differences Dostoevsky sees between human freedom and rational explanations and arguments.

When the Inquisitor condemns Jesus for refusing the temptations of the Devil, thereby leaving humankind without "reason" for choosing to follow or believe in him, Jesus cannot in any rational sense defend himself. While the Inquisitor can give humankind "reasons" for believing in Jesus and the Church—specifically the reasons of miracle, mystery, and authority—Jesus can use no such justifications. He cannot appeal to any such reasons because these would then be the objective standards on which the Inquisitor and humankind would make their decisions. That would remove the need for a free, faith-governed choice, which is what Jesus seeks from human beings. If he were to say one word in rational defense of his position against the charges of the Inquisitor, he then would not allow for the Inquisitor's right and ability to make a free subjective choice. He would show that his own acts are not subjectively and freely determined, because they would then be open to rational debate and questioning.

Is there then no reply open to an existentially governed individual? What type of reply could Jesus, or any individual, make in defense of his or her subjective choices? Since Jesus cannot use a rational argument, his reply must be by means of an action or deed. He must show the legitimacy of his choices by his actions. One of the endings Ivan proposes for "The Grand Inquisitor" emphasizes just this fact:

> When the Inquisitor ceased speaking he waited some time for his Prisoner to answer him. His silence weighed down upon him. He saw that the Prisoner had listened intently and quietly all the time, looking gently in his face and evidently wishing to reply. The old man longed for Him to say something, however bitter and terrible. But He suddenly approached the old man in silence and softly kissed him on his bloodless aged lips. That was all his answer.[6]

Jesus shows his willful choice and "defends" his way of life through an act of love—a kiss—and not through a rational justification. To act according to one's free subjective choices, to stand and act as an example of the worth of one's choices: that is the only existential answer that can be given to a rational challenger and critic. While Dostoevsky's Underground Man, who calls himself a "sick man," chooses spite as the ground for his actions, Jesus, who for the Christian is the ideal of what a human being should be, is governed by love. Dostoevsky's question to himself and humanity seems to be: which will we choose?

QUESTIONS FOR STUDY AND DISCUSSION

1. What is the "duality" of the Russian character, and what are some prominent historical examples of how it has manifested itself from Peter the Great to the Russian Revolution?
2. Characterize the Westernizer-Slavophile controversy, and how it manifested itself in nineteenth-century Russian cultural life.
3. How is the development of Russia different from that of Western Europe?
4. What is the geographic position of Russia in relations to the centers of Eastern and Western civilization?
5. Discuss the need for modernization in Russia. Why does this imply Westernization?

6. How does Underground Man describe the relation between reason and will in human life? Why is his outlook representative of existentialism?
7. What are Underground Man's criticisms of the Enlightenment legacy of the supremacy of science, utopian schemes for improving society, and proper education as a cure for social ills?
8. What role does Lisa play in *Notes from Underground*? How does her relationship with Underground Man reflect his lifelong struggle between the "highest and best" and his lower impulses?

SUGGESTIONS FOR FURTHER READING

Billington, James H. *The Icon and the Axe: An Interpretive History of Russian Culture.* New York: Random House Vintage, 1970.

Brower, Daniel R. *Training the Nihilists: Education and Radicalism in Tsarist Russia.* Ithaca and London: Cornell University Press, 1975.

Florinsky, Michael T. *Russia: A History and an Interpretation,* vol. II. New York: Macmillan, 1955.

Gleason, Abbott. *Young Russia: The Genesis of Russian Radicalism in the 1860s.* New York: Viking, 1980.

Hingley, Ronald. *The Russian Mind.* New York: Charles Scribner's Sons, 1977.

Pipes, Richard. *Russia under the Old Regime.* New York: Charles Scribner's Sons, 1974.

Raeff, Marc. *Origins of the Russian Intelligentsia: The Eighteenth-Century Nobility.* New York: Harcourt, Brace and World, 1966.

Riasanovsky, Nicholas V. *The Image of Peter the Great in Russian History and Thought.* New York and Oxford: Oxford University Press, 1985.

_____. *Russia and the West in the Teaching of the Slavophiles: A Study of Romantic Ideology.* Cambridge: Harvard University Press, 1952.

Venturi, Franco. *Roots of Revolution: A History of the Populist and Socialist Movements in Nineteenth Century Russia.* New York: Universal Library, 1966.

---

[1] In the Norton Critical Edition of *Notes from Underground*, translated and edited by Michael R. Katz (New York: W. W. Norton & Co., 1989), 93-94.

[2] Dostoevsky, Fyodor. *Notes from Underground.* Translated and annotated by Richard Pevear and Larissa Volokhonsky. New York: Vintage Classics, 1993, 28.

[3] Ibid., 17.

[4] Ibid., 13.

[5] Ibid.

[6] Fyodor Dostoevsky, *The Brothers Karamazov*, translated by Constance Garnett. New York: W. W. Norton & Co., 1976. 243.

LIFE OF FRIEDRICH NIETZSCHE

1844
Born in Röcken, a village in Saxony

1864
Matriculation at University of Bonn

1869
Awarded a position teaching classical philology at University of Basel. Receives doctoral degree from University of Leipzig. Becomes a close friend of Richard Wagner, the German composer, and his wife Cosima.

1870
Serves as medic in Franco-Prussian War; becomes seriously ill

1871
German unification under Prussian auspices

1872
Publishes the *Birth of Tragedy*

1873–76
Publishes *Untimely Meditations* (four essays)

1874
Withdraws from association with Wagners and is critical of their anti-Semitism and "pseudophilosophy."

1878–81
Publishes other early works, including *Human, All-Too-Human*, *Mixed Opinions and Maxims*, *The Wanderer and His Shadow*, and *Daybreak*

1879
Physical breakdown, resigns his position at the University. Embarks on a ten-year period of wandering that is lonely but enormously productive. The catalogue of his writings from this period are:

> *The Gay Science* (1882)
> *Thus Spake Zarathustra* (1883)
> *Beyond Good and Evil* ((1886)
> *Genealogy of Morals* (1887)
> *The Wagner Case* (written and published 1888)
> *The Antichrist* (written 1888; published 1895)
> *Nietzsche Contra Wagner* (written 1888; published 1895)
> *Twilight of the Idols* (written 1888; published 1889)
> *Ecce Homo* (written 1888; published 1908)

1888
Highly productive last year of sanity and writing

1889
Complete physical and mental collapse from which he never recovers; cared for by mother and then by sister

1900
Death

CHAPTER ELEVEN

FRIEDRICH NIETZSCHE

INTRODUCTION: THE UNIFICATION OF GERMANY

The life and writings of Friedrich Nietzsche (1844–1900) must be understood against two backdrops: the modern history of Germany on the one hand, and the intellectual currents of the European **Enlightenment** and of the reaction to it, **Romanticism**, on the other.

The key to modern Germany is the unification of Germany in 1871. At the beginning of the nineteenth century, Germans had a common language and culture but not a common government. "Germany" consisted, as it had for centuries, of a number of independent states. By the end of the nineteenth century, Germany was a unified nation, industrially and militarily the most powerful one in Europe. In the seventeenth and eighteenth centuries, one German state, the Kingdom of Prussia, had gradually emerged under the rule of successive members of the Hohenzollern dynasty, who were all named Frederick (Friedrich in German), to become the most powerful of the several German states then in existence. Prussia, which played the key role in unifying Germany, had a long history of authoritarian rule and militarism. It combined an absolute monarchy with a powerful, militarized aristocracy (called Junkers) who ruled with an iron hand a peasantry that lived in a state of serfdom. The state developed a powerful army, and military-style discipline permeated every aspect of the government. Dominating the fortunes of the other German states throughout the nineteenth century, Prussia imposed its character and will on the shape of German reunification.

The man who more than anyone else brought about German unification was Prussia's prime minister, Otto von Bismarck (1815–1898), a political genius, staunch Prussian patriot from the Junker class, and ruthless, thoroughgoing pragmatist. William I (1797–1888) became king of Prussia in 1861 and named Bismarck Chancellor of the kingdom in 1862. It was a politically brilliant tactic with fateful consequences for Germany and Europe. Bismarck either crushed the reform-minded liberals among the Prussian political and intellectual elites or he won them over, thereby gaining control of the Prussian parliament. In time-honored Prussian fashion, Bismarck introduced "top-down" social reforms explicitly designed to cripple liberal and radical reform efforts and to insure undivided loyalty to the state. For example, he introduced the most advanced social legislation for workers in Europe, providing insurance for sickness, disability, accidents, and old age, thereby co-opting progressive sentiments and winning the political loyalty of the working classes.

It was Bismarck's remarkable success in foreign policy, however, that chiefly won him German hearts and minds, confirmed Prussia's leadership, and brought about German unity. In the teeth of parliamentary resistance, he reorganized and strengthened the army, and in 1866 Prussia waged war against its chief foreign competitor, the Austro-Hungarian Empire. Prussia speedily won the Seven Weeks War, eliminating Austria as a player in German politics. Also in 1866, and under Bismarck's direction, Prussia organized a Confederation of North German States. In 1870, in order to bring the southern German states into the Confederation and under Prussian control, Bismarck deliberately provoked hostility between Prussia and France, whereupon Prussia invaded France. The war, called the Franco-Prussian War, ended with the siege of Paris and France's surrender in January 1871. As Bismarck had calculated, the south German states came to the aid of the Prussians.

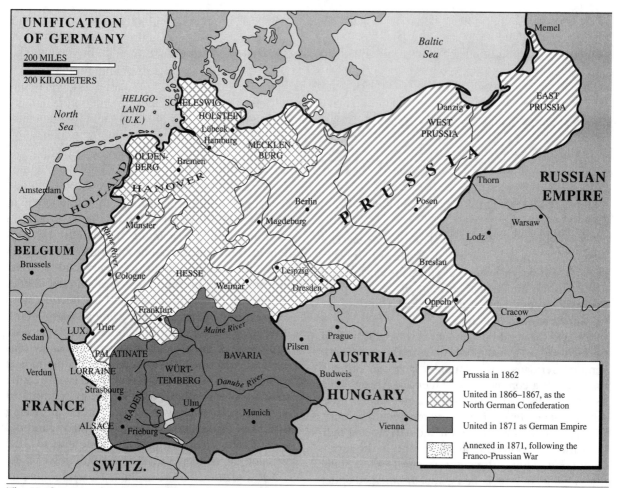

The Unification of Germany. Redrawn from *The Western Heritage,* Sixth Edition, Combined Edition, by Donald Kagan, Frank Turner, Steven E. Ozment, Frank Turner, Steven E. Ozment, and Frank M. Turner, (1998), Prentice-Hall, Inc.

The war completed the unification of Germany. On January 18, 1871, at Versailles, the German princes granted the title of Kaiser (from the Latin caesar, emperor) to King William I, creating the German Empire (Reich). By this act, Bismarck and Prussia created the most powerful industrialized nation in Europe, with an educated, hard-working, and disciplined population and the finest army on the continent. This formidable new state was also thoroughly authoritarian, molded in the Prussian image, and its people had been largely denied much experience with democratic ideas and institutions, such as representative government and the guarantee of individual rights. (In the twentieth century, this inexperience would seriously hamper German attempts at democracy until after its defeat in World War II). The united Germany quickly became a major player in the intense imperial competition among the great powers of Europe that led to World War I.

We cannot understand Nietzsche's often critical remarks about his fellow Germans, which occur throughout his writings, including *Twilight of the Idols,* except against this background of German unification. Nietzsche was born in Prussia and was twenty-seven and a young professor when Germany was united, and he became increasingly critical of the militarism, chauvinism, and anti-Semitism that characterized the new Germany.

GERMAN THOUGHT AND CULTURE

Germany had a great cultural and intellectual tradition of which Nietzsche was also the heir, and he deplored what he considered its decline under the new Reich. The paradox of modern Germany is that the political developments described above were taking place while Germany was the home of some of the most creative and daring intellectual and artistic developments in Europe. The flowering of German literature, philosophy, religious thought, historical study, art, and music in the late eighteenth and early nineteenth centuries was so remarkable it has been called the "German Renaissance." It was a dazzling outpouring of intellectual and artistic creativity. Among the great names of that renaissance were Johann Wolfgang von Goethe, Heinrich Heine, Friedrich Schlegel, and Friedrich Schiller in literature; Immanuel Kant, Johann Fichte, G. W. F. Hegel, and Friedrich Schelling in philosophy; Friedrich Schleiermacher and David Strauss in religious thought; Caspar David Friedrich in painting; and Ludwig van Beethoven, Karl Maria von Weber, and Franz Schubert in music. This renaissance produced some of the most influential and creative achievements in thought and art in the modern West.

The leading figure of the "German Renaissance" was Johann Wolfgang von Goethe (1749–1832), one of the greatest writers of the Western world. He is considered a "universal genius." Poet, novelist, playwright, essayist, statesman, scholar, and scientist, he was a modern "Renaissance man" who, like Leonardo Da Vinci, developed the many sides of his personality, intelligence, and talent to the highest degree. In literature Goethe is ranked with Homer, Virgil, Dante, and Shakespeare. His best-known works include the poetic drama, *Faust*, one of the great works of Western literature, his very popular romantic "Sturm und Drang" ("Storm and Stress") novel *The Sorrows of Young Werther*, and *The Roman Elegies*. Nietzsche had the greatest admiration for Goethe.

The **Romantic movement** in German arts and letters, which was part of the "German Renaissance" and in which Goethe participated but which he eventually rejected, was an important part of the dominance of **Romanticism** throughout western Europe in the first part of the nineteenth century. Reacting against the rationalism and "neoclassicism" of Enlightenment thought and art, the romantics emphasized feeling and intuition, affirmed individuality and spontaneity, exalted nature as the organic context of human life, celebrated the diversity of peoples and cultures, and often nostalgically evoked a pre-modern, pre-industrialized past (such as the Middle Ages) as a "golden age." A prominent example of German romanticism in literature was the group known as the *Frühromantiker* (early romantics), which included the writer-philosopher Friedrich Schlegel, his wife the novelist Dorothea Mendelssohn Schlegel, the religious thinker Friedrich Schleiermacher, and the novelist and poet Ludwig Tieck. Nietzsche read extensively in and was quite critical of the Romantic writers of Germany and also of France.

Every German in the nineteenth (and indeed in the twentieth) century who claimed to be philosophically literate had to read and come to grips with the work of Immanuel Kant and G. W. F. Hegel. These two thinkers have been among the most important shapers of modern European thought—not only in philosophy, but also in a wide variety of fields including history, psychology, political science, religious studies, anthropology, sociology, and literary criticism. Nietzsche was very critical of Kant, and it is useful to know what he was criticizing. He wrote less about Hegel directly, but he was certainly critical of his ideas as well.

Immanuel Kant (1724–1804). Kant's ideas became such a watershed in the history of modern philosophy that we speak of "pre-Kantian" and "post-Kantian" in referring to philosophical developments. In his *Critique of Pure Reason* (1781) he constructed a new model for understanding the mind in its relation to the world. On the one hand he argued, against the rationalists like Descartes, that human understanding is not simply a mirror that reflects intuitively the structure of things as they are in themselves. On the other hand, against the empiricists like Hume, he argued that the mind is not simply a "blank tablet" deriving all its knowledge from sense experience. What we call the "mind," Kant said, must be viewed as an active agent that constructs the raw material of sense experience into an ordered and intelligible world through principles inherent in the mind. In no sense do human minds *create* the universe of physical objects and relations, which are realities other than ourselves that are simply "given" to our sense. But it is entirely our minds that construct them into an ordered and intelligible world.

Nor are the principles in our minds simply subjective to each individual. They are universal and objective characteristics shared by all normal humans by virtue of their reasoning ability, and that it why we share a common world and science is possible.

Central to Kant's philosophy is his distinction between the *phenomenal* and the *noumenal*. What we perceive through our senses are things as they *appear* to us—what Kant called *phenomena*. What things are *in themselves*, apart from our experiencing their appearances through our senses, cannot be known to the human mind. But Kant insisted that we must assume the existence of things in themselves, even though we can have no knowledge of them. He called things in themselves *noumena*. He also believed that the realm of noumena may include realities such as God. But noumena, Kant said, cannot be known, and human understanding has nothing to say about them. Human knowledge is limited to organizing and making sense of the physical universe (phenomena) as we perceive it through our senses. Kant believed that that was exactly what we see in the work of scientists such as Sir Isaac Newton, and Kant believed he had provided a philosophical explanation of Newton's theories about nature.

In his moral philosophy Kant argued that a human being is free or autonomous to the extent that she transcends passions and desires and acts out of duty to the moral law or, as he called it, the *categorical imperative*: those moral principles that can be applied universally and recognize the autonomy and dignity of persons. The moral law is the law of our own being as rational creatures. But the ability to act autonomously means that persons have free will. Unless I am free either to do or not to do what the moral law commands, then morality is an illusion. Kant argued that insofar as we understand ourselves simply as physical organisms, as we do when we study humans scientifically, there is no way of thinking of ourselves as free. The world of Newtonian science is deterministic. All we can *know*, through science, is that we are phenomena operating in space and time and thus entirely subject to the laws of physics and physiology. But since we must believe that our will is free in order to make rational sense of morality, we can consistently believe that as moral beings we are noumenal. We belong to a moral realm "outside" the phenomenal world of space and time.

So while Kant believed we could have genuine *knowledge* only of the world of phenomena, he argued that certain *beliefs* that go beyond the phenomenal world are necessary as practical *"postulates"* or affirmations in order to make sense of the moral life. The first such postulate, as we have seen, is *free will*. The second is *immortality*. If morality is to make sense, then ought entails can: if the inner moral law commands, I must be able to obey. But it is obvious that because of the lifelong struggle in humans between duty and desire, none of us perfectly obeys the moral law. So we require an indefinitely long period of time in order to make our wills perfectly good. The third postulate is the *existence of a God* who is the good and purposeful source and goal of both the phenomenal and the noumenal realms. Such a supreme reality alone has the power to guarantee our immortality and to overcome the inevitable split or dualism in this world between duty and desire: between our duty to the moral law and the happiness we naturally seek.

Georg Wilhelm Friedrich Hegel (1770–1831). Hegel was very influenced by Kant, but believed Kant was arbitrary in leaving us with a complete dichotomy between phenomena and noumena. If, as Kant had showed, the mind actively constructs the meaning of the universe of phenomena through categories within itself, then, Hegel reasoned, is not the mind the clue to the whole of reality-phenomenal and noumenal alike? Hegel developed a philosophical perspective known as *absolute idealism*. Individual human minds are manifestations of a cosmic or univesal Mind, which Hegel called the Infinite, the Absolute, or Spirit. Reality as a whole is the total process of Spirit's self-expression. Spirit is the Universal Agent that is disclosed in the unfolding processes of nature and history and can be known by human minds, which are Spirit "thinking itself." The kind of reasoning that enables us to understand the laws of the development of the world-process is what Hegel called *dialectic*, in which concepts generate and pass into their opposite, uniting in a higher synthesis yet without canceling their differences. The dialectic is both the inner meaning and the driving force of the unfolding of Spirit, manifested in the emergence of conflicts and contradictions in nature and history that move the process—the life of Spirit—to a higher level that is both continuous with what went before and yet truly new and unprecedented.

According to Hegel, there are two stages in the cosmic life of Spirit. (1) One is the realm of nature, which is Spirit making an object of itself, or becoming its own "other." Nature is an objective, physical order of things that is a necessary basis for the development of subjects—of human consciousness. (2) The second stage is the emergence of human consciousness, which is Spirit "returning to itself" as self-knowledge. Since what we know as history is precisely the story of human consciousness, Hegel was supremely interested in history. He believed that world history, as the manifestation of Spirit, was the unfolding of a rational process exhibiting principles discoverable by the mind. The rise and fall of nations, and the impact of great men—what Hegel called "world-historical individuals" such as Alexander the Great, Julius Caesar, and Napoleon—together with the varieties of human cultural experience, all contribute integrally to Spirit's unfolding purpose.

History, rightly understood, manifests a purpose, a *telos*: the progress of freedom—from ancient societies in which only the ruler was understood as free, through the Greek and Roman worlds in which some but not all were free, to the modern recognition that all individuals simply as human beings (spirit or subject) ought to be free. But true freedom, the full development of human consciousness and identity, can be achieved only within concrete political communities. Only the loyal, civic-minded citizen of the political community is the truly free person. In the state's laws and institutions, which are manifestations of Spirit, the individual has a basis for rationally determining his or her own life. Thus public and private interests are fully harmonized. The state is the highest human association, joining individuals together into a community and replacing the rule of instinct with the rule of law. Hegel found in the modern nation-state the fullest historical embodiment of universal reason, the supreme manifestation of Spirit, and the fullest expression of individual freedom. Its highest expression, he believed, was the Prussian state of his day, combining absolute monarchy with the principle of the individual's inherent worth and dignity.

NIETZSCHE'S LIFE

Friedrich Nietzsche lived and thought against the background of the cultural and political developments in eighteenth and nineteenth-century Germany that we have described so far. Nietzsche was one of the most original, provocative, and controversial of modern philosophers. Mention of his name evokes a cluster of phrases associated with him and often misinterpreted, such as "the death of God," "master and slave moralities," and "the will to power." Despite his repeated expressions of contempt for the rise of extreme German nationalism in the unified Germany and for the anti-Semitism that accompanied it, and despite his conviction of the generally negative effect of political power on cultural life, Nietzsche's ideas were later distorted and appropriated by the National Socialists or Nazis (1921–1945) to their purposes. This came about through a combination of circumstances. One was his dramatic language and an aphoristic prose style that lent itself to quoting him out of context. Another was the unfortunate control his sister Elisabeth Förster-Nietzsche, an active anti-Semite and German racialist, had over the publication of his writings as his literary executor during his period of insanity and after his death. A third factor was the willful romanticizing and distorting of Nietzsche as the "prophet" of a new Germanic "mythology" by some of his admirers.

Nietzsche was born in 1844 in Röcken, a village in Saxon Germany. His father and both his grandfathers were Lutheran ministers. His father died from a brain hemorrhage when Friedrich was four (which may be a medical clue to Nietzsche's later physical ailments), and he and his sister Elisabeth were raised by their mother, a grandmother, and two aunts. After an excellent classical education in one of the finest preparatory schools in Germany, Nietzsche attended the Universities of Bonn and Leipzig. At Bonn he began by studying theology, but he gave it up when he lost his faith and "majored" in classical philology instead. So impressive was Nietzsche's achievement as a student in that field that he was appointed to a professorship at the University of Basel, in Switzerland, at the age of twenty-four and before he had completed the doctorate (which the University of Leipzig then awarded him without examination)—an almost unheard-of action. He became a Swiss citizen and taught at Basel for ten years.

During his Basel years (1869–79) Nietzsche published his earliest books, beginning with The *Birth of Tragedy* (1872), a highly original and startlingly "revisionist" reinterpretation of ancient Greek tragic

Friedrich Nietzsche. By Stephen Lahey.

drama. Nietzsche interpreted Greek drama and culture as a conflict and synthesis between the Dionysian (unbridled passion that breaks down barriers and constraints) and the Apollonian (reason that bestows order, balance, individuation). Nowadays students of ancient Greek civilization take for granted the powerful Dionysian elements in Greek life, but it was a daring hypothesis in a time when the most influential European classical scholars (and also Goethe) interpreted the Greeks entirely in Apollonian terms. His book, which concluded with praise of the composer Richard Wagner as the creative renewer of German culture, was not well received by his fellow classicists.

While at Basel Nietzsche became a close friend and ardent admirer of Richard Wagner, the operatic genius who was revolutionizing German music, and his wife Cosima, who lived in Tribschen near Basel. At first Nietzsche was like a son to Wagner, and he later considered the time he spent with the Wagners one of the happiest periods of his life. But Nietzsche soon became disillusioned with Wagner, who was becoming the self-appointed cult figure of the strident German nationalism and anti-Semitism that were emerging in the early years of the country's unification. Nietzsche, by contrast, always called himself a "good European" and an "anti-anti-Semite," and he criticized the Germans unmercifully. He spent the rest of his career "working through" his relationship with Wagner; two of his last writings are directly about Wagner.

Nietzsche served as a medic in the Franco-Prussian War of 1870–71, where he contracted dysentery and diphtheria from nursing wounded soldiers in a boxcar for three days. Previously a mostly healthy although extremely near-sighted person, Nietzsche was progressively debilitated by ill health for several years, until in 1879 he suffered a serious physical breakdown. He decided to resign his university professorship and spent the next nine years "wandering," living mostly in temporary lodgings and hotel rooms in Switzerland and northern Italy. He endured recurrent and severe migraine headaches, stomach cramps and vomiting, and episodes of almost complete blindness.

Astonishingly, it was precisely those nine years (1879–1888) that were the most productive and creative of Nietzsche's life: in the writings of that period he developed a uniquely life-affirming philosophy. He wrote all his greatest and best-known books during those years, such as *The Gay Science* (1882–87), in which his famous parable of the "madman" who announces the death of God appears; *Thus Spoke Zarathustra* (1883–85), a highly imaginative "prose-poem" that he always considered his greatest work and that contains some passages of remarkable beauty; *Beyond Good and Evil* (1886), a general critique of the ideas and values of his time; *On the Genealogy of Morals* (1887), his historical and psychological analysis of morality in which he developed the typology of "noble" and "slave" moralities; *Twilight of the Idols* (1889), perhaps the best summary of his final views; *The Anti-Christ* (not published until 1895), his all-out attack on Christianity; and *Ecce Homo* (Latin for "behold the man," which were Pilate's words concerning Jesus addressed to the mob in Jerusalem; not published until 1908), in which he looks back over all he has written and responds to criticisms of his thought.

After receiving some early notoriety for his first books, Nietzsche wrote all his later works mostly ignored by critics and the reading public; he even had to pay for the publication of most of his books himself. His work was neglected until 1888, when some scholars and literary critics started reviewing his books and a noted Danish intellectual, Georg Brandes, gave a series of lectures on his thought.

After that, Nietzsche's rise to fame was meteoric, but he knew nothing of it, because by then he was living in a private world of madness. Early in January, 1889, Nietzsche suffered a complete mental collapse. Though he had brief periods of lucidity after that, he spent the rest of his life in a childlike mental darkness cared for by his mother and then Elisabeth Förster-Nietzsche, his sister.

After his mental breakdown, Elisabeth had published, with no critical editing, the disorganized, half-formed mass of notes and sketches he had made (some of which he had revised, polished, and used in his published books) for the abandoned work and entitled it *The Will to Power*. As it stands, the collection is full of important ideas that we do not find elsewhere in Nietzsche's writings, so that for many years interpreters of Nietzsche incorrectly regarded this undigested and unedited miscellany as his chief book and the main summary of his thought—with many unfortunate results.

GUIDE TO THE READINGS

Nietzsche had intended *Zarathustra* as his major philosophical statement. Continuing to develop his ideas, however, he collected notes during the 1880s for a major, even more comprehensive work that he thought of calling *The Will to Power*. But he abandoned this project in 1888 in favor of a different plan. 1888 was the last year before his collapse into mental illness, and it was an enormously productive period for Nietzsche. He wrote five books in which he succinctly and combatively expressed his developed philosophy. *Twilight of the Idols* was the last one he saw through to publication. At the end of the "Foreword" to *Twilight*, Nietzsche writes: "Turin [the town in northern Italy where he was living], 30 September 1888, on the day when the first book of the *Revaluation of all Values* was finished."[1] At that time, Nietzsche had in mind the publication of four books with the collective title *Revaluation of all Values*, a phrase that can be taken as a kind of motto for his thought. The "first book" of the *Revaluation* was *The Anti-Christ*, which is published along with *Twilight of the Idols* in your edition of Nietzsche. *Twilight* was not part of the projected *Revaluation* series, but Nietzsche considered it an important summary of his ideas. On September 12, 1888, in a letter to his secretary and most devoted admirer, Peter Gast, Nietzsche had written that *Twilight* was "a very sharp, precise, and quick digest of my essential philosophical heterodoxies: this is so that the book can serve to introduce and whet the appetite for my *Revaluation of All Values*. . . . There is a lot in it of judgments on the present, on thinkers, writers and such."[2]

The "revaluation of all values" is for Nietzsche the radical ("root") critical examination of the most foundational ideas, beliefs, and values of the human race, especially as expressed historically and culturally in Western civilization from the ancient Greeks and Israel down to Nietzsche's own day. For example, he analyzed what the later philosopher Ludwig Wittgenstein called "the bewitchment of our intelligence by means of language." Language is uniquely human and essential to human life and knowledge, but language is also inherently deceptive. Through language we carve up and simplify the ceaselessly changing flux of reality and ourselves into objects, causes and effects, and selves consisting of "ego" and "will." Nietzsche was especially critical of philosophers, beginning with Socrates, for making idols of their concepts ("God," "being," "substance") and regarding them as more real than the concrete world of our sense experience. Nietzsche's "revaluation" extended to metaphysics, religion, morality, and to politics.

Although Nietzsche, like most modern thinkers, was indebted to Kant's metaphysical skepticism, he heaped unrelenting scorn on Kant's analysis of the moral life. He considered Kant a Christian in disguise and a hypocrite, with his universal ethics of duty to others and his "smuggling" freedom, immortality, and God back in as props for the moral life after getting rid of them in his philosophy of nature. Nietzsche believed that Kant had been a pernicious influence in nineteenth-century Germany, allowing people to perpetuate Christian belief and morality in a respectably "modern" and secularized form. Nietzsche considered Hegel's philosophy the basis of a widespread understanding of the course of history as progressive, which Nietzsche considered profoundly mistaken. However, we can see affinities with Nietzsche's thought in Hegel's conviction that truth is to be found only within nature and history, however differently Nietzsche interpreted them.

Broadly speaking, Nietzsche was a naturalist in his outlook. While he never denied the possibility of supernatural realities, he maintained that humans could know nothing about them. The only reality of which we have knowledge is nature, which is the spatio-temporal universe that is known through our senses and is in a process of endless change or becoming. This ceaseless flux of sensory appearance is reality or "being"; we know nothing of any invisible, unchanging order of reality behind or beyond it. Religions and many philosophers have constructed such a realm (for example, Christianity's God, Plato's Forms), but such ideas are simply that— human constructions. On this planet the natural process has produced biological life in all its multiform variety, and humanity is to be understood as a unique manifestation of life and the animal kingdom. Nietzsche, always trying to get at the roots or primary causes of human phenomena, traced human ideas, values, and behavior to their psychological and (more deeply still) physiological bases. At the same time, he was very concerned to analyze and appreciate human life in all the rich and varied ways in which it expresses its uniqueness in nature. Thus, Nietzsche ranged over human culture in all its aspects, from the arts to politics to education to religion and morality.

In religion and morality Nietzsche rejected the idea of God, not only as an abstraction referring to something "beyond nature" of which we can have no knowledge, but also as the supreme idea used by Christianity to deny everything that affirms life in this world. He famously used the phrase "the death of God," as in his "Parable of the Madman" in *The Gay Science* (aph. 125), not in the literal sense that there was once an eternal, infinite being who no longer exists, but as a metaphor to describe the modern decline of Christian belief as the foundation of Western society—a decline that he both welcomed as a liberation and recognized as a dangerous upheaval.

Nietzsche also laid upon Christianity the primary responsibility for the triumph of "slave morality," a morality that is rooted in resentment and revenge (he always used the French word *ressentiment*) against the self-affirming values of superior or "noble" human beings by the inferior, the "herd," in societies. It is a morality that further expresses its negative basis by demanding of humans that they war against, rather than creatively sublimate, their biologically-rooted passions and drives. Nietzsche believed that different societies had developed different moralities expressing their distinctive social, political, and cultural life. His criterion for evaluating all moral codes or philosophies—indeed, his criterion for evaluating everything—was whether or not they were expressions of "ascending" or "descending" life, health or sickness (decadence), life-affirmation or life-denial. Moralities that arise from and creatively channel natural instincts and drives are healthy; those that war against our nature are unhealthy.

In his political thought Nietzsche was an unsparing critic of modern egalitarian movements such as democracy and socialism. Basing his views on the human place in nature, Nietzsche thought it was obvious that humans are not equal, nor should they be. Nature is a system of hierarchies of stronger and weaker (this is reminiscent of Aristotle), and human groups are no exception. There are those who naturally command and those who naturally obey. Interestingly, Nietzsche argued that it was precisely conservative societies, ruled by a "natural" aristocracy and characterized by a strong sense of tradition and rank, that best produced and allowed to flourish individual achievement and creative genius in thought and the arts. He sharply distinguished between political power and cultural greatness in a nation, and said that typically periods of cultural achievement have been periods of political decline. He wrote that the last great epoch in Europe was the Italian Renaissance, which took place in a region that was politically fragmented and weak. By contrast, the new and powerful German Reich represented everything Nietzsche considered bad about political power and its effect on individual expression.

Nietzsche was a highly experimental thinker, in both the form and the content of his writing. In the development of his literary style and philosophical ideas he was engaged in ceaseless "self-overcoming," as he called it, never content to rest with what he had been doing but constantly testing, questioning, and setting things in new perspectives. Nietzsche began in his earliest books by writing sustained essays. From there he went on to experiment with writings that were collections of "aphorisms," as he called them, and he became a master of the highly polished sentence and short paragraph. (Strictly speaking, aphorisms are typically very short, succinct sayings, whereas Nietzsche's "aphorisms" are everything from that to very long paragraphs.) In the works of his most fruitful period (1886–88), Nietzsche wrote books that were unified and connected collections of long and short aphorisms and, in the case of *The Genealogy of Morals*, of short essays.

As *Twilight of the Idols* demonstrates, Nietzsche's experimentalism means that he was never a "systematic" thinker, but that does not mean that his philosophical writings are incoherent. He adopted and experimented with styles of philosophical writing that were very different from the customary styles because of what he considered to be the bankruptcy of "philosophy as usual" and because these new styles best expressed what he believed philosophy to be: a problem-oriented approach to the basic issues that looks at everything from a variety of different angles and in as compressed a manner as possible. The philosophy that Nietzsche expressed through his experiments with style was also experimental, a series of "thought-experiments," and *Twilight* should be read with this stylistic intention kept in mind. The philosopher, Nietzsche believed, must be constantly willing to experiment with ideas, no matter how well-established or well-rewarded, and to question his or her own previous conclusions. This, approach, he said, is true science (the German word for science, *Wissenschaft*, refers to all forms of systematic, reasoned inquiry, from classical philology to physics): the "gay science" of cheerful but rigorous experimentation, holding everything up ceaselessly to investigation.

Nietzsche's earlier writings are the most experimental. In them we find a subtlety, an openness to looking at everything in both a positive and negative light, even a kind of tentativeness, a "holding in suspension," that we do not find in the later works. Out of the earlier works hypotheses emerged that later became his key ideas, and he worked out the implications of those ideas in such books as *Twilight of the Idols*. In these later works Nietzsche is more unqualifiedly assertive, and he trims everything down to what he considers to be its essential elements. Nietzsche's experimental approach to ideas was also an "existential" one. For Nietzsche, experimenting with ideas involved testing them in one's own life—"living" them. Experimenting to get at truth means calling into question, with an open mind, one's own taken-for-granted ideas, values, and beliefs.

Christian belief and morals, modern philosophy, the belief in progress, and popular ideas in modern politics—these were some of the great "idols" that Nietzsche sounded out—"touched with a hammer as with a tuning fork"—in books such as *Twilight of the Idols* and found to be hollow. As his German title, *Götzendämmerung*, a play on the title of Wagner's opera *Götterdämmerung* ("Twilight of the Gods") indicates, Nietzsche saw the reality and power of these foundational values as "dying" or fading into twilight in his own time, being challenged by the sciences and, through a variety of causes, progressively losing their hold on the consciousness of the Western world. Most people (including most philosophers) in the late nineteenth century were unaware or only dimly aware of it, but this fundamental upheaval in knowledge and values was taking place and its implications for the human future were fraught with both profound danger and extraordinary possibility. Nietzsche saw the internal contradictions produced in the modern West by this process as erupting into conflicts on an unprecedented scale in the twentieth century. At the same time, he saw himself as a herald of a time when out of the individual and social disintegration and chaos of his own day humans would create new, life-affirming values.

The original title of *Twilight* was "The Idle Hours of a Psychologist." Nietzsche often called himself a "psychologist," and his penetrating psychological insights (which Sigmund Freud, for example, clearly recognized as such) were central to his thought. He changed the title, but left a few references to the original title in the text of the book, which can be a bit confusing. For example, toward the end of the "Foreword," he writes, "This book too—the title gives it away—is above all a recovery, a sunny spot, a sidestep into a psychologist's idleness."[3] Peter Gast felt that the book needed a more "splendid" title, as befitted a work that in the "Foreword" Nietzsche called "a grand declaration of war." So Nietzsche came up with a title that, besides parodying a Wagnerian opera title, conveyed his belief that the ideas and values that most people have long taken for granted as permanent and fundamental are actually only human constructions.

The Foreword makes it clear that idols are the main topic of the book. In the Bible, idols are created things that are worshiped as gods, but are not really God. Nietzsche uses the term more broadly to suggest that most of what humans believe are illusions, and destructive ones at that. In the book he "sounds out" the great idols that have been worshiped by human civilization—and specifically in their Western versions—examining and exposing them for what they are and what they express about human life. Sounding out idols is simply another way of talking about the revaluation of all values. And what are the great idols Nietzsche sounds out? The beliefs about God (yes, for Nietzsche even God—especially God—is an idol), morality, philosophy, language, science, human nature, and psychology that have shaped and dominated the Western world and therefore who we are. Nietzsche also speaks in the "Foreword" of his "cheerfulness." He sees himself as a "happy warrior" battling on behalf of life and its affirmation, and not a gloomy pessimist just saying "No" to everything. The "Foreword" also provides a good example of the way in which Nietzsche uses certain metaphors for dramatic effect. When he speaks of "war," he simply means conflict generally—in this case intellectual conflict—which he considers essential to a robust life.

The first section of *Twilight*, "Maxims and Arrows," reveals Nietzsche as a master at writing those short, highly compressed statements we have noted and that we call proverbs or aphorisms. His aim, he says, is "to say in ten sentences what everyone else says in a book. . . ." Some of his most famous aphorisms are in "Maxims and Arrows," such as number 8: "What does not kill me makes me stronger." The aphorisms of "Maxims and Arrows" anticipate much of what is to come in the remainder of the book.

The main body of *Twilight* can be outlined as follows: (1) Idols of philosophy and Christianity ("The Problem of Socrates," "'Reason' in Philosophy," "How the 'Real World' At Last Became a Myth"); (2) Idols of morality ("Morality as Anti-Nature," "The Four Great Errors," "The 'Improvers' of Mankind"); (3) The decline of German culture and education ("What the Germans Lack"); (4) Miscellaneous reflections on nineteenth-century thinkers and writers and various topics ("Expeditions of an Untimely Man"); (5) Nietzsche's indebtedness to the cultures and ideas of ancient Greece and Rome ("What I Owe to the Ancients"); (6) Conclusion—from *Thus Spoke Zarathustra* ("The Hammer Speaks").

Let us consider a few highlights from the book in the order of the topics listed above as a way of focussing the reading of the book. These highlights and the reading of *Twilight* itself should be considered in light of the topical discussion of Nietzsche's writings given above. "The Problem of Socrates" starts the reader right off with a startling revaluation of an icon of Western civilization: by making an idol of reason and setting it over against instinct and passion, says Nietzsche, Socrates showed that he was a symptom of decline or decadence in ancient Greece. Nietzsche then goes on to argue, in "'Reason' in Philosophy," that virtually all Western philosophers since Socrates and Plato have made an idol of their ideas or concepts, regarding them as true "reality" and this tangible physical world of the senses as merely "appearance." In "How the 'Real World' Became a Myth," under the heading "History of an Error," Nietzsche tells the story of Western thought as the gradual emergence from the idolatrous illusions of Platonism (the Forms) and Christianity (God) to the modern secular and scientific outlooks that take nature, this world of the senses, as the truly real and reject the construction of purely abstract worlds beyond this one. Thus, he says, what began as the so-called "real world" of abstract ideas has in modern times increasingly become a myth, and the world of appearance has become the only reality we know.

In "Morality as Anti-Nature," Nietzsche succinctly states his criticism of almost all moral codes ever adhered to by human societies: they are literally "unnatural," demanding the suppression or denial of our natural instincts and passions instead of building positively on them and creatively sublimating or "spiritualizing" them. In section 4, Nietzsche singles out Christianity for special criticism as an extreme example of anti-natural morality, contrasting its understanding of love with what he regards as a healthy, life-affirming idea of love. He also observes—and this looks forward to the next part, on "The Four Great Errors"—that attitudes of people toward life are not objective truths but simply symptoms of either "health" (life-affirmation) or "sickness" (life-denial or decadence).

In "The Four Great Errors," Nietzsche describes four "idols" or illusions of the human race, all of which have to do with our judgments about the relationship between cause and effect: (1) mistaking causes for consequences ("Believe in God/obey the moral law, and it will make you happy"); (2) false causality (believing that human motives and decisions actually cause things to happen); (3) imaginary causes (ascribing feelings of well-being or suffering to God, evil spirits, faith, sin, etc.); and (4) free will (which was invented as an excuse to blame and punish people). In section 8 of "The Four Great Errors," we see a good statement of Nietzsche's naturalism: there is nothing but nature or the universe, with humans as one of its myriad manifestations, and nature is a process that is "innocent" and without ultimate purpose.

"The 'Improvers' of Mankind" is a continuation of Nietzsche's critique of traditional morality. Moral judgments are only symptoms or expressions of "ascending" or "declining" life, expressed differently in different human cultures; they have no objective validity. In this section, Nietzsche articulates his distinction, which he expresses at length in his book, *The Genealogy of Morals*, between "master" or "noble" morality and "slave" morality: the former values flow spontaneously from the strong and life-affirming; the latter arise from resentment of the strong by the weak and life-denying. Christianity, he argues, is a supreme example of slave morality.

In "What the Germans Lack," Nietzsche reflects on the negative effects the unification of Germany and the flexing of its muscles as a new great power in Europe have had. Germany, he says, used to be famous for its culture—its literature, thought, music, and art—during the age of the German Renaissance, but with political power its culture has sharply declined. "Power," he asserts, "makes stupid." He generalizes with the observation that there is always an incompatibility between political power and cultural greatness. (Since Elizabethan England would seem to be a counter-example, perhaps one should treat Nietzsche on this, and on other points, with the same skepticism that he enjoins upon his reader when considering other matters). Nietzsche's observations on what a university education ought to be and do (sections 6-7) may lead the reader to evaluate Nietzsche's comments in light of the reader's own experience of a university education.

In "Expeditions of an Untimely Man," Nietzsche includes miscellaneous reflections on important thinkers and writers of the nineteenth century and also on topics such as art and beauty, freedom, ethics, Darwinism, capitalism, democracy, and socialism. Among a few highlights: Nietzsche indicates in this part of the book what sort of writers and thinkers he admires and what sort he dislikes. He could be sarcastically critical of the English, and here he singles out prominent figures such as John Stuart Mill, George Eliot, and Thomas Carlyle. The section on George Eliot is a good statement of Nietzsche's view that you cannot, like George Eliot and many other nineteenth-century skeptics, reject Christianity and still consistently affirm Christian morality. By contrast to the English writers he mentions, Nietzsche admires the influential American essayist Ralph Waldo Emerson. In Section 17, Nietzsche describes the sort of persons he admires, which may illuminate aspects of his philosophy that we have laid out earlier. In sections 19 and 20, he discusses the categories of "beautiful" and "ugly." In these sections, and also in "Anti-Darwin," he hints at his emerging doctrine of the will to power, which includes an interesting criticism of Darwin. Nietzsche's discussion of the "natural value of egoism" in section 33, and his longer discussion of "whether we have grown more moral" in section 37 are examples of his "revaluation." His answer to the question that he raises in section 37 is definitely "No," and here he speaks critically of modern movements such as socialism and feminism as expressing human weakness and decline rather than strength. Nietzsche expresses his admiration for Dostoevsky in section 45, and in section 49 for Goethe, "the last German before whom I feel reverence."

Finally, in "What I Owe to the Ancients," Nietzsche summarizes what he has learned and appropriated from the ancient Greeks and Romans. Sharply rejecting the idolatry of reason that began with Socrates and Plato, Nietzsche identifies himself with the "Dionysian" spirit that animated earlier Greek culture and found artistic expression in Greek tragic drama. "Affirmation of life even in its strangest and sternest problems, the will to life rejoicing in its own inexhaustibility through the sacrifice of its highest types—that is what I called Dionysian . . . ." The god Dionysus has become the symbol for Nietzsche's whole philosophical outlook so that Nietzsche calls himself "the last disciple of the philosopher Dionysus. . . ."

The breadth of Nietzsche's genius and the range of his thought are considerable. He is best known as a philosopher who did not write in the usual manner of philosophers. But he was also a penetrating psychologist whose insights anticipated those of Sigmund Freud; a classical philologist (scholar of ancient Greek and Roman language and culture) who made original contributions to the interpretation of ancient Greek culture and its arts; a literary and art critic and cultural analyst; and a better-than-average musician and composer who helped the composer Richard Wagner establish the Bayreuth Music Festival in Germany, which continues to this day. Nietzsche also put the German language to use with a freshness, inventiveness, and clarity that have caused his leading translators and interpreters to regard him as one of the greatest writers of the German language. The flourishing of scholarship on and attention to Nietzsche's thought over the past forty years or so has enabled us to realize how remarkably his thought anticipated twentieth-century social and intellectual trends—from political trends and catastrophes such as world war to pragmatist and existentialist philosophies, philosophies of language, depth psychologies, and recent "post-modern" literary theories.

QUESTIONS FOR STUDY AND DISCUSSION

1. How did Prussia bring about the unification of Germany?
2. What was the "German Renaissance"?
3. What did Nietzsche mean by the revaluation of all values? What are some of the main values he revalues, and how does he deal with them?
4. Why was Nietzsche so critical of Christianity? What does Nietzsche think is wrong with Christianity? What value do you see in his criticisms?
5. Why does Nietzsche consider Socrates not truly "Greek"? What, according to Nietzsche, was Socrates' influence on later philosophers?
6. What is Nietzsche trying to show in "The History of an Error"? Does his characterization of Western intellectual development make sense on the basis of what you have read in works from Western civilization?
7. What, according to Nietzsche, are the "four great errors"? Give one example of each.
8. Nietzsche distinguishes between "freedom" and "free will." What does he mean by each, and what is the difference?
9. What is Nietzsche's criticism of morality as it is commonly understood and practiced? What would he substitute for it?
10. In what ways does Nietzsche say he is indebted to the ancient Greeks and Romans?
11. What does Nietzsche mean by calling himself a follower of Dionysus? Do you think the symbol of Dionysus expresses a positive or a negative outlook on the world?

SUGGESTIONS FOR FURTHER READING

Beiser, Frederick C. *Enlightenment, Revolution, and Romanticism: The Genesis of Modern German Political Thought,* 1790–1800. Cambridge, MA: Harvard University Press, 1992.

Blackbourn, David and Geoff Eley. *The Peculiarities of German History: Bourgeois Society and Politics in Nineteenth-Century Germany.* New York: Oxford University Press, 1985.

Danto, Arthur. *Nietzsche as Philosopher.* New York: The Macmillan Company, 1965.

Bruce Detwiler. *Nietzsche and the Politics of Aristocratic Radicalism.* Chicago: The University of Chicago Press, 1990.

Furst, Lilian. *Romanticism in Perspective: A Comparative Study of Aspects of the Romantic Movement in England, France and Germany.* London: The Macmillan Company, 1979.

Gilman, Sander L. *Conversations with Nietzsche: A Life in the Words of His Contemporaries.* Translated by David J. Parent. New York: Oxford University Press, 1987.

Graham, Ilse. *Goethe: Portrait of the Artist.* Berlin & New York: de Gruyter, 1977.

_____. The Social Foundations of German Unification: 1858–1871. Princeton: Princeton University Press, 1972.

Karl Jaspers. *Nietzsche: An Introduction to the Understanding of His Philosophical Activity.* Translated by Charles F. Wallraff and Frederick J. Schmitz. Chicago: Henry Regnery Company, 1965.

Kaufmann, Walter. *Nietzsche: Philosopher, Psychologist, Antichrist.* New York: The World Publishing Company, 1950.

Alexander Nehamas. *Nietzsche: Life as Literature.* Cambridge, MA: Harvard University Press, 1985.

Nietzsche, Friedrich. *The Portable Nietzsche.* Selected and translated, with an Introduction, Prefaces, and Notes by Walter Kaufmann. New York: The Viking Press, 1954.

Tracy Strong. *Friedrich Nietzsche and the Politics of Transfiguration.* Expanded Edition. Berkeley and Los Angeles: University of California Press, 1988.

Talmon, Jacob L. *Romanticism and Revolt: Europe,* 1815–1848. London: Thames & Hudson, 1967.

---

[1] Nietzsche, Friedrich. *Twilight of the Idols.* Indianapolis, IN: Hackett Pub., 1997, 4.

[2] Ibid., ix.

[3] Ibid., 3.

LIFE OF SIGMUND FREUD

1856 Born in Freiberg, Moravia (now in Czech Republic)

1860 Freud family moves to Vienna

1873 Begins study at University of Vienna

1881 Awarded doctor of Medicine degree

1881–82 Research with Josef Brücke at University of Vienna

1882 Physician at Vienna General Hospital; meets Martha Bernays

1885–86 Research with Jean Charcot in Paris

1886 Marries Martha Bernays, daughter of a well-known Hamburg family; establishes himself in the private practice of neurology; begins professional relationship with Josef Breuer and together they publish *Studies in Hysteria* in 1895; begins his own self-analysis

1896 Coins the term "psychoanalysis" for his new science of mental life

1899 Publishes his first important work,*The Interpretation of Dreams.* Gathers around him a small group of interested people to read and discuss papers. Among the papers that Freud writes during this time are *The Psycopathology of Everyday Life* (1901) and *Jokes and Their Relation to the Unconscious* (1905).This is the beginning of the psychoanalytic movement, which would eventually grow to include many well-known persons, including Carl Jung,Alfred Adler, Karen Horney, and Otto Rank.

1905 *Three Essays on the Theory of Sexuality*

1908 Formation of the Vienna Psychoanalytic Society; psychoanalysis rapidly becomes a worldwide movement

1912–14 Defections of Adler and Jung from Vienna Society

1913 *Totem and Taboo*, the beginning of a series of books and articles in which Freud applies psychoanalysis to cultural problems

1914–18 World War I

1915 Freud writes "Reflections Upon War and Death"

1917 *Introductory Lectures on Psycho-Analysis*

1920 *Beyond the Pleasure Principle*, in which Freud introduces his theory of the death instinct

1923 Develops a cancerous growth in his jaw and undergoes the first of 33 operations. Publishes *The Ego and the Id*

1927 *The Future of an Illusion*

1930 *Civilization and Its Discontents*

1938 Flees Austria for London, England in the wake of the Nazi takeover.

1939 *Moses and Monotheism*

1939 Freud dies in London, having asked his physician to administer an overdose of morphine

1940 *An Outline of Psycho-Analysis* is published posthumously

CHAPTER TWELVE

SIGMUND FREUD AND PSYCHOANALYSIS

INTRODUCTION

The traditional model of human nature that dominated Western philosophy and science for two millennia tells us that the "essence" of being human is defined in terms of our conscious life and our ability to reason. We find this model, in various forms, in thinkers as diverse as Plato and Aristotle, Aquinas, Descartes and Locke, Kant and Hegel, Jeremy Bentham and J. S. Mill. Sigmund Freud (1856–1939) has been perhaps more influential than anyone else in bringing about a fundamental revaluation of this model in the Western world. Freud's emphasis on the primary role of the unconscious in human life, an unconscious dominated by instinctual drives rooted in our biological nature, represents a dramatic departure from the model of human nature in which reasoning and conscious decision-making rule the day. While Freud was by no means the first to question the primacy of reason and the traditionally subordinate place of the passions, and while he was also not the first to consider the role of the unconscious in human life, his questions and considerations gained weight because of the way in which he raised them and because of the cultural and historical context in which they appeared. To begin with, they appeared in their fully developed form in the shadow of a deeply traumatic event: the First World War (1914–1918).

The Great War and its impact. World War I was so profoundly disturbing in its disruptiveness and destructiveness that it is sometimes said that the nineteenth century really ended, not in 1900, but in 1914. This statement points out that it was the First World War, which began in August of 1914, that shattered the assumptions and institutions that had characterized nineteenth-century Europe. The "Great War," as it was called, was a cataclysm that shook

Western civilization to its foundations and produced fundamental changes in European life, thought, and art that shaped the cultural world we still inhabit. Many reflective Europeans, and some Americans, who lived through World War I, whether as participants or observers, had their lives and their outlook on the world turned upside down and they were never the same again. This upheaval is abundantly evidenced in biographies and autobiographies of famous writers, artists, historians, scientists, philosophers, and theologians who lived through the war. While Freud's work began long before the war, the disturbing experiences of the war and its consequences gave his work a new context and a new credibility. Thus, while the important twentieth-century intellectual movements we call **existentialism** and **psychoanalysis** had emerged well before the war, it was the war and its impact that gave both movements new resonance and influence. As we study the life and work of Freud, it is particularly important to have a basic grasp of the war and its impact.

The causes of the war lay in the feverish competition for empire and military hegemony among the Great Powers of Europe (Britain, France, Germany, Austria-Hungary, Russia) in the late nineteenth and early twentieth centuries. A burgeoning and promising internationalism during the period before the war was finally swamped by the forces of a new, right-wing nationalism in the European nations. The new nationalism also inspired and inflamed smaller nations in the Balkans such as Serbia that had been subject for centuries to the Ottoman Turkish Empire. It was a Bosnian nationalist who touched off the war in June of 1914 by his assassination of the Archduke Ferdinand, heir to the Austro-Hungarian throne, and his wife in Sarajevo.

The Great Powers were loosely grouped into competing alliances, so that when Austria-Hungary declared war on Serbia, Russia pledged to help Serbia, supported by its alliance partner France, which caused Germany to support Austria-Hungary; that in turn brought Britain into the war on the side of Russia and France.

It was the conduct of the war, particularly on what was called the "Western Front," that shattered the optimistic illusions of Europeans. In Western Europe, both sides soon became mired in the trench warfare that was to dominate throughout the war. The policy of the generals on all sides seemed to be one of attrition: each sought to win by killing more of the enemy soldiers than the enemy was killing of theirs. The losses in the great battles of the war were simply staggering: close to a million lives lost, for example, in the Battle of the Somme alone. A whole generation of young European men was nearly wiped out. The entry of the United States into the war in 1917 on the side of Britain, France, and Russia, along with a successful British naval blockade, finally tipped the balance. Germany surrendered and an armistice was declared on November 11, 1918. The Treaty of Versailles following the war subjected Germany, now with a new and struggling democratic government, to staggering and humiliating reparations that laid the foundations for the rise of the Nazis under Adolf Hitler. It also carved Europe up roughly according to Woodrow Wilson's principle of "self-determination," creating new states such as Yugoslavia and Czechoslovakia out of the old Austro-Hungarian empire.

The impact of World War I on the literature, art, and politics of Europe was profound, shaping some of the most characteristic features of the twentieth-century world. It shook to the foundations modern European assumptions about reason and progress, and created widespread disillusionment. Important novelists of the time were deeply influenced by the war and embodied it as a theme in their writings. **Dadaism** and **Surrealism**, which respectively celebrated the absurdity of life and explored the disturbing unconscious depths of the human personality, became leading movements in art. Politically, the war made possible the Bolshevik Revolution in Russia in 1917, and the post-war period saw the rise of right-wing authoritarian movements such as Fascism in Italy and Nazism in Germany. But it also led to a renewed commitment to peace and internationalism. The League of Nations was founded, full of hope, but ultimately foundered in the 1930s. Peace movements dedicated to the proposition that World War I must be "the war to end all wars" enlisted supporters throughout Europe and the U.S. during the 1920s and 1930s. Against the background of the First World War's devastation and the disillusionment and hope that followed it in the 1920s and 1930s, the philosophical and literary movement called **existentialism** and the revolutionary psychology that was developed by Freud and called **psychoanalysis** seemed to make sense to many educated people. While psychoanalysis began in the nineteenth century, it had its major impact in the twentieth.

FREUD AS SCIENTIST AND HUMANIST

Freud certainly did not invent the ideas of the unconscious and the power of the non-rational in human life. All the way back to the origins of Western civilization we find profound testimony, typically in literature and in religious writings, to their importance—for example, in Sophocles' plays, the *Book of Job*, the letters of Paul of Tarsus, Augustine's *Confessions*, and Luther's writings. Modern writers such as the three main pioneers of existentialism—Kierkegaard, Dostoevsky, and Nietzsche—have likewise perceptively explored the power of the unconscious and the non-rational in our lives.

Freud, however, is distinctive in having believed wholeheartedly that natural-scientific investigation in particular could lead to such conclusions. He considered himself a medical scientist pursuing a rigorously rational and empirical examination of human mental life, and a clinician helping his patients by bringing repressed memories and desires into the daylight of consciousness so that they could deal with them rationally. Freud concluded his book on religion, *The Future of an Illusion*, with the statement that "an illusion it would be to suppose that what science cannot give us we can get elsewhere."[1]

There are, therefore, two cultural contexts for Freud's psychoanalytic investigations and doctrines: (1) the **scientific worldview** that emerged from the Enlightenment, and (2) the more traditional perspectives of **classical humanism**. First, Freud clearly carried on the legacy of the Enlightenment, with its emphasis on our ability rationally to understand the world and ourselves and thereby to improve our

World War I in Europe. Redrawn from The Western Heritage, Sixth Edition, Combined Edition, by Donald Kagan, Frank Turner, Steven E. Ozment, Frank Turner, Steven E. Ozment, and Frank M. Turner, (1998), Prentice-Hall, Inc.

condition. Many interpreters have seen the "Freudian revolution" as one of the great "paradigm shifts" in Western thought, following on the Copernican and the Darwinian revolutions. Copernicus (as confirmed empirically by Galileo) dislodged the earth from the center of a finite universe of crystalline spheres to a small planet orbiting a star in a universe that is for all practical purposes infinite. Darwin replaced the prevailing view of a relatively "young" world of fixed species hierarchically arranged by God and crowned by humankind, with the picture of an unimaginably long process of evolution by natural selection and of humanity as a very recent species among the many that exist today and the many that are extinct. Freud, who saw his work as building on and somewhat akin to that of Darwin, inaugurated the next stage in the modern reassess-

ment of the human place in nature, by showing the powerful role that nature, in the form of our unconscious and instinctual drives, plays even in the highest expressions of the human mind.

Like Dostoevsky and Nietzsche, then, Freud emphasized the importance of the nonrational in human life and he opposed many of the traditional theories that have emphasized human rationality and neglected the power of desires and emotions. Unlike Dostoevsky and Nietzsche, however, Freud saw his approach to the investigation of human nature as entirely scientific and considered himself to be a natural scientist and a physician. (He was also, unlike Dostoevsky and Nietzsche, a determinist, as we will see below.) Psychoanalysis was for him a scientific theory and also a therapeutic technique that enabled a patient, by using the methods of what

Freud called **free association**, to become aware of the unconscious motives and forces that played a crucial role in his or her life. Freud's scientific investigation produced the view that human beings are not primarily rational, but are governed to a large degree by non-rational—unconscious, and instinctual—forces. At the same time, he believed that it is only through scientific reason that we can establish the truth of this view of human nature, and that psychoanalysis is essentially a rational process of bringing these forces into the light of consciousness so that the patient can deal with them and is no longer dominated by them.

Freud believed that human mental life grew out of and reflected our bodily existence as organisms produced by the evolutionary process. What differentiated him strikingly from most of his scientific contemporaries was his recognition that there are many psychological problems that have mental rather than physiological causes. At the same time, Freud very much reflected the science of his day in interpreting all human behavior—psychical as well as physical—as (a) manifesting a certain quantity of energy, and (b) governed by Newton's first law of motion: for every action there is an equal and opposite reaction. He saw the human organism's physical and psychic energy as directed toward *equilibrium* or *stasis*, the quiescence that comes from the complete satisfaction of desires. Finally, like the other scientists of his day, Freud was a **determinist**: all events result from causes that, if known, fully explain them. Freud's **determinism** was distinctive because of the way in which he applied it to human mental life and behavior. He assumed that there are no accidents in our mental life. Everything we desire, think, or do, whether conscious or unconscious, has a reason or reveals a meaning that fits together with everything else in our mental life. There is no unmotivated behavior; it is just that the motives of much of our behavior are hidden from us in our unconscious life. In his determinism Freud clearly differs from Dostoevsky, although not entirely, perhaps, from Nietzsche.

The theory and practice of psychoanalysis grew out of the scientific assumptions of Freud's day, his clinical work with his patients, and his career-long self-analysis. Although he developed the basic ideas of his theory of personality and therapeutic technique during the last decades of the nineteenth century, he continued to develop and revise his ideas throughout the rest of his life.

Second, however, there is another side to Freud that makes his thought so richly textured and at the same time so exasperating to those who have tried to find "hard science" in his theories. This is the Freud who stands in the tradition of **classical humanism**, with its focus on the richness and complexity of the human self as expressed in literature and the visual arts. Freud was steeped in ancient Greek and Roman as well as modern literature, and he loved painting and sculpture. His theory of the dynamics and development of the human personality was a vision of the heights and depths of the drama of the self that transcended the science of his day, including his own scientific assumptions. It is significant that in naming the crucial stage in the child's early relationship to its parents the "Oedipus complex," Freud reached back to ancient Greek mythology and the story of Oedipus's unintentional but fateful killing of his father and marrying of his mother. Freud referred to what he called the "love instinct" with the Greek word *eros*—the love that is desire. He admired the penetrating psychological insight of Dostoevsky and Nietzsche. A passionate lover of the art of the city of Rome, with its many layers of pagan and Christian civilization, Freud wrote psychoanalytic studies of Michelangelo and Leonardo da Vinci. He was an assiduous collector of art objects and filled his famous consulting room with them.

FREUD'S LIFE AND INFLUENCE

Freud grew up in Vienna, the capital city of the Austro-Hungarian Empire and, during Freud's lifetime, a center of European scientific and cultural activity. He lived there until a year before his death. As a boy he experienced discrimination growing up Jewish in a strongly Catholic country. Although he never practiced the Jewish religion, his Jewish cultural background and tradition were important influences in his life and thought. As a schoolboy Freud had an excellent education in the humanities, and throughout his life he read widely and had broad interests in literature and the arts.

Freud studied medicine at the University of Vienna, a leading institution of the time, receiving his degree in 1880. After showing considerable early promise as a neurologist, he studied in Paris with

Jean Charcot, who aroused his interest in the study of hysteria and hypothesized that its origins were psychological rather than organic. Freud returned to Vienna, established himself in private practice, and in 1887 married Martha Bernays. The Freuds had six children, one of whom, Anna Freud, worked closely with her father and became a world-famous psychiatrist in her own right.

Stimulated by the ideas and therapeutic techniques of his older colleague and friend Josef Breuer, Freud began to develop the theory and practice of what he came to call **psychoanalysis**. He developed his revolutionary new ideas out of his own clinical work with patients, often women suffering from hysterical symptoms, and out of his intensive self-analysis. Central to Freud's theory were the hypotheses of the unconscious, of repression, of infantile sexuality, and of the fundamental influence of early childhood and especially the relationship with one's parents in personality development. His first great published work on psychoanalysis was *The Interpretation of Dreams* (1900), a study of dreams as keys to unlocking repressed experiences and desires based largely on Freud's self-analysis.

By the early decades of the twentieth century Freud had begun to achieve international fame and notoriety, initiated the institutionalization of psychoanalysis as a science and a healing profession, and attracted to himself students from around the world, many of whom went on to become leaders in the psychoanalytic movement. While continuing to develop and revise his theory, Freud also began to apply the ideas of psychoanalysis to larger cultural issues such as religion, art, politics, and the nature of civilization itself. Perhaps the best-known book of this period is *Civilization and Its Discontents* (1930). A writer with an excellent prose style, Freud won the prestigious Goethe Prize for Literature in 1930 and was nominated for the Nobel Prize.

Freud spent the last sixteen years of his life in frequent pain from cancer of the jaw, undergoing thirty-three operations, but he continued to develop his theory, to write, and to lead the psychoanalytic movement. With the Nazi takeover of Austria in 1938, Freud was expelled from the country and spent the last year of his life in London. His four older sisters were all murdered by the Nazis.

Freud's influence on twentieth-century Western civilization has been profound and far-reaching. His ideas, and the many other "depth psychologies" to which they gave rise, have fundamentally altered our understanding of human nature. Psychoanalysis has had a dramatic impact on both high and popular culture. Surrealist artists drew directly on psychoanalytic ideas for inspiration, and much modern art has implicitly or explicitly reflected such ideas in its portrayal of the human image. Freud's influence on major twentieth-century novelists, poets, and playwrights has likewise been extensive, as for example in the plays of Eugene O'Neill and the novels of Hermann Hesse. At a popular level, not only our consciousness of ourselves but our language has been shaped by Freud. We familiarly talk about the unconscious, drives, repression, complexes, fixation, projection, rationalization, libido, the Oedipal situation, neurosis and psychosis, the id, ego, and superego. We generally assume that our dreams are clues to our unconscious self, as well as conscious mistakes such as slips of the tongue—which we call "Freudian slips." Psychiatrists, psychoanalysts, clinical psychologists, and other psychotherapists and counselors became a new kind of priesthood" in the twentieth century, offering help with personal problems and "salvation" in the form of the ability to cope with life more positively.

MAIN IDEAS OF PSYCHOANALYSIS

In order to understand the basic arguments of *The Future of an Illusion*, it is useful to outline Freud's basic ideas and assumptions. This introductory sketch of the central ideas and practice of psychoanalysis will closely follow his last book, *An Outline of Psycho-Analysis*. Freud wrote it between July and September of 1938, at the age of 82, after he had been forced into exile in London. Published posthumously in 1940, it is his final statement of his fully developed ideas.

In the *Outline*, Freud shows that he believed to the end that psychoanalysis was a thoroughly scientific theory, and he tries whenever possible to use familiar scientific language and to draw analogies with fields such as physics. But he regarded psychoanalysis as a young science, still in need of considerable development and elaboration. He also confessed his ignorance about certain aspects of the human psyche, and he candidly distinguished between what he thought he could confidently assert and what he thought needed much further

Sigmund Freud. Courtesy of the World Health Organization.

instincts, which originate from the somatic organization [the body] . . . ."[2]

Through interaction with the external world, a portion of the id develops into the **ego**, which mediates between the id and the world. The ego's main purpose is self-preservation. In this task, the ego calls upon its powers of perception, thought, choice, memory, and adaptation in coping with the external world, while internally it controls the demands of the instincts by deferred gratification and suppression. Like the id, the ego seeks pleasure and the avoidance of discomfort or pain, but unlike the blindly-operating id, it must do so in a conscious and realistic way.

In addition, the long period of parental dependence of the human child contributes to the creation of the **superego**. The superego is the internalization of the influence of one's parents, and through them of one's society: ". . . not only the personalities of the actual parents but also the family, racial and national traditions handed on through them, as well as the demands of the immediate social milieu which they represent."[3] The influence of later parent-like models such as teachers and admired public figures are also part of the superego. What we commonly call conscience is, according to Freud, the superego. The id reflects our biological nature and genetic inheritance, the superego our social inheritance, and the ego what we individually do with these "givens" as we cope with life in the world.

The superego exercises severe and arbitrary demands on the ego, usually at the expense of the id. Hence the ego's function includes not only reconciling the id's pursuit of pleasure with external reality, but also mediating between the desires of the id and the restrictions of the superego. The mature, healthy, adult ego succeeds in accepting the demands of both the id and the superego in ways that are not destructive to the human personality. "An action by the ego is as it should be if it satisfies simultaneously the demands of the id, of the super-ego and of reality. . . ."[4] Such reconciliation is, according to Freud, what maturing and education are essentially about. When an individual has failed to succeed at this task of psychically growing up, it then becomes the job of the psychoanalyst to try to help that individual develop a healthy and harmonious self.

The instincts. The id expresses the basic purpose of the human organism's life, which is the satisfaction

investigation. He looked to the future, anticipating that others would come after him to shed light on the things of which he claimed ignorance, and to carry forward and revise various aspects of psychoanalysis. He speculated on the likelihood that in the future "chemical substances" might be used in therapy, a possibility that has been actualized in the extensive use of drugs in the treatment of both neuroses and psychoses, not as a substitute for the traditional "talking" forms of therapy, but as an additional method of healing to bring to bear on mental problems.

The structure of the self. Freud begins by describing, on the basis of his clinical study of individual human development, what he calls the "psychical apparatus." Here he introduces his influential threefold division of the personality into **id**, **ego**, and **superego**. The **id** is the oldest and most fundamental part of the self, the "archaic" foundation of everything else. The id "contains everything that is inherited, that is present at birth, that is laid down in the [individual's] constitution—above all . . . the of its innate needs without regard to inner restraint or the demands and dangers of the external world. The ego must transform this pursuit of satisfaction into realistic behaviors. The powerful needs of the id are the expression of instincts, which arise from our bodily nature and are the ultimate cause of all our activity. Freud substantially revised his theory of the instincts over many years, concluding that there are two basic instincts: (1) **Eros** or the **love instinct**, the aim of which is to unite, "to bind together"[5]; and (2) the destructive or **death instinct**, which aims at undoing or destroying connections and ultimately at extinction. For some time he had believed that eros alone was the fundamental instinct and could explain the destructive as well as the unifying aspects of human behavior. In his 1920 book, *Beyond the Pleasure Principle*, Freud first articulated his view that alongside the erotic or love instinct, and mixed together with it in various and subtle ways, is a separate destructive or death instinct.

The total instinctual energy available to Eros is called **libido**. Freud never developed a term for the corresponding energy of the death instinct. All our knowledge of libido is based on its manifestations in the ego, where it can be observed. When a child is born, it is characterized by **primary narcissism**, in which the total energy of the libido is absorbed in the newborn's undifferentiated ego-id. In a short time the emerging ego begins to transfer some of its libido onto objects (other persons and things) outside itself, transforming **narcissistic libido** into **object libido**. On the one hand, object libido is very mobile, able to attach itself to many different objects. On the other hand, it can easily become fixated on specific objects, such as the child with its mother or the adult who falls "head over heels" in love with someone else.

The destructive or death instinct only reveals itself when it is directed outward toward people, things, and situations in the world, where it manifests itself as aggression and hostility. But it also continues to function within a person; with the development of the superego, the destructive instinct's energy often turns in upon the self with an aggressiveness that would otherwise be directed outward. This in turn exacerbates the self-destructive tendencies already present within, as when a person bottles up and turns against him- or herself the rage he or she feels toward someone else or things in the world.

Personality development: infantile sexuality and the Oedipus complex. The single most controversial feature of Freud's psychoanalytic theory was undoubtedly his conclusions about **infantile sexuality**. According to Freud, a person's sexual life begins very soon after birth, and not at puberty as the traditional wisdom had it. " . . . [In] early childhood there are signs of bodily activity to which only an ancient prejudice could deny the name of sexual and which are linked to psychical phenomena that we come across later in adult erotic life—such as fixation to particular objects, jealousy, and so on."[6] But it is very important to be clear about what he means by "sexual life." "Sexual life includes the function of obtaining pleasure from zones of the body,"[7] and Freud always sharply distinguished between the *sexual* and the *genital*. The sexual refers generally to obtaining pleasure through any of a number of what Freud called *erotogenic zones* of the body, of which the genitals are only one.

The mother is the first love object of the child—first her breast and then, with the emergence and differentiation of the ego, the mother herself. This is true of both boys and girls. However, the further development of the two sexes differs:

Male development. Prior to the emergence of the phallic stage, the male child loves his mother and identifies with his father. With the increase of sexual impulses in the phallic stage, focused now on the penis, the boy wants exclusive sexual possession of his mother and develops an antagonism toward his father as his rival for the love of the mother. Drawing on the story in Sophocles' *Oedipus the King*, Freud called this the **Oedipus complex**, and regarded it as a crucial stage in the child's development. The male child fears the father's anger, a fear that takes the specific form of fearing that the father will cut off the offending penis. It is a fear that is driven home to the boy when he sees that females indeed lack a protruding sexual organ. This is *castration anxiety* or the *castration complex*, which Freud called "the severest trauma of . . . [the boy's] young life."[8] It causes the boy to repress his incestuous desire for his mother and his hostility toward his father. Freud assumed that all human beings are constitutionally bisexual, inheriting the tendencies of the opposite sex as well as of their own sex. When the boy gets through the Oedipus phase, he will tend to identify either with his mother or with his father, depending on the relative strength of the feminine and the masculine in his makeup, and this will shape his personality and relationships throughout his life.

Female development. Freud saw the developmental process differently for female children. The mother is also the girl's first love object, but she does not come to identify with her father the way the boy does. When the girl enters the phallic stage and discovers that she does not possess the external genitals of the male, she feels what the boy-child fears—castrated. She tends to blame her mother, anatomically like her, for this condition, and begins to focus her love more on her father. The father possesses the organ she is lacking, which makes her love also envy—what Freud called *penis envy*, which is the female counterpart of the male's castration anxiety. But whereas with the boy the castration complex brings the Oedipal phase to an end, with the girl penis envy *introduces* the Oedipus complex. She loves her father and regards her mother as a rival for his love. Unlike the boy's resolution of the complex, the Oedipus complex does not disappear for the girl, although with maturation it weakens and she comes to accept the impossibility of possessing her father. Like the boy, the girl will identify more with the father or with the mother depending on the predominance of masculine or feminine elements, although for both it is not an exclusive identification with one parent or the other.

Through his work on infantile sexuality Freud was a pioneer of twentieth-century theories of personality development, which in a variety of ways describe the individual's mental development as taking place through a series of more or less well-defined stages. After Freud, psychologists such as Jean Piaget applied the concept to cognitive development and (more recently) Lawrence Kohlberg and Carol Gilligan to moral development, while others who remained broadly in the Freudian tradition, such as Erik Erikson, carried forward and revised Freud's more general approach to personality development.

The unconscious and repression. Traditionally, psychology was concerned almost entirely with people's conscious states. Freud overturned this focus in the name of science, arguing on the basis of his case studies and self-analysis that the foundational, the most powerful, and by far the largest part of the human self is the unconscious. While some things in the unconscious can be called to mind without great effort or resistance—as when we remember what we had for breakfast this morning—many things are buried deeply and can only be made conscious with the assistance of a trained therapist who helps us bring them to light and interpret their meaning. That is because of **repression**, a defense mechanism by which the ego forces out of consciousness memories, ideas, and perceptions that it considers dangerous. They are repressed into the id, which is entirely unconscious. The superego can have a large influence on what the ego represses, and the stronger the superego, the more repressions there are likely to be. The most powerful repressions are memories from early childhood, which can include such things as "forbidden" sexual desires and experiences and hostility toward one or both parents. Repression is a necessary part of normal development, but it can manifest itself in a variety of abnormal ways such as psychosomatic illnesses, hysterical paralysis, sexual impotence or frigidity, suicidal guilt feelings, and uncontrollable rage.

Dreams, jokes, and slips of the tongue. The repressed material in the unconscious manifests itself in indirect and symbolic ways in our dream life, which Freud called a harmless form of psychosis. All of us are aware of the fact that our dreams have a life and logic of their own that often seems to have nothing to do with our waking life. While some dreams seem reasonably straightforward, prompted, say, by something from the previous day, others are extremely puzzling and sometimes bizarre. Freud considered the interpretation of dreams to be an absolutely key element in unlocking the unconscious through psychoanalysis.

Neurosis and psychosis. **Neurosis** and **psychosis** are weakenings of the ego in its formidable task of mediating among id, superego, and the external world. A relative weakening or disturbing of the ego in its organization and functions is a neurosis. An absolute weakening, one which brings the ego's "proper relation to reality" to an end, is a psychosis. The neurotic's ego is crippled but can be helped by therapy to return to its normal functioning. As Freud writes: "The analytic physician and the patient's weakened ego, basing themselves on the real external world, have to band themselves together into a party against the enemies, the instinctual demands of the id and the conscientious demands of the super-ego. We form a pact with each other."[9] In order to be helped by psychoanalysis, a person's ego must retain a certain degree of connection with reality and inner coherence. In the case of psychosis, the ego has retreated so completely from reality and become so inwardly fragmented that Freud confessed frankly that such persons could not be helped with the knowledge available at that time. Psychoanalysis could help neurotics; it could not help psychotics.

Relative strength or weakness of ego is a "given" in a person's development, so that by nature, so to speak, some people are more susceptible to neurosis and even to psychosis than are others. There is also a very wide range of behaviors that fall under the category of neurosis. According to Freud, all human beings, even the most "normal" ones, are to some degree neurotic, while some have such severe forms of neurosis as to border on psychosis. Even "normal" persons, if they observe themselves closely, turn out to be repressed in unhealthy ways about certain things, acting out patterns of relationships established in the Oedipal phase, or manifesting quirky compulsions, impulsions, and obsessions.

Reality-testing and treatment. Notice the importance to Freud of the idea of relationship to "the real external world" as a benchmark of mental health or illness. The concept of *reality-testing* is important in his approach to self-analysis and therapy. The external world is the world of objects and other persons which we commonly perceive and inhabit and which we understand properly through reason. Freud always saw the aim of psychoanalysis as restoring persons to a normal working relationship with the world thus understood. The psychoanalyst assists persons in bringing repressed memories and desires to consciousness through the technique of free association, talking about anything that comes to the patient's mind including the sharing of dreams. By facing their inner "demons" and understanding them both rationally and emotionally, individuals are liberated to function more adaptively and live more healthily in the "real world."

The individual and civilization. Around 1912 Freud began applying the psychoanalytic theory of the structure and dynamics of the human personality to the interpretation of wider social and cultural issues, such as the psychosocial functions of religion and the arts and the problematic character of human civilization. He never thought that psychoanalytic theory provided the last or the only word on these cultural phenomena, but he did believe that it could shed significant new light on old human institutions.

An essay Freud published in 1915, "Reflections upon War and Death," belongs among these wider studies, as he reflected on what the Great War (World War I) was revealing about the relationship between the individual and civilization and about people's attitudes toward death. Freud was stimulated to write only several months into the war, because the unexpected ferocity and carnage of the war were already evident and arousing widespread horror over how this could happen among what Europeans considered the most civilized nations of the world. Responding to the shock and disillusionment created by the war and its savagery, he argued that war dramatically unmasks deep-seated human desires, such as aggression and desiring the death of others, which we can otherwise pretend we have contained or diminished. The basic idea of the essay is one that Freud would develop extensively in his later works: "Civilization is the fruit of renunciation of instinctual satisfaction. . . ."[10]

In two of Freud's most important later books he applied psychoanalytic theory to the understanding of religion and of the general problems of civilization. His general study of religion is *The Future of an Illusion* (1927) while his chief study of the problems of civilization is *Civilization and Its Discontents* (1930). In both books Freud recounts how our instinctual desires are made to suffer under the forces of society, and how such restrictions inevitably produce neurosis and anti-social behavior.

The theme of *Civilization and Its Discontents* is the ambivalence of the individual human being toward civilization. "Discontents" in the title translates the German *Unbehagen*, which Freud uses to refer to the "uneasiness" or malaise that pervades the lives of human beings living together in society. He defines "civilization" or "culture" (*Kultur*) as encompassing all the distinctively human ways in which we set ourselves apart from nature, such as language, political, social, and economic organization, customs and mores, religion, art, war, and the accumulation of knowledge. Civilization has two purposes: (1) to protect us against the vicissitudes of nature, and (2) to regulate our relations with one another.

Civilization has a variety of means of reconciling the individual to its demands, not all of which require instinctual repression. One means is **sublimation**, the displacement of instinctual desires from their original objects onto "higher" objects. (We have already seen how Nietzsche anticipated Freud in recognizing the importance of sublimation). Freud describes this "subliming" of the instincts as "an especially conspicuous feature of cultural development; it is what makes it possible for higher psychical activities, scientific, artistic or ideological, to play such an important part in civilized life."[10] So, for example, the sexual drive is often creatively sublimated into artistic expression and enjoyment. Another means is aim-inhibited love, the ability of some people living in society to universalize the love instinct beyond either the sexual or even family ties over to friendship and even to love of humanity generally, and to inspire others to move in a similar direction.

But in the final analysis, says Freud, civilization is possible only through a considerable renunciation of individual humans' instinctual drives:

> . . . it is impossible to overlook the extent to which civilization is built up upon a renunciation of instinct, how much it presupposes precisely the non-satisfaction (by suppression, repression or some other means?) of powerful instincts. This "cultural frustration" dominates the large field of social relationships between human beings. . . . it is the cause of the hostility against which all civilizations have to struggle.[11]

We have seen, in summarizing Freud's theory of the personality, that the id seeks only its own pleasure; it is governed by what Freud called the **pleasure principle**. The demands of civilization, as expressed through the external world and the superego, force the ego to control these powerful instinctual desires, which it does through conscious suppression and unconscious repression.

In *Civilization and Its Discontents*, Freud fully utilizes his developed theory of the instincts. The life of the id is dominated on the one hand by Eros, the love instinct, which leads persons toward one another in bonding, compassion, and community; and on the other hand by the destructive or death instinct, which manifests itself in alienation, hostility, aggression, cruelty, and destruction. It is the death instinct, which manifests itself as "the inclination to aggression," that "constitutes the greatest impediment to civilization."[12]

Civilization uses both *external* and *internal* means to try to restrain and control the individual's impulse to aggression and destruction. *Externally*, the societies we live in confront us as a powerful authority whose rules are accompanied by the threat and the reality of punishment. But external sanctions alone are not enough, and if they were all that was available, civilization would be impossible. The other, and more effective, means by which societies control the destructive instinct is the superego, the internal appropriation by the individual self of society's rules and values through the influence of parents and others. In this way conscience and the sense of guilt, beginning in early childhood, play a crucial role in controlling the individual's hostile impulses. A person, experiencing the demands of authority and punishment entirely from within, exercises self-control quite apart from external authority and sanction. But the superego is a relentless taskmaster, severely repressing the individual's id and creating excessive guilt and self-punishment.

As Freud saw it, societies develop in somewhat the same manner as individuals: Like individuals, societies develop a "cultural superego," embodied in an ethical code that may make impossible demands on individuals. It is the psychic tension and inner conflict produced by these individual and social demands that creates a general unhappiness or malaise toward the burdens of civilization. Freud found with his patients in turn-of-the-century Vienna that he frequently had to relieve the terrible pressures on their ego of unhealthily repressive demands of the superego and the crippling guilt that accompanied it. Here is Freud's own account of the problem:

> In our research into, and therapy of, a neurosis, we are led to make two reproaches against the super-ego of the individual. In the severity of its commands and prohibitions it troubles itself too little about the happiness of the ego, in that it takes insufficient account of the resistances against

obeying them—of the instinctual strength of the id . . ., and of the difficulties presented by the real external environment. . . . Consequently we are very often obliged, for therapeutic purposes, to oppose the super-ego, and we endeavour to lower its demands. Exactly the same objections can be made against the ethical demands of the cultural super-ego. It, too, does not trouble itself enough about the facts of the mental constitution of human beings. It issues a command and does not ask whether it is possible for people to obey it. On the contrary, it assumes that a man's ego is psychologically capable of anything that is required of it, that his ego has unlimited mastery over his id. This is a mistake, and even in what are known as normal people the id cannot be controlled beyond certain limits. If more is demanded of a man, a revolt will be produced in him or a neurosis, or he will be made unhappy.[13]

Writing in 1930, with the memory of the European-wide devastation produced by the modern weaponry of World War I still fresh and the ominous rise to power of Adolf Hitler and his National Socialist Party beginning to take place in Germany, Freud concluded Civilization and Its Discontents on a somber note:

The fateful question for the human species seems to me to be whether and to what extent their cultural development will succeed in mastering the disturbance of their communal life by the human instinct of aggression and self-destruction. It may be that in this respect precisely the present time deserves a special interest. Men have gained control over the forces of nature to such an extent that with their help they would have no difficulty in exterminating one another to the last man. They know this, and hence comes a large part of their current unrest, their unhappiness and their mood of anxiety. And now it is to be expected that the other of the two "Heavenly Powers," eternal Eros, will make an effort to assert himself in the struggle with his equally immortal adversary. But who can foresee with what success and with what result?[14]

We are reading Freud's reflections more than seventy years later. During that time the world has seen World War II, including the Nazi Holocaust and the use of nuclear weapons against Japan, the Gulag Archipelago in the Stalinist U.S.S.R. and the Cultural Revolution in Maoist China, both of which killed millions, the development of huge stockpiles of nuclear weapons, the Cold War, further wars in Korea and Vietnam and elsewhere, genocides in Cambodia, central Africa, and former Yugoslavia, serious environmental damage, and new, destructive forms of terrorism. On the other hand, the world has also witnessed the founding of the United Nations, dramatic improvements in the rights of women and minorities in the U.S. and elsewhere, the collapse of communism in Europe and the spread of democracy in Latin America, and environmental concern and action on a global scale. Would we want to revise Freud's outlook in a more optimistic direction, or would we instead want to "put it in italics" for emphasis? Is the future of the struggle between love and death as uncertain for us as it was for Freud?

Because he saw the tension between the individual and civilization as largely irreconcilable, Freud believed that therapy would largely have to be directed to self-cure. Hence individuals, although needing the comfort and support of others, will have to come by their own efforts to understand themselves, and will need more self-knowledge if they are to be cured. This pursuit of self-knowledge as a means to a healthy self—the modern, idiosyncratically re-translated version of Socrates' "know thyself"—is perhaps the most important legacy that Freud and psychoanalysis have given us.

THE FREUDIAN LEGACY

The combination of, and also the tension between, the scientific and the humanistic sides of Freud's pioneering theory, together with specific aspects of the theory itself, have made his methods and conclusions controversial ever since they first became well known. Some of his most famous students—such as Carl Jung, Alfred Adler, Otto Rank, and Karen Horney—broke away from Freud, significantly modified some of his ideas, and in some cases founded their own movements and training institutes. Others who remained within the Freudian tradition—such as Melanie Klein, B. F. Winnicott, and Karl Menninger—developed some of Freud's ideas in new and fruitful ways. All psychoanalysts and many psychiatrists in the United States have remained broadly Freudian in their theory and therapy. (Psychoanalysts are usually physicians who are trained specifically in psychoanalytic theory and practice and undergo extended psychoanalysis at a certified psychoanalytic institute. Psychiatrists are physicians who have qualified through a residency in psychiatry to treat psychological problems and disorders). The psychoanalytic tradition founded by Freud, as represented for example at the Menninger Foundation in Topeka, Kansas, has undergone many developments and modifications in its details over the years. Among other things, it has been open to influences from other theories, other forms of therapy, and physiological and pharmacological research. Today's mental health specialists typically utilize a variety of resources in treating patients. That is precisely what we should expect of any pioneering system of psychological theory and therapy such as Freud's: the capacity to generate new insights, corrections, and elaborations.

Lively controversy continues over Freud's theory and his therapeutic techniques. In 1993 a *Time* magazine cover story asked the question, "Is Freud dead?" In 1995, the planning of an exhibit on Freud, scheduled to open in 1998 at the Library of Congress (which has the largest collection of original Freud documents in the world), became embroiled in heated and bitter debate. In universities Freudian ideas are much more likely to be encountered among faculty in the humanities than among psychology faculty. The past decade has seen a spate of books both criticizing and defending Freud. Some criticize psychoanalysis as a theory on the grounds that it is not truly scientific; others criticize it as a therapy, charging that it is protracted and expensive and not any more effective than other kinds of therapy. Some scholars and scientists accuse Freud of having distorted or suppressed some of his clinical data, and of having changed his theory for personal or ideological rather than for scientific reasons. Many feminists have long objected to Freud's characterization of personality development in women, seeing the idea of "penis envy" as perpetuating in modern form Aristotle's view of women as defective males. There are learned and articulate exponents of these criticisms, and learned and eloquent defenders of Freud on all these issues. Most recently, a group of American neurologists who use brain imaging are claiming to offer truly scientific, empirical evidence for some of Freud's core ideas—including his theory of unconscious drives or instincts, such as sex and aggression, rooted in the most primitive part of the brain, and even his work on dreams. They even have a journal called *Neuropsychoanalysis*. The fact that Freud continues, a hundred years after he developed psychoanalysis, to generate both creative revision and development and lively controversy, is impressive testimony to the importance and influence, if not correctness, of his ideas.

GUIDE TO THE READINGS

In *The Future of an Illusion* Freud examines the ideas of religion: where do they come from, and what value do they have? Freud's answer is that an examination of the psychical origin of religious ideas shows that they are "illusions," by which Freud means that they are not fact-based beliefs but rather "fulfillments of the oldest and strongest and most urgent wishes of mankind."[15] Religion is an expression of humanity's deepest desires, beginning with the desire of the helpless infant for protection from insecurity and danger and including the desire to overcome death by living eternally with the gods, the desire for justice in an an unjust world, and the need to understand the origins of the universe and human life and to explain the inexplicable.

Socially, religious beliefs arose during the childhood of the human race, and individually they grow out of the child's long period of dependence upon his or her parents. Beliefs in the gods, who are imaged as divine parents, prolong throughout adult life our childhood dependence on our parents. Although religions have played a key role historically in robbing nature of its terrors and reconciling individuals to society, Freud believes that in the present and even more in the future they will be seen by an increasing number of people as survivals from a prescientific world that are in conflict with what we know of reality through reason and investigation. Furthermore, in their task of making people more moral religions have failed. Since they perpetuate childhood dependence and illusion rather than encouraging autonomy, they are social forms of neurosis.

If we are to live a life governed by reason and face the world as it is—what Freud calls "education to reality"—then we must see our religious beliefs not as expressions of reason but as irrational hopes and wishes that promote a life of illusion. For some this may turn out to be a harsh truth, since giving up our fondest wishes about ourselves and the world can be a wrenching experience. While science itself is a finite human enterprise that often makes mistakes, the strength of science over religion, says Freud, is that science seeks to be self-corrective and dynamic rather than dogmatic and unchanging.

QUESTIONS FOR STUDY AND DISCUSSION

1. What was the cultural and political legacy of World War I?
2. What does it mean to say that Freud drew on the traditions of both the scientific worldview and classical humanism?
3. How does Freud characterize the structure of the self?
4. Describe Freud's theory of personality development. What does he mean by "sexuality" in talking about infants and young children?
5. What is the role of repression in personality development?
6. What does Freud believe dreams reveal to us about ourselves?
7. What does Freud mean by "civilization"? How does he use his theory of the instincts in analyzing the relationship between civilization and the individual?
8. How does Freud account for the emergence and development of religion in human history? What roles do the individual and society respectively play in this development?
9. What does Freud see as the function of religion as one of the ways in which civilization reconciles individual humans to itself? Does he think it has worked?
10. What does Freud mean by calling religious beliefs "illusions"?
11. How does Freud see the future of religion?

SUGGESTIONS FOR FURTHER READING

Freud, Sigmund. *An Outline of Psycho-Analysis*. Translated and edited by James Strachey. New York: W. W. Norton & Co., 1949.

Freud, Sigmund. *The Interpretation of Dreams*. Translated and edited by James Strachey. New York: W. W. Norton & Co., 1965.

Fussell, Paul. *The Great War and Modern Memory*. New York: Oxford University Press, 1975.

Gay, Peter. *Freud: A Life for Our Time*. New York: Doubleday, 1989.

Jones, Ernest. *The Life and Work of Sigmund Freud*. Edited and abridged by Lionel Trilling and Steven Marcus, with an Introduction by Lionel Trilling. New York: Basic Books, 1961.

Kiernan, Victor G. *European Empires from Conquest to Collapse, 1815-1960*. Leicester: Leicester University Press, 1982.

Tuchman, Barbara. *The Proud Tower: A Portrait of the World Before the War, 1890-1914*. New York: Macmillan, 1966.

---

[1] Sigmund Freud, *The Future of an Illusion*, translated and edited by James Strachey. New York: W. W. Norton & Co., 1961, 56

[2] Freud, *An Outline of Psycho-Analysis*, translated and edited by James Strachey. New York: W. W. Norton & Co., 1949, 2

[3] Ibid., 3.

[4] Ibid., 3.

[5] Ibid., 5.

[6] Ibid., 10.

[7] Ibid., 9.

[8] Ibid., 47.

[9] Ibid., 30.

[10] Freud, "Reflections Upon War and Death," translated by E. Colburn Mayne, in *Character and Culture*, edited by Philip Rieff. New York: Macmillan Publishing co., 1963, 115.

[11] Freud, *Civilization and Its Discontents*, translated and edited by James Strachey, New York: W. W. Norton & Co., 1989, 51.

[12] Ibid., 82.

[13] Ibid., 108-109.

[14] Ibid., 111-112.

[15] Freud, *The Future of an Illusion*, translated and edited by James Strachey, New York: W. W. Norton & Co., 1989, 38.

LIFE OF VIRGINIA WOOLF

1882

Birth in London, England, third child of Leslie Stephen and Julia Prinsep Duckworth. Her father begins work as the editor of the *Dictionary of National Biography*. In 1881, Leslie Stephen purchased the lease to Talland House in St. Ives, where the family would spend its summers until 1899. This is the setting for Woolf's book *To the Lighthouse*.

1895

Death of Julia Stephen. Woolf experiences her first breakdown later that year

1897

Marriage of stepsister, Stella, who dies six months later

1904

Death of Leslie Stephen. Woolf with brothers, Thoby, Adrian and George Duckworth and sister Vanessa travel abroad. Upon their return they leave the family home at 22 Hyde Park Gate for Gordon Square in the Bloomsbury area of London. Woolf experiences a second breakdown during this year. Woolf has by this time had her first review (unsigned) published in *The Guardian*, and she is actively pursuing her writing as a vocation.

1906

Woolf siblings travel again abroad. Thoby contracts typhoid fever and dies. Vanessa marries Clive Bell, becomes a well-known artist.

1908

Inauguration of "Thursday Evenings" the core group of what would become the Bloomsbury Group. Among the members of the group were J. Maynard Keynes, one of the most influential economist of the twentieth century; Lytton Strachey, a historian who revolutionized the art of biography; Roger Fry, a prominent artist and art critic who introduced Post-Impressionist art to Britain and the U.S. and Vanessa Bell and Duncan Grant, who became noted British artists and designers. Associated with Bloomsbury were notable figures such as the philosopher Bertrand Russell and the writers D. H. Lawrence and Katherine Mansfield.

1909

Death of Aunt Caroline from whom Woolf receives a legacy of £2500

1912

Marries Leonard Woolf

1913

The Voyage Out is accepted for publication. Woolf has another serious breakdown.

1914–1918

Years of World War I

1915

Woolfs move to Richmond area of London and start Hogarth Press. Establish a country residence in Asham. They later purchase Monk's House in Rodmell which will remain their country residence throughout Viriginia's lifetime and Leonard's.

1918

Night and Day

1920

Jacob's Room

1924

Woolfs leave suburban London and return to live in Bloomsbury

1925

The Common Reader, Mrs. Dalloway

1927

To the Lighthouse. Period of most intense friendship with Vita Sackville-West. Starts to write *Orlando.*

1928

Woolf reads two papers at the women's colleges in Cambridge which will be the basis for *A Room of One's Own*

1931

The Waves

1936

Publishes *The Years* and begins her anti-war statement *Three Guineas*

1939

Outbreak of World War II

1941

Woolf depressed over war. Following the completion of her final novel, *Between the Acts*, feels the "madness" returning and drowns herself in the River Ouse not far from her home in Rodmell.

CHAPTER THIRTEEN

"A PLACE OF THEIR OWN": VIRGINIA WOOLF

INTRODUCTION

How can I further encourage you to go about the business of life? Young women, I would say, . . . you are, in my opinion, disgracefully ignorant. You have never made a discovery of any sort of importance. You have never shaken an empire or led an army into battle. The plays of Shakespeare are not by you, and you have never introduced a barbarous race to the blessings of civilization. What is your excuse? It is all very well for you to say . . . we have had other work on our hands. Without our doing, those seas would be unsailed and those fertile lands a desert. We have borne and bred and washed and taught, perhaps to the age of six or seven years, the one thousand six hundred and twenty-three million human beings who are . . . at present in existence . . . . There is truth in what you say . . . But at the same time may I remind you that . . . . the excuse of lack of opportunity, training, encouragement, leisure and money no longer holds good. . . . Thus, with some time on your hands and with some book learning in your brains . . . . surely you should embark upon another stage of your very long, very laborious and highly obscure career.[1]

With these words, Virginia Woolf (1882–1941) encouraged the fictional, all-female audience of her narrator in *A Room of One's Own* to pursue a life of reading and writing literature. Woolf actually delivered two lectures in October, 1928 at the two women's colleges—Girton and Newnham—then attached to Cambridge University. *A Room of One's Own* was loosely based on these lectures and on the experiences Woolf had while at Cambridge to deliver them. The book was published in 1929. It became a famous and highly influential feminist work, especially in the United States after 1970. Woolf, who wrote mostly experimental novels, was also a journalist, and an original member of the Bloomsbury group, an influential group of loosely affiliated writers, artists, and intellectuals who met at the Woolf residence and other homes in Bloomsbury, a London neighborhood, from 1904 to the 1930s. She produced her major writings in the 1920s and 1930s, and she died at her own hand in 1941. She was neither a leader in the post-World War II feminist movement, nor was she active early enough to have been a major influence in the suffragist movements either in the United States or in Britain. She was "rediscovered" by feminist scholars in the 1970s, and her nonfiction work, *A Room of One's Own*, is now considered by many to be a brilliant and witty critique of patriarchy. In recent years, it has been given a prominent place in the feminist "canon." *Three Guineas*, another of her non-fiction works, contrasts patriarchy and war with feminism and pacifism, which has become another common theme among contemporary feminist writers. Among Woolf's most important predecessors are Mary Wollstonecraft and the woman suffragists of the nineteenth century. Her intellectual contemporaries among women writers and thinkers include especially Simone de Beauvoir, the existentialist author of *The Second Sex*, as well as the several female writers, artists, and activists associated in varying degrees with the Bloomsbury group.

FEMINIST FOREMOTHERS

Mary Wollstonecraft (1759–1797) is undoubtedly the most important intellectual predecessor to Woolf. In her best-known work, *A Vindication of the Rights of Woman* (1792), Wollstonecraft makes a plea, based on the philosophical and political principles of Enlightenment thought, for the equal rights of women to education and moral development. The Enlightenment, or Age of Reason, you will recall, was a period in which Western humanity, through a newly-found faith in the powers of human reason, dared to question and shake off the authorities—philosophical, political, and religious—which had governed its development since the Middle Ages. Despite its intense faith in the power of reason to lead to the betterment of human life, both individual and social, and despite its calls for individual emancipation and self-determination, the social milieu of the Enlightenment period dictated that most women of intellect and learning remain in the private sphere. Wollstonecraft, however, spoke out with power and conviction about the situation of her sex. Her words would become one of the foundational documents for the feminist movement in the nineteenth and twentieth centuries.

Mary Wollstonecraft was born in London in 1759 into a working-class family. She had little formal education, but she had wit and intelligence and set forth to pursue what avenues were open to a woman of her class and circumstances: teaching, being a hired companion or governess, and writing. She worked at all three until she achieved success—even notoriety—as a writer and translator. Her first foray into political writing, *A Vindication of the Rights of Man* (1790), was a response to Edmund Burke's famous *Reflections on the Revolution in France*. Like Thomas Paine, she defended the Revolution against Burke's attacks as the political realization of Enlightenment hopes for government founded on reason. But as a small manual on education she had published previously demonstrated, Wollstonecraft had long been concerned about women's education, so from this first essay it was a natural progression to an essay devoted exclusively to the rights of women. *Vindication of the Rights of Woman* blends her ideas about the education of women with natural rights theory.

In *Vindication*, Wollstonecraft takes the traditional and Enlightenment view that reason is the definitive characteristic of human beings—a view expounded by such thinkers as Plato, Aristotle, Seneca, Thomas Aquinas, Pico, Descartes, the *philosophes*, and Wollstonecraft's contemporary Kant—and argues that that is no less true of the female than of the male half of the human race. The alternative would seem to be to say that women are somehow deficient as human beings—a position which many writers in Western history have in fact taken. Wollstonecraft's book was to become an influential document in the long feminist struggle to overcome the deeply entrenched view that the differences between the behavior of men and women were the result of differences in their inherent natures rather than the circumstances of their nurture. The central argument of the *Vindication* is that the attainment of virtue is the proper goal of human life. But reason is essential to the cultivation of virtue, and education is essential to the development of reason. Unless we are to say that women are incapable of virtue, then women's reason must be developed through the same sort of education by which men's reason is made capable of virtue.

Wollstonecraft proposed revolutionary solutions to the plight of women. Women should of course have the same kind of education and educational opportunities as men. Marriage would be far happier if there were greater equality between the partners rather than the slavish dependence of the woman upon the man. The prevailing inequality in marriage does not produce a healthy relationship either between husband and wife or for the children. Wollstonecraft criticizes the double standard of society regarding male and female sexual impropriety. Although her critics would accuse her of advocating "free love," she actually recommended chastity for both males and females. Wollstonecraft suggests that women with proper education could be trained as physicians or be able to run their own business. Women should also study politics and be allowed to participate in decision-making in public life. She did not really deal much with the economic factors in sexism and the special plight of working class women; and she continued to regard marriage and children as the natural or "normal" situation for

Elizabeth Cady Staton and Susan B. Anthony. The Library of Congress.

women. But both her basic principles and many of their applications were radical and far-reaching in their implications for social change. Some of them have not yet been fully realized.

Wollstonecraft died shortly after childbirth in September, 1797, and her writings were neglected for a time. (The daughter she gave birth to was Mary Godwin Shelley, author of *Frankenstein*.) By the mid-nineteenth century, however, women intellectuals such as George Eliot and Margaret Fuller "rediscovered" *Vindication* and were amazed to find that it was a severely moral and serious work. Some of the nineteenth-century mothers of the feminist movement, notably Elizabeth Cady Stanton and Lucretia Mott, were enthusiastic about the book and hailed Mary Wollstonecraft as a pioneer of the women's movement. Indeed, *Vindication* was read by early leaders in the American women's rights movement and reprinted after the American Civil War (1861–1865) in *The Revolution*, published by Elizabeth Cady Stanton, Parker Pillsbury, and Susan B. Anthony. But other feminists of the Victorian period distanced themselves from her, highly critical of her life and considering her an unworthy example of the emancipation of women. It has been only in our time, with the most recent phase of the women's movement, that Mary Wollstonecraft has been fully rehabilitated and vindicated as the first modern spokeswoman for the rights of women. This has resulted in the widely available publication of her work and new research into and biographies on her life.

Nearly sixty years after *Vindication*, on July, 1848, at Seneca Falls, New York State, a movement was begun in the United States that would continue for more than seventy-five years until the passage of an amendment enfranchising women in 1920 and the introduction of an ultimately unsuccessful equal rights amendment in 1923. It was the movement for women's suffrage. Like other long-lived reform movements, it developed by stages and shifted with events. A similar movement also began in Great Britain, but space does not permit a full recounting here.

The major source of American women's rights thinking at the time of Seneca Falls was the philosophy of natural right, as exemplified in the writings of John Locke, a body of belief refined in the Enlightenment and summed up in the U.S. Declaration of Independence. At base, women's rights claims were a demand for personhood, for inclusion in the cultural values that proclaimed that individuals had inalienable rights because they were persons, that it was government's function to protect those rights, and that to do so, government had to rest on the consent of the governed. Natural rights affirmed the right of individuals to equality of opportunity, and it presupposed that the highest good was the full development of each person's rational faculties.

Wollstonecraft's *Vindication* had been a statement for including women under this Enlightenment umbrella, and yet the kind of demands for educational opportunities that Wollstonecraft and the American feminists who followed after her made were controversial even though they were linked to women's traditional roles. Access to secondary and higher education was slowly obtained, and it prepared future leaders in the women's rights movement. Efforts to increase women's educational opportunities affected the movement for women's rights only indirectly. Other reform movements would have greater impact, particularly the movement to abolish slavery.

Women reformers confronted an impediment in America: the conflict between reform efforts and the "cult of true womanhood." The concept of "true womanhood" or the "woman-belle ideal," which defined females as "other," as suited only to be wives, mothers, sisters, and daughters, arose in response to the urbanization and industrialization of the nineteenth century that separated "home" and "work," a separation that would also inform Karl Marx's earliest economic and social analyses. By 1850, distinct ideas about "men" and "women" had emerged. Man's place was public, the world outside the home, the brutal environment of uncontrolled capitalism, the realm of the mechanical, political, and monetary, and his "nature" was violent, lustful, and competitive. Woman's place was "home," a haven from amoral capitalism and dirty politics, where "the heart was," where the spiritual and emotional needs of husband and children were met by a "ministering angel." Woman's "nature" was defined as pure, pious, submissive, and domestic; however, she retained her moral purity only so long as she remained at home. If she entered the public sphere, she was defiled. "True womanhood" was possible only for middle-class women, but as an ideal, it affected working-class women and slave women, making their lives even harder, since they came to be seen as wicked and unnatural.

This concept of "woman" contained a contradiction that became apparent as women responded to such moral evils as prostitution, alcohol abuse, and slavery. Despite their supposedly natural moral superiority, women were condemned for acting to end these evils. Women who joined moral reform, temperance, and abolition societies and made speeches, held conventions, and published newspapers entered the public sphere and thereby lost their claim to purity and piety. What became the woman's rights movement arose out of this contradiction, because as women became competent public figures and were condemned for it, they began to demand equal standing so that they, like men, could be publicly active and effective in addressing social problems.

The Protestant clergy was a major source of resistance to women's public reform activities. At the same time, Protestantism was also a major source of woman's rights ideology. The core of Protestantism is the idea that worshipers need no priest to intercede to God for them; they can read and interpret the Scriptures for themselves. Instead of a priesthood, there is a priesthood of believers. That idea underscores the individualism in natural rights theory, and women used it to justify their challenges to scriptural interpretations that reduced woman's sphere of activities. Biblical passages enjoining women to submission and silence were used as a weapon against women's reform activities, but many deeply religious women activists, like **Lucretia Coffin Mott** (1793–1880), a Quaker minister and an early leader of the woman's rights movement, also presented biblical evidence to legitimate their work, arguing that the Bible legitimated women's reform activities. Clergymen, too, were sometimes sympathetic. On the other hand, some women saw an irresolvable conflict between the church and women's rights.

Alongside religious texts, biology or, rather, ignorance of biology was also used to justify woman's limited role. On average, women were smaller then men. Presumably, then, they had smaller brains, brains too small to sustain the rational deliberation required in politics and industry, and their smaller, more delicate and excitable nerves could not withstand the pressures of politics or the marketplace. Menarche, the onset of menstruation, was viewed as a physical cataclysm that rendered women unfit for normal activity. Harvard medical professor Dr. Edward Clarke argued against higher education for women on the grounds that the blood needed to sustain development of the ovaries and womb would be diverted to the brain, causing serious illness. Children belonged to their fathers because it was believed that the child-to-be existed in male sperm and was merely incubated in the mother's womb. As biological knowledge increased, and as women attained higher education, they tested and refuted such claims as those of Dr. Clarke. The poor health of middle-class women was explained by the effects of childbirth, complicated by limited medical knowledge, and by lack of exercise, which was unfashionable and virtually impossible in women's clothing of the nineteenth century. Whalebone corsets constricted breathing and circulation, and skirts that weighed twenty pounds and trailed on the floor limited movement severely. Women attempted to bring about clothing reform and argued that only if given training and opportunity could women's physical abilities be determined.

Suffrage Parade, New York City, May 3, 1913. Sophia Smith Collection, Smith College, Northampton. Mass.

Opponents sometimes made a third argument. In a rare contradiction of individualism, they claimed that the family was the fundamental unit of society represented in public by the husband. Women commented that, according to natural rights theory, no one could be represented by another without her consent, and they pointed to the laws that oppressed married women as evidence of how poorly husbands had represented their wives. In New York in 1848, at the time of the Seneca Falls convention, for example, a married woman had no legal right to her own earnings, to her children, to make a contract, to bring suit, or to make a will. She owned only what she inherited or received as a gift; such holdings could not be sold without her consent or to pay her husband's debts. However, she could not will her property to anyone, and if it were sold (because she could not make a contract, including a deed of sale, it had to be sold by her husband) the proceeds belonged to her husband. Her husband had absolute control of the children; in the rare case of divorce, they belonged to him, no matter how unfit he might

be and regardless of fault. He might will them to another guardian, along with the entirety of the estate amassed in marriage. If a husband died without leaving a will, the law was ruthless. The survivor received a "widow's portion," at best one-third of the estate. The remainder reverted to trustees, if there were children, or to the state, if there were none. In *A Room of One's Own* Woolf points retrospectively to British versions of such laws.

In the period prior to the Civil War, these oppressive laws were the major target of woman's rights activities. They were attacked at their conventions, which called public attention to the dire condition of married women. Efforts for change were directed at state legislatures. But the legal changes that occurred were not due solely to the efforts of woman's rights activists. Rapid industrialization created pressure for legal reforms that would ease commercial transactions. In this period, many states altered their laws to give women a right to their earnings, to joint guardianship of children, and to legal standing such that they could sue, bear witness, and make some contracts. However, many states made no such changes, and the temperance movement that grew so phenomenally in the 1880s and 1890s was fueled by the problems of married women who were legally and economically at the mercy of their drunkard husbands.

When the Civil War came in 1861, women ceased their agitation for increased rights and devoted themselves to ending slavery and supporting the Union effort. **Elizabeth Cady Stanton** (1815–1902) and **Susan B. Anthony** (1820–1906) headed a drive to gather signatures on petitions in support of what became the thirteenth amendment abolishing slavery. Large numbers of women took part in massive developments of relief agencies, hospitals, and other medical facilities to alleviate the suffering of the war. Many believed that their efforts would be rewarded with enfranchisement. Instead, the fourteenth amendment was proposed that, for the first time, inserted the word "male" into the U.S. Constitution, an amendment that would necessitate passage of a further constitutional amendment to effect woman suffrage. A fifteenth amendment, prohibiting denial or abridgement of the right of citizens to vote, based on race, color, or previous condition of servitude, was ratified in 1870 without the inclusion of "sex." Women felt deeply betrayed when their former Republican and abolitionist allies abandoned them to argue that woman's enfranchisement should wait because it was "the negro's hour."

Suffragists did not surrender meekly in the face of these defeats. Woman's rights activists and suffragists were unsuccessful in their new protests and activities, however, because their causes were unpopular with a majority of men and women. For the most part, men and women accepted the tenets of true womanhood and viewed the efforts of reformers with displeasure. True women were unselfish, devoting themselves to others; women activists were selfishly working for themselves, and they were attacked as sour old maids (nearly all were married with many children) who wanted to wear the pants and consign men to the kitchen and the nursery. As long as women relied primarily on natural rights arguments in defense of their cause, resistance remained high. A second line of argument, based on benefits or expediency, became more prominent after 1880 and made woman suffrage popular by making it acceptable to conservative women and men.

The argument from expediency or benefits treated woman suffrage as a means to good ends rather than a fundamental right. **Frances E. Willard** (1839–98), president of the **Woman's Christian Temperance Union** (**WCTU**) from 1879 to 1898, called woman suffrage "home protection," the means by which women would protect themselves and their loved ones from the ravages of King Alcohol. The expediency argument rested on a belief that women were essentially different from men: purer, more spiritual, concerned for others, and naturally domestic—wives and mothers. These distinctive qualities meant that women would use their votes to purify politics (some called this "public housekeeping") and to protect women and children. In particularly, their votes would close the saloon and eliminate the brothels frequently housed above them. From this perspective, women were not moving into the public sphere, they were simply claiming it as theirs.

With passage of the fourteenth amendment, many suffragists, including Stanton and Anthony, in frustration and anger, made highly racist statements that attacked African Americans as well as recent immigrants. Willard, similarly, was ambivalent about the expanding incidence of lynchings in the South, which, along with segregation, black woman activists were particularly concerned to combat. As the white, northern movement focused on passage of a federal suffrage amendment, its racism increased. In their efforts not to alienate Southerners, needed for passage and ratification, suffragists rejected the appeals of African American women for support against segregation and asked African Americans not to appear at conventions or to march in parades. Although some African American women, such as Ida B. Wells and Mary Church Terrell, were active in promoting woman suffrage, African American experience with the fourteenth and fifteenth amendments made them recognize that suffrage solved few problems. They saw the ballot as a limited goal and directed most of their efforts to fighting against the evils of lynching and "Jim Crow." Their insights are echoed in Woolf's comments regarding the limitations of suffrage, and they would later be repeated in post-World War II feminist arguments.

After a period in the early twentieth century known as "the doldrums," suffragist protest gained new momentum and intensity during the first presidential term of Woodrow Wilson. This renewed

Simone de Beauvoir. From AP/Wide World Photos.

activity eventually bore fruit: on March 4, 1919, the American Congress adjourned without Senate action on a suffrage amendment that had been passed by the House, but when the new Congress convened, the House passed the amendment on May 21 and the Senate on June 4. The ratification campaign quickly followed, facilitated by the exceptional organizing of the **National American Woman Suffrage Association (NAWSA)**. U.S. women voted for the first time in the election of 1920. In Britain, similar activism by women such as Emmeline Pankhurst and her daughters Christabel and Sylvia achieved a limited franchise in 1918, which was extended in 1928 to all women over age 21. Despite years of persuasion, woman suffrage came about the United States and Britain only because of outstanding leadership, exceptional organization, political savvy, media sophistication, and an organized program of militant agitation, made more effective by the late American entry into the First World War.

Tragically, suffrage was only a minor achievement. Most women did not vote; those who voted did not vote as a bloc and so had little political leverage. As the Great Depression of the 1930s eroded most of the gains women had made in higher education and the professions, women learned how little could be achieved through the ballot. Women's legal and economic subjection continued, and a second movement became inevitable.

The movement for women's liberation after the Second World War assembled itself in the United States following the influence of Martin Luther King, Jr. Prior to the post-war American Civil Rights movement, feminism had been the passion of relatively few American women. Certainly nineteenth-century female abolitionists such as the Grimké sisters had seen the link between liberating blacks from slavery and gaining women consideration as full human beings. Certainly the work of Susan B. Anthony and Elizabeth Cady Stanton that led to women's suffrage had created a powerful feminist heritage. But the movement that by the mid-1980s had become so strong a factor in the popular American consciousness, and that was growing in many other parts of the world, only arose when ordinary women had their consciousness raised sufficiently to make them think they were indeed an abused species and really could improve their lot by banding together for emotional support and political action.

Following the Second World War **Simone de Beauvoir** (1908–1986) one of the notable figures of the French existentialist movement together with Jean-Paul Sartre, wrote a study of women's place in Western culture entitled *The Second Sex* (1949). De Beauvoir's main thesis was that women have functioned as the first instance of "otherness" in the male world. That is to say, men, who have controlled the major institutions of the historical cultures, have viewed women as an alien form of humanity. Because women have tended to be smaller and physically weaker than men, and because women have had the task of bearing children, men have dominated women, making them subservient to masculine wishes and projects. In line with her existentialist convictions that, whatever their conditioning by heredity and environment, human beings are free and so have the power to choose their values, indeed their very selves, de Beauvoir criticized the majority of women for freely agreeing with the prevailing male view of their otherness and affirming it for themselves. She studied the many inducements societies have tended to offer women to conform to this role, but she also criticized women for a certain dishonesty or bad conscience, urging them to contest their role as the "other" and assert themselves both to control their own destinies and to contribute to fashioning history.

While de Beauvoir had considerable influence among the intelligentsia and became something of a guru during the 1960s when feminism entered the mainstream, the credit for mothering a popular feminist liberation movement in the United States goes to Betty Friedan. Born in 1923 in Peoria, Illinois, in her 1963 book The *Feminine Mystique* she articulated the widespread discontent of women trapped in suburbia and the traditionally rather restricted roles of wife and mother. *Mystique* gave voice to the sources of what became the American women's movement. In 1966 she co-founded the **National Organization of Women (NOW)** and in 1973 she helped to found the First Women's Bank. Her books *It Changed My Life* (1976) and *The Second Stage* (1981) dealt respectively with her experience in the first phases of feminist political organizing and with her sense that by the end of the 1970s the women's movement needed to reassess itself and better address the aspirations of women who had chosen traditional domestic and political roles.

Friedan, the National Organization of Women, and *Ms. Magazine* edited by Gloria Steinem, feminist activist and writer, spotlighted the many ways in which women have long been treated as sex objects, denied equal pay for equal work, assigned most of society's menial work, and erased from history (both in the sense of having their contributions ignored in the records and being denied the chance to fashion social change by serving as political leaders, church officials, top-echelon educators, and the like). Under the general rubric of "consciousness raising," feminists sought to make women aware of their manipulation and arm them with practical strategies for claiming greater freedom and influence.

Primary among such strategies was women's banding together for both emotional support and collaborative efforts to gain the legislation and shifts of popular opinion that would improve their working conditions, access to leadership roles in business, government, education, and church life, self-confidence and a sense of freedom to explore whatever possibilities their talents afforded them. The National Organization of Women was a major force behind the **Equal Rights Amendment**, suffering considerable loss of prestige when the women's movement failed to get the ERA passed. NOW and other women's organizations also targeted women's reproductive freedom as a leading goal, rejoicing in the **Roe v. Wade** Supreme Court Decision of 1973 that greatly expanded the liberty to have abortions. In many communities the **Planned Parenthood Organization** took a feminist turn, coming to specialize in offering women counseling about contraception and abortion, while other social agencies, concerned with such topics as rape, domestic violence and incest, frequently also became feminist strongholds.

By the mid-1980s Women's Liberation had become a significant factor in virtually all segments of American public life and was establishing toeholds in most of the developed countries. Indeed, liberation movements in such third world areas as Latin America were starting to develop a feminist dimension, as revolutionaries realized that women tended to be the poorest of the poor. The same realization was affecting black liberation, and across most movements for social reform "the feminization of poverty" and women's status on the margins of social power had come into clearer focus. In business, law, religion, medicine, engineering, and the other professions, women regularly had formed organizations dedicated to fostering their professional interests and improving their professional standing. Women's Studies had become an academic specialty in colleges and universities, and such general feminist journals as *Signs* afforded outlets to those interested in either historical or theoretical issues bearing on women. Feminist theory had become a vital area, as scholarly women sought to turn such recent schools of thought as deconstructionism, structuralism, and neo-Freudianism to the illumination of women's experience, arguing that the history and theory developed in most areas had neglected women's voices and so produced a distorted or merely partial picture of the human reality they were supposed to illumine. Many presses began to publish series in Women's Studies, while *The Journal of Feminist Studies in Religion* was typical of the organs that individual scholarly disciplines developed to incorporate women's voices and the findings of feminist scholars.

WOOLF'S LIFE

While Virginia Woolf's life and career stands in this broad historical stream of activism and protest, she also stands somewhat apart from it. She was born in London in1882, the third of four children born to Leslie and Julia Stephen. Both her parents brought to their union children from a previous marriage, which meant that there were a total of eight children in the household. Leslie Stephen was a well-known intellectual figure of the times, so Virginia was exposed to the rarefied atmosphere of her father's literary and politically liberal friends. She was educated at home, unlike her brothers, who were sent to prep schools and then to Cambridge University. This disparity was something that she always resented and it is reflected in *A Room of One's Own* and *Three Guineas*. She vowed early in life to be a writer; as children, she and her brothers and sister published a family newspaper called the Hyde Park Gate News. It is generally agreed that some of the tragic and trying circumstances of her childhood and adolescence deeply affected her emotional health and precipitated a series of mental breakdowns in adolescence and adult life. Some of these circumstances include the death of her mother when Virginia was thirteen, the death of her stepsister a few years later, the unwanted affections of one of her stepbrothers, and the domineering and later morose figure of her father.

With the death of their father in 1904, the four Stephen children exchanged the dark and dreary house in Hyde Park Gate for a new house and a new life in the Bloomsbury area of London. It was here that they began to host a gathering of brother Thoby's Cambridge classmates, who would later constitute the core of the Bloomsbury group. This period from 1905 to 1912 was a formative one for Virginia. She began writing review essays for periodicals and started a novel. She traveled extensively throughout Europe and to Turkey. She studied Greek and continued to read voraciously. She taught classes to working women. Most importantly, she gained both intellectual stimulation and social confidence from her exposure to her new circle of friends. She herself would later describe this period as her "graduate education."

In 1912, she married Leonard Woolf, whom she had met through her brother, Thoby. Theirs was a marriage of deep and abiding friendship, but the physical side of the marriage ended soon after their honeymoon. Leonard was an anchor, a rock, and responsible both for preserving her life and providing her with the emotional security that would enable her to write. A year after their marriage, Virginia had one of her most serious breakdowns. Partly as therapy for her, the Woolfs purchased a printing press in 1917, and from their home in the Richmond area of London founded Hogarth press, which made its name as the first publisher of many new writers who would become famous (such as T. S. Eliot) and of the works of Sigmund Freud in English translation. Both the therapy and the Press were successful. Virginia went on to become a productive and successful author up to her death in 1941, and the Press exists to the present day.

The platonic nature of her relationship with Leonard and the labyrinthine sexual liaisons of a number of the participants in the Bloomsbury circle have led many scholars to speculate about Woolf's sexuality. Virginia always had close female friends, the relationships with some of whom were clearly romantic in nature. Her most famous friendship was with the aristocratic and openly lesbian Vita Sackville West, wife of British diplomat Harold Nicholson. In fact, *Orlando*, a fictional biography published in 1928, is reputed to have been written as a love letter to Vita.

Woolf achieved a reputation as a brilliant, highly creative writer. She wrote volumes of essays and reviews that appeared in some of the foremost British publications. There is also a substantial collection of short stories. Most scholars agree that as an essayist she was superb, but there is less unanimity regarding her novels. She took a highly experimental approach in most of them, and she is categorized as one of the early "stream of consciousness" writers. There is little emphasis on plot or action, and the story proceeds via the inner narrative of the character so that the reader has, more or less, a window on the soul. Her best-known novel in this style is *Mrs. Dalloway*, which was a commercial success. *To the Lighthouse*, which is modeled on her own family, was another commercial success. This book served as a healing catharsis for Woolf, for it allowed her to express many of her unresolved feelings toward her mother and father. Two other critically acclaimed novels are *Jacob's Room* and *The Waves*, but these are more difficult to read and therefore not as popular.

The completion of a novel was always fraught with emotional stress for Woolf. In 1941, she had just completed *Between the Acts*. Her popularity, which had peaked in the 1920s, had somewhat declined; she did not think this a good novel; she was depressed by the war; and she felt she was burdening her husband too greatly. Feeling the madness beginning to come upon her again, she took her own life in March, when she walked from her and Leonard's house in the country south of London into the River Ouse, a large stone in her pocket. Contrary to her wishes, her novel was published. It has a distinctly anti-war theme and has been judged one of her best.

Scholarly attention to Woolf's work, her life, and her circle of friends has grown over the past three decades to the point where there are now Virginia Woolf Societies in the United States, Britain, and France; her homes in England are tourist attractions; and there is a veritable industry in Woolf and Bloomsbury memorabilia. Her complete diaries have been published in five volumes, and volumes of her letters to family and friends continue to be uncovered and published. Woolf was at the center of the Bloomsbury Group named after the London suburb where Woolf and many of her friends lived. Attacked by their critics as snobs who thumbed their noses at convention, they did indeed reject Victorian manners and values, established new trends in literature and art, and generally espoused a liberal/socialist political agenda. A number of the leading artists and intellectuals of the time moved in and out of the Bloomsbury circle.

While Woolf was born as the women's suffrage movement in Britain was in full swing, she was active as a writer after that movement had achieved success and before the post-World War II feminist movements. Thus, while not an activist, Woolf considered herself a supporter of women's rights throughout her life and gave service to the British suffrage movement in the 1910s. She herself had felt deeply the strictures placed on females in upper-middle-class Victorian society. Woolf always believed that it was the liberation from this traditional

Portrait of Virginia Woolf. Reprinted by permission of Corbis Images.

Victorian family circle that allowed her to realize the full extent of her creativity. The role of women within society and the family, and male/female sexuality, are among the strongest themes in her novels. The 1993 film *Orlando* is an interpretation of one of Woolf's most unusual novels. Whether the theme of this work, as the director of the film claims, is androgyny or not, it does dare to explore in a whimsical way the different social roles of men and women in society and the perceptions of the privileges allowed to each.

GUIDE TO THE READINGS

On Saturday, October 27, 1928, Virginia Woolf wrote in her diary: "I am back from speaking at Girton [to] starved but valiant young women . . . intelligent, eager, poor, and destined to become schoolmistresses. I blandly told them to drink wine and have a room of their own."[2] Woolf did not like public attention and shied away from personal appearances. She declined all honorary titles, degrees, and awards, and she rarely spoke before groups. In 1928, however, she was persuaded to speak to the women at both Girton and Newnham Colleges at Cambridge on the topic of women and fiction. In *A Room of One's Own*, which is based on these lectures, she surveys literature and women of literary talent in an effort to answer the question: Why have there been so few women writers? From this seemingly narrow focus, she exposes aspects of the condition of all women that have stunted their lives and stifled their abilities. The conclusion is all-too obvious: throughout history patriarchal society has subordinated women and devalued their work. She proposes that in order to exercise their talents to the fullest, women, like men, need personal freedom and financial independence—a room of one's own and five hundred pounds a year.

The book is divided into six chapters that fall roughly into two parts. Chapters one to three make the case against patriarchy. Here we find themes that had been raised early by writers such Wollstonecraft, Harriet Taylor and J. S. Mill, and by the women of the suffragist and women's rights movements of the nineteenth century. In Chapters four through six, Woolf examines women authors and their writing. These chapters are essentially an exercise in feminist theory and criticism, which has been picked up and greatly elaborated by feminist literary scholars during the latter decades of the twentieth century.

Woolf opens the book with a direct address to her audience and then she slips into the third person as Mary Beton, which sets up a trialogue between the female writer, the audience to whom the writer is lecturing, and the reader of the book. Ms. Beton has been invited to lunch at a men's college at "Oxbridge" (a fictional representation of Cambridge University), and to dinner at "Fernham." The latter is a loosely-based fictional representation of Girton College. Founded by the English suffragist Emily Davies in 1873 and originally called Hitchin College, Girton was the first women's residential college in Great Britain. Newnham College, where Woolf gave the second of the lectures on which *Room* is based, was the second such residential college, also at Cambridge University, founded in 1874 and established on curricular principles that differed from those of Girton. By contrasting the male Oxbridge and the female Fernham in the way that she does, Woolf reveals the inequality of educational opportunities between men and women. And even Fernham, as cold and austere as it is, has been a giant leap forward, for, as we learn in the after-dinner conversation between the two Marys, it came into being only in the last half of the nineteenth century and then only after a long, hard struggle (which is a roughly accurate representation of the actual work that was required to establish Girton). In the 1920s there were only two residential options for women at Cambridge (Oxford began admitting women to full student membership in 1920, but Cambridge did not), compared to multiple, better endowed options for men. Throughout the book, Woolf touches on other issues that are of concern to her. One that appears here in the first chapter is the problem of war. Mary Beton catches sight of a Manx cat out of the window following her luncheon at Oxbridge, and this prompts her to muse about life before World War I. Woolf, like most of her contemporaries and as we have read in the previous chapter on Freud, was deeply affected by this conflict and many of her writings expressed anti-war themes. Here Woolf states her belief that the "Great War" killed romance and romantic poetry.

In chapter two, Mary Beton resolves to pursue her topic in the appropriate way by researching it at the British Museum. She wants to uncover the answer to the question of why women are poor relative to men ("Why did men drink wine and women water?"), which has so strong a bearing on their further opportunities, as the disparities between Oxbridge and Fernham showed. In this especially delightful part of the book, we can observe Woolf's considerable wit in the descriptive passages. The mention of the young Oxbridge student who "has been trained in research" is a veiled, perhaps bitter, comment on Victorian society, which sent its men to universities and kept its women at home. Perusing the reference catalogue, she discovers that there are a vast number of books written about women by men, but no books about men by women. The title to the book by "Professor von X," which seems both absurd and appalling to most Westerners today, is representative of the attitudes and beliefs held by most men about women in the West for many centuries. Perceiving that her reaction to the pompous professor is one of anger, she is led to the conclusion that men are angry, and that the consequence of this anger is that women must become the mirrors through which men view themselves. Mary Beton's hypothesis has affinities with Simon de Beauvoir's argument concerning the non-reciprocal objectification to which men, as the dominant gender, subject the "Other"—women (or "woman"), the subordinate gender—as a way of giving themselves a superior or positive place and identity over against the negatively depict-

Jane Dunn, Photo: Leonard Woolf and Virginia.
Reprinted from A Very Close Conspiracy (1990),
Little, Brown and Co.

ed woman. Similarly, Mary's discovery of a multitude of books on women, sex, and gender in the British Library is echoed in French sociologist Michel Foucault's later finding that contrary to popular myth, Victorian society was not silent about sex and gender, but singularly loquacious, even if not openly so.[3]

At the end of the chapter, Mary tells us of an inheritance from an aunt that liberated her from the drudgery of newspaper work. Such an inheritance was a fact of Woolf's own life. Even though they both came from upper-middle-class families, neither she nor Leonard had much money, contrary to what one might have expected. It was therefore necessary for both of them to earn money from their writing. An annuity from Virginia's aunt Caroline Stephen—who did not die of a fall from a horse in Bombay as did the fictional aunt in *Room*, but from quite ordinary causes in her cottage near Oxford—provided a degree of financial security that allowed Woolf to give more attention to her novels. It was not until the late 1920s that Woolf would realize much financial reward from her writing. Here, as elsewhere in the book, Woolf points to economic dependence as a major source of women's subjection.

The topic narrows in chapter three to an examination of English literature in the time of Queen Elizabeth I. Still searching for answers to why women are poor and why they do not write (or, at least, publish), and still speaking in the voice of Mary, Woolf reviews legal codes related to women in Elizabethan times and later. Her method reflects the method of many contemporary historians who have sought to write the history of women and, like many of them, she uncovers some interesting information. We learn that women were at the mercy of both husband and family and could be "beaten and flung about the room without any shock being inflicted upon public opinion." Mary ponders why in literature some of the most profound thoughts fall from the lips of women, yet in real life women could neither read nor write. Women did not write, not because they lacked the ability, but because they were prevented from writing. She imaginatively illustrates this in her tale about Shakespeare's sister, Judith. Anonymity and chastity have been demanded of women if they are not to share the tragic fate of the fictional Judith Shakespeare. The psychological impact of family and society on women was so great, Mary concludes, that it is astonishing that there were any women writers at all, and yet there were a few.

In the concluding three chapters, Woolf/Mary introduces us to the works of several British women writers. Aphra Behn was a novelist and popular playwright in seventeenth-century London. She earned her living by her pen at the expense, as was usual for women of the time, of a respectable reputation. Passing over a number of writers, Mary/Woolf focuses on well-known nineteenth-century women authors Emily and Charlotte Brontë and Jane Austen. Mary/Woolf speculates that when women began to write, they wrote novels because the conditions under which they lived were more conducive to novels than to poetry. She is of the opinion that writing is not solely the product of the individual, but rather emerges out of a corporate or cultural voice and experience. A truly superior author submerges his or her personality, Mary claims, pointing to William Shakespeare as perhaps the best and best-known example among male authors. Emily Brontë and Jane Austen accomplished this same end, but Charlotte Brontë let her anger show through her writings in a way that lessened their quality. Furthermore, because of the paucity of women writers over the centuries, there is no established tradition of a women's language. She suggests that women must develop such a language and write in it so that whatever books women write may be adapted to a woman's body, that is, to feminine rather than masculine rhythms. One of her arguments here is that women need to learn more about women, physiologically and psychologically, and not trust to the analyses of women by men. Such analyses as we learned in the case of "Professor von X," and as she repeats using other examples, have not only been grossly unfair, but inaccurate and damaging. Woolf anticipates in Mary's discussion aspects of contemporary feminist dialogue, especially in the work of some contemporary French scholars.

In chapter five, Mary/Woolf moves from a consideration of nineteenth-century women authors to that of a recent author, Mary Carmichael. Woolf reminds us in this chapter that Mary is speaking to an all-female audience, which allows her certain public freedoms—concerning the discussion of sexuality, at least—that would not be available to her if men were present in the room. Mary Carmichael is one of the names that the narrator of *Room* says her audience may call her; like the character, her novel, *Life's Adventure*, is fictitious, but its description does closely follow the opening of *Love's Creation*, a 1928 novel by Mary Stopes. The discussion centering around this new young author may reflect the type of discussion that Woolf carried on with herself concerning her own writing. Woolf's novels, recall, were often experimental in nature, and she worked with "stream of consciousness" writing. Woolf was an exacting writer and gave her books up to print with trepidation and only after careful and repeated revisions. She struggled to find her own novelistic form, once defining it as "elegy." At least one critic had commented that her prose is as much poetry as prose, a judgment that applies most accurately to *Jabob's Room* (1922) and *Waves* (1931).

In chapter six, Mary/Woolf arrives at a conclusion about what an author must have in order to produce the best writing. The best authors—she cites Shakespeare, Coleridge, and Jane Austen—are those who reveal neither male nor female sexuality in their writing (much as in chapter four they don't treat their work like a form of confessional), but rather have such a unity of mind that their writing is androgynous. This conclusion may seem to contradict somewhat the arguments in the previous chapters concerning the need for a women's language, and a new genre of novel built around the rhythms of women's bodies. Perhaps. These last three chapters, however, are a kind of further experimentation for Woolf. Mary has meandered over the course of her discussion, first expressing this idea and then that until she finally comes to her theory of androgyny. We have, in a way, been part of her inner dialogue, and thereby a part of Woolf's as well.

Mary Beton ends her somewhat meditative journey, and the narrator then sums up in her own voice, as good lecturers should. Surprisingly, she advises against making judgments on the merits of writers of either sex, and if judgments are made, an aspiring author should ignore them. One must do things for the sake of doing them, not for the rewards, be those praise or money. This conclusion seems clearly to reflect Woolf's personal experience. She was intensely sensitive to criticism (a hint is given in chapter four), which is one reason why she found it so difficult to bring closure to her books. Again expressing the testimony of personal experience, Woolf claims that the value of writing is that, through writing, the writer sees life more intensely, permitting her to live more intensely. The "gates" or opportunities have now been opened for women, and they must act. But, to recap her opening and a theme that she raises several times throughout the book, it may still be necessary to have a room of one's own, and perhaps also £500 a year!

QUESTIONS FOR STUDY AND DISCUSSION

1. Mary Wollstonecraft makes this statement in *Vindication of the Rights of Woman:* "Friendship is a serious affection; the most sublime of all affections, because it is founded on principle, and cemented by time. The very reverse may be said of love." Wollstonecraft was saying that marriages should be based on friendship not love, or at least the type of "passionate love" that one associates with marriage vows. If you think that there is some wisdom behind this statement, consider how "love and marriage" are portrayed in contemporary times through television, movies and books. Is "friendship" presented as one of the essential factors to a successful marriage?

2. What was the concept of "true womanhood"? Are women still expected to live up to that image of femininity?

3. In what ways are the core ideas of natural rights philosophy, Protestantism, and social evolution linked? Do these ideas still influence beliefs about the nation and the role of government in relation to the individual?

4. Why is the ballot such a limited tool for social change? Why was suffrage such a small achievement for women? What issues brought a second movement into existence?

5. Explore the history and varied definitions of the word "feminism." Consider why that term has consistently been associated with more radical challenges to woman's role.

6. What is the question Woolf tries to answer in *A Room of One's Own?* Describe generally the approach she takes to answering it.

7. What is the ideal of "androgyny" that Woolf uses as a criterion for evaluating works of fiction? How does she apply it to leading women writers of the nineteenth century? What writers dos she believe have embodied it? Do you seen any tension between the androgynous ideal and her emphasis on women writers developing their own language?

SUGGESTIONS FOR FURTHER READING

Bell, Quentin. *Virginia Woolf: A Biography.* New York: Harcourt Brace Jovanovich, Inc., 1972.

Cott, Nancy F. *The Grounding of Modern Feminism.* New Haven: Yale University Press, 1987.

Flexner, Eleanor. *Century of Struggle: The Woman's Rights Movement in the United States.* New York: Athenaeum, 1968.

Giddings, Paula. *When and Where I Enter: The Impact of Black Women on Race and Sex in America.* New York: William Morrow, 1984.

Hussey, Mark. *Virginia Woolf A to Z: The Essential Reference to Her Life and Writings.* New York and Oxford: Oxford University Press, 1995.

Nicholson, Nigel. Virginia Woolf. New York: Penguin Putnam Inc., 2000.

Smith-Rosenberg, Carrol. *Disorderly Conduct: Visions of Gender in Victorian America.* New York: Oxford University Press, 1985.

---

[1] Woolf, Virginia. *A Room of One's Own.* New York: Harcourt, Inc. 1981, 112-113.

[2] Woolf, Virginia. *A Moment's Liberty, the Shorter Diary.* New York: Harcourt Brace Jovanovich, 1984, 250.

[3] Foucault, Michel. *The History of Sexuality: Volume I: Introduction.* Trans. Robert Hurley. New York: Random House, 1980, 12-35.

LIFE OF GERDA WEISSMAN KLEIN

1924

Born May 8: lived in Bielitz, a town in the part of Poland that had been part of the Austro-Hungarian Empire; grew up speaking German; father part owner of a fur processing factory; mother and brother Arthur the other family members.

1939

September 3: Germans take control of Bielitz, having invaded Poland September 1. In the days following the synagogue burned down, all Jewish men 16-50 must register and Arthur leaves, never to be seen again. Just before Christmas: Weissmann family is forced to move into their basement. Niania, an old Gentile friend, remains loving and loyal.

1940

January: Nazis order that all Jews remaining in Bielitz must wear the yellow star of David. By Spring only 300 Jews left out of 8,000 in Bielitz. The family survives by making clothing. In June France falls to the Nazis.

1941

Gerda's English lessons result in her arrest but the German police official spares her. This German is one of two who behaved "as though they were human." Gerda comes to know Abek Feigenblatt and later his family. Abek loves her very much but she never finds it possible to return his love. Best friend Ilse Kleinhälzer.

1942

January: Gerda receives a desperate letter from friend Erika which is the last communication from her. April 19: The remaining Bielitz Jews are forced to move into ghetto. The Weissmann family leaves their home. There are only 250 Jews now left; the old are sent to Auschwitz. May 8: Gerda's last birthday with her parents. Her last birthday gift is an orange. June: Her father is deported and Gerda never sees him again. Shortly afterwards she is separated from her mother never to see her again. Gerda taken by truck with other young women to work in Sosnowitz, Abek's home town. She visits with his parents, who arrange a work card for her to enable her to remain in Sosnowitz, but she refuses it. July 2: Gerda meets Suse Kunz, who becomes a close friend throughout the rest of the war. Gerda transported to Bolkenhain, in eastern Germany, to work in a weaving mill. German official in charge of the women is Frau Kügler, the second German who is kind to her. Through August and September Gerda writes to Abek and is still hearing from Arthur. Yom Kippur: discussion among the group about whether or not to fast. They are threatened if they do.

1943

January: last message from Arthur. Gerda has corresondence with Abek and receives gifts from uncle in Turkey. Gerda writes and produces plays for the other women, later saying that this is the "greatest thing" she has ever done. The war turning against Germany. August: with Ilse, she is transferred to weaving mill at Märzdorf; very bad situation—and she contemplates suicide. Is moved to Landeshut where she is reunited with Suse, friend Lotte, Frau Kügler; conditions better. November: Abek is in men's camp, Burgberg, nearby; a terrible place, but he has had himself placed there to be near Gerda; they see each other regularly but Gerda remains very ambivalent about him. German situation deteriorating.

1944

May: transfer to concentration camp; sees Abek for the last time, says farewell to Frau Kügler; taken to Grünberg camp for women; another weaving factory; meets new friend, Liesel Stepper. November: Gerda gets hold of small packets of poison for her and Ilse.

1945

January: Germans are rapidly losing war. Gerda believes that she will be freed; Allies closing in from east and west. January 29: Death march begins; 4000 women forced to walk west; out of 2000 in Gerda's group, 120 will survive. Gerda and friends develop plan to escape, but give it up after seeing fourteen other women shot. The prisoners apparently witness the firebombing of Dresden. They walk through German cities of Chemnitz, Reichenbach, Plauen; they have marched 500 km (about 300 miles) over two months since Grünberg. April: Death of Roosevelt announced. They cross into Czechoslovakia. Death of Ilse. Death of Hitler. They reach Volary, Czechoslovakia. The remaining women prisoners are locked in a factory in which the SS has put a bomb; freed by Czech partisans. War in Europe is over May 8, Gerda's birthday. American soldiers take over area. Gerda is very frail and ill. Meets, gets to know, falls in love with American Captain Kurt Klein.

CHAPTER FOURTEEN

MODERN JUDAISM AND THE HOLOCAUST

INTRODUCTION: JEWS IN CHRISTIAN EUROPE

In this chapter we will examine the historic struggle of Jews to define and maintain their identity as a religious and cultural minority within the discriminatory and often hostile environment of Christian anti-Semitism, and the fundamental challenges to both Jews and Christians posed by the Nazis' systematic destruction of six million European Jews between 1939 and 1945.

The historical background to Hitler's anti-Jewish ideology is to be found in many centuries of Christian anti-Semitism. Up until the nineteenth century "anti-Semitism" is more properly to be understood as "anti-Judaism": discrimination against and persecution of Jews as adherents of a rival religion with which Christianity shares its historical and theological roots.

The earliest Christians were one of many sects within the Judaism of the first century of the Common Era, so that initially it was a matter of disagreement with fellow Jews over whether or not the Messiah had appeared and was to be identified with the man Jesus. It was a fateful day for the future relationship between the two faiths when, in the fourth century of the Common Era, Christianity became the official religion of the Western world, accelerating and intensifying Christian hostility toward Jews into a long tradition of theological and popular anti-Judaism. Christians believed that Jews had been condemned by God because they had rejected their own Messiah, despite the fact that Christian acceptance of Jesus as the Messiah had required a complete reinterpretation of the prevailing messianic expectations. To the whole of the Jewish people was assigned the corporate responsibility for being "Christ-killers," despite the fact that it had been specific people and groups within Palestinian Judaism who had both rejected and accepted Jesus and that the Roman authorities in Judea bore substantial responsibility for Jesus' death.

Christians saw the Jewish *Diaspora*, the scattering of Jews throughout the world, together with the Roman destruction of the Jerusalem Temple in 70 C.E., as divine punishment for their spiritual blindness; while the scattering of the Christian community throughout the Mediterranean world and the periodic persecution of Christians by Roman authorities were interpreted as vindication of Christian claims and holy martyrdom. Theologians such as Augustine accepted Paul's idea in Romans 11 that God had a continuing purpose for his originally-chosen people until the end of the world, but unlike Paul they viewed that purpose as to suffer whatever a Christian world had to mete out to them until they saw the light and became Christians.

Through the Christian centuries in Europe, every Holy Week (the week preceding Easter, when the gospel accounts of Jesus' trial and crucifixion are read on a daily basis in many churches) the worshippers would hear the cry of the crowd when Pilate asked what he should do with Jesus: "Crucify him!" followed by the crowd's statement, "His blood be upon us and upon our children." (Matt. 27:20-26) Everyone interpreted those verses as applying corporately to all Jews past and present, that minority in the midst of Christendom who stubbornly insisted on adhering to the "old" religion. Easter was often a time of outbreaks of violence against Jews by Christians in Europe. All sorts of superstitions—indeed, a whole mythology—about Jews grew up beginning in the twelfth century in Christian Europe, many of them bound up with the idea that Jews were in league with Satan: they drank the blood of Christian children in their rituals, they poisoned wells, they caused the periodic outbreaks of bubonic plague, they secretly practiced all sorts of satanic arts against Christians. Among the Protestant Reformers in the sixteenth century, Martin Luther toward the end of his life, frustrated over continued Jewish refusal to convert despite the reform of Christianity, wrote a notorious book *On the Jews and Their Lies* in which he called for harsh measures against Jews who remained in Europe.

European Jews lived as a "client people" throughout the Middle Ages. They were exploited by the Christian nobility, persecuted by the masses, and excluded from citizenship in society as a whole. In general, three avenues of religious living were open to them: (1) a life confined by the traditions, laws, and customs of their people; (2) a life vitalizing those traditions through philosophical exploration; and (3) a life based on a mystical interpretation of Jewish existence as necessary to the world's salvation. As Jews interacted with European civilization they evolved their own expressions of beauty and knowledge. In response to the culture of Muslim Spain, Jews created poetry, art and song, and philosophy. Under the heel of Christendom, Jews learned to erect monuments of faith—lives devoted to God's word through study and interpretation of Torah, and deaths sanctifying God's name by testifying to the loyalty Jews had toward their faith.

The two types of Jewish culture that developed in the Middle Ages came to be called *Ashkenazic* and *Sephardic*. **Sephardic Judaism** emerged in Spain and Portugal, Turkey, Egypt, and North Africa; **Ashkenazic Judaism** developed in Germany. Sephardic Judaism was deeply influenced by Islamic culture and produced philosophers and poets.

The mostly Ashkenazic Jews of medieval Christian Europe learned to adapt to an uncertain and shifting environment by turning inward rather than outward. They interpreted God as speaking a special language—that of the law codes, the tradition of rabbinic interpretation of Torah embodied in the Talmud. They believed that living strictly according to Jewish law was both the highest service to God and a wall of security around the Jewish community in a hostile environment.

Between the end of the eleventh century and late in the thirteenth century, Christian Europe launched a series of ultimately unsuccessful Crusades against the Muslim Turks who controlled Palestine and other parts of the Near East. The crusading fervor inevitably directed itself also against Jews both in Europe and in the Near East, where they generally enjoyed much greater toleration in Islamic societies. A mystical form of Judaism arose in response to the new and destructive circumstances often produced by the Crusades. A group of pious Jews in Germany formed a "Hasidic" (from *Hasid*, meaning "pious") or saintly sect. Spanish Jews wrote esoteric mystical interpretations of the Bible, the most famous of which, *The Zohar*, determined the shape of all subsequent Jewish mysticism. Much later, in eighteenth-century Poland, a new movement called Hasidism arose out of the Jewish mystical and Hasidic traditions that had emerged in the Middle Ages.

The Middle Ages were marked by the widespread growth throughout Europe of repressive laws against the Jewish people during the Middle Ages. Typically Jews were not allowed to own property in land, effectively forcing them into joining the emerging middle class, becoming primarily artisans, merchants, and bankers. At various times and places Jews were required to wear an insignia, such as a yellow star of David (later revived by the Nazis), in public. There were laws regulating Christian fraternization with Jews and Jewish use of public facilities. In short, Jews were at best "second-class" citizens, actively discriminated against; at worst, as often during the crusades and when Christian society sought a scapegoat for plague and famine, they were actively persecuted and killed.

THE CHALLENGES OF MODERNITY TO JEWS AND THE RELIGIOUS RESPONSE IN MODERN JUDAISM

With the growth of knowledge and toleration fostered by the Scientific Revolution of the seventeenth century and the eighteenth-century Enlightenment, many Jews were eager to "modernize," but only if it allowed them to remain Jews. Acceptance of Jews by the surrounding Christian society, however, usually included stipulations and conditions. In 1806, for example, before Napoleon would extend liberty to the Jews of France, he summoned an "Assembly of [Jewish] Notables" to answer twelve questions regarding their loyalty to France. While other offers of citizenship—like that made by Wilhelm von Humboldt of Prussia in 1809—were made more graciously, they still included explicit as well as implicit conditions. Jews accepted these, but insisted that they could remain distinctively Jewish.

In the modern West, Jews have differed over how and in what way they should preserve and affirm their distinctiveness. Three major movements in modern Jewish religion—Reform, Conservative, and Orthodox—represent such a response. Finally, after the *Shoah* or Holocaust, the Nazi slaughter of six million Jews, some Jewish theologians have advocated a more mystical response: Jews are the conscience of the world.

Reform Judaism. Reform Judaism emerged in the early nineteenth century in Germany as the earliest of the modern Jewish movements. Pioneers of Reform claimed that Jewish distinctiveness lay in its capacity for change and development. This view places thinking and belief at the center of Jewish identity. To be a Jew means to hold certain ideas to be true rather than to perform any particular action. Judaism represents an ideology and not a set of deeds (*halakha*).

The Reform understanding of Jewish distinctiveness facilitated entrance into modern culture. Reform Jews could eat with non-Jews, join their friends for activities scheduled on the Jewish Sabbath, and accommodate themselves to values far removed from those sanctioned by the tradition. Reform Jews boasted that they had left the inequality of the sexes behind as an antiquated doctrine, and polemicized against their opponents as benighted and sexist. Serious studies of the Reform movement in Judaism, however, suggest that practice did not live up to rhetoric. Women were granted equality in name, but not in opportunity. They were barred from becoming rabbis until the 1970s; their contributions were indispensable to Reform Jewish life, but women themselves were often relegated to the sidelines.

Conservative Judaism. Another group, called the Positive-Historical School of Judaism in Europe and Conservative Judaism in the U.S., attracted individuals who tended toward Reform Judaism, but who withdrew from such radical actions as abandoning the Hebrew language in worship and study, denying

traditional Jewish hopes for a restored national home in Zion (Palestine), and ignoring the strong sentimental attachment of Jews to their ancestral practices. The keynote of the movement was respect for the consensus of the Jewish people, for the ideals and values reflecting communal concerns, or the collective consciousness of educated Jews.

Perhaps the most important aspect of Conservative Judaism is its insistence on the centrality of learning. Additionally, Conservative Judaism integrated women into its institutional structure at an early period. Women were teachers, workers, and builders of Conservative synagogues. They won concessions on various modern concerns from marriage, divorce, and abortion to participation in religious ceremonies. Women could study at a school of Jewish education. However, they were not initiated into the higher Jewish learning. After their sisters in the Reform movement had achieved the goal of rabbinic ordination, Conservative women had to wait nearly two decades and engage in countless battles before they gained the privilege.

Neo-Orthodox Judaism. Traditional Jews looked askance at both Reform and Conservative Judaism as deviations from a divinely revealed view of reality. Leaders of Orthodox Judaism charted a path between assimilation into and withdrawal from the modern world that has been called "Neo-Orthodoxy." According to a leading spokesman, Emmanuel Hirsch, Orthodox Judaism would embrace the legacy of the Enlightenment "as affording a greater opportunity for the fulfillment of its task, the realization of a noble and ideal life," but would reject it when it demands "capricious abandonment of the chief element of our very being." The chief element was defined as accepting the Torah "as the fountain of spiritual and ethical life."[1] The modern world was a special challenge. And the Jew was to become the teacher of humanity. The emancipation that the Enlightenment had brought allowed the Jew a new environment for communicating the Jewish message of Jewish distinctiveness. A Jew who assimilated could not be an ambassador to a wayward world but could serve as an ideal vision of reality with others.

One aspect of this ideal included a traditional social, economic, and psychological place for women within the scheme of reality. Women were to be the submissive helpmates to men. While powerful in their own domain—the home and the family—they were to allow men to determine the shape and pattern of their lives. Feminist liberation, from this perspective, is not even an ideal worthy of lip service. Women who seek "equality" are abandoning their own Torah-ideal, their true nature and purpose, and substituting the false values of the modern age in its place. Since the philosophy of Judaism presents the truth for all reality, the Neo-Orthodox Jew such as Hirsch cannot accept any alternative model of sexual roles than those given in early rabbinic codes and in the commentaries on them.

Whether formulated by Reform, Conservative, or Neo-Orthodox leaders, the approach to Judaism as a philosophy of life provided Jews with a groundwork upon which to build a new Judaism. Jews were led to recognize common interests shared with other religions and in the twentieth century they have cooperated with non-Jews in advancing social justice, in probing the meaning of faith, and in trying to establish world peace. Particularly since the Nazi Holocaust, religious Jews, even the Neo-Orthodox, have begun dialogue with non-Jews, and non-Jews seem to have responded positively. Relationships particularly with Christians—both informally and formally—seem to have improved, as Christians confront the anti-Semitism that has pervaded their theology and history.

ZIONISM

Another group of Jews in the modern period rejected such a belief-oriented approach and advanced a more "realistic" alternative. These Jews contended that Jewish distinctiveness grew out of a shared culture and national loyalty. Jewish identity depends on affirmation of the communal goals of the Jewish people. The long centuries of exile had robbed Jews of their true national heritage. The modern world, these Jews argued, would provide an opportunity to rebuild the Jewish national home in what had been the land of Israel. These Jews did not believe that Jews could ever exist comfortably as a small minority in societies dominated by Christianity. As long as Jews remained entirely a dispersed people, without a homeland of their own, they would be despised and persecuted. When they asserted their national strength, however, they would be respected and treated as equals. Furthermore, they viewed their rebuilt homeland as an experiment in human culture.

They would create a society in which equality became a reality, not merely a dream. Although often appearing to outsiders as a monolithic nationalism, in fact Zionism represented many different perspectives: deeply religious, frankly political and opportunistic, and cultural.

The *kibbutz* movement, founded by Zionist settlers in Palestine, offered its own interpretation of Jewish identity, Jewish interaction with non-Jews, and the status of women. Jewish distinctiveness depended on a completely Jewish culture. The Jewish language, Hebrew, the Jewish worker, and Jewish folkways—special songs, dances, and even food—characterized Jewish life in Palestine. That distinctiveness had implications for Jewish relations with non-Jews. It was determined that non-Jews, such as the Arabs who lived in Palestine, would respect Jews only when they did things for themselves. As an expression of this a boycott was declared on Arab goods and services, and these tactics seemed to work. Jews in Palestine created an independent, self-contained community, and won grudging respect from a world prepared to see them defeated again and again in history. Within that community it appeared that ideals would be concretely realized. On the kibbutzim women worked side by side with men, sharing the same jobs, reaping the same rewards.

BACKGROUND TO THE HOLOCAUST

In the nineteenth century there was a gradual lifting of restrictions against Jews. As Jewish men were allowed to study at universities, so the Jews experienced their own Enlightenment or *Haskalah*. This thinking gave rise to the Reform Judaism that reinterpreted Judaism as an essentially rational faith and sought to modernize Jewish practices. Assimilation became the watchword, and some Jews—notably Karl Marx's family—underwent what might be considered nominal conversion to Christianity. All this was based on the belief that if Jews could enter fully into citizenship and cultural and social participation in their countries it would minimize their distinctiveness and demonstrate that they were patriotic citizens of their "host" countries. Ironically from our post-Holocaust vantage point, in no country did Jews assimilate more fully than in Germany.

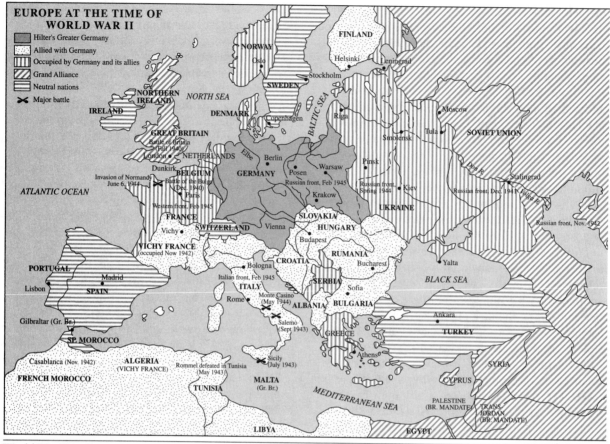

World War II in Europe.

A counter-movement to the Enlightenment was the Romantic movement in philosophy, history, literature, and the arts. Romanticism in some of its expressions accentuated the *differences* among nations and peoples. Each nation or people was thought to have certain distinctive generalizable characteristics which could be ascertained and were to be highlighted. At its best, Romantic emphasis on differences was a celebration of human diversity in all its richness. At its worst, it gave intellectual and moral sanction to invidious generalizing about and stereotyping of human groups, to categorizing in terms of superior and inferior, "civilized" and "primitive."

The idea of *race* came to play a prominent role in this sort of thinking, and our contemporary preoccupation with and ways of thinking about race are largely a product of nineteenth-century thought. There were thought to be clearly distinct racial

groups, and to each group were ascribed certain inherent characteristics. In the hands of Social Darwinists, Darwin's theory of evolution seemed to give solid "scientific" grounding to the notion that some races (notably white Europeans) were more "fit" or successful in the struggle for survival than others, or had evolved to a higher plane. Leading biologists and anthropologists of the late nineteenth and early twentieth centuries solemnly set forth and elaborated these ideas as scientific truth. Western ideas of the natural superiority of the white "race" and the natural primitiveness and inferiority of black, brown, and yellow "races" were widely believed and used as rationalizations of Western imperialism and colonialism. This was applied to the Jews despite the fact that what links Jews with Jews is a common religious tradition and culture. The term "anti-Semitism," meaning hatred of Jews as the "Semitic race," was first used in the 1870s.

There also arose political theories of an international Jewish conspiracy that supposedly operated secretly in all sorts of ways to undermine European social stability, Christianity, and racial purity. For example, alternatively Jews were seen as a main force behind communism, which was a movement to be reckoned with throughout Europe at this time, and as comprising an international banking cabal. The conspiracy theories about Jews were a modern secularized version of the traditional Christian interpretation of Jews as in league with Satan and the secret cause of the various troubles and disasters that were visited upon Christians. It was the old scapegoating of Jews dressed up in new forms.

The unification of Germany in 1870, under Chancellor Otto Von Bismarck, brought with it a strong new spirit of German nationalism. For some the new nationalism found expression in the creation of a new mythology exalting the superiority of the "Germanic" or "Aryan" race that over many centuries had made Germany great, and the denigration of German Jews as insidious pollutants, cancers within the otherwise healthy body of racially pure Germanhood. The composer Richard Wagner (1813–1883) was one such figure who was very influential, and in some of his operas he sought to revive some of the old pre-Christian Teutonic mythology to glorify the German past.

Nationalism was a dominant theme throughout Europe in the nineteenth century. Italy had also recently become unified for the first time in many centuries, and long-unified countries like the United Kingdom, busily building a world empire upon which the sun never set during the long reign of Queen Victoria, were enjoying periods of strongly nationalistic sentiment. Competition in capitalist colonial expansion played a large role in this new nationalism, which by the beginning of the twentieth century had the great European powers on a collision course culminating in World War I.

A notorious case in France at the end of the nineteenth century showed the depth and virulence of the centuries-old legacy of anti-Semitism in modern Europe. When it was discovered that an officer on the general staff had been selling secrets to Germany, attention turned to Captain Alfred Dreyfus. Although there was no evidence to justify suspicion of him, he was the only Jew on the staff. Dreyfus was court-martialed on trumped-up evidence and condemned to penal servitude on Devil's Island. While he was later released and vindicated, his innocence championed by leading figures such as the writer Emile Zola and the statesman Georges Clemenceau, the incident brought to a head years of persistent anti-Semitic agitation by militarists, monarchists, and clergy hostile to the democratic institutions of the French Republic.

Treatment of Jews in Russia and Eastern Europe, always bad, became worse during the latter part of the nineteenth century. Russia and Poland had the largest Jewish populations in Europe, together with the most conservative autocracies and large Christian populations of illiterate peasants little better off than serfs. From 1881 until the outbreak of the Revolution in 1917, tsarist Russia essentially declared war on Russian Jews, following the traditional pattern of diverting Christian Russians' attention from their serious economic and social problems by focussing their pent-up resentments on Russian Jews. Unhappily, it must be said that the great Russian writer Fyodor Dostoevsky was as virulent an anti-Semite as he was a devoted supporter of the Russian Orthodox Church and the tsar.

Russia, Poland, and other eastern European countries enacted increasingly repressive legislation against Jews. Thus the word *pogrom* entered our vocabulary. It is a Yiddish word from the Russian word meaning "devastation," and refers to an organized massacre against helpless people. (Yiddish, short for *yidisch daytsch* or Jewish German, is a German dialect usually written in Hebrew characters. It became the dialect of eastern European Jews, and through them a kind of international Jewish dialect.) A vivid fictional portrayal of Jewish life under the tsars and the racist and conspiratorial ideas and religious superstitions which made up Christian Russian attitudes toward Jews can be found in Bernard Malamud's novel *The Fixer*.

NAZISM AND THE HOLOCAUST

Pogroms and other forms of attack against Jews were often used, in Russia and eastern European countries, by those in power as political propaganda to gain popular support and take the masses' minds off their own impoverished conditions. It was, however, only in Germany in the 1930s, with the growth of the National Socialist (Nazi) Party and Adolf Hitler's rise to power that racial anti-Semitism was adopted as an official ideology and policy by a major European country.

The background to the rise of Nazism was Germany's defeat in World War I (1914-1918) and the harsh terms imposed by the victorious Allies in the Treaty of Versailles after the war. Looking for an excuse for their defeat, some Germans blamed Jewish disloyalty and conspiratorial machinations. Others resented the democratic Weimar Republic, which had to struggle not only to create unfamiliar democratic institutions but also to deal with staggering economic problems. The heavy reparations payments imposed by the victorious allies contributed to severe economic conditions in Germany during the 1920s. The humiliation and frustration of a proud people combined with economic hard times to make the soil fertile for the rise of radical right-wing nationalist groups during this period.

The group that emerged to dominance was the National Socialist Party under the leadership of Adolf Hitler (1889-1945), one-time artist and World War I corporal who developed into a kind of demonic genius with remarkable skills at creating and implementing a complete ideological worldview, symbolized in powerful trappings such as the *Hakenkreuz* (swastika) and the mass rallies where he held audiences spellbound with his appeal to the greatness and destiny of German "blood and soil." He outlined the program of the Nazi movement in *Mein Kampf* (1925). It contains the most extreme sort of anti-Semitic hatred, sounding the familiar racial and conspiratorial themes, and calling for a strong "Aryan" Germany purified of Jews and other undesirable elements.

Despite favorable conditions and Hitler's skills, the Nazi Party did not make all that much headway in German elections throughout the 1920s. What tipped the scales was the worldwide economic crisis that began in 1929 and continued throughout much of the 1930s. Nazi representation in the Reichstag or Parliament improved dramatically in 1930, to 18.3 per cent of the votes, and from then on they made steady progress. But the party still did not have an absolute majority even in 1933, when the German president, Field Marshal von Hindenburg, appointed Hitler Chancellor (Prime Minister) of the Reich. The move was intended to capitalize on Hitler's and Nazi popularity and to put him in a position where he could be controlled by powerful political and economic interests. Once in power he seized full control, treated the existing democratic institutions with contempt, and came to call himself simply *Fuehrer* (leader) with all power. He also began the systematic implementation of his anti-Jewish ideology.

Nazi policy against Jews began to be enacted immediately upon Hitler's accession to power. There were three stages in the development of the Third Reich's treatment of what was euphemistically called "the Jewish Question."

1. 1933-39: Persecution of German Jews. During this period German Jews were deprived of their rights as citizens, had their property confiscated, and were excluded from all educational institutions and cultural life in Germany. The definition of "Jew" was explicitly based on Nazi racist ideology: Jews were persons of "impure blood," as the Nuremberg Laws of 1935 stated, in contrast to those of "pure" or "Aryan" or "German" blood. It made no difference that a Jew might be entirely secularized, completely non-observant of the Jewish religion; it made no difference that a Jew had become a Christian. All one needed to be classified as Jewish was a grandparent who had claimed to be Jewish. The legal, economic, and cultural deprivation of German Jews—500,000 people or about 0.8 per cent of the population—all took place, of course, within the context of ceaseless and effective anti-Jewish propaganda and official incitement to violence against and looting of Jews. Hitler played skillfully upon the psychological legacy of centuries of Christian anti-Judaism, and once told some Christian bishops that he was simply carrying out what Christians had always wanted done with Jews.

The rapid succession of anti-Jewish legislation, however, swiftly created a strong sense of solidarity among German Jews. They formed a national representative body *Reichsvertretung der Juden in Deutschland* (National Jewish Agency in Germany) and established their own social, educational, and cultural institutions in the face of their exclusion from the larger life of the nation. This representative body was chaired by Rabbi Leo Baeck (1878-1956), the universally acknowledged leader of German Jewry throughout the Hitler era and one of the most eminent Jewish figures of the twentieth century, who stayed with his people despite repeated opportunities to leave. Sent to Theresienstadt concentration camp in 1943, where he continued to teach and inspire his fellow Jews, he escaped death by a fortunate mistake and continued to write and teach in England and the U.S. following the war. Another leader of the German Jewish community during this period was Martin Buber, one of the most influential religious thinkers of the twentieth century. Buber was in charge of developing Jewish adult education institutions during the 1930s until he was forced out of Germany in 1938. He spent the rest of his career in Israel, where he was professor of social philosophy at the Hebrew University.

During the first phase of Nazi persecution many Jews believed that if they were content to remain apart, those in power would come to ignore them or regard them as harmless. Others believed that given time the Nazis would either be forced out or would moderate their policies in the face of opposition both within and without Germany. Still others, mainly Zionists, saw the situation as far more grave, and insisted that the only sensible solution was emigration to Palestine. To that end they made a considerable effort to evacuate Jewish children and young people from Germany.

Emigration of Jews was also the official Nazi policy during this period, although Nazi officials were equally dedicated to pillaging and confiscating Jewish property and reducing Jews to poverty. Many German Jews were in fact able to emigrate. Of the half million Jews living in Germany when Hitler came to power, approximately 300,000 emigrated, freely or forcibly, in time to escape the "Final Solution": the all-too-successful Nazi attempt at full-scale genocide throughout the continent of Europe. Of those Jews who remained in Germany after 1939, 90 per cent perished. Many more German Jews could have been saved before the outbreak of the war in 1939 had the free nations been willing to take in Jewish refugees or assisted them in emigrating to Palestine, which was controlled by the British. Groups of exiled German Jews were literally turned away by countries, including the U.S., on the basis of immigration laws.

2. 1939–41: Restriction and internment of Jews all over Europe. Germany invaded Poland on September 1, 1939, plunging Europe into the Second World War. Anti-Jewish policy during the earliest years of the war can be characterized as a kind of transition from the pre-war policy of forced emigra-

tion to the "Final Solution." Germany had already annexed Austria and Czechoslovakia in 1938. Now making an all-out war effort to conquer Europe, Germany in swift succession occupied all or part of most of the countries of the European continent: Poland, France, Belgium, Holland, Denmark, Norway, Yugoslavia, Greece, Lithuania, Latvia, and Estonia. Italy was a German ally, and the governments of Rumania and Hungary were pro-Nazi satellites. Switzerland and Sweden were neutral.

The Reich Security Main Office was established in 1939 and given the task of solving the "Jewish Question." It was headed by Reinhardt Heydrich, a close associate of Heinrich Himmler, head of the dreaded S.S. (*Schützstaffel*, "defense corps"). Officers and troops of the S.S. played the key role in implementing Nazi policy against Jews during the war. Anti-Semitic decrees issued against Jews in occupied Poland, which had a Jewish population of over three million, imposed the wearing of a special Jewish badge (the "yellow badge" in the shape of the star of David, a revival of medieval practice, which had been imposed on German Jews in the 1930s), forced labor, the looting of Jewish property, and expulsion of Jews to labor camps.

Central to Nazi policy in the 1939–41 period was the isolation and internment of Jews in occupied areas; over time Jews throughout Europe were sealed off from outside help and contact. In Poland many Jews were rounded up and isolated together in forced ghettoes. The first large ghetto in Poland was Lodz. The largest, set up in 1940, was in Warsaw. Eventually half a million Jews were forced into the Warsaw ghetto, where many died from malnutrition and disease. The Warsaw Ghetto revolt in 1943 was the largest Jewish uprising, and the first armed revolt, against the Nazis in occupied Europe. Throughout this month-long revolt Jews fought tenaciously against their Nazi tormentors despite few weapons, overwhelming odds, and the debilitating physical effects of life in the ghetto. The Warsaw Ghetto Uprising was an attempt to halt or slow down Nazi deportation of Jews from the ghettos to the death camps, which was where most Jews confined in the ghettoes ended their lives.

3. 1941–45: The Final Solution. The third and last phase of the Nazi "solution of the Jewish Question" began in June, 1941, and ended only with Germany's defeat in May 1945. During those four

Crematoria at a German concentration camp. AP/World Wide Photos.

years, Jews all over Europe were relentlessly and efficiently hunted down, rounded up, savagely persecuted, subjected to every conceivable torture and degradation, and murdered—first in mass shootings and then in the more efficient gas chambers of extermination camps. Millions of other unfortunate human beings who were not Jews also perished in Nazi camps: political opponents, Soviet prisoners of war, gypsies, homosexuals, the mentally ill and retarded. But no group was singled out in Nazi ideology from the beginning and hunted down with such single-mindedness and thoroughness as were Jews. Ridding the world of Jews was central to Nazi ideology in a way that few other commitments were. So important was the "Final Solution" to the Third Reich that the effort to destroy all Jews—which required a considerable commitment of personnel, planning, and materiel—often took precedence over the general war effort. For example, trains needed to pull boxcars full of Jews to concentration and death camps would sometimes be given priority over trains needed to carry troops to the front lines.

But German efforts to round up and deport to the camps all the Jews in Europe had to adapt to the size of the Jewish population in each occupied country, the degree of autonomy accorded its government by the Nazis, and very importantly the attitudes of the people regarding their Jewish fellow citizens. In some western European countries the Nazis found their task the most difficult. The most notable example of non-Jewish solidarity with and protection of Jews is Denmark. In 1943 the Nazis attempted to round up the 7,500 Danish Jews. The Danes not only warned their Jewish compatriots, but helped them to go into hiding and cross over to neutral Sweden. Similarly, the Norwegian people and the Norwegian national church defied the Nazis, and exerted every effort to prevent the arrests and deportations. By contrast, Poland, which the Nazis completely controlled, had a long tradition of vigorous anti-Semitism, Poles generally were suffering and dying at the hands of the Nazis, and there was a large measure of indifference to the fate of Polish Jews. Having established their

"General Government" in Poland, the Nazis built most of the extermination camps, including Auschwitz, in Poland. Rumania and Hungary likewise had strong anti-Semitic traditions and also pro-Nazi governments that willingly handed over Rumanian and Hungarian Jews to the Germans. At the same time, there were non-Jews in every European country—including Germany and Poland—who were what Jews call "righteous Gentiles," individuals and families who risked their lives hiding Jews and helping them escape. The people who hid Anne Frank and her family in Amsterdam and the efforts of Raoul Wallenberg, a Swedish diplomat, in rescuing thousands of Hungarian Jews, are among the best-known of many such "righteous Gentiles."

The Germans had built the first of the concentration camps, Dachau, in March 1933, shortly after Hitler's accession to power. Buchenwald was opened in 1937. After the war had begun the Nazis began establishing a number of concentration camps in Poland. Himmler issued a directive to build a camp at Oswiecim (German name "Auschwitz") in April of 1940. Before the implementation of the "Final Solution" in 1941, all the camps, including Auschwitz, were concentration camps, where Jews and other captives were crowded together under unspeakable conditions and often made to do slave labor. Beginning in 1941, some camps were built or designated as extermination or death camps, the only function of which was to destroy and dispose of as many people as possible as efficiently as possible in gas chambers and crematoria. Some camps, like Auschwitz, were mixed: both concentration and death camps. The names of the Nazi camps—Dachau, Buchenwald, Majdanek, Theresienstadt, Chelmno, Treblinka, Sobibor, Mauthausen, and many others—have become bywords for the inhumanity of which human beings have been capable in the twentieth century. Auschwitz, the largest of all, where over two million persons—most of them Jews—were destroyed, has itself become a universal symbol of the horror of the Holocaust. Remarkably enough, even in the camps, where humans were starved, beaten, forced to live in their own filth, worked as slave labor, tortured, and experimented on, there were a number of armed uprisings. At Treblinka, for example, the entire camp population poured out of the opened gates after revolting against their captors, and many who made it to the woods survived.

The Nazi war against the Jews achieved the appalling success it did through a high degree of bureaucratic and technological efficiency and hundreds of thousands of persons to fill all the needed positions. Many of these were ordinary people, often personally "decent" folk who loved their spouse and children, perhaps enjoyed classical music, went to church, and did not belong to the Nazi Party—people who were just "doing their job" as loyal Germans. To be sure, there were always sadists around, like the Auschwitz "Angel of Death," Dr. Josef Mengele, other Nazi Party and S.S. leaders, and persons in all ranks of the hierarchy. But the system could never have worked as well as it did without the cooperation of large numbers of "normal" persons. Those who imagine that this behavior is a "German" trait would do well to read the American theologian Reinhold Niebuhr's book *Moral Man and Immoral Society*, published in 1932, shortly before Hitler came to power. It is a penetrating analysis, with many specific examples, of the general social phenomenon that even persons who are morally upright and sensitive in their personal life will willingly participate in immorality as members of groups and causes—governments, corporations, churches, nations, movements. There are entirely too many examples from twentieth-century American life of this sort of split between private and group behavior to make one entirely confident that he or she would not have been a "good German" from 1933–1945.

What Hitler was doing to German Jews during the 1930s was known in official circles in other countries and to observant foreign visitors. By 1942 what was going on in the concentration camps and extermination camps was becoming widely known. It is now well documented that the Allied nations did nothing for the beleaguered and tortured Jews—neither before nor during the war. Private organizations, Jewish and non-Jewish, in many places did all they could to help Jewish refugees and call attention to what was going on. Their governments were silent, despite repeated appeals at high levels. During the war appeals were made, for example, simply to get Allied planes to bomb the railroad lines and bridges leading to Auschwitz and other camps, but other aspects of the war effort always took priority.

Gerda Weissman Klein at Book Signing. Courtesy of the United States Holocaust Memorial Museum.

Nazi Germany was utterly defeated in the war, and its surviving leaders were tried for crimes against humanity and convicted in international tribunals following the war. But the machinery of death ran efficiently up to the very end. To say only that the Nazis were defeated omits the fact that even in defeat they were extraordinarily successful, not only in devastating Europe, but in achieving one of the most important things they set out to do: annihilate every Jew in Europe. From the best estimates of the numbers of Jewish dead, here are a few statistics: Before the war there were 3,300,000 Polish Jews. The Nazis destroyed 3,000,000—ninety per cent of the total—in effect completely wiping out not only the largest but one of the most culturally and spiritually creative Jewish communities in the world. Ninety per cent of the Jews of the Baltic countries and those remaining in Germany were destroyed; seventy-seven per cent of the Jewish population of Greece; seventy-five per cent of Dutch Jews; sixty-five per cent of Russian Jews. Overall the Nazis murdered sixty-seven per cent of the Jews of Europe: over two-thirds of the entire Jewish population of Europe, or about 6,000,000 people.

"Holocaust" is a term that Jews themselves have chosen to describe what happened to European Jewry in World War II. Generally the word means a great destruction or devastation, but etymologically it bears a specifically Jewish interpretation. The word comes from the Greek *holokauston*, which in the Septuagint or Greek translation of the Hebrew Bible translates the Hebrew word *olah. Olah*, meaning literally "what is brought up," translates into English as "an offering made by fire unto the Lord," "burnt offering," or "whole burnt offering." For some the notion of "burnt offering" was particularly graphic in view of the millions of Jews whose bodies were literally burned to ashes and smoke in huge crematoria after they were gassed. Another term in the Jewish literature on the Holocaust is *Shoah*, a Hebrew word meaning "whirlwind."

JEWISH RESPONSES TO THE HOLOCAUST

The trauma of the Nazi Holocaust has confronted contemporary Jews with the reality of radical evil as well as the issue of Jewish survival. Ironically, there was little reflection on it in the first years after the war. Only when the distance of time allowed some perspective amid the pain did Jews confront the depth of evil embodied in the Holocaust and the necessity for a new response to it. The thrust of the newer Jewish thinking has been that ethics is more important than theology, the human response of seeking appropriate moral responses more important than views of God. Post-Holocaust Jewish theology has as one of its major themes the need to create a new ethical ideal for a humanity shaken to its roots by its own destructive power. The three problems that faced Jews earlier in the twentieth century have been reformulated in the light of the Nazi era. How does Jewish distinctiveness help explain the pain and suffering characteristic of Jewish history? Can Jews enter into any positive relationship with non-Jews after learning the depths of the anti-Semitism harbored by Gentiles? Dare Jews hope that any transformation of society, even of Jewish society, is possible in a world filled with radical evil?

The post-Holocaust years have intensified debate and diversity among Jews as all issues have seemed to require new questions and new perspectives. Judaism today tends toward internal polemic and polarization more than ever in its past. Worldwide Jewish support for Israel—whose existence is viewed as the one great positive outcome of the Holocaust—is nevertheless marked by heated internal controversy over Israel's relations with its Arab neighbors and with Palestinians within its own territories. Issues such as women's and minority rights, abortion and other biomedical ethical issues, pollution and overpopulation, and nuclear war are at the center of the agenda of much current Jewish thought.

Various Jewish thinkers have probed the specific issues raised for Jews by the Holocaust in a variety of ways. Richard Rubenstein uses the Nazi experience to illuminate a modern world in which everyone must live without illusion, recognizing that the old moral restraints no longer apply. The traditional God of the covenant, who saves and defends Israel, is "dead" after the Holocaust, and Jews must affirm and support the new nation of Israel as embodying the value of Jewish survival. Eliezer Berkovits offers a much more traditional Jewish counsel, consolation, and interpretation, appealing to the biblical notion of God's withholding of the divine presence

at times, and calling for a continuing Jewish religious commitment that has survived other disasters in the past. Emil Fackenheim believes that the *Shoah* has revealed a new divine commandment: Jewish survival. The Jew's distinctiveness lies in Jewish existence itself—not the nature of that existence, but its very persistence. The relationship of Jew to non-Jew is that of teacher and witness, one whose existence testifies to both the darkness and the light of the human situation. In the light of the new commandment the door is open to a newly shaped Judaism, a Judaism in which the community as a whole takes on new meaning, a Judaism that transcends gender roles, a Judaism in which the commandment affects all equally. These varied responses illustrate the continuing struggle of Jews to define their reason for being in a world in which the old assumptions, the old values, the old optimisms about the human future, can no longer be taken for granted.

GUIDE TO THE READING

There is a rich literature, both appalling and deeply moving in its descriptions of what being a victim of the Holocaust was really like, written by survivors of the Holocaust. Among the "classic" survivor-witness memoirs are Elie Wiesel's *Night*, Primo Levi's *If This Is a Man*, and Viktor Frankl's *Man's Search for Meaning*. Another is Gerda Weissmann Klein's *All But My Life*, a woman's account of her experience from the beginning of the war in 1939 until her liberation in 1945.

Born May 8, 1924, until the age of fifteen Gerda Weissmann had a happy childhood as a member of a close-knit, middle-class Jewish family in the small town of Bielitz, Poland. Her father, who had studied medicine as a young man, was part owner of a factory that processed furs and was devoutly religious. Her mother, a traditional homemaker, displayed great strength as she tried to hold the family together and make do with little as the Nazis deprived and humiliated them. Her older brother Arthur was a gifted student of great promise. All but Gerda perished in the Holocaust.

As part of their invasion of Poland, on September 3, 1939 the Germans took control of Bielitz. In the days following the synagogue was burned down, and former Gentile neighbors turned against their Jewish townsfolk. By mid-October all Jewish men had to register with the Nazi government, and on October 19 Arthur left, never to be seen again. Just before Christmas the Weissmann family were forced to move into their basement. Their old Christian friend Niania remained loving and loyal to them.

By January of 1940 all Jews remaining in Bielitz were forced to wear the yellow Star of David. By spring only 300 Jews were left out of 8,000. Gerda and her family survived by making clothing. The following year Gerda met Abek Feigenblatt, who fell deeply in love with her, proposed marriage to her, and did everything he could to see her even after both had been sent to work camps. Gerda was unable to love him, but felt guilty because he cared so much for her. Early in the book we are also introduced to her best friend Ilse Kleinhälzer, who would for the most part be with Gerda throughout the war. In April of 1942 the 250 Jews remaining in Bielitz were forced to move into a ghetto. In June Gerda's father was deported, and shortly afterwards her mother, along with all the older people, to one of the Nazi death camps. She never saw them again.

When she was forcibly separated from her mother because she was considered young enough to be slave labor for the Nazis, Gerda, together with Ilse and other young women from the area, were taken to work in Sosnowitz, Abek's home town. Although his family tried to help her, Gerda chose to stay with Ilse and the other

Gerda and Kurt Klein. Courtesy of Glenn Levy.

women. In Sosnowitz Gerda met Suse Kunz, who would also be a close friend the rest of the war. In the summer of 1942 the three friends were transferred to Bolkenhain, in eastern Germany, to work in a weaving mill. The German official in charge of the women, Frau Kügler, turned out to be a genuinely good person who did what she could for the women within the limits of her position. In Bolkenhain for a year, Gerda wrote and produced plays for the other women, and looked back on that as perhaps the finest thing she had done in her life.

In August of 1943, with the war turning against Germany and its allies, Gerda and Ilse were moved to the weaving mill at Märzdorf, where conditions were much worse, and Gerda considered suicide. Later in the year the two women were transferred to work at Landeshut, where they were reunited with Suse, another friend, Lotte, and Frau Kügler, and conditions were better. Late in the fall Gerda learned that Abek had had himself transferred to Burgberg, a men's work camp nearby, in order to see Ilse. They did manage to meet regularly, but Gerda remained very ambivalent about him.

May of 1944 saw the three women transferred to Grünberg camp for women and another weaving factory. There Gerda met another new friend, Liesel Stepper. By the beginning of 1945 the Germans were rapidly losing the war. On January 29 4,000 women prisoners, in two groups, were made to do a forced walk westward. Of Gerda's group of 2,000, only 120 survived the long march. In two months they were marched 500 km (about 300 miles), walking through German cities including Dresden, Chemnitz, Reichenbach, and Plauen. Crossing the Czech border, the remaining women prisoners were locked in a factory in which the SS had placed a bomb, but were freed by Czech partisans. Germany surrendered on May 8, Gerda's birthday, and American soldiers took over the area. Ilse had died on the march; Suse died the very day of their liberation. Gerda was extremely frail and ill. During her long recuperation she met, got to know, and fell in love with American Captain Kurt Klein. They were eventually married, and she spent the rest of her life in the U.S.

QUESTIONS FOR STUDY AND DISCUSSION

1. What are the roots of Christian anti-Judaism? How did it express itself in the Middle Ages?
2. What does it mean to say that the three religious paths in medieval Judaism were legalism, philosophy, and mysticism? Which paths predominated among Sephardic and Ashkenazic Jews respectively?
3. What was the impact of the Enlightenment on European Judaism?
4. Why have the questions of Jewish identity and relationship to the non-Jewish world taken on central importance in the nineteenth and twentieth centuries? Characterize the three main types of Jewish religious response to the challenges of modernity, and how each has sought to answer the questions of identity and relationship.
5. What role did nineteenth-century racial theories play in the development of modern anti-Semitism?
6. What were the three stages of Nazi policy toward European Jews between 1933 and 1945? How did Nazi policy define who was Jewish?
7. How does the phrase "the banality of evil" apply to the Nazi Holocaust? Are there also examples from twentieth-century American life?
8. What issues has the Holocaust posed for Jews and for Christians? What are some of the responses Jewish thinkers and writers have made?
9. What were the personal qualities that helped Gerda Weissmann Klein to survive the Holocaust?

SUGGESTIONS FOR FURTHER READING

Agus, Jacob Bernard. *Jewish Identity in an Age of Ideologies*. New York: Frederick Ungar, 1978.

Berenbaum, Michael. *The Vision of the Void: Theological Reflections on the Works of Elie Wiesel*. Middletown, CT: Wesleyan University Press, 1979.

Berkovits, Eliezer. *Faith After the Holocaust*. New York: KTAV, 1973.

Eckardt, A. Roy and Alice L. Eckardt, *Long Night's Journey into Day: Life and Faith After the Holocaust*. Detroit: Wayne State University Press, 1982.

Friedman, Maurice S. *Martin Buber: The Life of Dialogue*. Chicago: University of Chicago Press, 1976.

Isaac, Jules. *The Teaching of Contempt: Christian Roots of Anti-Semitism*. Trans. Helen Weaver. New York: Holt, Rinehart and Winston, 1964.

Katz, Steven T. *Post-Holocaust Dialogues: Critical Studies in Modern Jewish Thought*. New York: New York University Press, 1983.

Kellner, Menachem Marc, ed. *Contemporary Jewish Ethics*. New York: Sanhedrin Press, 1978.

Littell, Franklin H. *The Crucifixion of the Jews*. New York: Harper & Row, 1975.

Neusner, Jacob. *Death and Birth of Judaism: The Impact of Christianity, Secularism, and the Holocaust on Jewish Faith*. New York: Basic Books, 1987.

Novak, David. *Jewish-Christian Dialogue: A Jewish Justification*. New York: Oxford University Press, 1989.

Poliakov, Leon. *The History of Anti-Semitism*. London: Routledge and Kegan Paul, 1974.

Roth, John K. *A Consuming Fire: Encounters with Elie Wiesel and the Holocaust*. Atlanta: John Knox Press, 1979.

Rudavsky, David. *Modern Jewish Religious Movements: A History of Emancipation and Adjustment*. Newly rev. 3rd ed. New York: Behrman House, 1979.

Ruether, Rosemary Radford. *Faith and Fratricide: The Theological Roots of Anti-Semitism*. New York: The Seabury Press, 1974.

---

[1] P. 43

APPENDIX TO VOLUME II

DECLARATION OF THE RIGHTS
OF MAN AND OF THE CITIZEN

'The Representatives of the people of France, formed into a NATIONAL ASSEMBLY, considering that ignorance, neglect, or contempt of human rights, are the sole causes of public misfortunes and corruptions of Government, have resolved to set forth, in a solemn declaration, these natural, imprescriptible, and inalienable rights: that this declaration being constantly present to the minds of the members of the body social, they may be ever kept attentive to their rights and their duties: that the acts of the legislative and executive powers of Government, being capable of being every moment compared with the end of political institutions, may be more respected: and also, that the future claims of the citizens, being directed by simple and incontestable principles, may always tend to the maintenance of the Constitution, and the general happiness.

'For these reasons, the NATIONAL ASSEMBLY doth recognize and declare, in the presence of the Supreme Being, and with the hope of his blessing and favour, the following *sacred* rights of men and of citizens:

'I. *Men are born, and always continue, free, and equal in respect of their rights. Civil distinctions, therefore, can be founded only on public utility.*

'II. *The end of all political associations, is, the preservation of the natural and imprescriptible rights of man; and these rights are liberty, property, security, and resistance of oppression.*

'III. *The nation is essentially the source of all sovereignty nor can any* INDIVIDUAL, *or* ANY BODY OF MEN, *be entitled to any authority which is not expressly derived from it.*

'IV. Political Liberty consists in the power of doing whatever does not injure another. The exercise of the natural rights of every man, has no other limits than those which are necessary to secure to every *other* man the free exercise of the same rights; and these limits are determinable only by the law.

'V. The law ought to prohibit only actions hurtful to society. What is not prohibited by the law, should not be hindered; nor should any one be compelled to that which the law does not require.

'VI. The law is an expression of the will of the community. All citizens have a right to concur, either personally, or by their representatives, in its formation. It should be the same to all, whether it protects or punishes; and *all being equal in its sight, are equally eligible to all honours, places, and employments, according to their different abilities, without any other distinction than that created by their virtues and talents.*

'VII. No man should be accused, arrested, or held in confinement, except in cases determined by the law, and according to the forms which it has prescribed. All who promote, solicit, execute, or cause to be executed, arbitrary orders, ought to be punished; and every citizen called upon, or apprehended by virtue of the law, ought immediately to obey, and renders himself culpable by resistance.

'VIII. The law ought to impose no other penalties but such as are absolutely and evidently necessary: and no one ought to be punished, but in virtue of a law promulgated before the offence, and legally applied.

'IX. Every man being presumed innocent till he has been convicted, whenever his detention becomes indispensable, all rigour to him, more than is necessary to secure his person, ought to be provided against by the law.

'X. No man ought to be molested on account of his opinions, not even on account of his *religious* opinions, provided his avowal of them does not disturb the public order established by the law.

'XI. The unrestrained communication of thoughts and opinions being one of the most precious rights of man, every citizen may speak, write, and publish freely, provided he is responsible for the abuse of this liberty in cases determined by the law.

'XII. A public force being necessary to give security to the rights of men and of citizens, that force is instituted for the benefit of the community, and not for the particular benefit of the persons with whom it is entrusted.

'XIII. A common contribution being necessary for the support of the public force, and for defraying the other expenses of government, it ought to be divided equally among the members of the community, according to their abilities.

'XIV. Every citizen has a right, either by himself or his representative, to a free voice in determining the necessity of public contributions, the appropriation of them, and their amount, mode of assessment, and duration.

'XV. Every community has a right to demand of all its agents, an account of their conduct.

'XVI. Every community in which a separation of powers and a security of rights is not provided for, wants a constitution.

'XVII. The right to property being inviolable and sacred, no one ought to be deprived of it, except in cases of evident public necessity, legally ascertained, and on condition of a previous just indemnity.'

OLYMPE DE GOUGES
The Declaration of the Rights of Woman
September 1791

Marie Gouze (1748–1793) was a self-educated butcher's daughter from the south of France who, under the name Olympe de Gouges, wrote pamphlets and plays on a variety of issues, including slavery, which she attacked as based on greed and blind prejudice. In this pamphlet she provides a declaration of the rights of women to parallel the one for men, thus criticizing the deputies of the National Assembly for having forgotten women. She addressed the pamphlet to the queen, Marie Antoinette, although she also warned the queen that she must work for the Revolution or risk destroying the monarchy altogether. In her postscript she denounced the customary treatment of women as objects easily abandoned. She appended to the declaration a sample form for a marriage contract that called for communal sharing of property. De Gouges went to the guillotine in 1793, condemned as a counterrevolutionary and denounced as an "unnatural" woman.

To be decreed by the National Assembly in its last sessions or by the next legislature.

PREAMBLE

Mothers, daughters, sisters, female representatives of the nation ask to be constituted as a national assembly. Considering that ignorance, neglect, or contempt for the rights of woman are the sole causes of public misfortunes and governmental corruption, they have resolved to set forth in a solemn declaration the natural, inalienable, and sacred rights of woman: so that by being constantly present to all the members of the social body this declaration may always remind them of their rights and duties; so that by being liable at every moment to comparison with the aim of any and all political institutions the acts of women's and men's powers may be the more fully respected; and so that by being founded henceforward on simple and incontestable principles the demands of the citizenesses may always tend toward maintaining the constitution, good morals, and the general welfare.

In consequence, the sex that is superior in beauty as in courage, needed in maternal sufferings, recognizes and declares, in the presence and under the auspices of the Supreme Being, the following rights of woman and the citizeness.

1. Woman is born free and remains equal to man in rights. Social distinctions may be based only on common utility.

2. The purpose of all political association is the preservation of the natural and imprescriptible rights of woman and man. These rights are liberty, property, security, and especially resistance to oppression.

3. The principle of all sovereignty rests essentially in the nation, which is but the reuniting of woman and man. No body and no individual may exercise authority which does not emanate expressly from the nation.

4. Liberty and justice consist in restoring all that belongs to another; hence the exercise of the natural rights of woman has no other limits than those that the perpetual tyranny of man opposes to them; these limits must be reformed according to the laws of nature and reason.

5. The laws of nature and reason prohibit all actions which are injurious to society. No hindrance should be put in the way of anything not prohibited by these wise and divine laws, nor may anyone be forced to do what they do not require.

6. The law should be the expression of the general will. All citizenesses and citizens should take part, in person or by their representatives, in its formation. It must be the same for everyone. All citizenesses and citizens, being equal in its eyes, should be equally admissible to all public dignities, offices, and employments, according to their ability, and with no other distinction than that of their virtues and talents.

7. No woman is exempted; she is indicted, arrested, and detained in the cases determined by the law. Women like men obey this rigorous law.

8.   Only strictly and obviously necessary punishments should be established by the law, and no one may be punished except by virtue of a law established and promulgated before the time of the offense, and legally applied to women.

9.   Any woman being declared guilty, all rigor is exercised by the law.

10.   No one should be disturbed for his fundamental opinions; woman has the right to mount the scaffold, so she should have the right equally to mount the tribune, provided that these manifestations do not trouble public order as established by law.

11.   The free communication of thoughts and opinions is one of the most precious of the rights of woman, since this liberty assures the recognition of children by their fathers. Every citizeness may therefore say freely, I am the mother of your child; a barbarous prejudice [against unmarried women having children] should not force her to hide the truth, so long as responsibility is accepted for any abuse of this liberty in cases determined by the law [women are not allowed to lie about the paternity of their children].

12.   The safeguard of the rights of woman and citizeness requires public powers. These powers are instituted for the advantage of all and not for the private benefit of those to whom they are entrusted.

13.   For maintenance of public authority and for expenses of administration, taxation of women and men is equal; she takes part in all forced labor service, in all painful tasks; she must therefore have the same proportion in the distribution of places, employments, offices, dignities, and in industry.

14.   The citizenesses and citizens have the right, by themselves or through their representatives, to have demonstrated to them the necessity of public taxes. The citizenesses can only agree to them upon admission of an equal division, not only in wealth, but also in the public administration, and to determine the means of apportionment, assessment, and collection, and the duration of the taxes.

15.   The mass of women, joining with men in paying taxes, have the right to hold accountable every public agent of the administration.

16.   Any society in which the guarantee of rights is not assured or the separation of powers not settled has no constitution. The constitution is null and void if the majority of individuals composing the nation has not cooperated in its drafting.

17.   Property belongs to both sexes whether united or separated; it is for each of them an inviolable and sacred right, and no one may be deprived of it as a true patrimony of nature, except when public necessity, certified by law, obviously requires it, and then on condition of a just compensation in advance.

POSTSCRIPT

Women, wake up; the tocsin of reason sounds throughout the universe; recognize your rights. The powerful empire of nature is no longer surrounded by prejudice, fanaticism, superstition, and lies. The torch of truth has dispersed all the clouds of folly and usurpation. Enslaved man has multiplied his force and needs yours to break his chains. Having become free, he has become unjust toward his companion. Oh women! Women, when will you cease to be blind? What advantages have you gathered in the revolution? A scorn more marked, a disdain more conspicuous. During the centuries of corruption you only reigned over the weakness of men. Your empire is destroyed; what is left to you then? Firm belief in the injustices of men. The reclaiming of your patrimony founded on the wise decrees of nature; why should you fear such a beautiful enterprise? . . . Whatever the barriers set up against you, it is in your power to overcome them; you only have to want it. Let us pass now to the appalling account of what you have been in society; and since national education is an issue at this moment, let us see if our wise legislators will think sanely about the education of women.

Women have done more harm than good. Constraint and dissimulation have been their lot. What force has taken from them, ruse returned to them; they have had recourse to all the resources of their charms, and the most irreproachable man has not resisted them. Poison, the sword, women controlled everything; they ordered up crimes as much as virtues. For centuries, the French government, especially, depended on the nocturnal administration of women; officials kept no secrets from their indiscretion; ambassadorial posts, military commands, the ministry, the presidency [of a court], the papacy, the college of cardinals, in short everything that characterizes the folly of men, profane and sacred, has been submitted to the cupidity and ambition of this sex formerly considered despicable and respected, and since the revolution, respectable and despised. . . .

Under the former regime, everyone was vicious, everyone guilty. . . . A woman only had to be beautiful and amiable; when she possessed these two advantages, she saw a hundred fortunes at her feet. . . . The most indecent woman could make herself respectable with gold; the commerce in women was a kind of industry amongst the highest classes, which henceforth will enjoy no more credit. If it still did, the revolution would be lost, and in the new situation we would still be corrupted. Can reason hide the fact that every other road to fortune is closed to a woman bought by a man, bought like a slave from the coasts of Africa? The difference between them is great; this is known. The slave [that is, the woman] commands her master, but if the master gives her her freedom without compensation and at an age when the slave has lost all her charms, what does this unfortunate woman become? The plaything of disdain; even the doors of charity are closed to her; she is poor and old, they say; why did she not know how to make her fortune?

Other examples even more touching can be provided to reason. A young woman without experience, seduced by the man she loves, abandons her parents to follow him; the ingrate leaves her after a few years and the older she will have grown with him, the more his inconstancy will be inhuman. If she has children, he will still abandon her. If he is rich, he will believe himself excused from sharing his fortune with his noble victims. If some engagement ties him to his duties, he will violate it while counting on support from the law. If he is married, every other obligation loses its force. What laws then remain to be passed that would eradicate vice down to its roots? That of equally dividing [family] fortunes between men and women and of public administration of their goods. It is easy to imagine that a woman born of a rich family would gain much from the equal division of property [between children]. But what about the woman born in a poor family with merit and virtues; what is her lot? Poverty and opprobrium. If she does not excel in music or painting, she cannot be admitted to any public function, even if she is fully qualified. . . .

Marriage is the tomb of confidence and love. A married woman can give bastards to her husband with impunity, and even the family fortune which does not belong to them. An unmarried woman has only a feeble right: ancient and inhuman laws refuse her the right to the name and goods of her children's father; no new laws have been made in this matter. If giving my sex an honorable and just consistency is considered to be at this time paradoxical on my part and an attempt at the impossible, I leave to future men the glory of dealing with this matter; but while waiting, we can prepare the way with national education, with the restoration of morals and with conjugal agreements.

Form for a Social Contract Between Man and Woman

We, _____ and _____, moved by our own will, unite for the length of our lives and for the duration of our mutual inclinations under the following conditions: We intend and wish to make our wealth communal property, while reserving the right to divide it in favor of our children and of those for whom we might have a special inclination, mutually recognizing that our goods belong directly to our children, from whatever bed they come [legitimate or not], and that all of them without distinction have the right to bear the name of the fathers and mothers who have acknowledged them, and we impose on ourselves the obligation of subscribing to the law that punishes any rejection of one's own blood [refusing to acknowledge an illegitimate child]. We likewise obligate ourselves, in the case of a separation, to divide our fortune equally and to set aside the portion the law designates for our children. In the case of a perfect union, the one who dies first will give up half his property in favor of the children; and if there are no children, the survivor will inherit by right, unless the dying person has disposed of his half of the common property in favor of someone he judges appropriate. [She then goes on to defend her contract against the inevitable objections of "hypocrites, prudes, the clergy, and all the hellish gang."]

Source: Olympe de Gouges, *Les Droits de la femme. A la Reine.* (Paris, 1791).

Declaration of Sentiments and Resolutions

When, in the course of human events it becomes necessary for one portion of the family of man to assume among the people of the earth a position different from that which they have hitherto occupied, but one to which the laws of nature and of nature's God entitle them, a decent respect to the opinions of mankind requires that they should declare the causes that impel them to such a course.

We hold these truths to be self-evident: that all men and women are created equal; that they are endowed by their Creator with certain inalienable rights; that among these are life, liberty, and the pursuit of happiness; that to secure these rights governments are instituted, deriving their just powers from the consent of the governed. Whenever any form of government becomes destructive of these ends, it is the right of those who suffer from it to refuse allegiance to it, and to insist upon the institution of a new government, laying its foundation on such principles, and organizing its powers in such form, as to them shall seem most likely to effect their safety and happiness. Prudence, indeed, will dictate that governments long established should not be changed for light and transient causes; and accordingly all experience hath shown that mankind are more disposed to suffer, while evils are sufferable, than to right themselves by abolishing the forms to which they were accustomed. But when a long train of abuses and usurpations, pursuing invariably the same object, evinces a design to reduce them under absolute despotism, it is their duty to throw off such government, and to provide new guards for their future security. Such has been the patient sufferance of the women under this government, and such is now the necessity which constrains them to demand the equal station to which they are entitled.

The history of mankind is a history of repeated injuries and usurpations on the part of man toward woman, having in direct object the establishment of an absolute tyranny over her. To prove this, let facts be submitted to a candid world.

He has never permitted her to exercise her inalienable right to the elective franchise.

He has compelled her to submit to laws, in the formation of which she had no voice.

He has withheld from her rights which are given to the most ignorant and degraded men—both natives and foreigners.

Having deprived her of this first right of a citizen, the elective franchise, thereby leaving her without representation in the halls of legislation, he has oppressed her on all sides.

He has made her, if married, in the eye of the law, civilly dead.

He has taken from her all right in property, even to the wages she earns.

He has made her, morally, an irresponsible being, as she can commit many crimes with impunity, provided they be done in the presence of her husband. In the covenant of marriage, she is compelled to promise obedience to her husband, he becoming, to all intents and purposes, her master—the law giving him power to deprive her of her liberty, and to administer chastisement.

He has so framed the laws of divorce, as to what shall be the proper causes, and in case of separation, to whom the guardianship of the children shall be given, as to be wholly regardless of the happiness of women—the law, in all cases, going upon the false supposition of the supremacy of man, and giving all power into his hands.

After depriving her of all rights as a married woman, if single, and the owner of property, he has taxed her to support a government which recognizes her only when her property can be made profitable to it.

He has monopolized nearly all the profitable employments, and from those she is permitted to follow, she receives but a scanty remuneration. He closes against her all the avenues to wealth and distinction which he considers most honorable to himself. As a teacher of theology, medicine, or law, she is not known.

He has denied her the facilities for obtaining a thorough education, all colleges being closed against her.

He allows her in Church, as well as State, but a subordinate position, claiming Apostolic authority for her exclusion from the ministry, and, with some exceptions, from any public participation in the affairs of the Church.

He has created a false public sentiment by giving to the world a different code of morals for men and women, by, which moral delinquencies which exclude women from society, are not only tolerated, but deemed of little account in man.

He has usurped the prerogative of Jehovah himself, claiming it as his right to assign for her a sphere of action, when that belongs to her conscience and to her God.

He has endeavored, in every way that he could, to destroy her confidence in her own powers, to lessen her self-respect, and to make her willing to lead a dependent and abject life.

Now, in view of this entire disfranchisement of one-half the people of this country, their social and religious degradation—in view of the unjust laws above mentioned, and because women do feel themselves aggrieved, oppressed, and fraudulently deprived of their most sacred rights, we insist that they have immediate admission to all the rights and privileges which belong to them as citizens of the United States.

In entering upon the great work before us, we anticipate no small amount of misconception, misrepresentation, and ridicule; but we shall use every instrumentality within our power to effect our object. We shall employ agents, circulate tracts, petition the State and National legislatures, and endeavor to enlist the pulpit and the press in our behalf. We hope this Convention will be followed by a series of Conventions embracing every part of the country.

RESOLUTIONS

WHEREAS, The greater precept of nature is conceded to be, that "man shall pursue his own true and substantial happiness." Blackstone in his Commentaries remarks, that this law of Nature being coeval with mankind, and dictated by God himself, is of course superior in obligation to any other. It is binding over all the globe, in all countries and at all times; no human laws are of any validity if contrary to this,

and such of them are as valid, derive all their force, and all their validity, and all their authority, mediately and immediately, from this original; therefore,

Resolved, That such laws as conflict, in any way, with the true and substantial happiness of woman, are contrary to the great precept of nature and of no validity, for this is "superior in obligation to any other."

Resolved, That all laws which prevent woman from occupying such a station in society as her conscience shall dictate, or which place her in a position inferior to that of man, are contrary to the great precept of nature, and therefore of no force or authority.

Resolved, That woman is man's equal — was intended to be so by the Creator, and the highest good of the race demands that she should be recognized as such.

Resolved, That the women of this country ought to be enlightened in regard to the laws under which they live, that they may no longer publish their degradation by declaring themselves satisfied with their present position, nor their ignorance, by asserting that they have all the rights they want.

Resolved, That inasmuch as man, while claiming for himself intellectual superiority, does accord to woman moral superiority, it is preeminently his duty to encourage her to speak and teach, as she has an opportunity, in all religious assemblies.

Resolved, That the same amount of virtue, delicacy, and refinement of behavior that is required of woman in the social state, should also be required of man, and the same transgressions should be visited with equal severity on both man and woman.

Resolved, That the objection of indelicacy and impropriety, which is so often brought against woman when she addresses a public audience, comes with a very ill-grace from those who encourage, by their attendance, her appearance on the stage, in the concert, or in feats of the circus.

Resolved, That woman has too long rested satisfied in the circumscribed limits which corrupt customs and a perverted application of the scriptures have marked out for her, and that it is time she should move to the enlarged sphere which her great Creator has assigned her.

Resolved, That it is the duty of the women of this country to secure to themselves their sacred right to the elective franchise.

Resolved, That the equality of human rights results necessarily from the fact of the identity of the race in capabilities and responsibilities.

Resolved, therefore, That, being invested by the Creator with the same capabilities, and the same consciousness of responsibility for their exercise, it is demonstrably the right and duty of woman, equally with man, to promote every righteous cause by every righteous means; and especially in regard to the great subjects of morals and religion, it is self-evidently her right to participate with her brother in teaching them, both in private and in public, by writing and by speaking, by any instrumentalities proper to be used, and in any assemblies proper to be held; and this being a self-evident truth growing out of the divinely implanted principles of human nature, any custom or authority adverse to it, whether modern or wearing the hoary sanction of antiquity, is to be regarded as a self-evident falsehood, and at war with mankind.

Resolved, That the speedy success of our cause depends upon the zealous and untiring efforts of both men and women, for the overthrow of the monopoly of the pulpit, and for the securing to woman an equal participation with men in the various trades, professions, and commerce.

Seneca Falls, N.Y., 1848

THE SADLER REPORT

The industrial revolution had a two-fold effect on England in the first part of the 19th century. On the one side it gave her a position of wealth and affluence which no other nation in history had enjoyed, and on the other it created terrible and wretched working conditions for her laboring force. The difference between these two sides was so great that a future Prime Minister of England dubbed them "The Two Nations."

The first factories were lacking in the most elementary sanitary and safety facilities, and the factory worker was subject to long hours of monotonous and unalleviated drudgery. Among the most unfortunate victims of this unhappy situation were the children, some of whom began work at four or five years of age. They were used in coal mines to carry buckets of coal up ladders and in other similarly dismal occupations. They received little or no education and often had to toil more than twelve hours per day under the most horrible working conditions.

In the early 1830s the House of Commons decided to investigate this situation, and a committee was formed, headed by Michael Thomas Sadler. The following dialogue is an excerpt from the Committee's report, given to the House of Commons in 1832 in the *Bill to Regulate the Labour of Children* which was then being debated.

VENERIS, 18° DIE MAII, 1832

Michael Thomas Sadler, Esquire, in the chair

* * *

MR. MATTHEW CRABTREE, *called in; and Examined.*

What age are you?—Twenty-two.

What is your occupation?—A blanket manufacturer.

Have you ever been employed in a factory?—Yes.

At what age did you first go to work in one?—Eight.

How long did you continue in that occupation?—Four years.

Will you state the hours of labour at the period when you first went to the factory, in ordinary times?—From 6 in the morning to 8 at night.

Fourteen hours?—Yes.

With what intervals for refreshment and rest?—A hour at noon.

Then you had no resting time allowed in which to take your breakfast, or what is in Yorkshire called your "drinking"?—No.

When trade was brisk what were your hours?—From 5 in the morning to 9 in the evening.

Sixteen hours?—Yes.

With what intervals at dinner?—An hour.

How far did you live from the mill?—About two miles.

Was there any time allowed for you to get your breakfast in the mill?—No.

Did you take it before you left home?—Generally.

During those long hours of labour could you be punctual; how did you awake?—I seldom did awake spontaneously; I was most generally awoke or lifted out of bed, sometimes asleep, by my parents.

Were you always on time?—No.

What was the consequence if you had been too late?—I was most commonly beaten.

Severely?—Very severely, I thought.

In whose factory was this?—Messrs. Hague & Cook's, of Dewsbury.

Will you state the effect that those long hours had upon the state of your health and feelings?—I was, when working those long hours, commonly very much fatigued at night, when I left my work; so much so that I sometimes should have slept as I walked if I had not stumbled and started awake again; and so sick often that I could not eat, and when I did eat I vomited.

Did this labour destroy your appetite?—It did.

In what situation were you in that mill?—I was a piecener.

Will you state for this Committee whether piecening is a very laborious employment for children, or not?—It is a very laborious employment. Pieceners are continually running to and fro, and on their feet the whole day.

The duty of the piecener is to take the cardings from one part of the machinery, and to place them on another?—Yes.

So that the labour is not only continual, but it is unabated to the last?—It is unabated to the last.

Do you not think, from your own experience, that the speed of this machinery is so calculated as to demand the utmost exertions of a child, supposing the hours were moderate?—It is as much as they could do at the best; they are always upon the stretch, and it is commonly very difficult to keep up with their work.

State the condition of the children toward the latter part of the day, who have thus to keep up with the machinery.—It is as much as they can do when they are not very much fatigued to keep up with their work, and toward the close of the day, when they come to be more fatigued, they cannot keep up with it very well, and the consequences is that they are beaten to spur them on.

Were you beaten under those circumstances?—Yes.

Frequently?—Very frequently.

And principally at the latter end of the day?—Yes.

And is it your belief that if you had not been so beaten, you should not have got through the work?—I should not if I had not been kept up to it by some means.

Does beating then principally occur at the latter end of the day, when the children are exceedingly fatigued?—It does at the latter end of the day, and in the morning sometimes, when they are very drowsy, and have not got rid of the fatigue of the day before.

What were you beaten with principally?—A strap.

Anything else?—Yes, a stick sometimes; and there is a kind of roller which runs on the top of the machine called a billy, perhaps two or three yards in length, and perhaps an inch and a half, or more,

in diameter; the circumference would be four or five inches; I cannot speak exactly.

Were you beaten with that instrument?—Yes.

Have you yourself ever been beaten, and have you seen other children struck severely with that roller?—I have been struck very severely with it myself so much so as to knock me down, and I have seen other children have their heads broken with it.

You think that it is a general practice to beat the children with the roller?—It is.

You do not think then that you were worse treated than other children in the mill?—No, I was not, perhaps not so bad as some were.

In those mills is chastisement towards the latter part of the day going on perpetually?—Perpetually.

So that you can hardly be in the mill without hearing constant crying?—Never an hour, I believe.

Do you think that if the overlooker were naturally a humane person it would be still found necessary for him to beat the children, in order to keep up their attention and vigilance at the termination of those extraordinary days of labour?—Yes, the machine turns off a regular quantity of cardings, and of course they must keep as regularly to their work the whole of the day; they must keep with the machine, and therefore however humane the slubber may be, as he must keep up with the machine or be found fault with, he spurs the children to keep up also by various means but that which he commonly resorts to is to strap them when they become drowsy.

At the time when you were beaten for not keeping up with your work, were you anxious to have done it if you possibly could?—Yes; the dread of being beaten if we could not keep up with our work was a sufficient impulse to keep us to it if we could.

When you got home at night after this labour, did you feel much fatigued?—Very much so.

Had you any time to be with your parents, and to receive instruction from them?—No.

What did you do?—All that we did when we got home was to get the little bit of supper that was provided for us and go to bed immediately. If the supper had not been ready directly, we should have gone to sleep while it was preparing.

Did you not, as a child, feel it a very grievous hardship to be roused so soon in the morning?—I did.

Were the rest of the children similarly circumstanced?—Yes, all of them; but they were not any of them so far from their work as I was.

And if you had been too late you were under the apprehension of being cruelly beaten?—I generally was beaten when I happened to be too late; and when I got up in the morning the apprehension of that was so great, that I used to run, and cry all the way as I went to the mill.

That was the way by which your punctual attendance was secured?—Yes.

And you do not think it could have been secured by any other means?—No.

Then it is your impression from what you have seen, and from your own experience, that those long hours of labour have the effect of rendering young persons who are subject to them exceedingly unhappy?—Yes.

You have already said it had a considerable effect upon your health?—Yes.

Do you conceive that it diminished your growth?—I did not pay much attention to that; but I have been examined by some persons who said they thought I was rather stunted, and that I should have been taller if I had not worked at the mill.

What were your wages at that time?—Three shillings [per week].

And how much a day had you for over-work when you were worked so exceedingly long?—A halfpenny a day.

Did you frequently forfeit that if you were not always there to a moment?—Yes; I most frequently forfeited what was allowed for those long hours.

You took your food to the mill; was it in your mill, as is the case in cotton mills, much spoiled by being laid aside?—It was very frequently covered by flues from the wool; and in that case they had to be blown off with the mouth, and picked off with the fingers before it could be eaten.

So that not giving you a little leisure for eating your food, but obliging you to take it at the mill, spoiled your food when you did get it?—Yes, very commonly.

And at the same time that this overlabour injured your appetite?—Yes.

Could you eat when you got home?—Not always.

What is the effect of this piecening upon the hands?—It makes them bleed; the skin is com-

pletely rubbed off, and in that case they bleed in perhaps a dozen parts.

The prominent parts of the hand?—Yes, all the prominent parts of the hands are rubbed down till they bleed; every day they are rubbed in that way.

All the time you continue at work?—All the time we are working. The hands never can be hardened in that work, for the grease keeps them soft in the first instance, and long and continual rubbing is always wearing them down, so that if they were hard they would be sure to bleed.

Is it attended with much pain?—Very much.

Do they allow you to make use of the back of the hand?—No; the work cannot be so well done with the back of the hand, or I should have made use of that.

Is the work done as well when you are so many hours engaged in it, as it would be if you were at it a less time?—I believe it is not done so well in those long hours; toward the latter end of the day the children become completely bewildered, and know not what they are doing, so that they spoil their work without knowing.

Then you do not think that the masters gain much by the continuance of the work to so great a length of time?—I believe not.

Were there girls as well as boys employed in this manner?—Yes.

Were they more tenderly treated by the overlookers, or were they worked and beaten in the same manner?—There was no difference in their treatment.

Were they beaten by the overlookers, or by the slubber?—By the slubber.

But the overlooker must have been perfectly aware of the treatment that the children endured at the mill?—Yes; and sometimes the overlooker beat them himself but the man that they wrought under had generally the management of them.

Did he pay them their wages?—No; their wages were paid by the master.

But the overlooker of the mill was perfectly well aware that they could not have performed the duty exacted from them in the mill without being thus beaten?—I believe he was.

You seem to say that this beating is absolutely necessary, in order to keep the children up to their work; is it universal throughout all factories?—

I have been in several other factories, and I have witnessed the same cruelty in them all.

Did you say that they were beaten for being too late?—Yes.

Is it not the custom in many of the factories to impose fines upon children for being too late, instead of beating them?—It was not in that factory.

What then were the fines by which you lost the money you gained by your long hours?—The spinner could not get on so fast with his work when we happened to be too late; he could not begin his work so soon, and therefore it was taken.

Did the slubber pay you your wages?—No, the master paid our wages.

And the slubber took your fines from you?—Yes.

Then you were fined as well as beaten?—There was nothing deducted from the ordinary scale of wages, but only from that received for over-hours, and I had only that taken when I was too late, so that the fine was not regular.

When you were not working over-hours, were you so often late as when you were working over-hours?—Yes.

You were not very often late whilst you were not working over-hours?—Yes, I was often late when I was not working over-hours; I had to go at six o'clock in the morning, and consequently had to get up at five to eat my breakfast and go to the mill, and if I failed to get up by five I was too late; and it was nine o'clock before we could get home, and then we went to bed; in the best times I could not be much above eight hours at home, reckoning dressing and eating my meals, and everything.

Was it a blanket-mill in which you worked?—Yes.

Did you ever know that the beatings to which you allude inflicted serious injury upon the children?—I do not recollect any very serious injury, more than that they had their heads broken, if that may be called a serious injury; that has often happened; I, myself, had no more serious injury than that.

You say that the girls as well as the boys were employed as you have described, and you observed no difference in their treatment?—No difference.

The girls were beat in this unmerciful manner?—They were.

They were subject, of course, to the same bad effects from this over-working?—Yes.

Could you attend an evening-school during the time you were employed in the mill?—No, that was completely impossible.

Did you attend the Sunday-school?—Not very frequently when I work at the mill.

How then were you engaged during the Sunday?—I very often slept till it was too late for school time or for divine worship, and the rest of the day I spent in walking out and taking a little fresh air.

Did your parents think that it was necessary for you to enjoy a little fresh air?—I believe they did; they never said anything against it; before I went to the mill I used to go to the Sunday-school.

Did you frequently sleep nearly the whole of the day on Sunday?—Very often.

At what age did you leave that employment?—I was about 12 years old.

Why did you leave that place?—I went very late one morning, about seven o'clock, and I got severely beaten by the spinner, and he turned me out of the mill, and I went home, and never went any more.

Was your attendance as good as the other children?—Being at rather a greater distance than some of them, I was generally one of the latest.

Where was your next work?—I worked as a bobbin-winder in another part of the works of the same firm.

How long were you a bobbin-winder?—About two years, I believe.

What did you become after that?—A weaver.

How long were you a weaver?—I was a weaver till March in last year.

A weaver of what?—A blanket-weaver.

With the same firm?—With the same firm.

Did you leave them?—No; I was dismissed from my work for a reason which I am willing and anxious to explain.

Have you had opportunities of observing the way in which the children are treated in factories up to a late period?—Yes.

You conceive that their treatment still remains as you first found it, and that the system is in great want of regulation?—It does.

Children you still observe to be very much fatigued and injured by the hours of labour?—Yes.

From your own experience, what is your opinion as to the utmost labour that a child in piecening could safely undergo?—If I were appealed to from my own feelings to fix a limit, I should fix it at ten hours, or less.

And your attribute to longer hours all the cruelties that you describe?—A good deal of them.

Are the children sleepy in mills?—Very.

Are they more liable to accidents in the latter part of the day than in the other part?—I believe they are; I believe a greater number of accidents happen in the latter part of the day than in any other. I have known them so sleepy that in the short interval while the others have been going out, some of them have fallen asleep, and have been left there.

Is it an uncommon case for children to fall asleep in the mill, and remain there all night?—Not to remain there all night; but I have known a case the other day, of a child whom the overlooker found when he went to lock the door, that had been left there.

So that you think there has been no change for the better in the treatment of those children; is it your opinion that there will be none, except Parliament interfere in their behalf?—It is my decided conviction.

Have you recently seen any cruelties in mills?—Yes; not long since I was in a mill and I saw a girl severely beaten; at a mill called Hick-lane Mill, in Bately; I happened to be in at the other end of the room talking; and I heard the blows, and I looked that way, and saw the spinner beating one of the girls severely with a large stick. Hearing the sound, led me to look round, and to ask what was the matter, and they said is was "Nothing but paying [beating] 'his ligger-on."

What age was the girl?—About 12 years.

Was she very violently beaten?—She was.

Was this when she was over-fatigued?—It was in the afternoon.

Can you speak as to the effect of this labour in the mills and factories on the morals of the children, as far as you have observed?—As far as I have observed with regard to morals in the mills, there is every thing about them that is disgusting in every one conscious of correct morality.

Do you find that the children, the females especially, are very early demoralized in them?—They are.

Is their language indecent?—Very indecent; and both sexes take great familiarities with each other in the mills, without at all being ashamed of their conduct.

Do you connect their immorality of language and conduct with their excessive labour?—It may be somewhat connected with it, for it is to be observed that most of that goes on toward night, when they begin to be drowsy; it is a kind of stimulus which they use to keep them awake; they say some pert thing or other to keep themselves from drowsiness, and it generally happens to be some obscene language.

Have not a considerable number of the females employed in mills illegitimate children very early in life?—I believe there are; I have known some of them have illegitimate children when they were between 16 and 17 years of age.

How many grown-up females had you in the mill?—I cannot speak to the exact number that were grown up; perhaps there might be thirty-four or so that worked in the mill at that time.

How many of those had illegitimate children?—A great many of them; eighteen or nineteen of them, I think.

Did they generally marry the men by whom they had children?—No; it sometimes happens that young women have children by married men, and I have known an instance, a few weeks since, where one of the young women had a child by a married man.

Is it your opinion that those who have the charge of the mills very often avail themselves of the opportunity they have to debauch the young women?—No, not generally; most of the improper conduct takes place among the younger part of those that work in the mill.

Do you find that the children and young persons in those mills are moral in other respects, or does their want of education tend to encourage them in a breach of the law?—I believe it does, for there are very few of them that can know anything about it; few of them can either read or write.

Are criminal offences then very frequent?—Yes, theft is very common; it is practiced a great deal in the mills, stealing their bits of dinner, or something of that sort. Some of them have not so much to eat as they ought to have, and if they can fall in with the dinner of some of their partners they steal it. The first day my brother and I went to the mill we had our dinner stolen, because we were not up with the tricks; we were more careful in the future, but still we did not always escape.

Was there any correction going on at the mills for indecent language or improper conduct?—No, I never knew of any.

From what you have seen and known of those mills, would you prefer that the hours of labour should be so long with larger wages, or that they should be shortened with a diminution of wages?—If I were working at the mill now, I would rather have less labour and receive a trifle less, than so much labour and receive a trifle more.

Is that the general impression of individuals engaged in mills with whom you are acquainted?—I believe it is.

What is the impression in the country from which you come with respect to the effect of this Bill upon wages?—They do not anticipate that it will affect wages at all.

They think it will not lower wages?—They do.

Do you mean that it will not lower wages by the hour, or that you will receive the same wages per day?—They anticipate that it may perhaps lower their wages at a certain time of the year when they are working hard, but not at other times, so that they will have their wages more regular.

Does not their wish for this Bill mainly rest upon their anxiety to protect their children from the consequences of this excessive labour, and to have some opportunity of affording them a decent education?—Yes; such are the wishes of every humane father that I have heard speak about the thing.

Have they not some feeling of having the labour equalized?—That is the feeling of some that I have heard speak of it.

Did your parents work in the same factories?—No.

Were any of the slubbers' children working there?—Yes.

Under what slubber did you work in that mill?—Under a person of the name of Thomas Bennett, in the first place; and I was changed from him to another of the name of James Webster.

Did the treatment depend very much upon the slubber under whom you were?—No, it did not depend directly upon him, for he was obliged to do a certain quantity of work, and therefore to make us up keep up with that.

Were the children of the slubbers strapped in the same way?—Yes, except that it is very natural for a father to spare his own child.

Did it depend upon the feelings of a slubber toward his children?—Very little.

Did the slubbers fine their own spinners?—I believe not.

You said that the piecening was very hard labour; what labour is there besides moving about; have you anything heavy to carry or to lift?—We have nothing heavy to carry, but we are kept upon our feet in brisk times from 5 o'clock in the morning to 9 at night.

How soon does the hand get sore in piecening?—How soon mine became sore I cannot speak to exactly; but they get a little hard on the Sunday, when we are not working, and they will get sore again very soon on the Monday.

Is it always the case in piecening that the hand bleeds, whether you work short or long hours?—They bleed more when we work more.

Do they always bleed when you are working?—Yes.

Do you think that the children would not be more competent to this task, and their hands far less hurt, if the hours were fewer every day, especially when their hands had become seasoned with the labour?—I believe it would have an effect for the longer they are worked the more their hands are worn, and the longer it takes to heal them, and they do not get hard enough after a day's rest to be long without bleeding again; if they are not so much worn down, they might heal sooner, and not bleed so often or so soon.

After a short day's work have you found your hands hard the next morning?—They do not bleed much after we have ceased work; they then get hard; they will bleed soon in the morning when in regular work.

Do you think if the work of the children were confined to about ten hours a day, that after they were accustomed to it, they would not be able to perform this piecening without making their hands bleed?—I believe they would.

So that it is your opinion, from your experience, that if the hours were mitigated, their hands would not be so much worn, and would not bleed by the business of piecening?—Yes.

Do you mean to say that their hands would not bleed at all?—I cannot say exactly, for I always wrought long hours, and therefore my hands always did bleed.

Have you any experience of mills where they only work ten hours?—I have never wrought at such mills, and in most of the mills I have seen their hands bleed.

At a slack time, when you were working only a few hours, did your hands bleed?—No, they did not for three or four days, after we had been standing still for a week; the mill stood still sometimes for a week together, but when we did work we worked the common number of hours.

Were all the mills in the neighbourhood working the same number of hours in brisk times?—Yes.

So that if any parents found it necessary to send his children to the mill for the sake of being able to maintain them, and wished to take them from any mill where they were excessively worked, he could not have found any other place where they would have been less worked?—No, he could not; for myself, I had no desire to change, because I thought I was as well off as I could be at any other mill.

And if the parent, to save his child, had taken him from the mill, and had applied to the parish for relief, would the parish, knowing that he had withdrawn his child from its work, have relieved him?—No.

So that the long labour which you have described, or actual starvation, was, practically, the only alternative that was presented to the parent under such circumstances?—It was; they must either work at the mill they were at or some other, and there was no choice in the mills in that respect.

What, in your opinion, would be the effect of limiting hours of labour upon the happiness, and the health, and the intelligence of this rising generation?—If the hours are shortened, the children may, perhaps, have a chance of attending some evening-school, and learning to read and write; and those that I know who have been to school and learned to read and write, have much more comfort than those who have not. For myself, I went to a school when I was six years old, and I learned to read and write a little then.

At a free-school?—Yes, at a free-school in Dewsbury; but I left school when I was six years old. The fact is, that my father was a small manufacturer, and in comfortable circumstances, and he got into debt with Mr. Cook for a wool bill, and as he had no other means of paying him, he came and agreed with my father, that my brother and I should go to work at his mill till that debt was paid; so that the whole of the time that we wrought at the mill we had no wages.

THOMAS BENNETT, *called in; and Examined.*

Where do you reside?—At Dewsbury.

What is your business?—A slubber.

What age are you?—About 48.

Have you had much experience regarding the working of children in factories?—Yes, about twenty-seven years.

Have you a family?—Yes, eight children.

Have any of them gone to factories?—All.

At what age?—The first went at six years of age.

To whose mill?—To Mr. Halliley's, to piece for myself.

What hours did you work at that mill?—We have wrought from 4 to 9, from 4 to 10, and from 5 to 9, and from 5 to 10.

What sort of mill was it?—It was a blanketmill; we sometimes altered the time, according as the days increased and decreased.

What were your regular hours?—Our regular hours when we were not so throng, was from 6 to 7.

And when you were the throngest, what were your hours then?—From 5 to 9, and from 5 to 10, and from 4 to 9.

Seventeen hours?—Yes.

What intervals for meals had the children at that period?—Two hours; an hour for breakfast, and an hour for dinner.

Did they always allow two hours for meals at Mr. Halliley's?—Yes, it was allowed, but the children did not get it, for they had business to do at that time such as fettling and cleaning the machinery.

But they did not stop in at that time, did they?—They all had their share of cleaning and other work to do.

That is, they were cleaning the machinery?—Cleaning the machinery at the time of dinner.

How long a time together have you known those excessive hours to continue?—I have wrought so myself very nearly two years together.

Were your children working under you then?—Yes, two of them.

State the effect upon your children.—Of a morning when they have been so fast asleep that I have had to go up stairs and lift them out of bed, and have heard them crying with the feelings of a parent; I have been much affected by it.

Were not they much fatigued at the termination of such a day's labour as that?—Yes; many a time I have seen their hands moving while they have been nodding, almost asleep; they have been doing their business almost mechanically.

While they have been almost asleep, they have attempted to work?—Yes; and they have missed the carding and spoiled the thread, when we have had to beat them for it.

Could they have done their work towards the termination of such a long day's labour, if they had not been chastised to it?—No.

You do not think that they could have kept awake or up to their work till the seventeenth hour, without being chastised?—No.

Will you state what effect it had upon your children at the end of their day's work?—At the end of their day's work, when they have come home, instead of taking their victuals, they have dropped asleep with the victuals in their hands; and sometimes when we have sent them to bed with a little bread or something to eat in their hand, I have found it in their bed the next morning.

Had it affected their health?—I cannot say much of that; they were very hearty children.

Do you live at a distance from the mill?—Half a mile.

Did your children feel a difficulty in getting home?—Yes, I have had to carry the lesser child on my back, and it has been asleep when I got home.

Did these hours of labour fatigue you?—Yes; they fatigued me to that excess, that in divine worship I have not been able to stand according to order; I have sat to worship.

So that even during the Sunday you have felt fatigue from your labour in the week?—Yes, we felt it, and always took as much rest as we could.

Were you compelled to beat your own children, in order to make them keep up with the machine?—

Yes, that was forced upon us, or we could not have done the work; I have struck them often, though I felt as a parent.

If the children had not been your own, you would have chastised them still more severely?—Yes.

What did you beat them with?—A strap sometimes; and when I have seen my work spoiled, with the roller.

Was the work always worse done at the end of the day?—That was the greatest danger.

Do you conceive it possible that the children could do their work well at the end of such a day's labour as that?—No.

Matthew Crabtree, the last Witness examined by this Committee, I think mentioned you as one of the slubbers under whom he worked?—Yes.

He states that he was chastised and beaten at the mill?—Yes, I have had to chastise him.

You can confirm then what he stated as to the length of time he had to work as a child, and the cruel treatment he received?—Yes, I have had to chastise him in the evening, and often in the morning for being too late; when I had one out of the three wanting I could not keep up with the machine, and I was getting behindhand compared with what another man was doing; and therefore I should have been called to account on Saturday night if the work was not done.

Was he worse than others?—No.

Was it the constant practice to chastise the children?—Yes.

It was necessary in order to keep up your work?—Yes.

And you would have lost your place if you had not done so?—Yes; when I was working at Mr. Wood's mill, at Dewsbury, which at present is burnt down, but where I slubbed for him until it was, while we were taking our meals he used to come up and put the machine agoing; and I used to say, "You do not give us time to eat"; he used to reply, "Chew it at your work"; and I often replied to him, "I have not yet become debased like a brute, I do not chew my cud." Often has that man done that, and then gone below to see if a strap were off, which would have shown if the machinery was not working, and then he would come up again.

Was this at the drinking time?—Yes, at breakfast and at drinking.

Was this where the children were working?—Yes, my own children and others.

Were your own children obliged to employ most of their time at breakfast and at the drinking in cleansing the machine, and in fettling the spindles?—I have seen at that mill, and I have experienced and mentioned it with grief, that the English children were enslaved worse than the Africans. Once when Mr. Wood was saying to the carrier who brought his work in and out, "How long has that horse of mine been at work?" and the carrier told him the time, and he said "Loose him directly, he has been in too long," I made this reply to him, "You have more mercy and pity for your horse than you have for your men."

Did not this beating go on principally at the latter part of the day?—Yes.

Was it not also dangerous for the children to move about those mills when they became so drowsy and fatigued?—Yes, especially by lamp-light.

Do the accidents principally occur at the latter end of those long days of labour?—Yes, I believe mostly so.

Do you know of any that have happened?—I know of one; it was at Mr. Wood's mill; part of the machinery caught a lass who had been drowsy and asleep, and the strap which ran close by her catched her at the middle, and bore her to the ceiling, and down she came, and her neck appeared broken, and the slubber ran up to her and pulled her neck, and I carried her to the doctor myself.

Did she get well?—Yes, she came about again.

What time was that?—In the evening.

You say that you have eight children who have gone to the factories?—Yes.

There has been no opportunity for you to send them to a day-school?—No; one boy had about twelve months' schooling.

Have they gone to Sunday-schools?—Yes.

Can any of them write?—Not one.

They do not teach writing at Sunday-schools?—No; it is objected to, I believe.

So that none of your children can write?—No.

What would be the effect of a proper limitation of the hours of labour upon the conduct of the rising generation?—I believe it would have a very happy effect in regard to correcting their morals; for I believe there is a deal of evil that takes place in one way or other in consequence of those long hours.

Is it your opinion that they would then have an opportunity of attending night-schools?—Yes; I have often regretted, while working those long hours, that I could not get my children there.

Is it your belief that if they were better instructed, they would be happier and better members of society?—Yes, I believe so.

INDEX